Public Debt Management

To Emma and Riccardo

Public Debt Management

ALESSANDRO MISSALE

OXFORD
UNIVERSITY PRESS

OXFORD
UNIVERSITY PRESS

Great Clarendon Street, Oxford OX2 6DP

Oxford University Press is a department of the University of Oxford.
It furthers the University's aim of excellence in research, scholarship,
and education by publishing worldwide in

Oxford New York

Athens Auckland Bangkok Bogotá Buenos Aires Calcutta
Cape Town Chennai Dar es Salaam Delhi Florence Hong Kong Istanbul
Karachi Kuala Lumpur Madrid Melbourne Mexico City Mumbai
Nairobi Paris São Paulo Singapore Taipei Tokyo Toronto Warsaw

and associated companies in Berlin Ibadan

Oxford is a registered trade mark of Oxford University Press
in the UK and certain other countries

Published in the United States
by Oxford University Press Inc., New York

British Library Cataloguing in Publication Data
Data available

Library of Congress Cataloging in Publication Data
Missale, Alessandro.
Public debt management / Alessandro Missale.
p. cm.
Includes bibliographical references.
1. Debts, Public. 2. Debts, Public—OECD countries. I. Title.
HJ8015.M57 1999 352.4'5—dc21 99–17544

ISBN 0–19–829085–3 (CIP)

Typeset by
Newgen Imaging Systems (P) Ltd., Chennai, India
Printed in Great Britain
on acid-free paper by
Biddles Ltd
Guildford & Kings Lynn

Preface

High levels of public debt are a common feature of modern economies. This fact, combined with the increased liberalization and sophistication of financial markets, has brought debt management to the forefront of economic policy issues.

As the debt ratio rises, the effects of alternative funding policies become as important as the effects of budget deficits. Managing debt inefficiently may seriously undermine any fiscal stabilization effort. Consider how dramatic the consequences of the 1992 EMS crisis would have been, had European debts been denominated in Deutsche Marks. Think of the budget impact of an unexpected rise in interest rates when the debt is greater than GDP and a large share of it is in short maturities or indexed to interest rates, as is the case in a number of OECD countries.

Faced with the problem of how to manage the public debt, policymakers turn to economic theory for guidance in the choice of debt instruments. Not surprisingly, academic interest in debt management has been revived. In recent years an increasing number of papers have dealt with the economics of debt management. Notwithstanding the many contributions, a general framework to contrast alternative strategies of debt management on welfare grounds has not yet emerged. Prescriptions for policymaking available in the literature are either hard to interpret or very specific.

The book aims at providing a theoretical framework that policymakers could use as a guide to debt management. The analysis focuses on policy issues and takes the perspective of cost and risk minimization that is familiar to policymakers. The effect of public debt management on financial markets, risk-sharing, policy credibility, interest costs and taxation are all discussed and evaluated within a unified theoretical framework. A large section of the book is devoted to the evidence on the composition and maturity of public debt of OECD countries and to the implications of security market structure for the choice of debt instruments. The analysis emphasizes the trade-offs involved in debt management, and shows how theory can be used to inform practical policy decisions.

The book grew out of a research project started many years ago with my Ph.D. dissertation at MIT; over time I extended this work to new ideas, new theories, new evidence. My first thanks go to Olivier Blanchard who first convinced me to work on debt management. Together we wrote the article on which Sections 6.7 and 6.8 in this book are based. More importantly, he taught me economics and intellectual honesty. I thank Bob Solow for invaluable advice and the friends and colleagues at MIT who shared with me ideas. I am particularly grateful to Andrea Ripa di Meana for many passionate discussions on debt management.

I owe a special thank to Marco Pagano who read an early version of this book, and decided to send it to the publisher without asking my consent. I am also grateful to Francesco Giavazzi, who always supported this project and to IGIER (the Innocenzo Gasparini Institute for Economic Research) which, over many years, provided me with an ideal research environment.

My greatest thanks are for Carlo Favero for his advice and for the time spent reading the book and answering my many questions about almost everything. I thank him and Francesco Daveri for their friendship and for making me see the good side of things—both in economics and in life.

I thank Pierpaolo Benigno, Daniele Checchi, Harris Dellas, Peter Englund, Ioannis Ganoulis, Jane Marrinan, Paolo Garella, Marco Pagano and Paolo Panteghini who added significantly to the quality of the book with their comments and suggestions. I thank Allyson Davies, Marco Pifferi and Giuseppe Cinquemani for skillful research assistance.

I am very grateful to my colleagues at the Department of Economics of the Universita di Brescia who worked more than they should have, during the period of leave that I took to finish the book.

The book was completed at the Bank of England during my tenure of a Houblon-Norman Fellowship. At the Bank I greatly benefitted from insightful discussions with Creon Butler, Andy Haldane, Paul Mills, Simon Price and Paul Tucker. The months spent at the Bank of England gave me a perspective on policymaking which would have otherwise been unobtainable. I am particularly indebted to Mervyn King who made this invaluable experience possible.

I thank all the people in the Treasuries, Ministries of Finance, Central Banks and Universities for providing me with data on debt composition and maturity: Mika Arola, Samuel Bentolilla, Benoît Coeuré, Jorge Correia da Cunha, Hendrik van Dalen, Mark De-Broeck, Francesco Drudi, Vítor Gaspar, Ilan Goldfajn, Jakob de Haan, Takashi Hanajiri, Eduard Hochreiter, Seppo Honkapohja, Lars Hörngren, Anja Kruijver, Karsten Jensen, Juan Jimeno, Jim Juffs, Zahir Lalani, Romana Lehner, Anabela Marques, Gian Maria Milesi-Ferretti, Alessandra Mongiardino, Kari Nars, Anders Paalzov, Ambrogio Rinaldi, Andreia Roldaõ, Gabriel Quirós Romero, Olivier Salvador, Stefano Scalera, Emmanuel Van der Stichele, Lars Strand, Maude Svensson, Stefan Theys, David Vestin, Roberto Violi, Oliver Whelan, Wiebe.

To write this book I took more time away from my family than I certainly should have. I thank Laura, Riccardo and Emma who gave me love and strength.

Contents

1

Policy issues

1.1 Policy issues and policy objectives

There are many different debt instruments which can be used to finance the budget deficit. A main distinction is the currency of denomination and, in particular, whether or not this is the domestic currency. Another important characteristics is the initial term to maturity, which among marketable instruments may range from few weeks to 30 years. The way the interest is computed is also important to determine the risk-return characteristics of financial instruments. Securities may promise to pay a fixed interest rate or have coupons which are indexed to another interest rate or to the price level. The marketability of debt instruments is also important. A policymaker may rely on marketable securities, as well as on loans from financial institutions and on savings bonds sold to personal investors. The composition of OECD countries' debts by type of instrument is shown for the year 1995 in Table 1.1.

Which instruments policymakers choose depends on the objective they pursue as well as on the circumstances in which the choice is made. Most of the literature on debt management is motivated by the normative issue of what type of debt governments should issue. This book, being written by an economist, will not escape the rule but, for a time, it is instructive to take a positive perspective and ask how debt instruments are actually chosen. A tentative hypothesis is that policymakers do behave as private borrowers and, thus, try to obtain the best possible conditions. We may expect policymakers to maximize the expected return of a debt strategy while avoiding to take much risk. "Funding at least cost and risk" is a primary objective of debt management policy in a number of OECD countries. This strategy is formally stated in the Report of Debt Management Review (1995) by the HM Treasury and the Bank of England:

The objective of debt management policy is to minimise over the long term the cost of meeting the government's financing needs, taking account of risk, whilst ensuring that debt management policy is consistent with monetary policy.

Interesting as it can be, the way public debt is managed in the United Kingdom may not be very representative of other countries' debt policy, at least if judged from the composition of the British debt. In the United Kingdom the share of the debt which is indexed to the price level is substantial and the average term to maturity of conventional fixed-rate securities is the longest in the OECD area.

Table 1.1. OECD:—composition by type of instrument, 1995

	T. Bills	Variable	Indexed	Fix-Bond	Foreign	Loans	Saving
Australia	13.3	3.5	3.0	76.4	3.1	0.7	—
Austria	1.6	6.4	—	45.7	22.0	24.3	—
Belgium	17.4	2.0	—	60.3	11.4	—	0.9
Canada	35.4	—	1.2	52.5	3.5	0.7	6.6
Denmark	7.6	2.7	—	73.9	15.6	—	0.2
Finland	10.2	—	—	38.3	46.4	5.1	—
France	8.9	2.7	—	70.3	3.7	2.1	11.9
Germany	0.4	0.8	—	49.2	—	40.5	3.9
Greece	26.5	35.3	—	—	22.8	15.4	—
Ireland	2.9	4.7	—	44.9	35.1	—	10.0
Italy	18.1	22.8	—	36.9	7.4	5.6	9.0
Japan	12.9	1.5	—	64.5	—	21.1	—
Netherlands	3.1	—	—	78.0	—	18.1	—
Portugal	12.7	26.9	—	20.9	17.4	0.9	21.3
Spain	32.3	—	—	54.4	8.7	3.1	—
Sweden	14.4	—	1.2	47.3	27.9	—	8.9
UK	3.2	1.7	13.6	59.6	5.0	—	15.4
USA	11.8	—	—	39.8	—	45.6	2.9

Notes: Data are for gross debt and include debt held by the Central Bank and government agencies except for UK data which are net of official holdings. Data for Canada refer to Paper Debt. Data for the US are gross of "Government Account series." T. Bills include other short-term debt. Index refers to price-indexed debt and Variable to variable-rate debt which excludes revisable-rate debt for Belgium. Saving comprises savings bonds and accounts with the Post Office.

Somewhat different is the composition of the Swedish debt. As price-index-linked bonds have been introduced only recently, the Swedish debt shows a considerable share of Treasury bills and a much larger share of foreign currency debt. However, objectives and overall strategy of government debt policy are strikingly similar to British ones. Quoting from the 1994–95 Report of the Swedish National Debt Office (SNDO):

The main role of the Swedish National Debt Office is to raise loans to finance the day-to-day deficits . . . . The aims is to provide this function at the minimum possible long-term cost . . . . The board (of the SNDO) has also laid down the permitted deviations, i.e. risks, from the benchmark portfolios . . . . The SNDO's strategy is to limit and weigh against each other the various type of risk concerned with government borrowing.

The results of a recent survey among representatives of OECD countries, which has been sponsored by the Swedish National Debt Office, also show that the objective of containing interest costs is shared by all country representatives.[1] Another uncontroversial factor motivating debt managers is the objective of avoiding the risk of refinancing, i.e. the risk of having to roll over a large amount of debt at unfavorable interest rates.

Though conceptually clear in their general purpose, the objectives of minimizing the expected cost of debt servicing and minimizing risk are of little help operationally.[2] For instance, the objective of minimizing interest costs suggests issuing benchmarks, that is, instruments for which an efficient and liquid market exists so as to save on liquidity premia, but without further qualifications it has no simple implication for most of the decisions which a debt manager must routinely take. Consider the choice between issuing 10-year bonds or rolling over a 3-month Treasury bill for 10 years. As the interest rate on the 10-year bond reflects the expected path for the 3-month interest rate over the next 10 years, the two borrowing strategies appear to be equally costly in expected terms. If a difference exists, it must be that either the path for future 3-month rates, as expected by the policymaker, does not coincide with market expectations or that a term premium on one of the two instruments has to be paid. Each possibility raises its own problems, and shows how limited in practice is the advice of minimizing interest costs. Does interest cost minimization mean that policymakers should try to guess future interest rates or even use private information in order to outperform the market? Important differences in debt policy would emerge depending on whether or not "taking views on interest rates" were considered a legitimate procedure in minimizing interest costs. Practical problems would also emerge in implementing cost minimization strategies based on debt instruments with low term premia. As a matter of fact, risk premia, being defined as the difference between current and expected interest rates, cannot be directly observed but must be identified out of market expectations. Estimation techniques can solve this measurement problem only to the extent that term premia are stable over time.

These problems are not peculiar to the choice of short-term versus long-term securities. The same considerations hold true for the choice of indexing government securities to the price level. For price indexation to make a difference in the costs of debt servicing, either expectations of future inflation must differ between the policymaker and private investors or investors must be willing to pay a premium in order to avoid the risk of inflation. Leaving aside the possibility of an active debt policy inspired to a "beat the market" strategy, whether interest savings can be expected by issuing price-index-linked bonds depends on the existence and magnitude of the inflation risk-premium. How difficult it is to measure such premium is witnessed by the economists' efforts to

---

[1] The reason why the word policymaker should not be used here is that, quite possibly, not all of the interviewed representatives are actually in charge of managing the debt.

[2] They are also unuseful as principles on which to construct benchmark portfolios against which the performance of debt managers could be evaluated.

Table 1.2. Factors motivating actual debt management—results from a questionairre: 16 OECD countries

	Interest cost reduction			Risk reduction		
	Bench-marks	Risk premia	Views on rates	Roll-over risk	Smooth redemption	Sum of last two
Yes	9	9	7	12	7	15
No	0	1	5	0	0	0
Indiff.	9	8	6	6	11	3

distinguish the inflation risk-premium from the expected inflation component of the interest spread between conventional and price-index-linked bonds in the United Kingdom.

These problems are in part reflected in the way OECD countries' representatives answer in the aforementioned survey. Policymakers express different views as the best way of reducing interest costs, as whether this should imply building benchmarks or issuing securities with a low risk-premium or taking views on interest rates. While no representative is opposed to the idea of issuing benchmarks in order to save on liquidity premia, whether interest cost reduction should be obtained by taking views on future interest rates is a very controversial issue. As shown in Table 1.2, such a strategy is suggested by only 7 representatives out of the 18 countries and, interestingly, quite a few managers are openly opposed to a "beat-the-market" policy.

A strategy of issuing securities with a low risk-premium—"satisfying market demand" in the survey words—finds a large consensus but, perhaps not surprisingly, a more detailed account of policymakers' replies would point out wide differences in terms of the specific policy indications regarding the maturity of the securities to issue and their diversification. For instance, in a few cases issuing short maturity debt is considered the cheapest policy, in others it is a particular maturity segment which is viewed as a source of strong demand, in others again it is by filling the entire maturity spectrum that term premia are believed to be avoidable.

Risk reduction is also a strong motivation of actual debt management: Table 1.2 shows that two-thirds of the debt managers are concerned with roll-over risk. Since avoiding the risk of refinancing appears to be the main reason for smoothing the redemption profile, an even stronger consensus emerges on the opportunity to insulate the government portfolio from interest rate shocks: 15 representatives are aware and concerned with the problem.

Then, a trade-off between the objective of reducing interest costs and the objective of containing risk is likely to arise. A conflict of objectives would emerge quite naturally in cases where cost minimization was pursued by relying on securities with a low risk-premium. In the example considered before, issuing

10-year bonds can be costly if investors are risk-averse and have short planning horizons, but rolling over of short-term bills is risky insofar as such strategy exposes the government budget to unexpected rises in the real interest rate.[3] Indeed, a more realistic representation of the policymaker's objective function implies a trade-off between the minimization of the expected cost of debt servicing and the minimization of budgetary risk. In many instances a policymaker would have to choose a combination of return and risk on such a trade-off. This is not so easy a task to accomplish in the absence of any theory of the proper degree of risk-aversion that a government should exhibit.[4]

Even more fundamental is to define which type of risk is relevant for debt management. When asked, policymakers indicate interest-rate risk as the only relevant type and, in particular, refinancing risk, that is, the risk of having to roll over short-term debt at a higher than expected real interest rate. Indeed, not only the survey of the Swedish National Debt Office but also the results of a recent OECD survey (see Broker 1993) rank the objective of avoiding interest-rate variations a priority of debt management. The fact that the Swedish National Debt Office is constrained in its policy actions by a minimum debt duration is another point in case; such a constraint sets a limit on the amount of debt which, on average, has to be refinanced.

There is no reason, however, why policymakers should only be concerned with interest-rate risk affecting government financial liabilities. For instance, changes in the real value of debt due to unexpected inflation should also be a matter of concern. More importantly, the interest-rate risk should be related to another important source of risk: the uncertainty of government revenues and spending. If anything, the uncertain path for taxes and expenditures affects the government borrowing needs and thus its exposure to interest-rate variations. As a private borrower, who aims at smoothing consumption, would take into account labor-income risk, a policymaker would have to pay attention to the relation between the returns on the various debt instruments and unexpected variations in revenues and spending. Indeed, modern portfolio theory would suggest government net worth, and its return distribution, as relevant variables for portfolio decisions. Put simply, decisions should be based as well on the return distribution of real activities such as revenues and spending commitments as on the return of financial assets. Taking up our motivating example, it would certainly make a difference in terms of risk, if unexpected rises in the real interest rate, making it costly to roll-over Treasury bills, were associated with unexpected falls in output and, hence, in revenues. Indeed, no government would be indifferent between two, otherwise identical debt instruments, if one

---

[3] However, if inflation is the main source of uncertainty it could well be that both the government and the private sector prefer short to long maturity debt.

[4] It is also difficult to think of ways to elicit the preferences of society on the matter.

paid low returns during recessions, when revenues are unexpectedly low and high returns during expansions, while the other did the opposite.

Before discussing optimal risk management, an important simplifying assumption underlying the present discussion must be taken care of: that the behavior of a debt manager can be inferred from the behavior of a private borrower. Such an analogy is misleading, at least in one but important respect: unlike a private borrower, a government is big; none of its policy actions is expected to be irrelevant to the equilibrium outcome. The choice of public debt may have potentially important effects on the allocation of risk and taxation. Only in one special case, under restrictive conditions such as intergenerational altruism and market completeness, and heroic assumptions on the rationality of individuals, such effects will not arise. However, under the same conditions the choice of financial instruments for deficit financing would be completely irrelevant, a case which is known to economists as Ricardian Equivalence.

The irrelevance theorem of debt management is presented and discussed in Chapter 2 of this book. Studying the conditions for the choice of debt instruments not to affect the real economy is a preliminary first step toward a better understanding of the effects of debt management. A number of effects are identified. The financial decisions of a sovereign borrower may have an impact on the expected returns, not only of government securities but also of private assets, especially if the economy is large and/or restrictions exist to capital mobility. Changes in the relative supply of debt instruments may affect risk premia and, in particular, the expected return that private investors require to hold equities and private debt. Through the channel of financial markets, government debt decisions may influence the cost of raising funds and, thus, real investment demand. This explains why debt management was traditionally viewed as an instrument to control aggregate demand. It was argued, for example, that rolling over Treasury bills, instead of issuing long-term bonds, stimulates real investment by reducing long interest rates and crowding equities in the portfolio of private investors.

Debt management also matters because it redistributes risk and changes the distribution of taxes across future contingencies. With incomplete markets for private financial assets, the introduction of a new government security would lead to a reallocation of risk and would possibly open up new opportunities for individuals to share risk. To continue with our example, in cases where a secondary market for private long-term debt did not exist, issuing 10-year government bonds could provide the necessary stimulus for such a market to develop. Even if private assets were actively traded, an efficient and liquid market for government securities would enhance hedging opportunities and improve risk sharing. For instance, government securities could be held by private investors as a necessary insurance against the risk of early liquidation of private assets. This suggests that the creation of benchmarks, say, by issuing substantial amounts of fixed-rate 10-year bonds, may be justified by insurance arguments in addition to interest-cost considerations.

Finally, debt management matters because it affects taxation. By choosing the type of debt to issue, the policymaker determines what will be the financing needs of the government in future contingencies. Alternative choices of government securities imply different distributions of debt returns across future states of the world and thus different taxes which will be levied depending on the realization of future events. Take the by-now-familiar choice between Treasury bills and 10-year bonds and suppose that an increase in the real interest rate occurs which was not expected at the time the strategy was decided (so that the higher rate was not discounted in the price at which 10-years bonds were issued). Had the government issued short-term bills instead of long-term bonds, it would end up paying a higher interest bill. Financing the correspondingly larger deficit would require taxes to be levied or public expenditures to be cut. As the opposite is true when the real interest rate falls, relying on short-term debt implies a greater uncertainty about future taxes which may lead to large variations in tax rates.[5] Since taxes distort the investment and labor choices of private agents, there is a theoretical rationale, or even better a welfare argument, for policymakers being concerned with the costs and risk of debt servicing. Indeed, high and variable tax rates are socially costly because they alter people's incentives to work and produce.

It is important to realize that the effect of debt management on taxation is not the consequence of a particular tax rule or way of financing budget deficits (or public spending); it could well be that the additional deficit, resulting from having borrowed short, is financed by issuing new debt. What the argument requires is that the government be prevented from borrowing indefinitely into the future in order to finance the interest payments on its debt, so that taxes will have to be raised eventually. This requirement is known as the "No-Ponzi Game condition."

The discussion thus far shows that many are the effects of debt management which a policymaker would have to consider when choosing the type of debt to issue. Evaluating the relative importance for social welfare of the various effects and thus concluding in favor of a specific debt policy is difficult. In Chapter 3, as a better approach to the problem, two alternative debt strategies are compared. A first strategy is to issue debt instruments which yield low returns in states where output and hence income are lower than expected so

---

[5] Suppose instead that an inflation surprise occurs. A capital loss will then be experienced on both securities, given that they are not indexed. However, to the extent that inflation is correlated over time and expected inflation is soon reflected in nominal interest rates, the real return on the roll-over strategy will remain relatively stable while a much lower return will be experienced on the strategy of issuing long-term bonds. In fact, the holding-period return on 10-year bonds would fall immediately, as future nominal rates are expected to be higher. In this case, a greater uncertainty about future taxes is induced by a longer maturity of the debt.

as to provide investors with insurance. The second strategy is to issue debt instruments which yield low returns when output is lower and public spending is higher than expected in order to hedge unexpected changes in government financing needs. The first policy minimizes the expected cost of debt servicing since lower risk-premia would be required by risk-averse investors to hold securities with returns negatively correlated to capital and labor income. The second policy implies higher interest costs but minimizes the overall risk in the government portfolio; i.e. the risk of having to change tax rates because of adverse shocks to government revenues and spending.

The analysis leads to the conclusion that, if risk premia on government securities just reflect their risk-return characteristics, the strategy of minimizing budgetary risk should be preferred to the strategy of minimizing interest costs. The ideal debt instrument would be positively indexed to output and negatively indexed to public spending so as to support a smoother path for tax rates and, thus, reduce tax distortions, relax liquidity constraints and enhance flexibility in conducting fiscal policy.

While output indexation is likely to be optimal if the prices of government securities reflect their risk-return characteristics, it may not be so in the presence of market inefficiencies, informational asymmetries, expectations failures and problems regarding the credibility of future policies. Even if market imperfections are limited to the frictions and delays associated with recording and reporting the relevant statistics, say GDP, output indexation can be particularly costly. It follows that policymakers must rely only on conventional securities, price and financial indexation.

The second part of the book deals with debt management by conventional securities. In Chapter 4 evidence on existing debt instruments and the compositions of public debts is presented for OECD countries over the period 1960–95. Since the real returns on conventional securities are implicitly contingent on future realization of the price level, the exchange rate and interest rates of different maturities, conventional debt instruments can provide substitutes for explicit output (and public spending) indexation.

Chapter 5 focuses on debt policy aimed at minimizing budgetary risk. Conventional securities are effective as hedging instruments to the extent that shocks adversely affecting government revenues, spending and refinancing costs also lead to lower than expected returns on public debt. The optimal choice of nominal versus price-index-linked bonds is shown to depend on the type of shocks hitting the economy, on whether supply or demand shocks prevail, on the importance of monetary disturbances, etc. The choice of debt denomination, i.e. domestic versus foreign currency debt, is also examined along the same lines. A special attention is paid to the maturity structure of domestic currency debt, a choice which finds a strong motivation in the objective of avoiding the risk of refinancing. Finally, evidence is provided on the relations between the returns on conventional instruments and the variables affecting the government budget. From the estimation of optimal debt compositions, a variety of patterns emerges across OECD economies regarding the composition between nominal, foreign currency and price-indexed debt which provides the best hedge against revenues and spending uncertainty.

Chapter 6 focusses on debt policy aimed at minimizing the expected cost of debt servicing. A concern for interest costs is justified if high risk-premia do not reflect the risk-return characteristics of debt instruments but result from market inefficiencies, informational asymmetries between the government and the private sector, expectational failures and the lack of credibility of future fiscal and monetary policy. A number of approaches to interest cost reduction are examined, such as "taking views on interest rates," issuing benchmarks, exploiting failures in the expectations hypothesis of the term structure, etc. A distinction is made between discretionary debt management and policies which enhance the transparency and regularity of government financial operations. Finally, the implications for debt management arising from the lack of credibility of government fiscal and monetary policies are spelled out. It is shown that the choice of debt instruments may signal the government resolution to carry out fiscal stabilization programs or set incentive for consistent, non-opportunistic, behavior. In particular, foreign currency debt, price indexation and short maturities may play a role in enhancing the credibility of the anti-inflationary policy.

Chapter 7 presents the main conclusions for policymaking.

2

The effects of debt management

2.1 The irrelevance of public debt management

Public debt management has important effects on the real economy. Only under restrictive assumptions about private agents' altruism and rationality, completeness and efficiency of financial markets and type of taxes, the government's choice of the composition of its outstanding liabilities and/or of the securities to issue does not matter. Studying such conditions is, however, important for two reasons. First, the neutrality result for tax-borrowing decisions known as Ricardian Equivalence (Barro 1974) has become a reference point in public finance. Second and more importantly, this analysis is a necessary first step toward a better understanding of the effects of debt management.

In what follows, an irrelevance theorem of debt management is derived and discussed. In fact, a number of neutrality propositions concerning government financial activity have been presented in the literature, but these results are obtained for specific examples concerning the structure of the economy and the debt-tax instruments available to the government. Hence, it is useful to outline a set of conditions sufficient for debt-management neutrality to hold under the most general assumptions about the structure of the economy. To this end it is helpful to think of the neutrality of debt management as extending the Ricardian Equivalence of tax-borrowing decisions to the choice of the financial instruments in which the government borrows.

The main difference with the decision between taxes and debt (as alternative means of financing public spending) is that, by definition, the choice of the debt instruments does not affect current taxes (and spending). Public debt management is the government's choice regarding the composition of its outstanding liabilities. It encompasses a variety of policies, including the choice of the denomination and maturity of the securities to issue; their indexation features; changes in the relative supply of existing securities; innovations in the menu of public assets. Such policies all leave current taxes unaffected. However, debt management does lead to changes in taxes across future periods and states of the world. The reason is that, for any given future event, the return on debt will differ depending on its composition. To take the simplest example, the decision to issue price-index-linked bonds makes the real return on debt invariant to the realization of future inflation, whereas issuing conventional fixed-rate bonds would make such a return contingent on inflation.

These considerations suggest an extension of the Ricardian Equivalence Theorem to debt management. The Ricardian proposition outlines conditions where the financing of a given path of government spending does not affect the real allocation of resources. If such conditions are satisfied, the choice of any of the possible combinations of current taxes and debt instruments compatible with funding needs does not matter. This is true, *a fortiori*, when attention is restricted to debt management: by holding current taxes fixed, we restrict the set of policy actions through which the government can affect the economy. It follows that the conditions for Ricardian Equivalence are sufficient for the neutrality of debt management. The discussion in the following sections will make it clear that conditions for debt-management neutrality are indeed less restrictive than those for tax-borrowing decisions.

Eliminating the unnecessary conditions of the Ricardian Equivalence, it is possible to identify a set of conditions sufficient to establish the following Neutrality Theorem of Debt Management:

Theorem of debt-management neutrality: Given current taxes and an exogenous path for public spending, public debt management does not affect the real allocation of resources if

(0) Private agents are rational;
(1) either current generations face any future change in taxation implied by government financial operations or else they are linked to future generations through altruistically motivated transfers;
(2) the share of future taxes to which each individual is called to contribute is state independent;
(3) capital markets are perfect. In particular, either there are no constraints on short sales of public assets or private substitutes for them exist;
(4) private asset markets are complete or, if they are incomplete, no new debt instrument is introduced that did not exist in the initial equilibrium;
(5) the use of debt cannot create value, i.e. debt Ponzi games are not viable;
(6) taxes do not distort incentives, for example, taxes are lump sum.

These conditions ensure that any conceivable financial operation of the government does not affect the equilibrium of the economy. Of course, failure of any of these conditions does not imply that debt management will necessarily have real effects. In particular, conditions (1), (2) and (5) may turn out to be unnecessary when financial operations do not change the return on the overall debt and thus taxes need not adjust. In this perspective, we can distinguish two classes of irrelevance propositions. The first class of results holds for operations which give rise to a change in the return on the overall debt. The second class of results —"pure" neutrality propositions—holds for financial operations not affecting the return on debt and, as a consequence, not requiring a change in future taxes (and spending).[1]

2.1.1 Debt-management neutrality

In general, changes in the composition of the outstanding debt, resulting from open market exchanges between debt instruments, or from alternative mix of debt instruments issued to finance the current deficit,[2] modify the pattern of future government liabilities across time and states of nature. As debt instruments with different risk characteristics yield different returns conditional on the same realization of the state of nature, the value of taxes, to be raised from next period on, depends on the current composition of the debt. This effect on taxation is not a consequence of a particular tax rule or way of financing budget deficits. It could well be that differences in debt returns do not lead to an immediate change in taxation, as higher (lower) interest payments can be financed by issuing new debt (or redeeming an old one). What the argument requires is that the government be prevented from borrowing (or lending) indefinitely far into the future in order to finance the interest payments on its debt: taxes will have to be raised (or cut) eventually. Formally, condition (5) must be satisfied, namely, debt Ponzi games must not be viable.

When changes in the debt composition affect the returns on debt across future states of world, debt management is neutral if (and only if) all the conditions stated in Section 2.1 are satisfied. In particular, to rule out intergenerational (and intragenerational) redistribution effects, people must be rational—take into account future tax liabilities—and either incur the change in future taxation themselves or care about the welfare of future generations. While this result looks familiar in view of Ricardian Equivalence, the following example adapted from Stiglitz (1983) may help the intuition.

Suppose that, starting from an initial equilibrium, the government undertakes an open market operation involving the purchase of government securities of type A in exchange for government securities of type B. Assume that the economy is stochastic and the return of these securities varies across states of nature; that security A yields a higher return in state X while security B in state Y. Hence, relative to the initial equilibrium, the open market operation increases government liabilities if state Y is realized and decrease them if state X is realized. Provided that debt Ponzi games are not viable, these changes in liabilities will eventually be serviced by levying taxes (by giving transfers in the state where liabilities decrease).

---

[1] Though fiat money is also a publicly issued asset, neutrality results for money, dominated in rate of return, are not reviewed. For a formal treatment see Sargent (1987).

[2] More precisely, here and in what follows what really matters is the financing of the overall deficit plus maturing debt.

An argument for this open market operation to be neutral is easily established if people currently alive either face the change in future taxation or are linked to future generations through a chain of altruistically motivated transfers. Suppose that both securities were in existence before the open market operation and that individual portfolio choices are not constrained, so that government financial activity does not change trading opportunities. Furthermore, assume that taxes are lump sum and that the share of the deficit (surplus) to which each individual (or her descendants) will be called to contribute is state independent. Since the change in the state-contingent distribution of debt returns implies the announcement of an offsetting change in the state-contingent distribution of taxes, agents' budget sets will be unaffected at initial equilibrium prices: any consumption plan which is feasible under the new debt composition was also feasible under the initial debt composition. Foresighted agents, realizing the change in their future fiscal position (or in the position of their descendants), will choose the same state-contingent consumption plans. Each agent can implement her desired plan by adjusting her asset portfolio to hedge against the change in tax liability risk. She can buy securities B and sell securities A in the same proportion of the share of the deficit (surplus) which she (or her descendants) will be called to contribute upon. As the demand for securities B rises and that for securities A falls to match exactly the new supply of these assets, all markets clear at the initial equilibrium prices. The argument can be easily extended to alternative mixes of debt instruments issued to finance a given current deficit.

This neutrality result is very general in the sense that it does not depend on the structure of the economy and on the risk-return characteristics of the securities considered. For instance, it holds for exchanges between securities with state-contingent returns and securities yielding safe returns (Stiglitz 1983); between nominally denominated and price-indexed securities (Levhari and Liviatan 1976); and for open market operations involving securities with different maturities (Chan 1983). It is also valid for exchanges of interest-bearing securities in monetary economies where fiat money is dominated in rate of return. However, because of the market imperfection needed for money to be valued, additional conditions must be met to extend the result to open market operations involving money.

The Say's law for debt management, that changes in relative supply of government bonds generate offsetting changes in relative demand of those assets, is clearly based on the the full set of neutrality conditions stated in the introduction. For debt management not to have redistribution effects, expectations must be rational and people currently alive must either face the corresponding changes in future taxes or be linked through (two-sided) altruism to future generations. In particular, in the absence of intergenerational transfers, the additional taxes (or transfers) which result from the change in the debt composition must be incurred at the time, or soon after, the uncertainty about debt returns is resolved. For redistribution not to occur, the share of the future deficit or surplus to which each individual is called to contribute must be state invariant. However, since current taxes are unaffected, the exact distribution of the imposition across individuals (or infinitely lived families) does not matter. Individuals must only know what fraction of the tax burden they will bear at the time of the open market operation, as pointed out by Chan (1983) and Stiglitz (1983).

Since neutrality hinges on offsetting changes in taxes and debt returns, debt Ponzi games must be explicitly ruled out for financial-tax operations to leave agents' intertemporal budget sets unaltered. If this were not the case, there would be no offsetting movements in the relative demand for public assets, and changes in the debt composition would affect the prices of public and private assets.

Importantly, securities A and B must already exist in the initial equilibrium for the invariance of agents' consumption opportunities. To undo government financial operations, agents must be able to buy and sell any desired amount of the government securities being exchanged, i.e. asset markets must be perfect.

Finally, the availability of non-distortionary taxation is important, not only to ensure that changes in future taxes implied by financial operations do not affect labor and investment choices but also to avoid incentive problems on the part of the government.

2.1.2   Neutrality with no change in debt returns

In general, changes in the composition of the public debt modify the distribution of debt returns across time and states of nature and, thus, imply different state-contingent paths for future taxes. However, under particular assumptions about the structure of the economy and the kind of assets considered, changes in the relative supply of existing public assets do not affect the overall returns (or value) of public debt and thus do not require a change in the path for future taxes (and public spending). As a result, conditions (1) and (2) turn out to be unnecessary for debt-management neutrality. Condition (5) also becomes unnecessary; as debt returns are not affected, neutrality does not require that debt Ponzi games be ruled out. However, if existing debt instruments allow for debt Ponzi games, they must not be retired, i.e. be put in zero supply.

The simplest case where debt management has no implications for future taxation, and is neutral provided that the other conditions are satisfied, is when there is no uncertainty. The reason is that, in the absence of uncertainty and market imperfections, all types of assets must yield the same rate of return per holding period (i.e. they are perfect substitutes) which implies that debt instruments with different characteristics, say denomination and maturity, are redundant as long as one asset is available to the government.

While the case of no uncertainty looks trivial, it serves to point out that even this extreme assumption is not sufficient to ensure neutrality by itself. Even with certainty the type of debt that governments issue matters if some other condition is violated. For instance, the condition that taxes are lump sum is still crucial for the neutrality of debt management if the government cannot credibly commit to a given tax plan. If taxes are distortionary, because of efficiency considerations the government may later want to deviate from its previously announced tax plan and reduce the value of the debt, say through inflation. The choice of the denomination and maturity of debt instruments is relevant insofar as it affects these future government decisions.[3]

Irrelevance theorems for government financial operations, which do not affect the overall return on the public debt, have also been derived under uncertainty for OLG economies with particular asset structures. Examples include Chamley and Polemarchakis (1984) who consider financial operations involving money and a productive investment technology with risky returns, Peled (1985) who treats money and non-contingent public bonds in an economy with random endowments, and Gottardi (1987) who considers one-period public bonds and an infinitely-lived risky asset yielding physical returns. Finally, as shown by Chamley and Polemarchakis (1984), neutrality with unchanged taxation would also obtain in Wallace (1981) although Wallace's result relies on unnecessary adjustments of taxes and transfers.

These results have all been obtained in OLG economies where investment opportunities have a particular characteristic and do not generalize to economies with arbitrary asset structures. The crucial aspect that they all share is that there must exist at least one infinitely-lived asset, like land or fiat money (held only as a store of value), while other assets must be claims on next period goods, like one-period real bonds or a productive investment technology.[4]

For neutrality it is important that the return on the long-lived asset be determined endogenously at the end of the saving period by intergenerational trade, while the return on the short-lived asset be given exogenously once the saving decision is made. Within this asset structure, the private portfolio return (or its value) depends linearly on the resale price of the long-lived asset as

---

[3] Whether the debt has a finite maturity or an infinite maturity also matters in overlapping generations (OLG) economies in the absence of uncertainty. Suppose that the competitive equilibrium is dynamically inefficient because of incomplete participation as in the OLG models of Samuelson (1958) or Diamond (1965). Then, the introduction of finite maturity debt, say, one-period debt, reduces the inefficiency but does not eliminate it completely if debt is not in adequate supply. On the contrary, issuance of infinite maturity debt like fiat money may lead to a Pareto-efficient allocation. This is because infinite maturity debt creates value by allowing for new trades between generations which are not possible with one-period debt. In fact, with one-period debt, each generation only trades with the government.

[4] Gottardi (1987) shows that the infinitely-lived asset needs not be government-issued money and be intrinsically useless.

determined endogenously by market equilibrium. This price can thus adjust to undo any effect on the portfolio return resulting from previous changes in its composition. Consider a price adjustment which leaves the portfolio return of the currently old generation unaffected. Clearly, this adjustment leaves the allocation of consumption between the currently old and young generations unaffected. More importantly, current changes in asset prices do not bind the overall return from saving of the currently young generation because such a return will depend on the resale value of the long-lived asset next period. Because of the infinite maturity of the asset and of the OLG structure of the economy a terminal valuation problem does not arise; the price of the long-lived assets can adjust indefinitely far into the future so as to replicate the initial equilibrium allocation of resources. Formally, for any given composition of the private portfolio there exists a price path of the long-lived asset which supports the same allocation of resources as a competitive rational-expectations equilibrium. Intuitively, each generation is indifferent about the composition of its portfolio since such a composition does not place any restriction on the portfolio return. Finally, because government financial operations do not affect the private portfolio return (or value), the return (or value) of the resulting government portfolio, i.e. net public debt, is also unaffected. So, financial operations do not require changes in future taxes and spending in any state of nature.

Therefore, within this class of neutrality results, government financial operations which modify the composition of the private portfolio lead to a change in the equilibrium path of prices of the long-lived asset but do not have real effects. This neutrality result can be generalized to economies with many assets, as shown in Sargent (1987), and to open market operations which involve only short-lived assets provided that a long-lived asset exists and is valued, as shown in Gottardi (1987). However, it fails whenever changes in the price of the long-lived asset alter other asset returns, as it would be the case if there were a nominal asset other than money in the economy, an implication shown in Chamley and Polemarchakis (1984), and in Detemple, Gottardi and Polemarchakis (1995). Obviously, since the equilibrium in OLG economies is typically not unique, this neutrality result does not ensure that all policies sharing the same path for taxes and spending result in the same allocation of resources, as pointed out by Peled (1985).

While conditions about tax-return redistribution effects are unnecessary to establish neutrality, it must be recognized that other conditions must be satisfied. Neutrality requires that no new asset is introduced into the economy and that individual portfolio choices are unconstrained; e.g. that short-selling is allowed. In particular, since market imperfections need to be assumed away, the neutrality proposition does not extend to monetary economies where money, dominated in rate of return, is held because of the inefficiency of the credit system. Finally, if the government is not able to precommit, neutrality requires that taxes are lump sum in order to rule out the incentive problems which have been discussed above for the case of perfect certainty.

Clearly, the very special asset structure required to establish neutrality lessens the practical importance of the result. Further doubts on the generality of this class of neutrality theorems emerge when one considers that for an equilibrium to exist, where both types of assets are traded, the asset structure must meet additional restrictions besides those considered so far. For instance, to insure the existence of an equilibrium where both money is valued and an investment technology is used the risk-return characteristics of the technology must be restricted; an equilibrium where money (or a long-lived capital good) is valued requires that bonds be supplied in limited amount, etc.

To conclude, "pure" irrelevance theorems, where government financial operations do not change the overall return on public debt and, thus, need not be coupled by changes in future taxes (or spending), are best viewed as interesting exceptions. If anything the sense in which debt management is neutral is limited: the type of debt that governments issue matters.

2.2 Why debt management does matter

Under general assumptions about the structure of the economy, the full set of neutrality conditions is needed to establish the irrelevance of public debt management. A closer examination of each of these conditions in turn explains why debt management affects economic activity and points to the welfare effects which can be expected from specific policies. The choice of debt instruments is shown to have important implications for the distribution of risk and for the efficiency of taxation and financial markets.

2.2.1 Distortionary taxation

In a world that is Ricardian in all respects except that taxes are distortionary, there is an optimal time profile of tax rates that minimizes the welfare losses of tax distortions (see Barro 1979). However, in the absence of uncertainty the characteristics of public debt, say denomination and maturity, would be irrelevant for taxation.[5]

With uncertainty, the risk-return characteristics of the debt have instead a crucial role in supporting the least distortionary tax scheme. Alternative mixes of debt instruments imply different distributions of debt returns across future contingencies. Since future taxes depend on debt returns, current changes in debt composition also lead to changes in the state-contingent distribution of tax rates on labor and capital income. If taxes distort incentives, such changes affect labor and investment choices both in future contingencies and in the current period.

---

[5] The argument abstracts from time consistency problems and from changes in the composition between money and interest-bearing debt.

Assume, for the moment, that tax rates on capital income are not contingent. Then, there exists a distribution of labor-income tax rates across time and states of nature which minimizes distortions in labor-leisure choices and is compatible with current and future funding needs. As the latter depend on the debt returns resulting upon the resolution of uncertainty, the welfare-maximizing policy calls for a joint determination of the state-contingent path for labor tax rates and debt returns. Corresponding to the optimal tax scheme there exists a unique risk-return structure of public debt which supports such a scheme. In particular, to implement the (second best) optimal tax plan, governments should issue a full set of state-contingent securities. Thus, in a dynamic stochastic environment the theory of optimal taxation is also a theory of optimal debt management, as first shown by Lucas and Stokey (1983) for an economy without capital.

The relevance of debt management extends to the case where governments can rely on state-contingent capital taxation except for the unrealistic case that there exists only one production technology. In fact, with only one technology the government could choose the state-contingent distribution of tax rates on capital income to support optimal labor taxation while issuing any type of security, for example, a safe asset, as shown by Zhu (1992), King (1990) and Chari, Christiano and Kehoe (1994). This is because the exact distribution of capital tax rates across states of nature does not affect investment incentives; only the expected value of tax rates does. In other words, with one production technology optimal taxation of capital income imposes only one constraint on the choice of capital tax rates. The government is free to choose the state-contingent tax rates on capital income in order to support optimal labor taxation. However, Bohn (1994) shows that debt management regains its role when the number of technologies and thus constraints implied by an efficient capital taxation increase. Efficient labor taxation requires a number of securities with different risk-return characteristics at least equal to the number of technologies. Specifically, it requires debt yielding returns explicitly contingent on at least N states of nature where N is the number of technologies.

The time inconsistency of fiscal and monetary policy is the second reason why debt management matters in the presence of distortionary taxation. The government may want to change the initially optimal tax plan at a later date, since the demand elasticities of debt and capital will be different from the viewpoint of this later date. Specifically, while the demand for government securities is very elastic with respect to expected net returns, it is zero after the securities have been issued; once in place debt provides an inelastic tax base for non-distorting taxation. Hence, issuing debt and announcing that it will be serviced by raising taxes on labor income might be the policy which is optimal conditional on the expectation that it will be carried out. But once the debt has been issued, the least distortionary policy may call for levying taxes on debt, or reducing its value by inflating or altering the path for real interest rates.

Obviously, debt management has no effect, if the government is able to set taxes for all future dates and contingencies, if it is able to credibly "precommit" to future policy actions. When precommitment is not possible, the choice of the denomination and maturity structure of public debt matters insofar as these characteristics affect the government incentives to depart from the original tax plan. To take a simple example, fixed-rate nominal debt creates a temptation for unanticipated inflation so as to reduce the real value of debt and hence the need for distorting taxes. If private agents realize the government incentive to inflate, the government cannot expect to obtain any revenue with surprise inflation. Anticipating inflation, rational agents ask for so high interest rates as to make the government unwilling to incur further inflation costs for lower tax distortions. Nominal debt only leads to an inflationary bias, a worse outcome than a government able to precommit would obtain. The problem does not arise, instead, if securities are either indexed to the price level or denominated in foreign currencies. On the other hand, if private agents are fooled into believing government announcements, nominal debt provides the government with an additional source of revenues.

While debt management matters irrespective of private sector's expectations, if expectations are rational the choice of debt instruments affects private agents' beliefs about future policy actions, for instance, it affects the expectation that policies will be carried over as announced. The relevant insight of the time consistency literature is that debt management allows the government to put in place incentives for consistent behavior, thereby establishing the "credibility" of a particular policy. In the previous example, issuance of foreign currency debt or price-indexed debt removes the incentive to inflate, thus enhancing the expectation that monetary policy will be anti-inflationary.

However, to the extent that debt management can influence private sector's expectations, it opens the possibility for a strategic use of debt characteristics. Milesi-Ferretti (1995) shows that an incumbent government may choose the type of debt so as to improve its chances of being re-elected. For example, an inflation-averse government could lengthen the maturity of nominal debt in order to shift the voters' preferences in its favor when the opposition government bears a relatively lower cost from inflating than from raising conventional taxes (see also Uhlig 1997). Pecchi and Piga (1999) contend that in a number of countries the monetary authorities oppose the introduction of price-index-linked debt in order to build a larger constituency against inflationary policy.

An interesting role for debt management emerges when the government's inability to precommit and private agents to coordinate create a potential for multiple rational-expectations equilibria. In such cases debt management may coordinate individual agents' expectations on the "good" equilibrium. In a model where both taxes and inflation are costly, Calvo (1988) shows that an equilibrium with low inflation and low nominal interest rates may coexist with an equilibrium with high inflation and high interest rates. If private agents expect high inflation and thus demand high interest payments on nominal debt, their inflationary expectations are self-fulfilling. Ex post the government can do no better than relying more heavily on inflation the higher is the debt burden.

The idea that debt management can remove temptations for opportunistic behavior can be formalized in the absence of uncertainty. However, the introduction of uncertainty leads to substantially different policy implications. With uncertainty, anti-temptation motives interact with efficient taxation in the choice of the risk-return characteristics of the debt. As discussed later, the current literature on distortionary taxation holds that the choice of the debt characteristics should hinge on the trade-off between credibility gains and the costs of adjusting taxes in response to shocks adversely affecting the government budget.

For the purpose of supporting an efficient tax scheme the type of debt available to governments is important, since it determines the extent to which tax distortions are avoidable. Obviously, if asset markets were complete, i.e. if there existed a full set of state-contingent securities, the government would be in an ideal position to implement the optimal policy. In fact, what matters is not so much whether private asset markets are complete but the government's ability to issue securities which are explicitly contingent on the relevant events.

The incompleteness and inefficiency of private asset markets are instead important *per se* as soon as the effects of debt management on the allocation of risk and on private borrowing opportunities are considered. Such effects become immediately relevant as we abandon the theoretical benchmark of a representative individual and examine limited access to financial markets and distributional issues.

2.2.2 Market imperfections

The notion of spanning is crucial for debt-management neutrality as much as for the other classical irrelevance theorems in the theory of finance. Security trades available to the private sector must span the same risk-return set of government financial operations. Intuitively, to undo the effects of financial-tax operations, the private sector must face the same opportunities as the government in choosing its portfolio strategy.

Allowing for unlimited short sales (and purchase) of government securities (at the prevailing price) is one way to ensure neutrality. An alternative sufficient condition is that private security markets provide private substitutes for government securities. Put simply, individual agents must have the possibility either to take short positions in the relevant government security or to borrow in a composite asset of private securities which replicates the state-contingent payoff structure of the government security. When there are binding constraints on negative holdings of public assets and a private substitute for them does not exist, debt management alters the tax-return opportunity set confronting investors. In that case government financial operations affect asset prices and resource allocation, as emphasized by Stiglitz (1983), Chan (1983) and Gale (1990) among others.

To see why constraints on short sales are important, consider the example of Section 1.1 where the government sells securities of type B and buys back an equal value of securities A. There it was implicitly assumed that the individuals, who will bear the change in taxation implied by the financial operation, hold a sufficient amount of securities A to exchange with securities B so as to leave their future net income unaffected across contingencies. To see what happens when this is not the case, suppose that the future change in taxation affects only some individuals, let's say of group i, but all the public debt is held by individuals of group j. Then to counter the government operation individuals i should buy securities B and finance the operation by selling securities A, which they do not have in the initial equilibrium. They must sell short securities A to individuals j, who in turn sell an equal value of such securities to the government to maintain their tax-return risk unchanged. For such trades to take place (possibly unlimited) short sales of the public asset A must be allowed. Alternatively, private debt with identical risk-return characteristics of the asset A must exist or be created.

Market imperfections can be a consequence of legal restrictions. Legal reserve requirements, portfolio constraints (Haliassos and Tobin 1990) and minimum denomination in which securities can be issued (Sargent and Wallace 1982) are examples often cited in the literature. In the past short selling of public debt was prohibited and only recently, with the introduction of futures contracts and "repos" markets for public bonds, has this constraint been relaxed. It is worth noting, however, that it is not so much the degree of perfection in private capital markets which matters for the irrelevance of debt management but rather the opportunities faced by the private sector relative to the government. Private agents may be unable to borrow at the same condition as the government, namely, to create private assets with the same characteristics of public debt because of informational asymmetries, verifiability and bankruptcy costs (see Stiglitz 1983 and Chan 1983). Indeed, it has long been argued, from Tobin (1963) to Stiglitz (1983), that the risk of default on private debt makes it impossible to create a private substitute for government debt.

While the current literature indicates capital market imperfections as a potential source for the effects of debt management, it has not yet provided insights on their implications. To find informal arguments for the effects of debt management based on market imperfections one must look at the literature of the 1950s and 1960s (Rolph 1957, Musgrave 1959 and Tobin 1963). However, if private agents are unable to borrow on the same conditions as the government, a role for debt management to relax borrowing constraints emerges quite naturally, even if the choice of government securities does not affect current taxes. For instance, liquidity constraints are likely to bind consumption choices in states of the world where aggregate and thus individual labor income are relatively lower. This implies that constrained agents may want to sell short government securities yielding high returns in high-income states in exchange for securities yielding high returns in low-income states. Insofar as constrained agents are prevented from implementing strategies involving short sales of government securities their relative supply matters. There is a clear role for the government to issue securities yielding returns positively indexed to labor income so as to allow for tax reductions in low-income states and thus relax borrowing constraints. Put it simply, the government can lessen liquidity constraints by issuing those securities which agents cannot sell short.

Liquidity constraints can alternatively be viewed as resulting from the absence of markets for future labor income or from private agents' inability to issue securities with the same characteristics as government securities. However, viewing liquidity constraints as being caused by market imperfections or incomplete markets does not change policy implications. The difference is conceptual in that, with imperfections, non-neutrality does not arise from missing markets in some kind of assets but from the fact that trades in such assets are constrained. Within an incomplete market framework the issues which arise are of a distributional nature; they regard risk sharing.

2.2.3   Incomplete markets

It has long been recognized that as long as the government does not create new securities the irrelevance of debt management can be established within an incomplete market framework (Chan 1983, Chamley and Polemarchakis 1984). Indeed, none of the arguments for neutrality reviewed so far relies on the existence of a full set of state-contingent claims. If government financial activity is limited to modify the relative supply of existing securities and people are free to trade, changes in the state-contingent distribution of debt returns and future taxes provide people with no new opportunities that were not available with the previous debt-tax mix. On the other hand, when private asset markets are incomplete, the introduction of a "new" government security alters the consumption opportunity sets of economic agents since it opens up trading opportunities which were absent in the initial equilibrium.[6] Then, nothing guarantees that people will choose the same consumption plan: the change in the set of traded public securities has a real impact on the economy.

However, it must be noted that public provision of a new security, though it changes the allocation of risk, is not like opening a private market because the distribution of future taxes also changes and so does the incidence of

---

[6] Obviously, the argument assumes that the security is not redundant, namely, that its return is not spanned by existing assets.

taxation across individuals. Unlike for a private contract where agents are free to join, participation in the public security-tax scheme is compulsory on the side of taxation (see Buchanan 1958). Therefore, the effect on risk allocation of introducing a new security very much depends upon how taxes will change and who will be liable for paying them (see Levhari and Liviatan 1976). On one hand, the possibility to use its taxing power allows the government to implement risk allocations which cannot be reached by the private sector. On the other hand, the compulsory aspect of taxation suggests that public provision of a new security will not replicate the outcome of the missing private market in that security, unless the incidence of taxation is carefully designed. Specifically, the "new-market" analogy holds only if the corresponding change in taxation does not alter each individual's tax share in any state of nature. As made clear by Campbell and Shiller (1996), in reviewing arguments for price-index-linked bonds, the introduction of a new public security can be welfare improving but the effect is certain only if a private market in the same security develops as a result of government innovation.

While the consideration of incomplete markets makes a strong case for the effectiveness of innovative debt management, it raises the issue of what type of debt governments should issue. Leaving aside the unrealistic case where the government issues a full set of contingent claims, this is a difficult issue to address. To evaluate whether government financial innovation is desirable one needs to know which and why markets are missing; how taxes will be affected by the innovation and who will be liable for them, as stressed by Levhari and Liviatan (1976) and Fischer (1983). In particular, financial innovation may not be welfare improving for every type of agent; it may just give rise to distribution trade-offs or even make everybody worse off (Hart 1975).

Research has progressed by considering whether particular public assets improve opportunities for sharing risk in OLG economies. In an OLG economy current generations cannot enter insurance contracts with generations yet unborn. Under certain specifications about uncertainty, the technology and the financial asset structure, the equilibrium is not Pareto optimal. Consequently there is scope for improving on the allocation of risk between different generations (see Gale 1990 and Blanchard and Weil 1992). Depending on the risk-return characteristics of the public assets being issued, government financial activity may be successful in providing intergenerational insurance. While general results have not yet been derived, there are several examples in the literature where even the introduction of relatively simple assets is welfare improving.[7]

This line of research raises the issue of what prevents long-lived private institutions from providing financial insurance in place of the government. Gale

---

[7] See Weiss (1980), Battacharya (1982) and Peled (1984) for the role of fiat money, Fischer (1983) and Peled (1985) for safe debt, Pagano (1988) for debt indexed to capital income, and Gale (1990) for the role of the maturity of safe debt.

(1990) suggests a motivation for government intervention based on the difficulties faced by private intermediaries in internalizing the positive externalities of financial innovation. Another reason is that the optimal insurance scheme may not operate without taxes. Fischer (1983) argues that the government has a natural advantage over private intermediaries which derives from its ability to tax future income and thus, to sell claims on future taxes.

The interaction between tax and financial decisions has been pointed out many times in the discussion. Indeed, the optimal insurance scheme can be implemented either through the choice of the risk characteristics of debt instruments or equivalently by means of a tax-transfer scheme. This raises the issue of why any public financial activity is needed when the government has lump-sum taxes and transfers at its disposal. The objection gains strength if we observe, as does Gale (1990) that there exist situations where the optimal allocation achievable with taxes and transfers cannot be decentralized as a competitive equilibrium with debt. A possible explanation is that tax-policy implementation presupposes a gathering of information which goes beyond the government capability. If the government knows the stochastic framework but cannot observe the realization of the state of nature, there is an advantage in relying on markets for public securities. The price of public debt may reveal valuable information needed to implement the insurance scheme. Furthermore, insurance policy relying on state-contingent taxes and transfers can easily run into incentive problems because people may not truthfully report the state of nature when the latter is private knowledge, as argued by Bhattacharya (1982).

While in the literature the scope for intergenerational insurance has been the main focus of the analysis, other opportunities for sharing risk can be thought of. Idiosyncratic taste and liquidity shocks are clear examples of risks which cannot be insured. This suggests a role for asset markets in providing liquidity services at the lowest transaction costs. Hence, in the absence of insurance markets for idiosyncratic risk, thin and illiquid markets for private securities give rise to a demand for "liquid" government securities with interesting implications for debt management. If the costs and inconveniences of exchanging interest-bearing debt for money vary across debt instruments, the liquidity of marketable government securities becomes an important consideration. For instance, with highly inefficient markets, short maturities may become a substitute for "liquidity," so that investors may require a lower expected return on short-term than on long-term securities. On the other hand, as efficient and thick secondary markets for long-term securities develop, as happened in most OECD economies, long maturities become more liquid than short maturities. The liquidity of government securities can be improved by promoting "benchmarks," that is, by issuing large amounts of securities with the same risk-return characteristics.

When the focus is on conventional fixed-rate securities differing only because of their coupon and term to maturity, this objective provides a rationale for the extensive use of consols in the past, since consols maintain the same infinite maturity over time. The recent practice of selling fungible bonds, namely, long-term bonds with coupons and maturities identical to those of existing issues, through subsequent auctions held at different dates, complies with the same logic.

2.2.4 Redistribution

In general, changes in the relative supply of government securities modify the distribution of debt returns across future states of the world and, hence, the risk-return set spanned by the private sector's portfolio. Only if the implied change in state-contingent future taxes (or transfers) falls on rational agents who are currently alive or on infinitely lived families, these operations have no real effects. [8] Changes in the relative supply of government securities may have redistribution effects, even when no new security is introduced into the economy. This happens if private agents do not hedge against the changes in tax liabilities implied by government financial operations, either because they do not rationally discount future tax changes or because such changes fall on future generations or alter the incidence of taxation across individuals of generations currently alive. [9] Incidentally, it is worth noting that government financial activity redistributes wealth risk across generations and individuals rather than wealth itself, since, current taxes being fixed, the pattern of redistribution depends on the realization of future events.

When private agents do not hedge against changes in tax risk (implied by government financial operations) risk-redistribution effects arise irrespective of the timing of taxation. With finite planning horizons redistribution effects do arise whenever the change in future taxes falls on generations yet unborn at the time of the operation. Financial operations may change the distribution of risk even if the time interval between the operation and the resolution of uncertainty about debt returns is small compared to the length of people's lives because governments can temporarily meet changes in their obligations by issuing new debt or by redeeming outstanding debt. That this is a relevant consideration is shown by the recent experience of most OECD countries where debt expansions and contractions have lasted about 20 years, as documented in Chapter 4.

[8] Note that debt-management neutrality does not require that all individuals, on whom taxes are currently being levied, be subject to future tax changes and thus relies on weaker conditions than those needed for the Ricardian Equivalence of financing public spending.

[9] Only if the asset structure is so special as to ensure that government financial operations do not affect debt returns and hence future taxation, redistribution is not an issue in spite of finite planning horizons and individual heterogeneity.

These considerations suggest that the timing of taxation is important and raise the issue of whether its choice interacts with debt management. As a way of organizing thoughts it can be said that, as long as taxes are lump sum, the risk-return characteristics of public debt do not impose a constraint on intertemporal tax decisions and hence on wealth redistribution policy. This is because financial operations imply a redistribution of the tax burden across states of nature but have no direct implications on how the burden is distributed over time. However, when taxes are distortionary the choice of the state-contingent tax scheme and hence the design of public debt can no longer be viewed as being independent from intertemporal tax decisions. Then, redistribution policy hinges on the joint determination of debt management and tax-borrowing decisions. Since in actual economies taxes are distortionary, redistribution should be a consideration as important as efficiency in evaluating government financial policy. Unfortunately, no attempt has been made yet to study the interaction of these two dimensions of debt management.

Exchanges of government securities may redistribute risk also within the same generation. Redistribution occurs if the share of taxes that each individual has to pay depends on the state of nature. This may happen if individual's tax shares are related to income, say because of proportional income taxation. In this case changes in taxes across states of nature, implied by financial operations, are equivalent to a redistribution of the incidence of taxation across individuals. For instance, the open market operation considered in the example of Section 1.1 would increase net wealth of individuals who earn a lower share of aggregate income in state Y than in state X. Only if individual's tax shares are state invariant private agents can easily hedge against tax liability risk; changes in the supply of government securities provide in the aggregate the perfect hedge for the corresponding changes in state-contingent taxation.

There is, however, an exception to this result. As shown by Chan (1983), redistribution may not take place if a complete set of markets for claims on future net income exist. This is because people could enter insurance contracts which nullify any redistributive impact of government financial operations. For example, risk-averse individuals could pool the risk of government intervention by transferring their holdings of government securities to a financial intermediary in exchange for claims equal to the future realization of their tax liability. Since government financial operations never give rise to aggregate risk, the intermediary would be in a position to hedge against tax redistribution risk. However, such insurance contracts are best viewed as an intellectual curiosity.

A separate issue arises when the timing and the incidence of future taxes across individuals is uncertain. In effect, while it has been implicitly assumed that governments announce the changes in taxation associated with financial operations, this is never the case in actual economies. Put simply, each individual may not know whether and how much she will be called to contribute to the change in future taxes. In fact, taxes can be raised on different types of income and/or at different future dates. Chan (1983) shows that in a Ricardian world the postponement of lump-sum taxes may lead to an increase in pre-cautionary saving when individuals' shares of future taxes are uncertain and the relevant insurance market is missing. A tentative extension of this effect to debt management suggests that an increase in the relative supply of government securities with riskier returns may increase saving. As aggregate tax variability increases under the new debt structure and individual tax shares are uncertain, individuals face more net wealth risk and, as a result, might save more as a precaution.[10]

Risk redistribution effects of debt management have been examined within the OLG economy structure. Although, with finite planning horizons effects on risk allocation do arise because of changes in the relative supply of existing assets and not only because of the introduction of new government securities, the literature has mainly focussed on the welfare implications of financial innovation (see however Stiglitz 1983 and Pagano 1988).

On the other hand, the effects of debt policy on financial market equilibrium have been extensively examined in the literature of the 1960s and 1970s. When planning horizons are finite and/or people do not take into account their future tax liabilities government debt policy has an impact on the expected returns, not only of government securities but also of private assets. This is because, changes in the relative supply of government securities would not be accommodated by offsetting movements in demand but would require a change in equilibrium asset prices. In other words, debt management may affect risk premia and, in particular, the expected return that private investors require to hold equities and private debt. Through financial markets government financial operations may influence the cost of raising funds and, hence, real investment demand (and savings decisions). This explains why debt management has been traditionally viewed as an instrument to control aggregate demand; the effects of changes in the maturity structure of conventional securities on investment have first been discussed by Tobin (1963) and Brownlee and Scott (1963) and formalized by Roley (1979).

2.3 Concluding remarks

The analysis of the preceding sections has identified a number of reasons as to why debt management affects economic activity. Each reason suggests a welfare improving role for debt management if not yet a specific debt strategy: (i) if

---

[10] This effect does not disappear when we consider that individual tax shares are uncertain because they are related to income. Unlike in the case of tax-borrowing decisions, examined in Barsky, Mankiew and Zeldes (1986), the consideration of proportional income taxation does not lead to the opposite result because the variability of the tax rate is what matters here, as opposed to the level of the tax rate.

taxes distort incentives, debt management may support the distribution of tax rates which minimizes the welfare loss of tax distortions. If time consistency is an issue, the design of public debt may enhance the credibility of policy announcements; (ii) if security markets are inefficient and markets for future labor income are missing, debt management has a role in relaxing borrowing constraints. With thin markets for private securities the liquidity of government securities can provide partial insurance against the risk of idiosyncratic liquidity and taste shocks; (iii) if private security markets are incomplete, the set of securities that the government issues, together with the implied distribution of taxes, determines the equilibrium allocation of risk. With unexploited opportunities for sharing the risk of generation-specific shocks, debt-tax schemes can be designed to improve intergenerational insurance; and (iv) if private agents do not take into account tax risk (either because of tax-myopia or because taxes fall on future generations) debt management changes the distribution or the perception of risk. In this case, the choice of debt instruments has an impact on the financial market equilibrium and may favor saving and investment decisions.

Since there are many reasons why debt management affects real outcomes, one needs to ask how this potential should be used. It is however hard to assess the relative importance for social welfare of the various effects of debt management and to make a case for specific policies. In Chapter 3 two debt strategies are identified and an attempt is made to evaluate how they fare in terms of tax distortions, liquidity constraints, risk allocation, saving and investment decisions.

3

How should the public debt be managed?

3.1 Expected cost versus risk minimization

How should the public debt be managed? This question has received different answers depending on the specific reasons considered as to why debt management matters. Each of these reasons suggests a policy objective: (i) distorting taxes—the design of public debt should support optimal taxation, also ensuring its time consistency; (ii) incomplete markets—debt management should improve risk sharing; (iii) imperfect markets—market efficiency should be enhanced; (iv) tax myopia and finite planning horizons—debt instruments should support stabilization policy.

Evaluating the relative importance for social welfare of the various effects of debt management so as to conclude in favor of a specific policy is far from straightforward. The absence of a general framework to contrast the welfare merits and drawbacks of specific policies sets a limitation to policy design. There is much to be gained from a unified approach to debt management which discusses and evaluates alternative debt strategies and their implications for taxation, risk sharing and market efficiency.

As a better approach to the problem, in this chapter two strategies are derived and compared in terms of the various effects of debt management. These strategies are suggested by the importance in policymaking of the following objectives:

1. minimization of the expected costs of debt servicing
2. minimization of the risk of debt servicing

As documented in Chapter 1, funding at the least cost and risk are goals explicitly stated in the official documents of many OECD countries. Policy measures to achieve such objectives are potentially many. However, cost and risk minimization lead to very simple implications for debt management when the least of inefficiencies and informational failures is assumed, namely, when:

(i) the government and private agents share the same information;
(ii) private agents make no systematic mistakes in forming expectations;
(iii) the government can credibly commit to future policy actions; and
(iv) markets are efficient (except for short-selling constraints on government securities).

These assumptions imply that risk premia on government securities just depends on their risk-return characteristics. Ruling out informational problems and severe imperfections ensures that differences in the expected returns of debt instruments are "fair," namely, that they reflect properly called risk premia asked by risk-averse investors who do not make systematic mistakes, are fully informed about the likelihood of future events, and confident that fiscal and monetary policy actions will be carried out as announced.

In such an ideal world, objective 1—the minimization of the expected cost of debt servicing—has a simple implication: the securities with the lowest risk premium should be issued. This can be accomplished by issuing securities which pay high returns in states of the world where labor and capital income are unexpectedly low, and low returns in states where income is unexpectedly high.

Which strategy minimizes risk is harder to say. A main complication is the absence of a satisfactory definition of risk. Conventional wisdom and policy practice identify in the risk of refinancing (maturing debt at higher than expected interest rates) the risk which is relevant for debt management. However, if containing the exposure of the government budget to interest-rate shocks is the rationale for avoiding "roll-over risk," then a broader and proper definition of risk is warranted. The definition proposed in Chapter 1 considers the risk of changes in government financing needs arising from shocks to output and public spending along with interest-rate shocks. This definition also shares a concern, but does not limit attention to refinancing risk; it views shocks to government revenues and spending as important as interest-rate shocks in determining financing risk. As a private investor takes labor income into account in deciding her portfolio, a government should be concerned not only with its financial liabilities but also with the net income from its real activity: tax revenues and public spending.

In view of these considerations, objective 2—the minimization of risk— implies a design of public debt with debt returns which are low when revenues are unexpectedly low and public spending is unexpectedly high, i.e. when financing needs turns out to be greater than expected. Thus, a strategy which aims to minimize risk does not only insulate the budget from interest-rate variations but also relies on debt instruments yielding low returns when revenues and thus income are unexpectedly low.

It follows that the risk-return characteristics which allow for the minimization of risk premia are the same characteristics which lead to an increased exposure of the budget to unexpected variations in financing needs. A trade-off emerges between the objectives of minimizing risk and minimizing interest costs. Then, the policy issue is: Should governments issue debt instruments which yield high returns in states where output is high (and spending is low) or should they follow the opposite strategy?

These two options provide a simple but exhaustive distinction between the available debt strategies in a framework where informational problems and market imperfections are ruled out. The choice amounts to positioning at an extreme point on the trade-off between cost and risk minimization.

What follows is an evaluation of these alternative strategies in light of the various effects of debt management. The examination of the arguments presented in the literature to date and the new arguments contained within Chapter 2 allows for an assessment of the welfare merits and drawbacks of these strategies, and provides a first important reference for policy decisions.

3.2 Finite horizons and capital accumulation

Securities which yield high returns in states where output is lower than expected are likely to meet the demand by risk-averse private investors as they provide valuable insurance against capital and labor-income risk. Since low risk-premia are required by investors to hold such securities, a strategy, which relies on high debt returns in states where ouput is lower than expected, minimizes the expected cost of debt servicing.

However, cost minimization falls short of providing a convincing argument for issuing debt with countercyclical returns. The effects of such a policy on social welfare must be considered. In particular, one needs to evaluate whether market efficiency is affected, how future taxes will change and how risk will be shared, say, between investors and taxpayers and/or between generations.

Is there any welfare argument for supplying debt that yields high returns upon the realization of bad shocks to output or capital income? In particular, is there a reason for providing insurance to asset holders? In this section, the implications of debt management for future taxes are left aside in order to focus on the effects which originate from changes in financial market equilibrium induced by government financial operations.

A candidate argument for high debt returns in low-output states is that this design of public debt could favor capital accumulation. While a positive effect on growth is not sufficient to conclude that a policy is socially desirable, the role of public borrowing for capital accumulation is a traditional theme of public finance. In what follows, effects on saving and investment decisions are examined to see whether the neoclassical concern for budget deficits to reduce capital accumulation, growth and future generations' welfare can be extended to debt management.

3.2.1 Saving decisions

Debt management can affect the accumulation and allocation of capital, if the corresponding changes in debt returns and taxes redistribute wealth-risk across and within generations. With finite planning horizons distribution effects arise when changes in tax-liability risk fall on future generations. There are, however, other reasons why this may happen. Taxpayers may not perceive the changes in tax risk resulting from changes in debt composition, i.e. they may suffer from tax myopia. Furthermore, taxpayers may not be able to undo these changes because of market imperfections.[1] In effect, most people do not offset tax risk either because of bounded rationality or limited access to financial markets. While we may expect people to anticipate future taxes, resulting from government borrowing, it is hard to believe that they unravel the link between financial operations and changes in the distribution of their tax liabilities across future contingencies and hence undo the consequences of debt management. Moreover, even if people did perceive and care about tax-liability risk, many individuals would be unable to implement hedging portfolio strategies because of transaction costs, minimum denomination requirements and short-selling constraints.

If agents fail to take into account the tax implications of debt management, changes in debt composition can affect saving and capital accumulation because they will be perceived as real changes in risk-return opportunities. For instance, public assets will be used as hedges against the return-risk of capital or private financial assets (instead of being held in anticipation of changes in tax liabilities). Then, the issue is: does debt yielding a high return, when the return on capital is low, increase saving and capital accumulation by providing insurance to asset holders?

As a first attempt to answer this question, consider a classical economy without imperfections where saving flows directly into productive investment. People can either save in a risky investment technology or in government securities with different stochastic characteristics. Suppose that changes in debt composition affect saving decisions either because tax changes fall on future generations or because of tax myopia. In either case, it is uncertain whether an increase in the relative supply of securities, which provide insurance against the return-risk of capital, will have a positive effect on saving. On the one hand, this operation can "crowd in" saving in risky capital because people may be willing to increase their holding of capital when its return-risk can be diversified away. On the other hand, the provision of insurance can reduce capital formation by reducing the need for precautionary saving. By building on a result in Devereux and Smith (1994), it can be shown that—with preferences characterized by constant relative risk-aversion—the effect on saving is positive only for elasticities of substitution greater than 1, that is, only if the substitution effect prevails over the income effect. Intuitively, a "safer" rate of return on overall saving has a similar effect of an increase in the rate of return. A safer return tends to increase saving through the substitution effect and to reduce it through the income

---

[1] In these cases debt management leads to risk redistribution, for example, between investors and taxpayers, insofar as investment opportunities and tax patterns differ across individuals.

effect, where the latter effect arises because a safer capital income lessens the precautionary motive for saving.

Hence, the risk-return characteristics of government securities which can possibly favor capital accumulation, if there are any at all, are unclear a priori. Paradoxically, low risk-aversion is needed to support the capital accumulation argument for providing insurance to savers (or current generations). However, one must concede that this ambiguity is a consequence of the stylized framework considered. In the real world, saving does not flow directly into productive investment but is intermediated through financial markets. The link between investment and saving decisions can be weak and the impact of debt management on the decisions of financial intermediaries may have important implications for capital accumulation.

3.2.2 Investment and Tobin's q: the portfolio approach

Debt-management literature from the 1960s and early 1970s provides a reference point to examine whether debt management can favor capital accumulation by affecting financial market equilibrium. Effects on asset prices hinge on the implicit assumption that people fail to take into account tax risk associated with government financial activity. While tax myopia appears a strong assumption, effects on asset prices are likely to arise if people have no direct access to financial markets. In effect, it is sensible to assume that financial institutions do not take into account human capital and hence labor-tax risk in their portfolio decisions.[2]

If public debt is perceived as net wealth, changes in its composition can affect portfolio decisions and possibly favor capital accumulation by reducing risk premia on corporate stock and private debt. The idea is that government securities provide hedges against the return-risk of private assets and this insurance function differ across government securities because of the different covariances of their holding returns with those of private assets. If this is the case, an increase in the relative supply of government securities which provide a better hedge against the return on corporate stock may reduce the risk of holding stock and private debt and thus increase their demand.

This potential channel for the real effects of debt management is suggested by the traditional portfolio approach which originates from the work of Tobin (1963) and finds a CAPM formalization in Roley (1979). In this literature debt management is mainly viewed as an instrument of stabilization policy. Tobin (1963) and Brownlee and Scott (1963) examine how changes in the relative supply of conventional government securities with different terms to maturity can enhance the government's control of real investment demand.

---

[2] Here, market imperfections matter as they provide a rationale for separating portfolio and saving decisions and for financial investors to not take into account taxes on labor income. Otherwise, imperfections play no role.

Tobin argues that the substitution of short- for long-maturity debt raises the price of equities and thus, stimulates investment demand, i.e. it leads the market valuation of existing capital to exceed its replacement cost. The explanation is that the holding-period return of short debt covaries more with that of money and less with that of equities than the holding return of long debt. Since short debt provides a better hedge against the return-risk of equities than long debt, an increase in its relative supply leads to an excess demand for equity (and long debt) and to an excess supply of short debt (and money). For asset market to clear, either the expected holding return on equity must fall—the prices of equities must rise—or the expected holding return on short debt must rise. To the extent that holding returns on money and short-term debt are correlated, the expected return on short debt cannot rise to make up for the whole adjustment. So, part of the adjustment comes from an increase in the prices of equities.

As shown by Roley (1979), within a CAPM (with a risk-free asset and constant absolute risk-aversion preferences) this result holds for open market exchanges between short and long discount bonds when certain conditions regarding the covariance structure of assets returns are satisfied. For instance, the result holds if the covariance between equity and long bonds is positive while that between equity and short bonds is negative. An alternative sufficient condition, when both covariances are positive (and that of long debt greater), is that the price of long bonds must not exceed the price of short bonds following the operation.[3]

This formalization is at odds with current finance theory. In particular, the state-contingent distribution of future asset prices is given, thus ruling out any possible role that expectations of future interest rates can play. However, the main problem with the capital accumulation argument is that the effect of debt management hinges on a number of conditions and thus appears unlikely. In particular, the insurance that the debt structure provides to institutional investors against the return-risk of corporate stock must reduce the wedge between their borrowing and lending rates in favor of the production sector. The effect on saving decisions of the implied distribution of taxes and debt returns should also be considered. Finally, as the relevant debt composition must be in place over a long horizon, tax myopia becomes an hardly justifiable assumption. In a sense the argument for providing insurance is based on a short-run analysis. Perhaps, a clearer role for debt management emerges for the purpose of conducting countercyclical policy. If output is demand-determined,

---

[3]   Roley (1979) finds that the price of equities increases only if the initial maturity compositions are sufficiently long. However, he considers a different experiment: a substitution of short- for long-maturity debt which leaves the value of the debt unaffected. As this experiment requires a change in current taxes or spending, it does not correspond to the relevant definition of debt management.

the effect on Tobin's q makes an argument for using the maturity composition of public debt to control investment demand.[4]

If it is theoretically unclear whether debt management can affect investment decisions, then evidence on the stochastic relation between the holding returns on corporate stock and conventional government securities with different maturities, has shed light on this issue.

3.2.3   An empirical assessment of the portfolio approach

If changes in the maturity composition of public debt can affect Tobin's q, the presumption is that such a relation must be weak. Even Tobin (1963), while arguing that long-maturity debt, unlike short-maturity debt, shares some of the "volatility" risks of private bonds and equities, points out that return covariations between conventional government securities and equity capital are not likely to differ much across maturities.

The presumption that changes in the maturity composition of public debt have little impact on the expected return on equities has been confirmed by empirical investigation. Empirical studies rely on the CAPM, or variants of it, to link changes in the relative supplies of government securities to the expected rate of return on corporate stock. Asset-demand parameters are estimated from the covariance structure of conditional holding returns on corporate stock (as measured by the stock market index), Treasury bills and long-term Treasury bonds.[5]

Empirical research on US data by Roley (1982), Friedman (1981, 1985, 1986), Frankel (1985) and Agell and Persson (1992) points to a weak relation between changes in the maturity composition of public debt and the expected rate of return on corporate stock.[6] The basic intuition that a substitution of short- for long-maturity debt reduces the expected rate of return on corporate stock is confirmed but the magnitude of this effect is small. For instance, with quarterly data Agell and Persson find that an unprecedently large 10% increase in the share of Treasury bills in investors' portfolio in exchange for long-term Treasury bonds would lower the conditionally expected rate of return on corporate stock by only 10 basis points, on a yearly basis, relative to Treasury bills (by 60 basis points with monthly data). This figure, although among the highest in the literature, is still very small if compared with equity return variability. It reflects a conditional

---

[4] The argument has lent support to US debt policy in 1961, known as "Operation Twist." Operation Twist consisted of open market operations and deficit financing directed toward shortening the maturity structure of the Federal debt with the intention of stimulating investment by reducing long interest rates, i.e. by twisting the yield curve.

[5] The results of these studies are derived under the maintained assumption that changes in relatives supplies of securities will not be accommodated by offsetting movements in demand. Hence, they cannot provide any evidence on the neutrality of debt management.

[6] See Frankel (1985) and Agell and Persson (1992) for an overview of the empirical literature.

return correlation between stock and long-term debt not significantly different from that between stock and short-maturity debt (besides being both positive and small).

To conclude, evidence on the demand for corporate stock suggests that the ability of debt management to affect investment is very limited.[7] It leads to the conclusion that debt management should be more concerned with implications for risk sharing, market efficiency and distortionary taxation.

3.3   Risk distribution: incomplete markets

A second argument for government securities yielding high returns in low-output states (or in states where the return on private assets is low) is that such a policy may improve the allocation of risk, say, between generations or between investors and taxpayers. The idea to be explored is that securities negatively indexed to labor or capital income may not only provide debt-holders with an insurance that could not otherwise be obtained, but also lead to a welfare improvement in the allocation of risk. This section examines whether incomplete markets for private securities offer arguments for providing explicit insurance against macroeconomic risk.

When private asset markets are incomplete, the type of debt that governments issue matters; as government securities have no private counterparts, the simple fact that governments issue securities with specific return characteristics and raise taxes accordingly determines the equilibrium allocation of risk. This is because a state-contingent pattern of taxes and public-debt returns gives rise to a state-contingent pattern of transfers across individuals, as much as private debt contracts. If private markets are incomplete, private contracts cannot replicate or undo the transfers between taxpayers and public-debt-holders implemented under alternative debt-tax schemes. A different allocation of risk corresponds to each choice of the debt-tax scheme. It is also clear that, when markets are incomplete, the introduction of a "new" public asset with its implied change in taxation will change the allocation of risk.

Incomplete markets suggest welfare-improving debt management as an interesting theoretical possibility. In principle, a government could choose the debt-tax scheme which generates the same transfers as the missing insurance contract. The issue is whether a debt-tax scheme with debt returns negatively indexed to (labor and) capital income enhances risk sharing, besides redistributing risk.

There are at least three missing-market arguments suggesting a potential role for debt management in risk sharing: (i) the missing market problem (or

---

[7] This conclusion is robust to different estimating procedures, holding periods and data sets considered in the various studies. However, such evidence cannot completely dispose of the argument. A positive effect on capital accumulation could be obtained if governments were to issue explicitly contingent securities, designed to enhance hedging opportunities against the return-risk of private assets.

incomplete participation) in overlapping generations economies; (ii) missing markets for human capital; and (iii) absence of insurance markets for unobservable idiosyncratic shocks, like taste or liquidity shocks.

3.3.1 Intergenerational risk-sharing

Among the possible reasons for public-debt management to improve risk sharing, the literature has focused on the lack of intergenerational insurance in overlapping generations (OLG) economies. Indeed, incomplete participation arising because of finite lifetimes provides the simplest reason preventing people from fully exploiting risk-sharing opportunities. The insurance role of debt-tax schemes is studied in Stiglitz (1983), Fischer (1983), Peled (1984, 1985), Pagano (1988) and Gale (1990).

A main finding of this literature is that the maturity of the debt instead of the type of indexation is important for intergenerational insurance: long-maturity debt allows generations to endogenously share either labor or capital income risk.[8] As long-term debt is sold before maturity, the relevant return for investors depends on the market value of the debt at the end of the holding period. Thus, "long maturities" make the holding-period return on government securities contingent on shocks affecting their future demand, even when they specify a fixed real payoff at redemption date. This property is valuable to society since generation-specific shocks are shared through the resulting change in demand of young generations for the assets supplied by old generations.

Suggested by Stiglitz (1983), this mechanism is easily understood in a pure exchange OLG economy, where generations live two periods, receive a random endowment in the first period of their lives and save in government debt. If the initial term to maturity of the debt exceeds one period, the old generation will sell debt to the young generation. When the young experience a positive shock to their income, the demand for government debt rises so that the old obtain a capital gain and the benefit of the positive shock is shared. The introduction of long-term debt opens a new market, in the sense that it allows for intergenerational trade. By contrast, with short-term debt no trade between generations would ever take place.

Although, for pure exchange economies the properties of long maturities of interest-bearing debt have not been formalized, we can draw parallels from the role of money. In effect, within the OLG framework money is an infinite maturity asset acting only as a store of value. With uncertain first-period endowments the return on money is fully contingent on the demand of the young generation. Endowment risk is shared by the old generation since when

---

[8] Obviously, governments could just rely on taxes and transfers if the relevant distribution of risk and the contingencies which shape the insurance scheme were easy to identify. In fact, this remains a theoretical possibility because the information needed to implement such schemes is beyond the capacity of governments and/or incentive problems may occur. See Gale (1990) for an insightful discussion of these themes.

the endowment of the young is high so is the return on money and vice versa. For i.i.d. shocks to endowments Peled (1984) shows that, if a stationary monetary equilibrium exists, it is conditionally Pareto optimal, i.e. it is optimal when individuals born in different states of nature are viewed as being different. Even though asset markets are incomplete, there is no room for improving on the allocation of risk. The intuition for this result is given by Peled (1985) who considers the introduction of one-period safe bonds. In spite of providing insurance against the risky return of money, safe debt cannot increase welfare because someone has to bear the tax-cost of this reduced uncertainty. Intuitively, when the current value of money is lowest, a positive rate of return on money is expected in all future states of nature (since shocks are i.i.d.). As a result, the young generation (born with the lowest endowments) buys safe debt at a discount, and taxes must increase to make up for the difference between redemptions and proceeds from new sales of safe debt. Obviously, it can be argued that the conditional criterion is too strong and leaves open the possibility of improving on the allocation of risk according the unconditional (or ex-ante) criterion.[9] Nevertheless, Peled's result is suggestive of the welfare gains which arise when long-maturity debt allows for intergenerational trade.

A number of conditions must be satisfied for long-maturity debt to be effective as a risk-sharing solution. For instance, people must be willing to transfer resources from the first to the second period of their lives. This possibility is considered by Fischer (1983), who examines unconditionally Pareto-improving schemes in a pure exchange economy, where the aggregate endowment is constant but its distribution between generations is random. Since in some states of nature the optimal scheme calls for transfers from the old to the young (the young want to transfer resources from the second to the first period of their lives) money cannot be used to allocate risk efficiently. A possible solution is for the government to purchase from the young generation its second-period random endowment in exchange for one-period safe bonds. To make up for possible gains (losses) the government makes transfers to (raises taxes on) the next young generation. While the scheme is a transparent example of risk sharing, it cannot operate without taxes and it is clearly unpractical for policy purposes. It shows the limitations which pure government financial intermediation encounters in practice.

Another case where long-maturity debt loses its risk-sharing role is when uncertainty is introduced via i.i.d. shocks affecting the returns from a linear investment technology and the first-period endowment is constant. As successive generations always face the same investment problem, when technological shocks are uncorrelated, asset demands and expected rates of return are state and time invariant. As a result the maturity of public assets becomes

---

[9]   See Peled (1985) and Fischer (1983) for insightful discussions in favor and against the conditional criterion respectively.

irrelevant: both expected and realized returns do not depend on maturity. In particular, any security yielding a real fixed return at redemption acts as a one-period safe bond regardless of its maturity. In a stationary equilibrium with a constant supply of money the value of money is also independent from technological shocks in spite of its infinite maturity.[10]

Within this framework, the existence of non-contingent debt may still allow the implementation of a better risk allocation than would otherwise be possible. In steady state, safe debt (financed by raising taxes on the young) allows each generation to receive a safe transfer from the successive generation, thus reducing the risk associated with technological shocks. Weiss (1980) points out that the introduction of money, if valued, leads to a welfare-improving reduction of risk since a safe return on saving becomes available. Gale (1990) shows that, with sufficiently high risk-aversion and/or return volatility, the introduction of safe debt can be conditionally Pareto optimal even if the economy is dynamically efficient, i.e. the expected rate of return on capital investment is positive.[11]

When shocks affecting the returns of the investment technology are persistent, long-maturity debt regains its potency by endogenously generating risk sharing. Serially correlated productivity shocks make the demand for long-term bonds, and hence the capital gain that the old generation realizes, contingent on the state of nature. Gale shows that in steady state the introduction of safe long-term bonds can be conditionally Pareto-improving, even when: (i) the introduction of one-period bonds would not be and (ii) one-period bonds are already being issued.[12] The key to this result is that the holding return on long-term debt rises because the real interest rate falls in states where productivity is low, given that productivity is serially correlated. Consider the case where the government issues only two-period bonds and raises taxes on the young generation to hold the amount of outstanding debt constant. In a stationary equilibrium while half of the debt is redeemed by the government, the other half (with one-period remaining maturity) is sold by the old to the young generation. If productivity shocks are positively correlated when a bad shock occurs it leads to the expectation of a low return on capital for the next period. As a result, the young shift their demand from capital to bonds, so that a capital gain is realized by the old. With two-period bonds each generation provides insurance to the preceding generation by paying, for its debt holdings, a price negatively correlated to the return on capital.

Interestingly, a necessary (and sufficient) condition for Gale's result is that the introduction of long-term bonds leads to a reduction of taxes in all states

---

[10] Money acts as a safe bond of finite maturity, with the exception that the size of the transfer from the young to the old generation is endogenously determined.

[11] The exact characterization is given by Zilcha (1990).

[12] The maturity of the bonds being introduced must, however, be limited; Gale shows that the introduction of consols is not welfare improving.

of nature. This is possible if investors are willing to buy long-term bonds at a premium, because such bonds provide a better hedge against productivity shocks than short-term bonds. Then, the government can reduce taxes or make transfers using the proceeds from bond sales which exceed the outlays for redeeming maturing bonds.

The possibility of improving risk sharing by issuing long-maturity debt is interesting in that no conflict arises between the alternative objectives of debt management. As taxes can be reduced in any state of nature, the provision of insurance is consistent with the objective of minimizing tax distortions. Long maturity debt is not only valuable as a hedge against the return risk of private assets but it also enables the government to decrease taxes in low-output states.[13]

Interestingly, for the purpose of evaluating alternative debt strategies, insurance can be provided through long-maturity debt without explicitly indexing debt returns to capital or labor income. However, examples where the insurance scheme relies on explicitly contingent debt, i.e. on securities providing a hedge against the return-risk of private assets, have also been provided in the literature.

Pagano (1988) examines the role of debt negatively indexed to the random returns on the investment technology. He considers a small open OLG economy where generations have constant absolute risk-aversion (CARA) preferences, live two periods, receive a fixed endowment and pay taxes in the first period of their lives. The government can either issue contingent bonds with returns negatively indexed to the return on capital or safe bonds yielding a constant, internationally determined, rate of return.

The introduction of contingent debt in this economy does not open a new market because its returns can be obtained as a linear combination between the returns on safe debt and capital. Nevertheless, indexed debt and the resulting changes in taxation lead to an unconditional Pareto improvement in the allocation of risk. Contingent debt allows the implementation of a debt-tax scheme where each generation is insured against capital income shocks through the taxes raised on the succeeding generation. Due to CARA preferences, the insurance provided by contingent debt leads to more investment in the risky productive technology and, thus, to higher expected output.[14] The additional risk is entirely borne by the young generation in the form of tax uncertainty,

---

[13] The debt-tax scheme appears to create "value" by replacing a missing market. This interpretation is suggested by Blanchard and Weil (1992) who relate intergenerational insurance to the viability of debt Ponzi games.

[14] Issuance of contingent debt crowds in investment in the productive technology for two reasons: (i) because of CARA preferences the provision of insurance increases risk taking and (ii) the transfer that each generation expects to receive in the second period of its life from the succeeding generation is reduced, since contingent bonds are issued at a lower expected return.

but this adverse effect on welfare is more than offset by the expected output increase. Intuitively, it is optimal for each generation to trade in more tax risk in the first period of its life (when it has none) for higher expected lifetime consumption (and lower expected taxes), before knowing the return on productive investment and hence, its tax liabilities.

The model is an interesting example where debt management, characterized by countercyclical returns and taxation, increases welfare. However, this result hinges on a number of assumptions which suggest its limited policy relevance. In particular, the desirability of providing insurance to the old, through the taxes raised on the young, depends both on the specification of preferences and on the allocation of risk in the absence of debt. These problems are common to explicitly contingent schemes; specific indications for the type of debt to issue are sensitive to the stochastic structure of the economy, that is, to the type of shocks and the life period when uncertainty occurs. The reason is that insurance, when provided by bonds negatively indexed to capital or labor income has to be financed by high taxes in bad states of nature. A strategy of high debt returns in low-output states may not increase welfare—according to the conditional criterion—because someone has to bear the tax-cost of the reduced uncertainty. For instance, in Pagano's model taxes increase in bad states of nature when bonds negatively indexed to capital income are introduced. This is because, if a safe asset yielding a non-negative return is already being issued, contingent debt must yield a positive rate of return in states where the return on capital is low in order to be valued. The same conclusion holds true if productivity shocks and thus capital income are serially correlated. This should be contrasted with the solution that long-maturity debt provides within the same framework. In Gale (1990) no distributional conflict arises between taxpayers and bondholders. Capital gains on two-period debt, realized by the old generation, do not require that higher taxes be levied on the young generation. On the contrary, even when a bad productivity shock occurs, the government can reduce taxes because the price of newly issued two-period bonds increases (the real interest rate falls). Intuitively, when people born in different states are viewed as being different, if the debt-tax scheme does provide insurance to everyone, instead of redistributing risk, a premium is paid by everyone (i.e. in any state of nature) to participate in the scheme.

3.3.2 Providing insurance to debt-holders: an assessment

Intergenerational risk-sharing makes a strong case for long maturities, but the result does not directly translate into a policy indication. One needs to ask whether the result, derived from highly stylized OLG economies, equally applies to real economies. As suggested by Fischer (1983), the substantial overlap of generations lessens the importance of government debt intermediation. Moreover, pension schemes already provide a less fanciful and more effective way to deal with generational risk. A more serious limit to the role of long-term debt is the extent to which shocks affecting different generations are positively correlated. For maturity to play a role people must not only be willing to transfer resources from current to future periods of their lives but also generation-specific shocks must prevail. In fact, most macroeconomic shocks, as well as demographic shocks, induce a positive correlation between labor and capital income, say, between first- and second-period life income.

While the scope for risk sharing is clearly exaggerated by simple OLG economies, theory is not without interest for policy. Research on intergenerational risk-sharing makes it clear that tax implications are crucial to evaluating the opportunity of issuing securities with specific risk-return characteristics. Although, optimal debt instruments can be characterized as providing insurance against the uncertainty of capital and/or labor income, introducing debt which yields high returns in states where private asset returns are low, can be socially costly. As shown by Levhari and Liviatan (1976) for price-indexed debt and stressed by Fischer (1983), one must consider how taxes will change and who will be liable for paying them, before saying anything precise on the welfare merits of government financial innovation.

An important feature that tends to characterize debt-tax schemes providing explicit insurance to asset-holders is the higher risk borne by taxpayers (in exchange for lower expected taxes). Public debt negatively indexed to private-asset returns implies high-interest payments in low-output states; it increases the present discounted value of taxes to be raised after the realization of a bad shock to output. To the extent that public debt and private assets are held by the "average" taxpayer, issuing such debt has no direct distribution effect. Otherwise the scheme implies a transfer from taxpayers to asset-holders in bad states of nature. If taxpayers' income is fixed, as in Pagano (1988), to transfer some risk on them is optimal. However, in reality incomes from different sources are fairly correlated. Therefore, it is unlikely that issuing debt negatively indexed to the return on private assets would provide an optimal risk-sharing solution. In particular, if taxation of labor income provides the main source of revenues and asset holdings are unevenly distributed across the population, such a scheme will burden more heavily taxpayers in states where their income is lower. Obviously, these redistribution effects are mitigated by the existence of proportional tax systems, which serve themselves as an important insurance function and by the fact that taxes can be considerably delayed. However, welfare-improving policies are hard to find.

Allowing the choice of debt instruments be guided by the demand for insurance, against the volatility of private asset returns, can adversely affect future generations or agents who do not hold such assets. Likewise, to observe the absence of privately supplied assets with certain risk-return characteristics is not sufficient to conclude that public provision of such assets is desirable, even when opening private markets in those assets would be. Issuing a new security changes the taxes to be levied conditional on the realization of future events and most likely the incidence of taxation. Because taxes are compulsory, public provision of a new security will not replicate the outcome of the missing private market in that security, unless the incidence of taxation is carefully designed.[15] As Campbell and Shiller (1996) observe in discussing the merits of price-indexed debt, the missing market argument for introducing a new public security holds true only if a private market in the same security develops as a result of the government financial innovation.

These considerations make an important point for policymaking: tax implications should be a main concern when evaluating innovations in the menu of public assets. If the absence of markets for insurance provides a rationale for government intervention, the emphasis should not be on the provision of the missing assets but rather on the distribution across states of nature of both taxes and debt returns. One may also conjecture that the risk-distribution effects arising from future tax contingencies, implemented, for example, through proportional income taxation, are more easily understood and, thus, more reliable in designing debt-tax schemes than the implications of financial intermediation. The correct approach to risk sharing may well be to choose a state-contingent distribution of taxes and transfers and use the appropriate debt instruments to support it.

While the scope for intergenerational insurance arising from finite lifetimes appears to be small, a potentially important role for debt management is suggested by missing markets for human capital.

3.4 Liquidity constraints

It is sensible to assume, as does Fischer (1983), that unexploited opportunities for sharing risk mainly result because of missing markets for human capital, i.e. for future labor income. As a consequence, people who receive their income only from labor are in a worse position to hedge against macroeconomic fluctuations than people who hold financial assets and have access to financial markets. In other words, labor income-earners are more likely to be liquidity-constrained than other agents in the economy.

If private agents cannot borrow at the same conditions as the government, a role for debt management in relaxing borrowing constraints emerges quite naturally. The argument for deficit financing to relax liquidity constraints, which has been made from Mundell (1971) to Woodford (1990), can be extended to debt management in an uncertain environment. It leads to the policy indication of issuing securities yielding low returns in low-output states, so as to support tax

---

[15] As discussed in Chapter 1, the "new-market" analogy holds only if the corresponding change in taxation does not alter each individual's tax share in any state of nature.

reductions in states where income is low and borrowing constraints are binding. This conclusion is based on the following argument.

Liquidity constraints are likely to bind consumption choices in states of the world where aggregate and thus individual labor income are relatively lower. As a result, private agents may want to hold securities yielding high returns in low-output states. With proportional income taxation this choice will benefit individuals whose income and share of taxes turn out to be lower than average (while leaving the average taxpayer unaffected). Their interest income net of taxes will be positive and increasing with the return on debt.[16] This debt-tax solution can be viewed as an insurance scheme where labor-income earners pool their risks of an income shortfall. In effect, conventional wisdom is that securities yielding countercyclical returns would provide valuable insurance against labor-income risk.

However, this insurance scheme can provide a solution only if agents, who expect to be liquidity constrained, are able and willing to buy debt in the first place. If agents have no financial wealth and are not currently saving, they have to borrow in order to finance the long position in government securities. Equivalently, agents may want short-sell government securities yielding high returns in high-income states in exchange for securities yielding high returns in low-income states. If implementing strategies involving short sales of government securities is costly, i.e. if private agents cannot borrow at the same conditions as the government, then securities yielding countercyclical returns are useless. There is instead a clear role for the government to issue securities with returns positively indexed to output in order to support acyclical labor taxation (see Section 2.2.2). This design of public debt implies low debt returns and taxes in states where income is low, thus allowing agents to consume more when liquidity constraints are binding.[17] The optimal policy calls for issuing those securities which liquidity-constrained agents cannot sell short to debt-holders. By doing so and using its taxing power the government implements the optimal but unfeasible security trade on behalf of constrained agents.

The conclusion that debt should yield low return in low-output states gains strength as we observe that in the real world people may not save over a long spell of time, for example, in early periods of life. In such cases, debt-tax schemes relying on low returns in low-output states would be of no use because liquidity-constrained agents would not be in a position to buy debt in the first place.

Missale (1996) provides an example where debt positively indexed to output helps to relax liquidity constraints. This result is derived in a simple two-period

[16] More precisely, countercyclical debt returns increase the size of transfers from high- to low-income earners in bad states of nature, i.e. when liquidity constraints are binding.

[17] Obviously, there are alternative solution to the problem. One is to tax capital income in bad states of nature. Non-uniqueness arises because of similar reasons of those examined in Section 2.2.1 and need not be investigated further.

OLG economy, where agents can be constrained in the first period of their life depending on the realization of income. Liquidity constraints are modeled as the impossibility for young generations to borrow against their future labor income from old generations (i.e. from asset-holders), a constraint that naturally arises in OLG economies. In a stationary equilibrium, positive output indexation allows for a smoother consumption path by supporting tax reductions in states where labor income is low and constraints are binding, i.e. by supporting acyclical labor tax rates. The optimal scheme involves transfers from debt-holders to constrained agents in low-output states and can thus be interpreted as a purchase of insurance by the government from debt-holders on the behalf of constrained agents. The scheme is effective even if risk-averse investors require a high expected return to hold securities positively indexed to output. Buying insurance from debt-holders increases the expected cost of debt servicing and the average level of taxes, but does not offset the benefits of procyclical taxation on liquidity-constrained agents.

The fact that procyclical debt returns may help to relax liquidity constraints is an important finding. Reducing the cost of market inefficiencies preventing agents from borrowing against their future income provides a first relevant reason why the low-output, low-return characterization of debt management could be the optimal debt strategy. Policy implications are interestingly similar to those suggested by the objective of reducing tax distortions.

3.5 Efficient taxation

Within a neoclassical framework where taxes distort labor and investment choices of infinitely lived identical agents and there is no other inefficiency, the objective of debt management is to minimize the welfare losses of tax distortions.

Since debt returns implement non-distorting transfers between the government and the private sector, the amount of revenues to be raised through distortionary taxation can be controlled by the choice of debt instruments. The optimal distribution of debt returns depends on the least distortionary distribution of tax rates across time and states of nature. Although complete smoothing of tax rates may not be optimal, insofar as consumption demand and labor supply elasticities do not change dramatically across time and states of nature, slight variations in labor income tax rates are required to minimize distortions. As a result, the optimal debt design specifies low returns in states where revenues from labor income are lower and/or government spending is higher than expected and vice versa. This debt design supports lower tax rates than would be possible otherwise in low-output and high-spending states, that is, in states where financing needs are higher than expected.

With explicitly contingent debt, the government would be in the ideal position to support the optimal path for tax rates. Securities with returns explicitly contingent on the state of nature implement non-distorting transfers between the government and the private sector whose direction and magnitude are conditional on the realization of future events. Contingent debt can thus be used to perfectly control the amount of revenues to be raised through distorting taxes in each state of nature. The optimal policy can be characterized as the government's purchase of insurance against having to increase tax rates in high-spending or low-revenue states.

Lucas and Stokey (1983) first showed the role of negative indexation of debt returns to public spending shocks. They consider an economy without capital, where taxes distort the labor-leisure choice of infinitely lived identical agents and government spending is the only source of uncertainty. The key to their result is that, in high-spending states, negative interest payments provide the government with a non-distorting source of financing which allows redistribution of tax rates from high- to low-spending states. This redistribution offers incentives for work and production in those states where this is most valuable; it increases output in states where private consumption and leisure are low because resources are diverted to government's use. In particular, contingent debt allows for a smoother consumption path than would be possible by deficit financing alone. This is because, with non-contingent debt, the present value of taxes to be raised after the realization of a bad shock increases and vice versa. While deficit financing allows the distribution of tax distortions over all future periods, it cannot eliminate the need for a change in tax rates in some future period and, thus, a change in work effort and consumption.

King (1990) and Chari, Christiano and Kehoe (1994), also using the neoclassical model, show that issuing debt negatively indexed to government spending is optimal, even when capital and productivity shocks are considered. The new important result is that the optimal contingent contract also involves transfers from the private sector to the government upon realizations of adverse productivity shocks. Intuitively, if government securities are positively indexed to productivity, fluctuations in revenues can be hedged by lower (higher) debt returns in bad (good) states, without sharp changes in labor tax rates. These results follow from the quantitative presumption that tax rates on labor income should fluctuate very little to minimize the welfare losses of tax distortions. In fact, simulations carried out by King and Chari *et al.* show that procyclical or countercyclical tax rates on labor income (as well as a positive or negative correlation with spending shocks) may result depending on the elasticities of consumption demand and labor supply. However, the contribution of changes in tax rates to government financing is negligible for a wide range of parameter values characterizing consumer's preferences. Most of the change in revenue needs, resulting from shocks affecting the government budget, is smoothed away in contingent security markets for public debt.

State-contingent debt is not the only instrument which governments can use to hedge against budgetary uncertainty in economies with capital. Zhu (1992), Judd (1991), King (1990) and Chari, Christiano and Kehoe (1994) stress that capital income taxation provides governments with an alternative shock absorber, possibly making contingent debt useless for the purpose of smoothing labor tax rates. The idea is that the exact distribution across future contingencies of tax rates on capital income has no distortionary effect, since only the expected value of tax rates affects investment incentives. As the government can freely choose capital tax rates to implement non-distorting transfers across contingencies and thus smooth labor tax rates, there is no need for contingent debt.

Bohn (1991) shows, however, that the above result can be obtained only in an economy with a single production technology. In this case, efficient taxation of capital income is consistent with infinite choices of the distribution of capital tax rates across states of nature. On the contrary, with more than one technology the state-contingent distribution of capital tax rates must be designed so as to ensure the same expected value of the tax rate for all technologies. Each technology imposes one constraint on capital taxation to be satisfied for an efficient allocation of investment (see Section 2.3). As the objective of avoiding distortions in investment decisions imposes constraints on capital taxation, state-contingent debt regains its role in supporting optimal labor taxation.

Obviously, other arguments for contingent debt exist. For instance, some smoothing of capital tax rates could be desirable because of increasing marginal losses from tax collection as in Judd (1991). In fact, one can think of many reasons for non-contingent capital taxation as well as for non-contingent debt, but the idea that contingent debt could provide valuable flexibility in the conduct of fiscal policy is appealing regardless of the aforementioned possible indeterminacy. This conclusion is reinforced by empirical evidence on US tax rates. As discussed in King (1990), there is too much persistence in capital tax rates and too much volatility in labor tax rates.[18]

Distortionary taxation provides a strong argument for debt yielding low returns in states of the world where financing needs turns out to be greater than expected. Implications for debt management are interestingly similar to those suggested by the objective of relaxing borrowing constraints. The fact that positive output indexation emerges as the optimal solution to "Keynesian" as well as to neoclassical distortions is a comforting result for policymaking.

However, one may wonder whether this strategy is still optimal when we abandon the unrealistic assumption that government securities are priced by fully informed, rational investors who do not make systematic mistakes. The next section extends the analysis to the consideration of market imperfections.

---

[18] See Barro (1986, 1990), Sahasakul (1986) and Judd (1989) for evidence on the US.

3.6   Optimal debt management in the absence of informational and credibility problems

The preceding analysis has identified some general principles which tend to characterize efficient debt management. Tax distortions and borrowing constraints suggest issuing debt with low returns in states where output is lower and public spending is higher than expected. This design of public debt avoids having to increase tax rates on labor income when bad shocks to output and public spending occur. As it limits the need for tax adjustment, this strategy reduces tax distortions and helps to relax borrowing constraints by increasing disposable income in states where constraints are binding. This strategy can also be viewed as providing flexibility to fiscal policy.

Issuing securities which yield low returns in low-output states, is not without consequences for the allocation of risk. Most likely, this policy does not improve everyone's welfare, but redistributes macroeconomic risk from debt-holders to taxpayers and from current to future generations.[19] It is "as if" the government purchased insurance from private investors on the behalf of taxpayers. However, specific arguments against this strategy cannot be found. A distributional trade-off may be necessarily involved in the choice of the debt-tax scheme. Pareto-improving solutions, if they exist, have only been suggested for intergenerational risk-sharing, and even in this case the policy implication is to issue long-maturity debt rather than debt negatively indexed to output. Most importantly, the fact that taxation is compulsory, while investing in public debt is voluntary, suggests buying insurance from investors as a better policy than forcing taxpayers to supply insurance to investors. This conclusion is reinforced if market imperfections prevent or make it costly for taxpayers to undo the effects of government financial operations.

Issuing securities which yield low returns in low-output states minimizes budgetary risk but increases the expected cost of debt servicing. High-interest costs have to be paid for a policy which insures the government against the risk of having to adjust tax rates in response to macroeconomic shocks affecting its budget. Risk-averse investors will ask a risk premium in order to hold securities with return positively correlated to capital income. As the government has to pay for insurance, the expected cost of debt servicing and the average tax rate will rise.

Could a strategy which does not reduce interest costs ever be optimal? This question arises quite naturally, given that in non-academic debate minimizing the costs of debt servicing is considered a main goal of debt management. In fact, there is no theoretical reason why attention should fall on the expected return of public debt rather than on its entire return distribution. For instance, issuing securities positively indexed to output may increase the expected cost of debt

---

[19] The degree of risk aversion of investors relative to taxpayers matters.

servicing and the expected level of taxes, but does not offset the benefits of lower taxes for liquidity-constrained agents. As optimal taxation is concerned, the least distorting distribution of tax rates must be supported by contingent securities yielding high returns in states where output is higher than expected and vice versa. Such securities may sell at discount, but high expected rates of return are fully consistent with efficient taxation, and the other objectives of debt management, if they result from properly called risk premia asked by private investors who are informed and "rational" in forming expectations about future events.

Indeed, the absence of informational asymmetries, expectations failures and market imperfections has been an important assumption of the preceding analysis. This suggests the importance of distinguishing the causes of debt-servicing costs. High expected rates of return are worth being sustained if they reflect the risk-return characteristics of government securities. On the contrary, a concern for interest costs is theoretically justified if risk premia follow from: (i) market imperfections; (ii) informational asymmetries between the government and private agents; (iii) systematic mistakes by private agents in forming expectations; and (iv) the government's inability to commit to future policy actions.

While market imperfections, and short-selling constraints in particular, have already been examined as possible determinants of borrowing constraints, the efficiency of the markets where government securities are traded is also crucial to ensuring that risk premia properly reflect the risk-return characteristics of government securities. Further implications of market inefficiencies are examined in the following section.

3.6.1 Market imperfections and idiosyncratic risk

Imperfections of private-asset markets suggest a role for debt management. Efficient secondary markets for government securities can provide liquidity and information which private markets cannot offer because of imperfections and/or externalities. In this way, government security markets may allow individuals to share the uninsurable risk of idiosyncratic shocks, like taste and liquidity shocks. For example, government securities can be held to avoid the "risk of early liquidations" of private assets. This role is important especially when, due to risk heterogeneity of private borrowers, thin security markets for private debt and informational asymmetries involve high costs from unexpected sales (see Pagano 1989). If setting up a market to meet liquidity needs is costly or benefits cannot be internalized, a well-functioning secondary market for government securities may fill this role. While financial intermediaries diversify liquidity risk, they also hold public debt to cope with the risk of early withdrawals.

Policies which provide insurance against idiosyncratic risk have, at first approximation, no adverse consequences in terms of taxation. This is an important difference between policies providing insurance against macroeconomic risk and those against idiosyncratic risk. Issuing securities which can be held as a hedge against income risk, for instance, which yield high returns in states where output is lower than expected, is not always desirable since the implied tax redistribution must also be taken into account. On the contrary, there is substantial merit in reducing idiosyncratic liquidity risk, say, by improving the efficiency of secondary markets for government securities.

A variety of policies, reviewed in the next chapter, exist which can enhance the efficiency of security markets. These policies comprise: market liberalization to foreign residents; transparent and predictable primary issuing policies; organization of well-functioning secondary markets; the introduction of hedging and borrowing facilities; etc. However, as attention is restricted to the choice of debt instruments, deep and liquid markets can be created by issuing instruments with standard characteristics which can be more easily priced and traded. Liquidity can be further promoted by issuing "benchmarks," namely, large amounts of securities with the same risk-return characteristics. Although, the effects of specific debt instruments on the efficiency of government security markets have not so far been formally investigated, arguments in favor of "standardization" have been made since the work of Friedman (1959). The consideration of idiosyncratic risk even suggests that standardization can be socially desirable.

In principle, while improving marketability limits the diversification in the menu of public assets, it should not affect the choice of the type of instrument, since liquidity and standardization are consistent with any risk-return characteristics of government securities. In practice, however, the cost of financial innovation favors the status quo. Innovating the inherited financial structure can be difficult and costly, a fact which biases the choice of debt instruments toward conventional financial assets. Until a thick market is established, high risk premia would be paid on unconventional securities because of the difficulties associated with pricing and hedging their return risk and because of the illiquidity of the markets where they would be exchanged. Even Campbell and Shiller (1996), who argue in favor of price-index-linked bonds, refer to the risk of "Balkanization" of financial markets as a main argument against price indexation. In the case of securities indexed to output and public spending, the frictions associated with the delay in recording and reporting the relevant indexation parameter would represent an even stronger obstacle to their introduction.

To conclude, the ideal debt instrument would have return positively indexed to output and negatively indexed to government spending. However, introducing such assets would be so costly that the implied tax burden would outweigh the benefits of the innovation. This suggests that the hypothesis that governments conduct their fiscal policy in a full set of state-contingent securities should be abandoned in order to examine debt management by conventional financial instruments: fixed-rate securities denominated in domestic currency with different maturities; variable-rate debt; price-index-linked securities; non-marketable loans; and securities and loans denominated in foreign currency.

The second part of this book examines whether and to what extent the optimal design of public debt, as characterized so far, can be obtained by the choice of conventional securities. Before doing so, in Chapter 4 evidence is provided on the choice of debt instruments and their relative amounts in OECD countries.

4

Debt composition and debt maturity: the evidence

4.1 Why contingent debt is not issued

In the absence of informational asymmetries, expectations failures and market imperfections, the ideal debt instrument would be negatively indexed to public spending and positively indexed to productivity or output. Shiller (1993, ch. 4) suggests issuing debt positively indexed to output as the socially optimal solution. This debt design would minimize tax distortions by limiting variations in labor tax rates, which would otherwise be needed to meet changes in financing needs. It would also help to relax borrowing constraints, by allowing for lower labor tax rates than would otherwise be possible in states where output is low and constraints are binding.

Introducing output-indexed bonds would however be difficult and costly because of the frictions associated with the delay in recording and reporting the relevant indexation parameter. In general, market imperfections and externalities tend to bias the choice of debt instruments towards "existing," conventional, instruments. Until a thick market is established, high risk premia would have to be paid on unconventional securities because of the difficulties associated with pricing and hedging their return risk and because of the illiquidity of the markets where they would be traded. Introducing output-indexed bonds would be so costly that the implied tax burden would outweigh the benefits of the innovation. It is also likely that a liquid market for such debt would never be established.

The gains from "standardization," and the costs of financial innovation may explain why securities with returns explicitly indexed to output or government spending are not being issued in the real world. In fact, in the recent past OECD governments have issued substantial amounts of debt indexed to short-term interest rates, price indexes and the ECU exchange rate. By contrast, no government has ever issued debt explicitly contingent on government spending, productivity and output, or on proxies for them.

If market imperfections offer one reason for non-existence, other explanations for the absence of debt indexed to real contingencies have been suggested in the theoretical literature. For instance, Calvo and Guidotti (1990a) and Bohn (1990a) argue that the ideal debt contract creates a moral hazard problem because the government can affect the variables to which debt returns are indexed. For instance, since the ideal contract calls for lower debt returns in states where (exogenous) public spending is high, the government would have a strong incentive to manipulate debt payoff while claiming that an adverse shock has occurred.

No doubt issuing securities contingent on public spending is problematic, but the moral hazard argument does not explain why governments cannot issue securities positively indexed to output or to proxies for it. Imperfections and practical problems appear a more convincing explanation for the absence of output-indexed bonds. As Fischer (1983) suggests, the frictions associated with the delay in recording and reporting the relevant indexation parameter are more important obstacles to the introduction of unconventional securities. The argument is mostly relevant for real aggregates and the more so the shorter the preferred holding period of investors. Not surprisingly, actual arrangements only contemplate financial and price indexation and, even within this restricted class, indexation to readily available interest rates and exchange rates has been preferred to price indexation.

Imperfections, illiquidity, and externalities of private-asset markets also suggest a role for government securities in providing insurance against the risk of idiosyncratic shocks, like taste and liquidity shocks. A debt policy which improves the efficiency of secondary markets for government securities and thus reduces idiosyncratic risk has a positive effect on social welfare, as opposed to policies which redistribute macroeconomic risk.

Policies concerning the organization of security markets in OECD countries over the last decade are reviewed in the next section. In the remaining part of the chapter evidence is presented on the debt structure by instrument and term to maturity for a number of OECD countries in the period 1960–95. The analysis aims to provide information on the risk-return characteristics and composition of public debts. Debt instruments are classified according to the main features which determine their risk-return characteristics: currency denomination, terms to maturity, indexation features, option provisions and marketability. Since inflation is a main determinant of debt returns, a proxy of the elasticity of the debt value to permanent changes in inflation is also constructed, which is called "effective maturity." Since a main objective is to examine how concerns over high levels of debt translate into actual policy decisions, the relation between the level of debt and its maturity is a point of focus.

In Section 4.3 information is provided on the main characteristics of debt instruments in a summary form, also to highlight similarities and differences among countries. The choice of the empirical measures of debt and debt maturity used throughout the analysis is discussed in Section 4.4 and related to the theoretical concepts. In Section 4.5 the evolution of the debt structure and the relation between the level of debt and its term to maturity are shown for each country separately. (Sources for the data, details of construction and data are given in the Appendix at the end of the book.)

4.2 Debt markets

In this section the structure of markets for government securities in OECD countries is briefly reviewed.[1] In fact, the main interest of the analysis is in the choice of debt instruments and in the composition and maturity structure of public debts, but the choice of instruments is not independent from the organization of the secondary market, primary issuing policy and the availability of hedging and borrowing facilities. For example, the cost of issuing long-term bonds can be reduced by the introduction of futures contracts in government securities since futures allow hedging against interest-rate risk.

Since the mid-1980s, governments in OECD countries promoted reforms of secondary markets for government securities. In order to enhance competition and minimize borrowing costs, financial markets were deregulated and liberalized to foreign investors. As a result of important organizational and regulatory changes, deep and liquid wholesale markets, where large volumes of debt can be traded at low transaction costs, have developed alongside traditional stock exchanges.

In most OECD countries, wholesale security markets are now organized as continuous dealer markets. In this market structure buying and selling orders are satisfied by intermediaries, called "primary dealers" or "market-makers." Primary dealers agree to quote continuous two-ways (bid and offer) prices, against which they are ready to satisfy buying and selling orders by the various traders. They make profit by maintaining a difference between bid and offer prices. Competing dealer systems are currently operating in Australia, Austria, Belgium, Canada, Finland, France, Ireland, Italy, Portugal, Spain, Sweden, the United Kingdom (UK) and the United States (US). They were introduced early in the 1940s in the US and in Canada, and recently in European countries; early in 1986 in the UK, lately in 1995 in Ireland. However, traditional order-matching (or order-driven) systems have not disappeared; their role has been confined to process retail (smaller size) trades.

The alternative to dealer markets is represented by auction-agency markets where trade takes place on a continuous "order-matching" basis, i.e. where buying and selling orders are recorded and then satisfied by mutual clearance. In Germany wholesale bond trade takes place through the "Inter-Bank Information System" a computerized continuous auction-agency market. The Danish market is made by (telephone trading and) the "Accept System," an electronic order-matching system, where trade is effected by broker-dealers accepting a bid or an offer posted on an electronic board. However, a quote-driven market has

---

[1] For a detailed analysis see Sundararajan, Dattels and Blommestein (1997) and Broker (1993).

also developed for benchmark issues, based on a voluntary agreement among dealers. In the Netherlands, buying and selling orders of sizeable amounts are sent, through a trading screen, to an interdealer broker whose task is to find a counterparty.[2] However, large volume orders can also be matched via two traditional floorbrokers. The Greek market is also organized as an auction-agency market, as it was the case in Ireland until recently, when the market was reformed to become a dealer system.

While, in their simplest form, dealer markets can be decentralized over-the-counter markets where dealers trade bilaterally with clients and other dealers, in almost all countries adopting this system, interdealer brokers have emerged. They provide trading networks connecting the various dealers. Services amount to telephonic and/or screen-based networks through which quotations are diffused and trades reported to other dealers. Trades are executed, possibly after negotiations, by the brokers. The number of interdealer brokers is naturally limited ranging from 1 broker in France to 7 brokers in the US. A notable exception to this system is represented by the Italian dealer market which is organized as an electronic market where demands and offers are automatically satisfied against the best quotation displayed on the screen. Interdealer systems clearly reduce search costs and price dispersion and thus lower transaction costs and improve price discovery.

Investment and trading, in particular, the market-making activity of primary dealers, have been supported by the introduction of hedging and borrowing facilities. Futures and option contracts in government bonds have been introduced in most countries so as to provide hedges against the interest-rate risk of securities holdings. More recently, "repurchase agreement (repos)" markets have been established in many countries allowing dealers to cover open positions which they have to take in the process of market making.

Secondary market design has also affected selling techniques and, more generally, the issuing policy of OECD governments. In most countries fixed-rate bonds are now issued through periodic auctions, either fully or in part, as in Japan where only a fraction of each 10-year bond issue is sold in this way, the other part being underwritten by the financial firms participating in the auction. In Germany, where a similar system has been in place for 10-year bonds, a full auction system was introduced only in 1998. A main exception is Denmark, where bonds are continuously sold by flexible-price taps, that is, by placing bids directly in the secondary market (on the "Match System") over an extended period of time, from 1 to 3 years. Ireland which followed the same technique has moved towards a full auction system, while in the Netherlands tap sales have become the main issuing method, after being introduced in 1990 to supplement multiple-price auctions.

---

[2] The interdealer broker acts as an intermediary and is not permitted to take positions of its own.

More importantly, as a part of eligibility requirements or informal relationships, the primary dealers (or the members of bank syndicates) are expected to take an active role in the bond auctions, so as to support *de facto* the demand for new issues.[3] The ability of primary dealers to absorb large quantities of new securities is valuable to the debt manager, in that it allows for an issuing policy which is not constrained by market conditions, say, by possible shortfalls of market demand. On the other hand, the regularity of the issuing process and the predictability of the type and amount of new issues are valued by the primary dealers which may pay a premium for the reduced uncertainty. With the goal of minimizing borrowing costs, in many countries, the authorities now hold auctions at regular intervals according to a predetermined calendar, they publicize the type of securities on offer and announce the size of issuance some days in advance. However, flexible issuing strategies are also adopted in a few countries, notably in Denmark, Germany and Ireland.

The promotion of liquid and efficient secondary markets has implications for the choice of debt instruments. Since simple instruments with standard characteristics are more rapidly priced and more easily traded, fixed-rate securities with bullet maturities and no options are clearly favored by dealers, a fact which gives a cost advantage to such instruments. Indeed, in OECD countries there has been a clear trend towards standardization (also by the use of standard maturities) with a reduction of the types of securities on offer.

Liquidity also requires thick markets, namely, that bonds be available for trade in large amounts. In many countries the authorities promote "benchmark bonds," that is, liquid, heavily traded bonds which are thus useful for pricing and term structure analysis. Benchmarks are created by "reopenings" of existing bond issues. In other words, fungible bonds, i.e. bonds with coupon and maturity identical to those of existing issues, are sold through subsequent auctions held at different dates. This technique allows the creation of large volumes of bonds with the same coupon and maturity date and thus to improve their liquidity.

Although, issues concerning the organization of markets and the choice of the market structure are not further discussed in the following chapters there is clearly an interaction between the structure of markets and the choice of debt instruments. While it appears that market design may limit the choice of debt, it only affects the relative costs of funding instruments. That no particular constraint is imposed by dealer markets, is witnessed by the successful introduction of new funding instruments in a number of countries: variable-rate bonds

---

[3] In exchange for this, in a number of countries primary dealers have access to a credit line at the central bank and are allowed to place non-competitive bids or participate in a second round auction. In Germany and Japan the syndicate of banks and financial firms underwrote a fraction of the bond issues.

in Australia, Belgium, the UK and, most notably, price-index-linked bonds in Sweden, Greece and the US.

4.3 Debt instruments

Government securities can be distinguished according to various characteristics: currency of denomination, type of interest rate, initial and remaining term to maturity, option provisions and marketability. These characteristics determine the distribution of debt returns across the future state of the world. For instance, fixed-rate securities denominated in the domestic currency have holding-period returns contingent on the realization of the price level, while foreign currency securities have returns contingent on the exchange rate of the corresponding currency. Indexation features are equally important: securities indexed to the price level yield a safe return while variable-rate (or floating-rate) securities yield a return contingent on future realizations of the interest rate used as the reference rate for indexation. Finally, the remaining term to maturity of a security makes its holding return contingent on future realization of the interest rate of the corresponding maturity and thus contingent on revisions in the expected path for inflation and real interest rates. Obviously, the latter contingency is altered by option provisions, that is, by whether the government (the holder) has the right to redeem (ask for repayment of) the security at a specified price before the maturity date.

Since the characteristics of debt instruments are not mutually exclusive, any decomposition will present some degree of arbitrariness. Here it has been decided to classify the debt instruments as follows:

(i) Debt denominated in foreign currency

(ii) Marketable securities denominated in domestic currency

(iii) Non-marketable debt denominated in domestic currency.

Foreign currency debt The decision of whether to borrow in domestic or foreign currency is traditionally considered an important dimension of debt management. However, in a number of countries foreign currency debt is not used for deficit financing but only for the purpose of raising foreign-exchange reserves. This is the case of Canada and the UK (and Sweden until 1992). In Denmark foreign currency debt is just rolled over for the purpose of leaving foreign-exchange reserves unaffected. Countries whose currencies are used as foreign reserves, Germany, Japan and the US, have no debt denominated in foreign currency. The same is true for the Netherlands and for France where, however, ECU indexed bonds and notes have been issued in preparation for European Monetary Union. From a different perspective, in Ireland and Sweden the debt is actively managed and foreign currency swaps are used, as in Belgium,

Finland, Italy, Portugal and Spain to control the exposure to exchange rate risk with respect to foreign currency debt.

Table 4.1 shows that foreign currency financing has been important in Austria, Denmark, Greece, Ireland, Portugal and Sweden, and was also significant in Belgium. It also points to a downward trend in the share of foreign currency debt since the mid-1980s. The notable exceptions are Austria, Sweden, Portugal and Spain, while in Italy there has also been a slow but continuous growth in the share of such debt.

Here all the liabilities denominated in foreign currency are grouped together, be they marketable securities or loans. ECU bonds and bills which are payable in domestic currency but are indexed to the ECU will be considered as foreign currency debt since both principal and interest payments are determined according to the prevailing exchange rate.

ECU bonds have been issued in Italy since 1982 and in Greece since 1986. In the late 1980s ECU bills with maturity up to one year have been offered in Italy and the UK. More recently, France has undertaken a program of ECU indexation, introducing ECU bonds and notes in 1989 and 1993, respectively. ECU bonds have also been issued in Spain since 1990 and in Denmark since 1992.

Table 4.1. Share of foreign currency debt

	1970	1975	1980	1985	1989	1991	1993	1995
Australia	n/a	6.7	17.4	17.7	16.4	9.9	7.6	3.1
Austria	32.1	33.3	28.1	22.7	15.7	15.8	19.2	22.0
Belgium	8.4	0.5	7.8	20.2	16.7	14.3	16.8	11.4
Canada	1.3	0.4	5.6	6.9	1.9	1.0	2.6	3.5
Denmark	53.9	55.7	33.3	20.5	23.5	16.6	24.1	15.6
Finland	37.1	45.4	57.6	54.7	43.1	47.4	58.6	46.4
France	1.5	0.4	0.0	4.0	0.8	2.8	3.6	3.7
Germany	1.1	0.3	0.0	0.0	0.0	0.0	0.0	0.0
Greece	n/a	n/a	16.1	30.6	27.9	27.5	25.7	22.8
Ireland	8.8	22.3	30.5	45.1	34.9	33.7	41.2	35.1
Italy	3.1	1.4	1.7	4.0	6.2	6.0	7.3	7.4
Japan	0.9	0.1	—	—	—	—	—	—
Netherlands	0.3	—	—	—	—	—	—	—
Portugal	26.8	18.5	20.3	31.4	16.8	7.4	11.5	17.4
Spain	6.6	6.0	9.4	7.9	2.8	4.3	8.2	8.7
Sweden	—	0.2	20.5	22.4	16.5	7.3	31.1	27.9
UK	6.5	6.2	2.8	2.3	3.4	4.1	5.6	4.4
USA	0.4	0.3	0.7	—	—	—	—	—

Notes: Per cent of total debt. Fiscal years ending in the same year or in March of the next year. Foreign currency debt includes ECU bonds and bills. For Canada data refers to Paper Debt. Data for the US are gross of debt in government accounts.

Marketable securities denominated in the domestic currency are the most used financing instrument. Their term to maturity at issue ("maturity" for short in what follows), as well as their remaining term to maturity when outstanding, are main objects of this study. Securities can be distinguished as:

(i) Short-term securities, mainly Treasury bills
(ii) Medium-term securities or notes
(iii) Long-term securities or bonds.

In turn, securities, usually with medium and long maturities, are of the following kinds:

(iv) Securities bearing a fixed interest rate
(v) Securities indexed to the price level
(vi) Variable-rate (or floating-rate) securities.

Among short-term, medium-term and long-term securities there is of course no sharp distinction, and often even the maturities offered for the same type of bond change substantially over time. Here each country's definition is adopted. In most cases the dividing line between short-term and medium-term debt is 1 year, while it is 2 years in the others.

Treasury bills   Treasury bills are the standard short-term instruments. They are sold at discount in typical maturities of 3, 6 and 12 months or 13, 26, 52 weeks or in 91 and 182 days as in Ireland, the UK and Portugal where a 364-day maturity is also available.

In addition to standard maturities, 1-month Treasury bills are issued in Finland, 5-week Treasury notes in Australia, and 60-day Financing bills in Japan. Cash management bills are issued with flexible maturities from few days up to 41 days in Canada while up to 6 months in the US.[4] Irish Exchequer Notes have also flexible maturities from 7 to 120 days. Treasury bills with maturities longer than 1 year, once common in Finland, Spain and Sweden, are now issued only in Germany. Dutch Treasury certificates introduced in 1992 now have maturities of 3 or 12 months but could be issued in maturities up to 2 years. Until the mid-1990s German discount bonds which were offered in maturities between 1 and 2 years (and 6 months since 1996), were more in the nature of money market notes and were not used for government's cash management.[5] In Austria, in addition to standard Treasury bills, one-year maturity bills with prolongation agreements up to 10 years were issued in the past, but such instruments were,

[4] In Belgium until the market reform of 1991, Treasury certificates with limited marketability had various maturities, ranging from 1 month to 1 year, and were sold to financial intermediaries at the demanded maturities without limitations on the amount requested.

[5] In Germany, non-marketable Treasury financing paper with maturities around 1 to 2 years is also offered to personal investors.

in fact, promissory notes privately placed with the banking sector. In Greece Treasury bills, issued in physical form, could be renewed for a period equal to their initial maturity at the same interest rate which was paid in advance at the time of renewal.

In almost all countries Treasury bills are sold through multiple-price auctions (or with uniform-price auctions as in Denmark and in Japan in the case of Financing bills or with a mix of the two techniques in Spain). Dutch Treasury certificates, Austrian, Irish and Greek Treasury bills, being sold via fixed-price subscriptions or on tap, are the only exceptions.

The traditional role of Treasury bills is that of government's cash management which explains why they have been introduced only recently in Denmark, Finland and the Netherlands, where the government used a current account at the Central Bank for cash management purposes. In these countries, bills have been introduced (or reintroduced as in the Netherlands) as a result of the EMU requirement of a non-negative balance of the Treasury account at the Central Bank. In a number of countries the role of Treasury bills or the use of a particular type of bills is limited to government's cash management. This is the case for Austria, the Netherlands and the UK, of Financing bills in Japan, and Cash Management bills in Canada and the US. In most countries Treasury bills can be used for deficit financing or refunding but only a few countries, notably those which experienced severe fiscal imbalances, have systematically relied on such instruments. As shown in Table 4.2, this has been the case in Belgium, Canada, Greece, Italy, Portugal, Spain, Sweden and the US.

The shares of bills reported in Table 4.2 do not provide a good indication of the maturity structure of the debt for two reasons. First, such shares are gross of Central Bank's holdings, so that privately held bills may differ sharply depending on the amount held in the bank's portfolio. For instance, Japanese Financing bills are almost completely held by the Bank of Japan, while the Bank of Finland holds a limited amount of Treasury bills, since it uses commercial banks' CDs for its open market operations. The second reason is that in some countries Treasury bills, being held by the household sector, seem to provide a clear substitute for non-marketable savings bonds (see below).

Fixed-rate notes and bonds   If the identification of short-term debt does not pose particular problems, the distinction between medium-term and long-term debt is more arbitrary—10 years in the US but 5 in Germany and Japan. Focusing on fixed-rate securities, Table 4.3 shows the share of debt made of medium- and long-term marketable securities, denominated in the domestic currency. For the reason given above, fixed-rate notes and bonds have been grouped together. Information on medium-term instruments, usually referred to as notes or certificates, will be presented in Section 4.5 for each country separately only in the cases where it is available.

Table 4.2. Share of Treasury bills and short debt

	1970	1975	1980	1985	1989	1991	1993	1995
Australia	n/a	17.4	13.3	5.2	16.7	23.7	20.1	13.3
Austria	19.6	23.6	12.0	9.6	6.7	6.0	6.3	3.2
Belgium	12.6	7.6	20.0	23.4	25.4	23.5	17.9	17.4
Canada	14.8	17.2	26.2	30.7	40.0	43.1	40.0	35.4
Denmark	—	—	—	—	—	8.9	8.0	7.6
Finland	—	—	—	3.3	0.5	5.6	8.6	10.2
France	19.6	19.7	19.9	29.8	10.1	7.4	7.4	8.9
Germany	1.4	4.8	1.3	1.3	1.3	3.0	2.0	0.4
Greece	n/a	n/a	39.1	33.2	45.2	36.9	23.0	26.5
Ireland	10.0	4.6	2.1	1.4	4.4	2.0	1.5	2.9
Italy	8.3	25.4	35.2	27.4	25.8	24.3	21.6	18.1
Japan	31.2	18.1	12.5	6.9	10.6	11.1	12.4	12.9
Netherlands	—	—	—	—	—	—	0.8	3.1
Portugal	—	—	—	6.4	16.5	21.5	11.3	12.7
Spain	—	—	—	53.1	63.3	52.5	36.6	32.3
Sweden	27.1	18.8	14.8	17.4	13.9	40.8	18.2	14.4
UK	3.9	11.6	1.3	0.9	5.8	5.2	1.1	3.2
USA	20.6	24.1	22.0	21.1	14.2	15.4	14.9	14.9

Notes: Per cent of total debt. Fiscal years ending in the same year or in March of the next year. Data for Austria include non-marketable T.bills converted into variable-rate notes at maturity but exclude floating-rate notes. Data for Germany include 1–2 year Treasury financing paper for personal investors. Until 1980 data for Sweden include 'old' T.bills held by the National Bank. Data for the UK are net of official holdings. For Canada and the US see Notes to Table 4.1.

Typical medium-term instruments are Dutch Treasury notes with maturities between 2 and 5 years, Danish Treasury certificates with a 2.5-year maturity, 4-year maturity German notes, Japanese notes with maturities of 2 and 4 years, French BTANs currently issued in maturities of 2 and 5 years, and recent Italian Zero-Coupon certificates with a 2-year maturity. Interest-bearing bonds/notes with a 2-year maturity have a long tradition in Canada and the US but they are not distinguished from, say, 10-year bonds in national statistics.

While it is impossible to give a summary overview of medium- and long-term securities for the last three decades as they varied widely across time and countries, it is easier to describe the current situation. In all countries notes and bonds now have "bullet" maturities, meaning that they are redeemed in one single payment at the final maturity. Sinking fund redemptions, according to which bonds are repaid in annual installments, were abandoned in the mid-1980s

Table 4.3. Share of fixed-rate notes and bonds

	1970	1975	1980	1985	1989	1991	1993	1995
Australia	n/a	67.8	56.1	64.5	59.4	62.2	69.2	76.4
Austria	40.7	36.8	47.5	36.6	37.8	39.8	43.3	45.7
Belgium	67.7	82.5	67.5	49.5	54.4	59.4	62.1	60.3
Canada	51.5	41.0	49.1	40.2	43.1	44.4	48.4	52.5
Denmark	36.8	41.7	65.8	73.0	58.0	58.9	62.0	73.9
Finland	29.5	22.9	29.6	31.9	45.6	33.7	26.8	38.3
France	10.1	16.3	26.7	29.3	56.1	60.5	68.8	70.3
Germany	16.3	14.6	17.6	27.3	39.8	45.0	48.8	49.2
Ireland	53.2	57.2	56.6	40.9	40.5	42.4	42.3	44.9
Italy	43.0	36.8	24.1	11.0	19.5	23.9	28.0	36.9
Japan	57.8	69.2	75.7	80.0	73.5	71.1	66.9	64.5
Netherlands	60.0	46.0	43.3	57.7	62.6	67.4	74.3	78.0
Portugal	72.3	80.7	17.8	4.3	4.0	7.9	15.9	20.9
Spain	35.0	22.4	21.3	11.7	28.9	36.5	49.8	54.4
Sweden	67.8	73.6	55.6	43.1	42.2	33.3	39.1	47.3
UK	70.9	69.8	79.5	71.4	58.0	56.7	61.0	59.6
USA	42.3	35.1	43.5	53.5	51.5	49.4	50.6	50.3

Notes: Per cent of total debt. Fiscal years ending in the same year or in March of the next year. For Denmark data include 2-year certificates. For Finland data exclude registered bonds. For France data exclude fixed-rate bonds exchangeable into variable-rate bonds. In Greece there were no fixed-rate bonds in 1995, their share was 6.4% in 1989. Data for UK are net of official holdings. For Canada and the US see Notes to Table 4.1.

in Austria, Finland and France and in the second half of the 1980s in Denmark, the Netherlands and Portugal.[6]

A summary overview of the maturities of long-term securities currently issued in OECD economies is also easy to provide. In fact, as a result of the deregulation and liberalization of financial markets to foreign investors since the mid-1980s, the markets for fixed-rate government bonds have become increasingly integrated. The creation of liquid markets and the promotion of "benchmark bonds" have led to a "standardization" of fixed-rate securities and to a reduction of the maturities on offer.

For all the countries considered, the 10-year maturity bond is now the main financing instrument. The emphasis on the 10-year bond is strongest in Austria, Belgium, Denmark, Germany, Japan, the Netherlands and to a lesser extent in the US. In other countries a greater maturity diversification is observed, but the maturities on offer are limited, usually to 3, 5, and 10 years as in Italy, Spain and Portugal, where 7-year bonds are also issued, as well as in Canada

---

[6] The repayments were at par value and could take place in equal or unequal installments, usually after an initial "grace period."

Table 4.4. Share of price-indexed debt

	1980	1983	1985	1987	1989	1991	1993	1995
Australia	—	—	0.0	0.8	1.3	1.5	1.9	3.0
Canada	—	—	—	—	—	0.3	0.7	1.2
Italy	—	0.2	0.2	0.1	0.1	0.1	—	—
Sweden	—	—	—	—	—	—	—	1.2
(face value)	—	—	—	—	—	—	—	(2.5)
UK	0.9	5.0	6.6	7.8	9.3	9.9	11.5	12.0

Notes: Per cent of total debt. Fiscal years ending in the same year or in March of the next year. Sweden bonds are deep discount bonds; face value is the redemption value without the capital uplift. In 1997 price-index-linked bonds have been introduced in Greece and in the US. For Canada see Notes to Table 4.1.

and the US where the 2-year maturity is important. Most countries also issue a 30-year maturity bond with few exceptions such as Belgium and Ireland, where the maximum maturity is 20 years, Finland and Portugal with 10-year and Greece with 7-year maximum maturity. In Belgium, the Netherlands and the UK the issuing activity is centered on the long end. For example, in the UK the focus is on the 5-, 10-, 20- and 25-year maturities, in the Netherlands on the 10-, 15- and 30-year maturities. In France a 55-year bond has been recently introduced.

Fixed-rate conventional bonds and notes are certainly the most common securities, but over the last two decades European governments have issued significant amounts of variable-rate bonds, i.e. bonds with coupons adjusted to prevailing interest rates, and bonds indexed to the price level.

Price-index-linked bonds   Price-index-linked bonds have either the coupons or the principal indexed to the consumer price index (the retail price index in the UK) with a lag which varies from 8 months in Australia and the UK to 2.5 months in Sweden.[7] Indexed bonds have been issued in the UK since 1981, in Australia since 1985, and more recently in Canada, Greece, Sweden and the US. The share of such debt is shown in Table 4.4.

Although alternative indexation mechanisms could be considered, almost all government bonds currently being issued are of the "capital-indexed" type. They are so called because the principal repayment at maturity is the product of the nominal value of the bond with the cumulative change in the price index. The interest payments are determined by applying the coupon rate, which is specified in real terms, to the inflation-adjusted principal amount, i.e. the sum between the nominal value of the bond and the capital uplift accrued up to the coupon-payment date. Swedish "zero-coupon indexed bonds" issued

[7] The only issue of Italian indexed bonds in 1983 was linked to the GDP deflator.

Table 4.5. Share of variable-rate debt

	1977	1980	1985	1987	1989	1991	1993	1995
Australia	—	—	—	—	—	—	—	3.5
Austria Security	n/a	n/a	n/a	6.4	9.4	11.0	7.9	6.4
Austria Loans	n/a	0.3	26.8	29.3	24.9	22.3	18.6	15.4
Belgium	—	0.1	2.1	1.7	1.4	1.6	2.3	10.0
Denmark	—	—	6.0	12.0	17.9	15.3	5.7	2.7
France	—	—	4.2	4.6	7.0	6.8	3.4	2.7
Germany	—	—	—	—	—	0.4	0.3	0.8
Greece	—	—	—	—	—	20.5	32.6	35.3
Ireland	—	0.8	5.0	3.6	7.8	8.6	5.5	4.7
Italy	4.6	13.6	41.6	41.9	33.1	30.3	27.9	22.8
Japan	—	—	2.9	2.4	2.3	2.1	1.8	1.5
Portugal	26.3	60.4	55.0	50.8	54.3	45.4	38.9	26.9
UK	1.1	0.7	—	—	—	—	0.8	1.5

Notes: Per cent of total debt. Fiscal years ending in the same year or in March of the next year. Data for Austria Security include non-marketable T.bills converted into variable-rate notes and floating-rate notes. Austria Loans also include variable-rate loans.

in 1994 are a special case of "capital-indexed bonds", i.e. bonds with a coupon rate equal to zero. Greek "interest-indexed bonds," introduced in 1997, are the relevant exception to this indexation mechanism. Interest-indexed bonds were first issued in Australia along with capital-indexed bonds between 1985 and 1987. They pay quarterly coupons (annual coupons in case of Greek bonds) indexed to the CPI and a fixed principal at maturity, i.e. the principal repayment is not adjusted for inflation.

Variable-rate bonds   With the exception of the UK the extent of price indexation has been fairly modest until recently. On the contrary, Table 4.5 shows that the share of variable-rate (or floating-rate) debt, i.e. bonds and notes with coupons indexed to prevailing interest rates has been substantial, especially in the 1980s. The use of variable-rate debt has been strongest in Portugal and Greece, but also very large in Austria, Italy, Denmark and, but to a much less extent, in France and Ireland.

Few countries, such as Australia, Belgium, Germany and the UK which did not rely on such debt in the 1980s are currently experimenting with floating-rate bonds.[8] Instead of relying on variable-rate instruments, in Canada, Denmark, Finland, Germany and Ireland interest-rate swaps are currently used to control the extent of indexation of public debt to market interest rates.

[8] Variable-rate bonds were introduced experimentally, but soon abandoned, in Japan in 1983 and in Spain in 1986, as well as in the UK and in Sweden in the late 1970s.

The indexation features and adjustment periods differ substantially across time and countries. Variable-rate notes and bonds can be classified according to the reference rate to which their coupons are linked or adjusted, i.e. depending on whether the reference rate is a money market rate, the auction rate of Treasury bill, or a long-term yield recorded on the secondary market.

Following the example of Ireland, in most countries variable-rate bonds are now issued with quarterly coupons indexed to the domestic interbank offer rate, usually the 3-month rate. This is the case of Austrian floating-rate notes and bonds, introduced in 1986 and 1992; Belgian 5-year bonds issued in 1994; German 10-year bonds of 1990; Irish variable-rate bonds issued since the early 1980s and Portuguese 1994 5-year bonds (to the 6-month rate). In Australia floating-rate notes introduced in 1994 have been indexed to the 3-month Australia bank bill rate while in the UK the London interbank bid rate is used as the reference rate.

The indexation mechanism which relies on simple or weighted averages of the issue rates from Treasury bill auctions is the one with the longest tradition. It was first adopted in the UK and in Italy in 1977, but, while in the former country the program was soon abandoned after 3 issues, in the latter it grew large.[9] Italian floating-rate notes now pay semi-annual coupons tied to the 6-month Treasury bill rate recorded in the last auction preceding the entitlement period. In the past, however, the reference rate was computed as the average of the rates in the auctions (of either 6-month or 12-month Treasury bills) held in the two months preceding by one month the entitlement period. Early issues of Irish variable-rate notes introduced in 1978 were indexed to 3-month Treasury bills. This form of indexation has been used in France where the average auction rate of 13-weeks Treasury bills has been taken as the reference rate. Coupons have been indexed to the issue rate recorded in the last auction preceding the payment of the quarterly coupon or to annual averages of the reference rate (or its bond equivalent) recorded during the year preceding the payment of the coupon. Greek bonds issued since 1992, with maturities of 3, 5 and 7 years, have annual coupons indexed to the 12-month Treasury bill rate. In Portugal "Public Investment Funds" (FIP) bonds issued between 1990 and 1994 had coupons adjusted to the average of the interest rates recorded in the last twelve auctions of Treasury bills of any maturity. In Austria the maturity of Treasury bills could be postponed (up to 10 years) in which case the interest rates were revised to the new issue rate.

Finally, indexation to secondary market yields was adopted in France and Denmark in 1984. Issued between 1984 and 1990, Danish bonds had coupons adjusted quarterly to the average yield on fixed-rate securities with a remaining

---

[9] UK bonds were indexed to market rates. They had semi-annual coupons indexed to daily averages of Treasury bills rates recorded during the 6-month period ending 1 month before each coupon payment.

term to maturity equal or less than three years, calculated over the 3 months preceding the entitlement period. In France the traditional form of indexation takes the weighted average of the yields on bonds with maturities equal or longer than 7 years as the reference rate (recorded weekly). The annual coupons are indexed to yearly averages of the values of the reference rate during the year preceding the payment of the coupon. A new variable-rate bond was however introduced in 1996 which has quarterly coupons indexed to a hypothetical 10-year yield obtained by linear interpolation of the yields of the two benchmark bonds with terms to maturity closest to 10 years. A Belgian 10-year bond issued in 1994 has step-up coupons revisable every 3 years to the average yield on bonds with a remaining term to maturity equal or less than 3 years.[10]

Maturity and interest-rate options   Government securities may also bear maturity and interest-rate options. Bonds exchangeable in other bonds with a different type of interest rate were issued on a large scale in France in the mid-1980s. A first type of fixed-rate bonds introduced in 1983 gave the holder the option to convert them (2 years after the issue date) into variable-rate bonds in any following year until maturity (at prespecified dates). A second type of variable-rate bonds introduced in 1984 gave the holder the option to exchange the bonds into fixed-rate securities during a limited period of time (usually 2 years) beginning 2 years after the issue date. A limited amount of variable-rate bonds exchangeable into fixed-rate bonds were issued in Italy in 1986, while a UK indexed bond of 1983 could be converted into a fixed-rate bond at the end of the same or the following year.

Maturity options on long-term securities had a much larger diffusion. The most important types of such securities are the following:

(i) Callable bonds
(ii) Putable bonds
(iii) Convertible and extendible bonds.

Callable bonds, which give the option to the borrower of an early redemption, usually at par value, have a long tradition. Indeed, perpetuals were of this kind. In the Netherlands, bonds and privately placed loans with maturities longer than 10 years were usually callable after 10 years. Examples of callable bonds are stocks issued with very long maturities in Ireland and the UK, known as "double-dated bonds" since they were redeemable (with 3 months notice) during the last 3 or 5 years of their lives. Austrian 10-year and 15-year bonds were also callable in the last 2 or 5 years prior to maturity. Few Canadian bonds

---

[10] Few indexation mechanisms do not fall in the above categories. In Portugal FIP bonds issued between 1977 and 1989 were indexed to the weighted average rate on deposit accounts between 6 months and 1 year by the three institutions with the largest accounts. In Sweden 10-year bonds introduced in 1977 had coupons revisable after 5 years to the new issue rate on comparable bonds and in 1979 a second experiment was made involving indexation to the central bank's discount rate.

issued in the 1980s and Belgian bonds, issued in the period 1986–91, included a call option clause. Thirty-year US bonds issued until 1984 were callable 5 years prior to maturity. While in all these countries call options are no longer used, in Portugal they have been attached to a few issues since 1991.

Put options on government securities, which enable the holder to ask for an earlier redemption (usually at half bond's life), are much rarer. Belgium is the country which used this instrument more extensively in the past, as putable bonds accounted for almost one-fourth of total bonds in 1983. In Belgium put options have been reintroduced on variable-rate bonds issued since 1994, after their use was suspended in 1991. A significant amount of putable bonds have also been issued in Italy between 1988 and 1992 for a share equal to 8% of total bonds in 1991.

Convertible securities offer the holder the option to convert them at pre-determined dates and interest rates into longer dated issues. Such securities have been issued on a large scale in the UK since the early 1980s and in France between 1983 and 1986. Extendible bonds, offering the holder the option of extending the maturity once or several times in the future, have been issued in the Netherlands and to a lesser extent in Canada where they were discontinued in 1984 and 1982, respectively. Greek Treasury bills and Austrian floating-rate notes can also be considered as short-term extendible notes.

Non-marketable debt   If the use of marketable securities is widespread, the reliance on non-marketable debt is more country specific. The most important instruments of this kind are the following:

 (i) Foreign currency loans
 (ii) Loans from financial institutions
(iii) Savings bonds for personal investors.

While most countries receive straightforward credits and loans from financial institutions, especially when borrowing in foreign currency, domestic loans are important only in few countries, those where the banking sector or other financial institutions played a major role in the sale and holding of debt: in Austria, Finland, Germany, Japan, and the Netherlands. Even in these countries the importance of loans is rapidly diminishing, as shown in Table 4.6.

In Germany loans are made against promissory notes, "Schuldschendarlehen" (or borrowers' notes), which are privately placed with banks and social security funds. They have a limited marketability in that they can be sold a limited number of times. In the Netherlands loans are made against registered non-marketable bonds, which can be transferred without limitations, and differ from marketable bonds only because they are privately placed with pension funds and insurance companies. In Finland the government also borrowed from such institutions through private placements of registered bonds.

Table 4.6. Share of loans and certificates of indebtedness

	1970	1975	1980	1985	1989	1991	1993	1995
Australia	n/a	2.7	2.3	1.8	1.4	1.6	0.9	0.7
Austria	7.5	6.3	12.4	31.1	34.8	31.2	26.4	24.3
Finland	33.5	31.7	12.8	10.1	10.9	13.3	6.0	5.1
Germany	62.0	68.8	72.3	65.9	53.8	47.4	40.0	40.5
Greece	n/a	n/a	15.3	15.3	8.1	3.6	3.5	3.2
Italy	19.0	18.2	8.6	5.8	5.0	5.7	6.1	5.6
Japan	10.2	12.6	11.8	10.2	13.6	15.6	18.9	21.1
Netherlands	30.4	42.0	49.4	41.1	36.2	31.5	24.2	18.1
Spain Mand.	56.6	62.5	65.2	21.4	1.8	2.1	3.5	2.5
Spain	—	—	—	1.7	0.6	2.4	0.1	0.6
Sweden	4.8	1.9	1.9	2.0	3.4	2.4	0.0	0.0
USA	22.6	28.0	25.6	21.1	29.6	31.5	30.6	30.6

Notes: Per cent of total debt. Fiscal years ending in the same year or in March of the next year. Data for Austria and Greece exclude non-marketable T.bills. Data for Finland include registered bonds, promissory notes, short-term loans and other borrowing. For Greece data exclude loans from the Central Bank. Spanish Mandatory loans are indicated as Spain Mand. Data for Spain excludes promissory notes (Pagarès). Data for the US consider debt held in government accounts. For Canada see Notes to Table 4.1.

Typically loans have long maturities: Dutch loans, "Ondherandse Leningen," now have maturities from 10 to 40 years with possible interest-rate adjustments after 10 years, while in Germany maturities are concentrated in the 5–10-year range. German loans are usually redeemable at final maturity, Dutch loans in annual installments. In Spain similar instruments, called Investment certificates of indebtedness, "Cedula para Inversíon," with a standard 10-year maturity were used until the last decade, but borrowing occurred under mandatory investment regulation on banks' deposits.

Savings bonds, unlike other government paper, are usually available only to private individuals, in effect small savers, and cannot be traded; they are disposable only by redemption at the Treasury.[II] Savings bonds are currently issued in Canada, Germany, Ireland, the UK and the US. Post Office certificates are issued in Italy while savings deposits or savings accounts with the Post Office are available in Belgium, France, Ireland and Italy and savings accounts with banks in Sweden (see Table 4.7).

[II] UK national savings certificates are available to all investors' groups but with a ceiling to the maximum amount which can be held.

Table 4.7. Share of savings bonds and deposits

	1970	1975	1980	1985	1989	1991	1993	1995
Australia	n/a	5.4	10.8	10.8	4.8	1.1	0.2	—
Belgium	9.2	7.5	4.3	1.7	1.5	1.2	0.8	0.9
Canada	31.0	41.1	19.0	22.0	13.8	10.1	7.6	6.6
Denmark	9.3	2.7	0.9	0.3	0.2	0.2	0.2	0.2
France	21.3	15.1	11.7	3.2	1.9	1.3	0.6	0.3
France Dep	45.3	46.5	37.8	24.3	18.1	16.6	12.7	11.6
Germany	0.5	3.8	5.2	3.4	3.6	3.0	3.1	3.9
Ireland	7.8	4.4	2.9	3.6	5.9	6.6	7.4	10.0
Italy	24.1	17.1	16.0	9.5	10.0	9.5	8.8	9.0
Portugal	0.9	0.7	0.4	0.7	7.5	13.7	21.3	21.3
Sweden	18.1	18.4	16.7	15.1	23.8	15.1	11.6	8.9
UK	10.7	7.8	10.4	14.1	15.4	16.3	14.5	13.5
USA	13.9	12.3	8.0	4.2	4.0	3.6	3.8	3.6

Notes: Per cent of total debt. Fiscal years ending in the same year or in March of the next year. Figures also include variable-rate and price-indexed savings bonds, prize and lottery bonds, deposits and accounts with the Post Office. Data for Germany excludes 1–2 year Treasury financing paper. France Dep distinguishes deposits with the Post Office from savings bonds. For Denmark data refer to lottery bonds. For Canada, and the US see Notes to Table 4.1.

Although savings bonds are issued with specific maturities, they are redeemable on demand before the final maturity date.[12] This makes the type of interest paid on such instruments a less important characteristic. The most common type are savings bonds with step-up fixed coupons. Flat interest rates apply only on Canadian bonds and some series of US bonds. Price-index-linked bonds have been issued in Ireland and the UK since the mid-1970s, while all Portuguese schemes and some Swedish accounts are at variable rates. Prize bonds or lottery bonds with interest payments determined by drawings are available in Denmark, Ireland, Sweden and the UK.

While savings bonds are redeemable on demand, certain restrictions apply. For instance, in Portugal early redemptions of savings certificates are possible only 3 months after the issue date and such period increases up to 6 months in the case of US bonds and to 1 year for German bonds. Moreover, early redemptions often involve some cost and delay of collection. In fact, with the exception of Canadian paper and some US series, savings bonds feature

---

[12] The typical maturity of savings bonds ranges from 3 to 7 years, but Canadian bonds have 12-year maturity and US bonds are issued with maturities of 20 and 30 years. Portuguese savings certificates have no maturity.

progressive interest rates or a combination of a flat rate and bonus payments. Furthermore, in most countries interest is not paid when the bond is returned during the first 12 months from the issue date, with the exception of Irish certificates and Canadian bonds where the initial period reduces to 6 and 3 months, respectively.

These features, aimed at discouraging investors from requesting redemption at an early stage, are coupled with the practice of changing the interest rates or introducing new series in which the old bonds can be converted when coupons go out of line with prevailing market rates. While in Canada the interest rate on outstanding bonds is reset each year to the rate of the new series and in the US the rate can be changed upward (there is a minimum rate), in all other countries a new series is required to change the interest rate. Obviously, the problem does not arise in the case of Portuguese variable-rate bonds and for savings accounts.

4.4   Debt maturity and debt duration

In the following sections evidence is presented on the average remaining term to maturity of fixed-rate securities denominated in the domestic currency. This statistic provides relevant information on the risk-return characteristics of the debt. In particular, since average maturity is inversely related to the amount of debt maturing at each date, the shorter this maturity the greater is the amount of new debt which must be refinanced in each period. Hence, in addition to the share of variable-rate debt, average maturity provides a summary indicator of the effect on the debt burden of changes in the real interest rate.

Furthermore, average maturity provides information on the sensitivity of the value of fixed-rate debt to changes in interest rates. The relevant concept in this case is Macaulay's duration which provides a linear approximation of the elasticity of the value of fixed-rate securities to unexpected changes in interest rates (see Shiller 1990). While duration is the relevant concept, the average remaining term to maturity, being closely related to duration, is the best alternative when data on the former are not available or require lengthy computations.

The market value semi-elasticity of a bond to an unanticipated change in its yield to maturity is approximated by:

$$-\frac{\partial P}{\partial i}\frac{1}{P} \simeq \frac{M}{1+i} \tag{4.1}$$

where M defines Macaulay's duration of the bond, P denotes the bond's price and i is the yield to maturity (interest rate) of such a bond. Duration, M, is the weighted average time to receive all interests and principal where the weights reflect the relative present values of the cash flows:

$$M = \frac{\sum_{j=1}^{n} [CP_j/(1+i)^{Tj}] Tj}{\sum_{j=1}^{n} CP_j/(1+i)^{Tj}}$$

where CP_j is the cash payment (interest plus principal) at period j, Tj is the time until cash payment j is made, n is the number of payments and i is the yield to maturity. Duration analysis can be improved by using the term structure of interest rates instead of the yield to maturity.

For a bond selling at par—i.e. for a bond whose price is equal to 1, $P = 1 = \sum_{j=1}^{n} CP_j/(1+i)^{Tj}$—duration simplifies to

$$M_{Par} = \sum_{j=1}^{n} [CP_j/(1+i)^{Tj}] Tj$$

which is equal to (minus) the derivative of the price with respect to the yield to maturity times $(1+i)$—i.e. Equation 4.1 holds exactly.

The duration of the fixed-rate component of the debt—i.e. the elasticity of the overall debt to changes in interest rates—could be computed as the weighted average time of meeting all outstanding commitments, that is, principals and interest payments. However, the lack of data on interest payments and the computational burden that such an estimate would imply suggest the use of the "average remaining term to maturity" as a proxy for debt duration.

The "average remaining term to maturity" of the debt (referred as average maturity for short in what follows) is the average weighted time to repay the principals of the outstanding securities where the weights reflect their relative nominal values. Formally:

$$\text{Average maturity} = \frac{\sum_{s=1}^{N} m_s X_s}{\sum_{s=1}^{N} X_s}$$

where N is the number of outstanding securities, m_s is the time to maturity of security s, and X_s is its redemption price.

To get an idea of the degree of approximation involved, it can be observed that the duration of a zero coupon bond coincides with its term to maturity while the duration of a coupon bond is shorter than its term to maturity due to the weight of interest payments. This implies that, in general, the average maturity of the debt overestimates debt duration.

For a class of recent theories of debt management the elasticity of the debt value to unexpected inflation is the relevant concept of debt duration. To obtain a measure of the debt elasticity to inflation consider a revision in expected inflation lasting until the bond's maturity. Assuming a constant real interest rate, this revision in inflationary expectations leads to an unanticipated shift in the yield curve and thus to a change in the bond price approximately equal to:

$$-\frac{\partial P}{\partial \pi}\frac{1}{P} \simeq \frac{M}{1+\pi}$$

where π is the inflation rate and M is the market value semi-elasticity of the bond, i.e. Macaulay's duration.

Although the assumption of a parallel shift of the yield curve is clearly a simplification, the average duration and thus the average term to maturity of the fixed-rate component of the debt are useful proxies for the price sensitivity of such debt to revisions in the expected inflation path.

The average maturity is instead inappropriate, as a measure of price sensitivity, when dealing with securities which have indexation features, maturity options, and with debt denominated in foreign currency. To take this into consideration, a maturity series is constructed, and referred as "effective maturity," which better approximates the market value elasticity of the debt to revisions in expected inflation. In constructing effective maturity, the average term to maturity is used to approximate the duration of fixed-rate securities and the following assumptions are made for other types of debt: (i) zero maturity is assigned to foreign currency debt and price-index-linked debt; (ii) the time before the next coupon adjustment is considered for variable-rate securities; (iii) the earliest redemption date is assigned to putable and convertible securities and (iv) the latest redemption date is assigned to callable securities.

These assumptions are based on the following arguments.[13] Except for the indexation lag, price-level indexed securities bear no inflation risk and their value should be considered as having zero elasticity to unanticipated inflation. The same holds true for foreign currency debt and ECU indexed securities as long as any inflation is reflected in currency depreciation. Here this is taken as a first approximation, which should be explored further, both theoretically and empirically.

Regarding securities with coupons indexed to a market rate, a change in inflation affects their value only for the time remaining before the next adjustment if, as it is assumed here, the reference rate is going to reflect future anticipated inflation.

---

[13] There are important differences between the above assumptions with the conventions adopted in the few countries which report data on the average maturity. For instance, in the case of option-bearing securities, to assign the maturity resulting from not exercising the option is the standard practice. More importantly, debt denominated in foreign currency or indexed to the price level is usually excluded from the calculation of debt maturity. Conventional measures take instead variable-rate debt into account, but its maturity is identified with the date of final redemption.

The earliest redemption date is the relevant maturity for putable bonds, since they enable the holder to ask for an early repayment when inflation, and thus interest rates, turn out to be higher than anticipated. For the same reason, the earliest conversion date is the relevant maturity for a convertible bond as the holder would not exercise the option to extend the bond's life. On the contrary, a government which has the option to call a security would not exercise its right when inflation turns out to be higher than anticipated; the latest redemption date is the relevant maturity in this case.

The last assumption concerns the maturity of non-marketable savings bonds. Though sold in specified maturities, these bonds are redeemable on demand but, as mentioned above, this entails costs and delay of collection. To avoid the arbitrariness implicit in assigning a given maturity to such debt it has been decided to follow conventional practice by excluding it from the stock of debt on which maturity is computed.

4.4.1 Debt

The net worth of the public sector is the definition which comes closer to the relevant theoretical concept of public debt. However, here the focus is on gross debt for a number of reasons which makes it a more reliable indicator. First, to compute future commitments, like those arising under public pension schemes, is difficult. Secondly, data on net debt are unreliable; they are sensitive to the criteria used to define public assets in national statistics. Especially if data on the market value of public assets are not available, as it is often the case, evidence on net debt can be particularly misleading because the quality of public assets is overestimated by book values.

Regarding to the level of government, the choice has fallen on the debt aggregate for which data on debt composition and maturity are available. Usually, this is the aggregate on which the debate has focused in each country. In any case, the present study aims to examine the joint evolution of debt and debt composition (by instrument and remaining term to maturity) rather than to compare figures across countries. Moreover, for most countries, the behavior of central and general government debt has been quite similar over the period considered.

Finally, a series is constructed that corresponds to the part of debt held by the private sector rather than by the central bank or in government accounts: "privately held debt" or, using British terminology, "market holdings" of debt. Indeed, claims by the central bank against the Treasury should not be counted as debt; borrowing from the central bank involves a substitution of money for interest-bearing paper, i.e. it does not increase the debt burden. It is also straightforward to exclude the debt held in government accounts, given that the government owes such liabilities to itself. However, central bank obligations, namely base money, are not counted as debt on the ground that money does not yield interest and thus cannot be viewed as a burden.[14]

As debt refers to gross privately held debt in what follows, the reader familiar with conventional debt figures will find in most cases the data provided here lower than those she is used to.

4.5　Debt composition and debt maturity in OECD countries

In this section evidence is presented on the type of instruments, the composition and the maturity structure of public debt and the ratio of debt to GDP ("debt ratio" for short in what follows), for 18 OECD countries: Australia, Austria, Belgium, Canada, Denmark, Finland, France, Germany, Greece, Ireland, Italy, Japan, the Netherlands, Portugal, Spain, Sweden, the United Kingdom and the United States.

Australia　Australia is one of least indebted OECD countries. In 1995 the central government debt, though on an upward trend, was still lower than 24% of GDP (the general government debt was higher at 43%). In fact, over the last two decades the debt ratio did not even reach 30%. This moderate dynamics reflects the effects of two stabilizations, one in the early 1980s and the other between 1986 and 1989, when reverse auctions were held to redeem outstanding bonds.

The Australian debt has attracted the economists' attention because of the issuance of price-index-linked bonds. Until the 1990s Australia was the only country with the UK to offer such bonds. Indexed bonds had been issued for the first time in 1985 with maturities of 10 and 20 years with either the principal or the coupons linked to the CPI.[15] Such bonds have never reached 4% of the debt, as the issuing program was soon suspended in 1989 to get new impulse only in 1993. The lack of success of the program is evident if compared to floating-rate debt. In 1995, one year after their introduction, variable-rate bonds already exceeded indexed bonds. Variable-rate bonds are issued with maturities of 3.5 and 5 years and have quarterly coupons indexed to the 3-month Australia bank bill rate.

Despite the attention which price indexation has received, Australia stands out for the large share of conventional bonds with initial maturities between 3 and 30 years. Bonds have been issued through multiple-price auctions since 1982, also using the technique of "reopening" existing issues in order

---

[14] In principle, debt management should not be kept distinct from monetary policy. Whether the borrowing requirement is financed by selling paper to the private sector or to the monetary authorities affects real outcomes. The same is true when open market operations are considered. While evidence on the composition between money and interest-bearing debt is not explicitly presented, episodes of substantial deficit monetization will be pointed out in the discussion.

[15] Capital-indexed bonds have fixed coupons and indexed principal with capital uplift paid at maturity, while interest-indexed bonds have fixed principal and indexed coupons (see Section 4.3).

to promote liquidity. Most of the trading activity is in the 3-year and 10-year issues.

Table 4.8 shows the composition of the privately held debt by type of instrument. Treasury bills, which have not been issued since 1982, are excluded from privately held debt because they were almost entirely held by the Central Bank, though precise data on the bank's holdings could not be found. Treasury notes, that is, new Treasury bills, are issued in maturities of 13, 26 weeks and, since 1991, 5 weeks. Long-term bonds have maturities between 3 and 30 years.

The share of fixed-rate bonds never fell below 55% over the last two decades and reached a remarkable 74% in 1995. Much of increase took place in the 1990s and mainly reflects a substitution of domestic currency for foreign currency debt. In fact, with the fiscal stabilization of 1986 borrowing in foreign currency was suspended and the share of such debt fell from a peak of 26% to less than 4% in 1995. In the second half of the 1980s Treasury notes became the

Table 4.8. Australia: composition by type of instrument

	1975	1980	1983	1986	1989	1992	1995
T.Notes	15.2	5.1	7.0	6.8	16.8	26.0	14.6
P-Indexed	—	—	—	0.4	1.4	1.4	3.4
Var-Bond	—	—	—	—	—	—	4.0
Fix-Bond	65.4	55.6	55.6	57.6	57.6	60.5	73.6
Foreign	8.7	22.4	20.7	25.9	17.5	9.8	3.7
Non-Mkt	10.7	16.9	16.7	9.3	6.7	2.3	0.8
o/w Savings	(7.1)	(13.9)	(14.1)	(7.4)	(5.1)	(0.7)	(—)
PH-Ratio	20.9	19.4	19.2	22.2	15.8	13.2	19.9
T.Bills	5.7	8.1	0.0	0.0	0.0	0.0	0.0
Off-Held	19.2	15.3	11.8	16.3	6.5	15.0	14.6
CB-Held	7.2	16.8	9.6	15.2	6.0	13.1	14.0
Debt Ratio	27.4	24.9	21.8	26.5	16.9	15.6	23.3
Average maturity of marketable PH debt							
Convention	8.8	6.5	4.7	6.7	5.5	5.5	6.3
All-Fixed	8.8	6.5	4.7	6.6	5.4	5.4	6.1
Effective	7.9	4.7	3.5	4.7	4.3	4.8	5.4

Notes: Data refer to privately held debt and are for fiscal years ending in June of the same year. Off-Held refers to official holdings of notes and bonds. Central Bank holdings include T.bills. General definitions: o/w means 'of which'; PH-Ratio denotes the ratio of privately held debt to GDP while Debt Ratio is the same ratio for total debt; Off-Held refers to official holdings of debt; CB-Held denotes Central Bank holdings; Convention denotes conventional average term to maturity; All-Fixed is average maturity for fixed-rate securities. For the definition of Effective maturity see Section 4.4.

main funding instrument; their share increased from 7% in 1986 up to 26% in 1992. In the most recent period the debt accumulation was instead entirely financed by fixed-rate long-term bonds. Marketable securities, notes and bonds, replaced savings bonds which declined from about 14% in 1983 to zero in 1995, a development which reflects financial innovation and the higher cost of borrowing on the retail market.

Not only the share of long-term bonds is large, but their maturity is also very long. In 1995 the conventional average term to maturity of marketable debt in private hands was as high as 6.3 years, a remarkable figure given that it comprises Treasury notes. When price-index-linked bonds are excluded from the aggregate, the average maturity of fixed-rate debt is slightly shorter at 6.1 years. As shown in Figure 4.1, the average maturity shows no trend over the last two decades, since the decline to 4.7 years in 1983 is rapidly reverted to 6.7 years in the following period, when the debt accumulation is financed by long-term bonds. The positive relation between debt and debt maturity clearly points to a policy of financing deficit accumulation with long-term bonds. The effective maturity series, which is constructed to approximate the sensitivity of the debt value to permanent changes in inflation, shows a remarkable stability over the last two decades, as it varies between 3.5 years in 1983 and 4.8 years in 1994 before reaching 5.4 years in 1995. Such variations mainly reflect changes in the share of foreign currency debt, since a minor correction is needed to take into account the small amount of variable-rate and price-index-linked bonds.

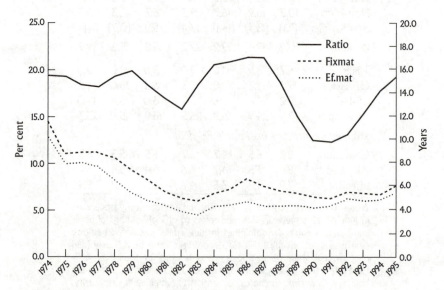

Fig. 4.1. Australia: debt ratio and debt maturity.

Table 4.9. Austria: composition by type of instrument

	1970	1975	1980	1983	1986	1989	1992	1995
T.Bills	19.6	23.6	12.0	11.4	8.7	11.4	10.9	8.0
o/w Var	n/a	n/a	n/a	n/a	n/a	(9.2)	(8.5)	(6.4)
Var-Bond	0.0	0.0	0.0	0.0	0.0	0.2	0.1	0.0
Fix-Bond	40.7	36.8	47.5	40.4	35.7	37.8	41.7	45.7
o/w Notes	n/a	(10.7)	(20.3)	(16.9)	(15.4)	(15.0)	(9.9)	(5.0)
Foreign	32.1	33.3	28.1	30.4	20.2	15.7	17.4	22.0
Fix-Loan	7.5	6.3	12.1	1.5	6.7	9.9	8.9	8.9
Var-Loan	n/a	n/a	0.3	16.3	28.7	24.9	21.0	15.4
CB-Held	10.8	4.0	1.0	0.6	0.2	0.0	0.1	0.0
Debt Ratio	11.2	14.7	26.0	34.4	43.3	47.8	48.5	57.4
Average maturity of marketable debt								
Convention	n/a	n/a	n/a	n/a	n/a	n/a	6.7	4.8

Notes: Data are net of the credit line at Central Bank but gross of the Bank's security holdings. T.Bills includes floating-rate notes. Fix-Bond includes long-term notes. Maturity for 1995 refers to 1994. For other definitions see Table 4.8.

Austria   Although the Austrian debt had been on an upward trend since the mid-1970s, in 1995 it was lower than 60% of GDP. The fiscal stabilization of the early 1990s temporarily interrupted this trend but the slow growth of the following years led the debt ratio to rise again up to 57% in 1995.

As in other OECD countries, in the 1990s fixed-rate long-term bonds have become the main financing instruments. New bonds issued since 1988 have bullet maturities and are not callable as was the case in the past.[16] They have been issued through multiple-price auctions since 1989. In 1991 the wholesale market was organized as a dealer market with the selected banks participating in the auctions acting as market-makers. By contrast, Treasury bills, which are more in the nature of short-term promissory notes, are still privately placed with banks. The role of the banking sector is reflected in the relatively high shares of loans and Treasury bills which in the early 1990s still accounted for 30% and 10% of the debt, respectively.

Table 4.9 shows the composition by type of instrument of the Austrian debt net of the credit line at the Central Bank but gross of the Bank's security holdings. The share of Treasury bills has been relatively small around 10% and relatively stable since the late 1970s. In the past, Treasury bills were issued with an initial maturity of 1 year which could be extended by prolongation agreements up to 10 years, in which case the interest rate became variable. National sources on debt composition thus distinguish three series of Treasury bills.

---

[16] Bonds had maturities of 10 and 15 years and could be called in during the last 2 or 4 years of their life. Sinking funds redemptions were abandoned earlier in 1985.

Conventional zero coupon Treasury bills are now issued with non-extendible maturities up to 1 year. A second type, "Primarmarkt-Orientiert Bundes-schatzscheine," refers to extended Bills which carried a fixed interest rate in their first year which was subsequently adjusted annually to the new issue rate. A third type, introduced in 1986 and known as floating-rate notes, "Bun-desschatzscheine Floater," bears coupons which are adjusted quarterly to the 3-month VIBOR. In the past "floaters" had a 3-year maturity and could be renewed, 2 or 3 times, for the same period.

Taking into account the large fraction of Treasury bills at variable rates, and variable-rate loans, the share of financially indexed debt, though declining, appears substantial; 24% in 1995 but still as high as 34% in the late 1980s. By contrast, long-term bonds with variable rates have played a minor role. A first issue of such bonds took place in 1989 and a new issue in 1992. The latter has a 10-year maturity and quarterly coupons indexed to the 3-month VIBOR, it is putable, callable and renewable.

Debt accumulation bears some relation to changes in the debt composition. Two instruments characterize the evolution of the Austrian debt: variable-rate loans and fixed-rate securities, notes and bonds with typical maturities of 5 and, especially, 10 years ("Bundesobligationen" and "Anleihen"). Since the early 1980s such instruments together account for more than 60% of the debt and their shares move in opposite directions. Between 1980 and 1986, during the period of faster debt accumulation, the share of fixed-rate bonds and notes decreases from 48 to 36% while the share of variable-rate loans, which was negligible at the beginning of the period, reaches a peak of 29%. Following the stabilization of the debt ratio in the late 1980s, notes and bonds increase up to 46% of the debt in 1995, while variable loans lose importance. Indeed, in the 1990s fixed-rate bonds become the main financing instrument as also shown by their increasing importance relative to notes which are now issued with a 10-year maturity.

Foreign currency debt has also played a role in financing recent deficits. Table 4.9 shows an increasing share of foreign debt from 16% in 1989 to 22% in 1995. This change does not reflect devaluation given the close link between the Schilling and the Deutsche Mark. In effect, funding in foreign currency has been traditionally important: in 1983 almost one-third of the Austrian debt was denominated in foreign currencies.

Published data on the average term to maturity of the Austrian debt are not available, though, debt maturity should be fairly long; a recent survey among representatives of OECD countries, sponsored by the Swedish National Debt Office, shows a conventionally measured average maturity equal to 4.8 years for 1994. In the absence of data on maturity, Figure 4.2 shows the relation between the debt ratio and the share of fixed-rate debt, i.e. fixed-rate notes, bonds and loans.

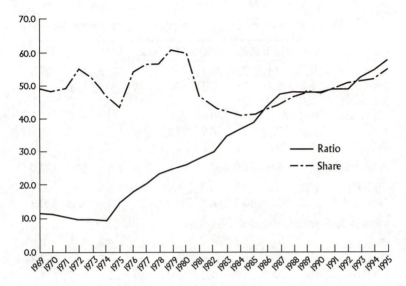

Fig. 4.2. Austria: Debt ratio and share of long fixed-rate debt.

Belgium   Belgium is one of the most indebted OECD countries with a debt ratio as high as 120% in 1995. The dynamics of debt accumulation have been similar to those of other European countries, with a sharp increase since the mid-1970s. After a strong fiscal correction in the mid-1980s, the debt ratio stabilized at 110% in 1988. The following rise in the early 1990s due to the cyclical downturn was halted in 1994 through renewed fiscal efforts.

As in other European countries, the reforms of the security market and of the primary market have been significant. The aim of the program has been to create a competitive secondary market, opening the financial system to foreign investors and reducing the intermediation of the banking sector. The market has been organized as a quote-driven market with primary dealers expected to make an active market in government securities.

While the new system was established in January 1991, important innovations had already taken place in the selling techniques and the characteristics of debt instruments. An important innovation was the introduction in 1989 of fungible bonds, "Obligation Lineaire." Such bonds are issued in the form of identical tranches of "OLOs-Lines" (lines in the bond issue listings) through subsequent auctions held at different dates within the same year. This allows the creation of large volumes of bonds with the same coupon and maturity and thus improves their liquidity. Belgian OLOs which have a typical maturity of 10 years (but also of 15 and 20 years) have been issued with multiple-price auctions since their introduction in 1989, while until then bonds were sold by public subscriptions through a syndicate of banks which negotiated coupon and maturities and guaranteed the firm placement of the issues.

Table 4.10. Belgium: composition by type of instrument

	1960	1970	1975	1980	1983	1986	1989	1992	1995
Short	17.7	11.4	7.5	15.4	21.1	23.1	24.5	22.1	17.3
Medium	5.1	2.2	2.0	0.3	1.3	1.9	0.5	0.0	0.0
Var-Bond	0.0	0.0	0.0	0.1	0.2	2.1	1.5	1.7	10.1
Fix-Bond	55.0	67.1	82.2	71.1	51.0	51.1	54.9	62.9	60.3
Foreign	13.0	9.2	0.5	8.5	23.9	19.9	17.1	12.3	11.5
Postal Dep	9.2	10.1	7.8	4.7	2.4	1.8	1.6	1.0	0.9
PH-Ratio	62.7	45.0	38.9	52.2	83.5	102.6	109.9	116.0	120.0
CB-Held	10.7	8.2	4.8	8.0	7.3	5.5	2.4	0.7	0.7
Debt Ratio	70.3	49.1	40.9	56.7	90.0	108.5	112.6	116.8	120.9

Average maturity of marketable debt

	1960	1970	1975	1980	1983	1986	1989	1992	1995
Convention	n/a	n/a	6.9	4.5	3.5	3.8	3.4	3.9	4.7
Fix-Bond	n/a	n/a	n/a	n/a	n/a	n/a	4.7	5.1	5.8
All-Fixed	n/a	n/a	5.6	4.0	3.0	3.3	3.3	3.9	4.7
Effective	n/a	n/a	5.6	3.7	2.3	2.6	2.8	3.4	3.8

Notes: Data refer to privately held debt. Its composition is estimated assuming that unclassified Central Bank holdings are all short-term. Data on maturity for 1975 refer to the year 1976. For other definitions see Table 4.8.

While reforms have been similar to other European countries, in Belgium, perhaps, the contrast with the past has been sharper than elsewhere. For instance, Treasury bills with maturities of 3, 6 and 12 months have been issued through auctions only since 1991. Until that time, Belgian "Certificats de Tresorerie" were either sold on tap in maturities of 1, 2, 3, 6, 9 and 12 months, or privately placed with money market intermediaries at negotiated yields and maturities.

In the early 1990s the issuance of bonds with put options was also suspended to recommence more recently on a small scale.[17] Putable bonds have a long tradition in Belgium and their use as a percentage of total bonds had been the largest in the OECD area reaching a peak of 24% in 1983. Callable bonds, which had been issued especially in the late 1980s, were instead discontinued in 1991.

Table 4.10 presents the evolution in the composition of the debt by type of instrument. The initial maturity of short-term debt is within 1 year, that of medium-term debt from 1 to 4 years and that of long-term debt (Fix-Bond) is longer than 4 years. Securities issued by public agencies, i.e. indirect debt, are included among bonds directly issued by the government since they are indistinguishable by characteristics and backing.

---

[17] Current putable bonds have step-up coupons every 3 years. Since coupons can also be adjusted to the average yield of OLOs with a remaining maturity of 2 and 3 years, the value of the put is clearly diminished.

The main developments of the debt structure are summarized by changes in the fixed-rate long-term component. The share of bonds increased from 55% in 1960 to 82% in 1975, as the debt decreased steadily, and then declined to 51% in 1986 after the period of more sustained debt growth. This inverse relation loosened in recent years, as the share of fixed-rate bonds started rising before the stabilization of the debt ratio in 1988. However, since the reform of the secondary market, the share of bonds shows only a moderate increase from 55% in 1989 to 60% in 1995.

Movements in short-term and foreign currency liabilities mirror the changes in long-term debt. The share of short-term debt, in particular, varies in similar fashion with the debt ratio until the most recent period. Short-term certificates have been issued to cope with structural imbalances and in 1989, following the period of faster debt accumulation, they account for almost one-fourth of the debt. Foreign currency debt was also important in the early 1980s when it reached a share of 25%, but it declined thereafter. Thus, except for the most recent period, the debt structure moved towards instruments whose value is less affected by inflation when the debt rises and vice versa.

Variable-rate debt has also been issued recently. While until 1992 the figures in Table 4.10 refer to liabilities of private companies assumed by the government, new variable-rate bonds were introduced in 1994. A first type has a 10-year maturity and annual coupons which are revised every 3 years according to the average yield of OLOs with 3-year remaining maturities. Such bonds have also minimum step rates and are putable at various future dates. A 5-year floater has also been issued with quarterly coupons indexed to the 3-month BIBOR. After 2 years their share has already reached 10%.

The relation between debt and maturity can be further investigated by looking at the average term to maturity of fixed-rate securities denominated in domestic currency from 1976 to 1995 which is shown in Figure 4.3. A negative relation between debt and average maturity is well documented until 1983. During this period, the average maturity of domestic currency debt fell substantially from 5.6 to 3 years in 1983 and then remained constant at 3.3 years until the end of the fiscal stabilization in 1989. In the most recent period, instead, maturity lengthened to a maximum of 4.7 years in 1995. When effective maturity is considered, the early shortening of maturity was more pronounced: from 5.6 to 2.3 years between 1976 and 1983. In the following period, however, the path for effective maturity was similar to that of fixed-rate securities; maturity remained short at around 2.7 years until 1990 before lengthening to 3.9 years in 1995.

Since detailed data before 1976 could not be found, the share of long-term fixed-rate securities is used as the best index of maturity to examine the relation over a longer period. Figure 4.4 shows the evolution of the share of long-term fixed-rate securities and of the debt ratio between 1960 and 1995.

As discussed above, until the late 1980s there is strong evidence of an inverse relation between debt and debt maturity.

Canada   In Canada the central government paper debt was 57% of GDP in 1995, but a higher ratio of about 77% was reached when all the liabilities are considered. Deficits accumulated rapidly in the first half of the 1980s and in the

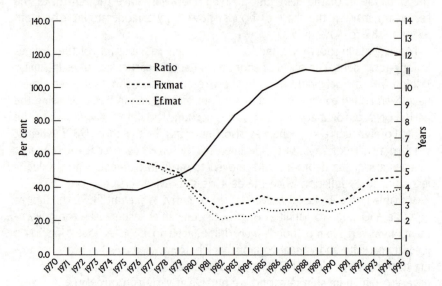

Fig. 4.3. Belgium: debt ratio and debt maturity.

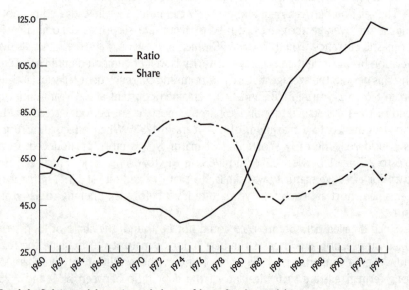

Fig. 4.4. Belgium: debt ratio and share of long fixed-rate debt.

1990s, after the public debt was temporarily stabilized at 42% of GDP in 1989 by the strong fiscal correction of the years 1986–9.

Debt management has always relied on simple instruments, that is, Treasury bills and bonds with bullet maturities and fixed coupons. Only a limited amount of callable bonds was issued in the 1980s and extendable bonds were discontinued in 1982. In the most recent period, however, fixed-rate issues have not prevented from indexing the debt to market rates, since swaps have been used since 1988 in place of variable-rate bonds.[18] A relatively large number of maturities are on offer: 2-, 3-, 5-, 10- and 30-year maturity bonds, but recently the issuing activity has concentrated on 2-, 5- and 10-year bonds in order to promote benchmarks. In 1991 price-index-linked bonds with a 30-year maturity have also been introduced, but in 1995 they accounted for less than 2% of the marketable debt denominated in the domestic currency.[19] With the exception of price-index-linked bonds, since 1992 all bonds are issued via multiple-price auctions (with "reopenings") according to a regular calendar for the typical maturities.

Table 4.11 shows how the composition by type of instrument of privately held government paper has changed over the last 30 years.[20] Canada stands out for the relatively high share of Treasury bills which now represents 33% of government paper but had reached a share as high as 41% in 1992. Two types of Treasury bills are issued: "Cash Management bills" with maturities between 1 and 41 days and Treasury bills with maturities of 3, 6 and 12 months. Their large share reflects the fact that banks use bills as instruments for liquidity management, but it also points out an important role in deficit financing. During the period of faster debt accumulation Treasury bills increased from 15% of the debt in 1975 up to 41% in 1992.

Except for a temporary increase in the late 1970s, the share of fixed-rate bonds moved in remarkably similar fashion with the debt ratio; it fell from 60% in 1960 to 33% in 1975, as the debt ratio declined and then increased from 34% in 1983 up to 54% in 1995 when the debt ratio rose from 31% to 57%. The increase of long-term bonds has been significant since 1992 when the funding policy aimed to lengthen the maturity of the debt. In fact, in the earlier period movements in the share of fixed-rate bonds also reflected a substitution for non-marketable savings bonds. The latter are issued with a typical maturity

---

[18] In March 1994 the interest-rate swap program amounted to 7.8 billion Canadian dollars which is equal to 2% of privately held "unmatured debt," shown in Table 4.11 and to 4% of privately held fixed-rate bonds.

[19] Such bonds have the capital indexed to the CPI. The capital uplift is paid at maturity and the interest rate, paid semi-annually, is calculated on the sum of the capital and the capital uplift accrued up to the coupon-payment date.

[20] The focus is on "unmatured debt," leaving aside other liabilities, since the latter, mainly "Superannuation Accounts," is a roughly constant fraction of GDP and thus its evolution is not informative about changes in the debt structure.

Table 4.11. Canada: composition by type of instrument

	1960	1970	1975	1980	1983	1986	1989	1992	1995
T.Bills	12.2	14.7	14.6	26.1	31.1	33.0	38.9	41.0	33.0
P-Indexed	—	—	—	—	—	—	—	0.4	1.3
Fix-Bond	60.4	44.5	32.6	43.5	33.6	39.6	43.0	46.6	54.3
Foreign	1.0	1.6	0.6	6.8	4.8	5.7	2.1	1.5	3.7
Savings	26.5	37.6	52.0	23.3	30.3	20.9	14.9	9.5	6.9
Gov-NoMKt	0.0	1.6	0.2	0.2	0.2	0.8	1.1	1.0	0.8
PH.Pap-Ratio	34.0	23.3	17.4	21.9	31.0	41.9	42.1	52.6	57.3
PH-Ratio	44.3	37.1	30.3	34.0	45.1	57.0	58.0	70.1	77.1
CB-Held	16.6	17.5	20.9	18.5	11.9	7.6	7.4	5.5	5.2
D.Pap-Ratio	40.8	28.3	22.0	26.8	35.3	45.4	45.5	55.6	60.5
Debt Ratio	51.0	42.0	34.8	39.0	49.3	60.4	61.4	73.1	80.2
Average maturity of marketable debt									
Convention	9.3	5.2	3.8	6.8	5.4	4.9	4.1	4.3	5.0
All-Fixed	9.3	5.2	3.8	6.8	5.4	4.9	4.1	4.2	4.7
Effective	9.2	5.1	3.8	6.3	5.1	4.6	4.0	4.1	4.5

Notes: Data refer to privately held paper debt and are for fiscal years ending in March of the following year. PH.Pap-Ratio is the ratio to GDP of privately held paper debt, while D.Pap-Ratio is the same ratio for total paper debt. PH-Ratio includes other debts, mainly Superannuation Accounts. For other definitions see Table 4.8.

of 12 years but redemption can be asked at any time and the interest rate is revised annually with the introduction of the new series. The share of savings bonds has moved in the opposite direction of marketable bonds, first increasing up to 52% in 1975 and then decreasing to 7% in 1995.

While foreign participation in the Canadian bond and bill markets has been traditionally important, borrowing in foreign currency has only served the purpose of raising foreign-exchange reserves; foreign debt never exceeded 7%, gaining importance only in the early 1980s.

The Canadian debt, in spite of a substantial share of Treasury bills, has a relatively long average maturity: 4.7 years in 1995. Figure 4.5 shows the evolution of the debt ratio and the average term to maturity of fixed-rate marketable debt which includes foreign currency debt.[21] Evidence on the effective maturity which corrects for foreign currency and price-indexed debt is also presented in the same figure. The relation between debt and maturity before and after 1980 is different. While in the earlier period debt and maturity move together,

[21] Evidence on the average maturity of fixed-rate securities denominated in domestic currency is not available but the exclusion of foreign currency debt, because of its low share, would result in minor differences.

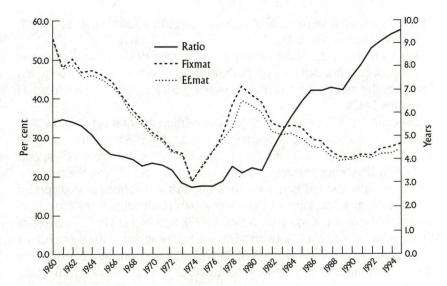

Fig. 4.5. Canada: debt ratio and debt maturity.

in the later period, as the debt rises, maturity falls from 6.8 to 4.1 years in 1990 and then lengthens slightly to 4.5 years in 1995. In the recent period effective maturity exhibits a similar pattern; it first falls from 6.3 years in 1980 to 4.1 years in 1992 and then rises back to 4.5 years in 1995. The dynamics of debt maturity is consistent with the increasing importance of Treasury bills as financing instruments in the 1980s, during the period of sustained deficit accumulation, and with the recent emphasis on long-term funding.

Denmark The Danish debt is among the highest in Europe, though stable just below 80% of GDP in 1995 after a rapid increase in the early 1990s. The recent events show how a debt problem, which appeared solved, may suddenly re-emerge because of weak economic conditions. In fact, in 1989 the debt ratio had dropped to a low 64% from 76% in 1984 by the virtue of the stabilization program started in 1982.

Interestingly, unlike in other European countries a system of primary dealers has not been established and notes and bonds are still sold by flexible-price "taps" by the National Bank directly in the secondary market (see Section 4.2). The bond market is liquid and efficient, also because a secondary market for private bonds has long been active as a result of the securitization of private loans which is a distinguishing feature of the Danish capital market.[22] Treasury bonds have been issued with bullet maturities of 5 and 10 years since 1980 and

---

[22] This is because of the tradition of financing residential and commercial construction and private housing by mortgage-credit bonds.

of 30 years since 1994 (the use of options and sinking funds redemptions was definitely abandoned in 1987).

Table 4.12 shows the evolution of the composition of the gross central government debt. Although data on National Bank holdings could not be found for the entire period, the securities in National Bank's portfolio never reached 2% in the 1980s.

Over the last 20 years a striking positive relation emerges between the debt ratio and its fixed-rate long-term component. Fast deficit accumulation until the early 1980s is financed with long-term bonds; their share rises from 42% in 1975 to 67% in 1984 when the debt ratio peaks at 76%. Focusing on the fiscal stabilization of the mid-1980s, it is worth noting that this episode is accompanied by a significant lengthening of the maturity structure. Indeed, the increase in the share of long-term bonds from 59% in 1982 to 67% in 1984 in the midst of the stabilization attempt is substantial. In the following years, the debt declines and the share of bonds falls to 45% in 1989. Debt accumulation in the early 1990s is also financed by long-term bonds which account for 61% of the debt in 1995.

Movements in long-term debt are mirrored by changes in foreign currency debt. Such debt was substantial in the 1970s (when it was used to finance current account deficits) and still one-fourth of the total during the 1980s. The share

Table 4.12. Denmark: composition by type of instrument

	1970	1975	1980	1983	1984	1986	1989	1992	1995
T.Bills	—	—	—	—	—	—	—	9.0	7.6
Notes	—	—	15.7	10.9	8.8	5.9	13.1	11.6	13.5
Var-Bond	—	—	—	—	0.8	8.5	18.0	9.3	2.7
Fix-Bond	36.8	41.7	50.1	61.5	67.3	60.1	45.1	51.5	61.1
Lott-Bond	9.3	2.7	0.9	0.3	0.3	0.2	0.2	0.2	0.2
ECU-Bond	—	—	—	—	—	—	—	1.6	1.1
Foreign	53.9	55.7	33.3	27.3	22.9	25.0	23.3	16.8	13.8
Comp.Sav	—	—	—	—	—	0.4	0.3	—	—
CB-Held	n/a	n/a	n/a	0.5	0.7	1.0	0.9	0.7	n/a
Debt Ratio	5.8	8.7	36.4	73.2	76.0	70.5	64.1	71.8	78.9
Average maturity of marketable debt									
Convention	n/a	n/a	3.3	4.3	4.3	4.0	4.0	4.2	5.0
All-Fixed	n/a	n/a	3.3	4.3	4.2	3.5	3.8	4.3	5.0
Effective	n/a	n/a	2.2	3.1	3.2	2.6	2.8	3.5	4.3

Notes: Until 1976 data are for fiscal years ending in March of the following year. The positive balance of the Credit Account of Treasury at the National Bank is not subtracted from gross debt. Data are net of government security holdings but gross of Bank holdings. Lott-Bond refers to lottery bonds; Comp.Sav to compulsory savings. For other definitions see Table 4.8.

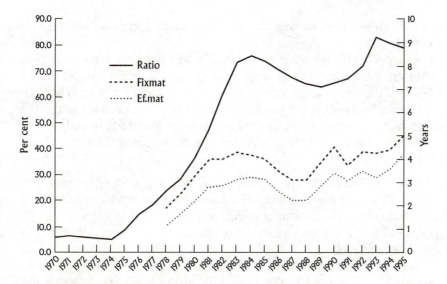

Fig. 4.6. Denmark: debt ratio and debt maturity.

of foreign currency debt is now rapidly declining, 14% in 1995, because of the policy of just renewing maturing debt in order to leave foreign-exchange reserves unaffected.

Treasury certificates or notes have recently gained importance. Introduced in 1976 with a standard maturity of 2 years and 50 days and now issued with a 2.5-year maturity, notes account for 16% of the debt in 1980. Then their importance diminishes, especially after the introduction of variable-rate bonds in 1984. Variable-rate bonds have quarterly coupons indexed to the average yield of government bonds with a remaining term to maturity lower than 3 years and thus are short as far as interest-rate sensitivity is concerned. Their share grows as high as 18% in 1989 before the indexation program is suspended in 1990. They are replaced by Treasury bills with maturities of 3, 6 and 9 months.[23]

Further insight in the relation between debt and debt maturity can be gained from Figure 4.6 that shows the effective maturity and the average maturity of the fixed-rate component of the debt denominated in the domestic currency. Evidence of a positive relation between debt and debt maturity is strong, even though the changes in maturity are not as large as expected. The maturity of fixed-rate securities increases by more than two years between 1978 and 1984, from 1.9 to 4.2 years, as the debt reaches a peak in 1984. The following decline in the debt ratio is associated with a shortening of debt maturity to 3.1 years

---

[23] Treasury bills are issued quarterly in fungible tranches. Their late introduction in 1990 reflects the fact that the Treasury used the credit account at the National Bank for cash management purposes.

in 1988. Over the last decades the debt rises and maturity lengthens to 5 years in 1995.

Changes in effective maturity also track quite closely the movements of the debt ratio. Effective maturity goes from 1.2 years in 1978 up to 3.2 years in 1984 and then down to 2.2 years in 1988 before reaching 4.3 years in 1995. The difference between the two measures of maturity is considerable, owing to the high share of foreign currency debt and variable-rate bonds. Indeed, effective maturity remained relatively short until the 1990s; shorter than in countries with no debt problems.

Finland   In Finland the central government debt soared in recent years from 11% of GDP in 1990 to 68% in 1995. Deteriorating economic conditions and legally mandated government expenditures produced large primary deficits. The capital losses on foreign currency debt due to the devaluation of 1992 added to deficit accumulation.

Reforms aimed at creating an efficient secondary market for government securities were enacted in the early 1990s at the same time as severe fiscal imbalances emerged. A group of primary dealers expected to make an active market in government securities was established in 1992. Innovations in debt instruments and in selling techniques had taken place earlier in 1989 with the introduction of Serial bonds with bullet maturities between 3 and 10 years and Housing bonds with maturities of 5 and 10 years. Both types of bonds are issued through uniform-price auctions, while Yield bonds with maturities of 2 and 4 years (but also up to 8 years) are sold via public subscriptions through the banking system to personal investors.

Despite the recent efforts to strengthen the domestic security market, Finland stands out for the very high percentage of public debt denominated in foreign currencies. As shown in Table 4.13, the share of such debt is the highest in the sample of countries under consideration: 46% in 1995. In the early 1980s the share of foreign debt was even higher at 60%, but at that time the debt did not even reach 15% of GDP.

Until the late 1980s foreign currency debt and long-term bonds account for the entire debt. The absence of Treasury bills is explained by the low level of debt and the traditional use of banks' Certificates of Deposit by the Bank of Finland for conducting open market operations. In fact, an old type of Treasury bill was introduced in 1985 with maturities between 1 and 18 months and soon discontinued in 1989.

In the 1980s, with a constant debt ratio not even reaching 15%, a substitution of bonds for foreign currency debt takes place; the share of bonds increases from 38% in 1980 up to 54% in 1989. In that year foreign debt interrupts its downward trend and becomes the main financing instrument of the large budget deficits which emerge since 1991. In fact, the sharp increase in the share of foreign debt, from 43% in 1989 to 61% in 1992, is only partly explained by

Table 4.13. Finland: composition by type of instrument

	1970	1975	1980	1983	1986	1989	1992	1995
T.Bills	0.0	0.0	0.0	0.0	4.0	0.5	8.4	10.2
Notes	0.0	0.0	0.0	0.0	0.0	1.7	3.4	5.0
Fix-Bond	56.2	45.3	38.4	38.0	42.4	54.1	21.7	33.7
o/w NoMkt	(27.8)	(24.0)	(9.1)	(13.3)	(7.8)	(10.2)	(2.0)	(0.3)
Foreign	37.6	46.3	60.2	59.2	52.0	43.1	60.7	46.4
Prom.Notes	1.2	0.0	1.1	2.8	0.9	0.7	5.8	4.8
Short-NoMkt	4.9	8.3	0.2	0.0	0.8	0.0	0.0	0.0
PH-Ratio	9.0	3.4	9.0	13.5	14.6	10.9	36.8	68.1
CB-Held	1.5	2.0	4.5	3.8	0.1	0.0	0.0	0.0
Debt Ratio	9.2	3.4	9.4	14.0	14.6	10.9	36.8	68.1
Average maturity of marketable debt								
All-Fixed	n/a	n/a	n/a	n/a	3.1	3.2	3.6	3.5
Effective	n/a	n/a	n/a	n/a	1.5	1.8	1.4	1.9

Notes: Data refer to privately held debt. Notes refer to "Yield Bonds"; Prom.Notes to promissory notes. o/w NoMkt stands for "of which non-marketable" and refers to "registered bonds," i.e. non-marketable privately placed bonds. For other definitions see Table 4.8.

the devaluation of the Finnish Markka in 1992; it also reflects voluntary deficit financing.

New Treasury bills (and HF bills) with maturities of 1, 3, 6 and 12 months, are also introduced in 1991 for borrowing purposes. One year later their share already reaches 8% and keeps rising to 10% in 1995. The move out of foreign currency borrowing into domestic currency financing which follows the 1992 crisis is highlighted by the rise in the share of long-term bonds from 25% in 1992 to 44% in 1995.

While the relative shares of domestic and foreign currency debt have changed dramatically over the period considered, the average term to maturity of the domestic currency debt, that is, Treasury bills and bonds, has remained fairly stable since the mid-1980s. The evolution of this maturity is shown in Figure 4.7 together with the effective maturity and the debt ratio. Average maturity has remained approximately constant with a moderate increase from 3.2 years in 1985 to 4.4 years in 1991 and then a reduction to 3.5 years in 1995. This path reflects the longer maturity of newly issued bonds and the late introduction of Treasury bills. Effective maturity has followed the same path, first increasing from 1.9 in 1985 up to 2.3 in 1991 and then back to 1.9 in 1995, with movements which are even less evident than those of domestic debt maturity. Its very low value is also worth noting.

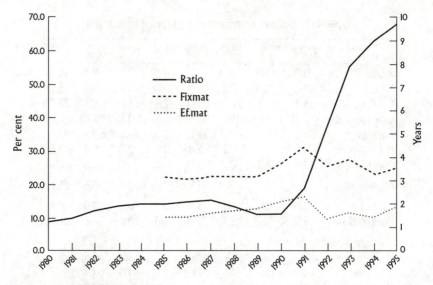

Fig. 4.7. Finland: debt ratio and debt maturity.

France   France is one of the least indebted OECD countries with a debt ratio equal to 43% in 1995. Although the debt has been on an upward trend since the early 1980s, its growth was very moderate until 1992 when the debt ratio was just above 30%.

In spite or, perhaps, because of the low debt ratio, debt management has always been innovative. The 1952/8 bond, the 4.5% bond of 1973 and the 8.8% bond of 1977, had the principal guaranteed by means of indexation to the price of gold. ECU bonds find a predecessor in the 7% bond of 1973 which was indexed to the European Unit of Account. Exchangeable bonds were introduced in 1983 and 1984 and used on a large scale until 1987. Exchangeable fixed-rate bonds gave the holder the option to convert them into variable-rate bonds 2 years after the issue date. A similar option gave the holder the right to exchange variable-rate bonds into fixed-rate bonds at prespecified dates and interest rates.[24] Renewable bonds bearing the option for an exchange into later issues at specified dates and conditions were also experimented in the period between 1983 and 1986. In 1986 fixed-rate bonds exchangeable into variable-rate bonds represented 17% of marketable securities. In the same year both shares of exchangeable variable-rate bonds and renewable bonds were 6%.

This strategy of designing debt instruments in order to satisfy the demand for specific contingencies was soon abandoned in favor of the simplicity and

---

[24] The option to convert fixed into variable-rate bonds could be exercised in any year after 2 years from the issue date. The option to convert variable into fixed-rate bonds could be exercised in a limited period of 1, 2 or 3 years after 2 years from the issue date.

marketability of fixed-rate long-term bonds. Debt management was again innovative: fungible bonds, "Obligations Assimilable du Trésor" (OATs) were introduced as early as 1985. The sale through subsequent auctions of fungible bonds, namely, bonds with coupon and maturity identical to those of existing issues, allows the creation of a thick, liquid market.

This technique, which was later extended to medium-term Treasury notes (BTANs) and even Treasury bills (BTFs), has been part of a far-reaching reform aimed at developing efficient markets for government securities. Since their introduction in 1985 OATs have been sold through multiple-price auctions which are now held with BTF and BTAN auctions according to a regular calendar. A futures contract on government bonds was also introduced early in 1986. More importantly, a group of specialists in government securities (linked by an interdealer broker system) was established in 1987 with the task of making markets in government securities.

These events are partly reflected in the evolution of the debt composition presented in Table 4.14. What is evident from the table is the strong reduction of short-term non-marketable debt, mainly savings bonds and Post Office deposits, from 68% in 1971 to just 12% in 1995. This process of securitization reflects financial innovation but also the need for alternative sources of financing when the debt grows.

Focusing on the marketable component of the debt, the lengthening of the maturity structure since the mid-1980s is noteworthy. The share of fixed-rate bonds which is 46% in 1995 has almost doubled since 1986. Medium-term notes BTANs, introduced in that year, now account for 22% of the debt. The change in the maturity composition since the first half of the 1980s is significant. In 1983 the share of Treasury bills (then "Bons en Compte Courant") had reached 32% up from 20% in the 1970s. In the following period a longer maturity structure is achieved by the use of variable-rate bonds and bonds with an exchange option into variable-rate bonds; their total share rises from 2% in 1983 to 14% in 1986. Such bonds have a short duration in that they provide holders with protection against increases in interest rates. It is only in 1986, when fixed-rate notes and bonds replace the former instruments, that duration starts increasing. Initially, a major role is played by BTANs, now issued in maturities of 2 or 5 years. Their share already represents 8% of the debt in 1986 and continues to rise up to 21% in 1989. In the 1990s fixed-rate OATs, with maturities of 10, 15, 20, and 30 years, become the most important funding instrument, reaching a share as high as 46% in 1995.

Variable-rate bonds (with and without convertibility options) have also been issued until 1990 but their role has been limited. Different indexation mechanisms and reference rates have been tried. The traditional and most common form of indexation (the one of earlier issues and exchangeable bonds) is based on the weighted average of the yields on fixed-rate bonds with a

Table 4.14. France: composition by type of instrument

	1971	1975	1980	1983	1986	1989	1992	1995
T.Bills	19.6	19.7	19.9	31.5	22.3	10.1	12.0	8.9
Notes	—	—	—	—	8.4	21.1	21.1	22.0
Var-Bond	—	—	—	—	4.3	7.0	5.5	2.7
Opt-Var	—	—	—	2.1	9.6	6.9	4.7	2.8
Fix-Bond	10.1	16.3	26.7	21.5	25.8	28.1	35.8	45.5
Long-NoMkt	n/a	n/a	1.4	5.5	3.3	4.9	2.3	2.1
Foreign	1.5	0.4	0.0	7.5	0.6	0.8	3.0	3.7
Savings	21.3	15.1	11.7	4.9	2.9	1.9	0.9	0.3
Postal Dep	47.5	48.5	39.8	25.4	22.8	19.2	14.7	12.1
Short-NoMkt	0.0	0.0	0.4	1.6	0.1	0.0	0.0	0.0
CB-Claim	3.9	−0.4	−4.5	−5.2	−3.3	−5.5	−5.3	−3.4
Debt Ratio	17.9	15.2	14.8	21.1	23.8	27.1	30.8	42.9
Average maturity of marketable debt								
Convention	n/a	n/a	n/a	n/a	n/a	5.5	6.4	6.3
All-Fixed	n/a	n/a	n/a	n/a	n/a	n/a	5.8	6.1
Effective	n/a	n/a	n/a	n/a	n/a	n/a	5.2	5.6

Notes: Central Bank holdings of securities are not available. Opt-Var refers to fixed-rate bonds giving the holder the option to exchange them into variable-rate bonds. Postal Dep refer to deposits with the Post Office. Non-marketable long-term debt, Long-NoMkt, is included in Fix-Bond until 1979. The conventional maturity of 1990 is indicated for the year 1989. For other definitions see Table 4.8.

maturity of at least 7 years (THE index) recorded weekly. The annual coupons of (past TRA bonds and) TME bonds are indexed to the yearly average of the weekly THEs recorded during the year preceding the payment of the coupon. However, different reference periods and interest rates have been used. For instance, the average auction yield on 13-weeks Treasury bills has been taken as the reference rate and coupons have been indexed to the rate recorded in the last auction prior to the payment of the quarterly coupon (TRB) or to the annual averages (TMB) of the reference rates (or their bond equivalent) recorded during the year preceding the payment of the coupon. Since 1996 new variable-rate bonds have quarterly coupons indexed to an hypothetical 10-year yield obtained by linear interpolation of the yields of the two benchmark bonds with terms to maturity closest to 10 years.

Since 1990 ECU bonds and notes are the only debt denominated in foreign currency but they do not even reach 4% in 1995, despite the emphasis on the issuing program.

Data on the average remaining term to maturity are not available before 1990. In 1995 the average term to maturity of fixed-rate bonds, notes and Treasury bills denominated in French francs was 6 years, among the highest in the OECD

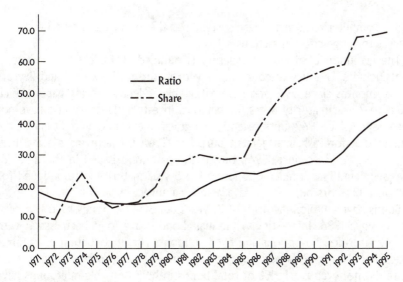

Fig. 4.8. France: debt ratio and share of long fixed-rate debt.

area. This long maturity reflects the large share of long-term bonds with initial maturities up to 20 and 30 years and an average remaining term to maturity of almost 10 years. Average maturity remains very long at 5.6 years even when zero maturity is assigned to ECU notes and bonds and the average time before the adjustment of the coupon is considered for variable-rate bonds. In the absence of data on maturity, Figure 4.8 shows the relation between the debt ratio and the share of fixed-rate long-term debt, i.e. fixed-rate notes, bonds and long-term loans denominated in the domestic currency.

Germany In Germany the general government debt rose substantially in the 1990s because of slow growth and German Unification; from 41% of GDP in 1991 to 57% in 1995. Despite the recent debt accumulation Germany remains one of the least indebted countries in the OECD area. Indeed, before the 1990s deficits accumulated at a rapid pace only between 1975 and 1982.

Attracting foreign investors has provided a main incentive to reform the primary and secondary markets for government securities. In 1986 foreign banks were admitted into the Federal Bond Consortium, the bank syndicate for issuing bonds. Since January 1998 the whole of each bond issue has been sold by auction; between 1990 and 1998 about one-third of each issue was placed with the members of the Consortium, which then bid in the auction where the second tranche of about 40% of the issue was sold. Up to 25% of each issue was reserved to the Bundesbank for tap resale on the secondary market since, in the absence of primary dealers, the Bundesbank performs the role of market maker. Interestingly, in 1997 a quote-driven market had not yet been established; the

IBIS, a computerized order-driven system, was the main alternative to the OTC market for large-size transactions.

The evolution of the debt structure is outlined in Table 4.15. Short-term debt includes Treasury discount notes with maturities between 1 and 2 years (and 6 months since 1996) and non-marketable Federal financing paper, which are 1- to 2-year maturity notes for personal investors. Treasury bills have not been issued since 1969; until recently the government used a credit line at the Bundesbank for cash management purposes. Treasury notes have a maturity of 4 years (2 years since 1996), but in the past were issued in the 2- to 6-year segment. Special federal bonds with a 5-year maturity were designed for personal investors but are now available to all investors.

Bonds have a typical maturity of 10 years but 30-year bonds have also been issued since 1986. Interestingly, German bonds have long been issued with bullet maturities, no options and fixed coupons. The introduction of variable-rate bonds late in 1990 was much in the nature of an experiment since their share did not even reach 4% of total bonds in 1995. Variable-rate bonds have quarterly coupons indexed to the 3-month FIBOR and an initial maturity of 10 years.

Table 4.15. Germany: composition by type of instrument

	1960	1970	1975	1980	1983	1986	1989	1992	1995
Short	3.5	1.7	5.3	1.3	2.4	1.1	1.3	2.9	0.4
Notes	2.9	3.2	2.8	4.1	3.0	4.3	5.5	8.7	11.6
5-year-Spe.	—	—	—	1.9	7.3	10.3	10.3	12.2	9.0
Var-Bond	—	—	—	—	—	—	—	0.4	0.8
Fix-Bond	12.5	16.8	11.6	11.7	11.0	17.9	24.4	28.0	31.2
Loans	56.1	76.4	75.8	75.5	73.8	62.9	54.8	44.9	42.8
Foreign	25.1	1.4	0.3	0.0	0.0	0.0	0.0	0.0	0.0
Savings	0.0	0.6	4.2	5.4	2.5	3.6	3.7	2.8	4.1
Others	34.6	12.6	4.6	1.9	1.2	0.8	0.6	5.3	4.7
PH-Ratio	14.3	16.9	23.7	30.9	39.3	40.8	41.2	43.1	57.3
CB-Held	17.0	9.2	5.1	2.9	2.3	1.9	1.4	1.4	0.5
Debt Ratio	17.2	18.2	24.9	31.7	40.2	41.4	41.7	43.6	57.5
Average maturity of marketable debt									
Convention	n/a	5.1	5.0	4.1	5.0	5.3	5.0	5.2	5.1
All-Fixed	n/a	4.8	4.2	4.0	4.6	5.2	4.9	5.0	5.1
Effective	n/a	4.5	4.1	4.0	4.6	5.2	4.9	4.9	5.0

Notes: Data refer to privately held debt. Other old debts are excluded for the purpose of computing the debt composition. The conventional maturity series includes savings bonds. For other definitions see Table 4.8.

Loans against borrowers' notes are negotiable private placements to banks and, to a lesser extent, to social security funds. While in the past their maturities were in line with those offered on bonds, in 1995 the average term to maturity of Federal borrowers' notes was 3.5 years, much lower than the 6.9 years maturity of Federal bonds. Unfortunately, detailed information on their maturity over a longer period of time and the distinction between fixed- and variable-rate loans is not available.

The very low share of short-term debt points to the long maturity of the German debt. In 1995 the conventional maturity of total Federal debt was 5.3 years (5 years excluding savings bonds, loans and variable-rate bonds). Despite the importance gained by notes and 5-year bonds, the maturity composition is still concentrated on the long end, with bonds and loans accounting for 74% of the debt.

Until the 1990s the structure of the German debt is characterized by the relative constancy in the shares of the different maturity groups. The share of long-term debt, bonds and borrowers' notes, declines steadily from 93% in 1970 to 80% in the late 1980s. During this earlier period the most significant change in the debt composition is the substitution of bonds for borrowers' notes taking place since the early 1980s. After reaching a peak of 79% in 1981 the share of notes falls to 55% in 1989 and then to 43% in 1995. Their funding role is taken up by fixed-rate bonds whose share goes up from about 10% in 1981 to 24% in 1989 and 31% in 1995.

In the 1980s the medium-term component of the German debt, i.e. 5-year special federal bonds and Treasury notes, gain importance along with long-term bonds. Introduced in 1979, 5-year special bonds account for 10% of the debt ten years later. More recently, the diffusion of Treasury notes has been particularly fast, as their share doubles from 6 to 12% between 1989 and 1995.

The shift towards marketable instruments has been favored by financial innovation and the lower cost of more liquid instruments, but a main role has been played by the strong demand for the Deutsche Mark by foreign investors: by 1987 more than half of bonds and medium-term notes was held by non-residents.

The joint dynamics of the debt ratio and the average term to maturity of fixed-rate securities and savings bonds is shown in Figure 4.9, and is the same relation which would emerge if the conventional maturity or effective maturity were considered. Data on maturity refer to all marketable securities (excluding variable-rate bonds) and non-marketable notes and savings bonds issued by the general government and by the Federal Railways and the Post Office. Because of the inclusion of saving bonds, which have an initial maturity of 6 and 7 years, the series is not directly comparable to those of other countries, but the low share of such paper makes it a minor problem. A more serious drawback is the

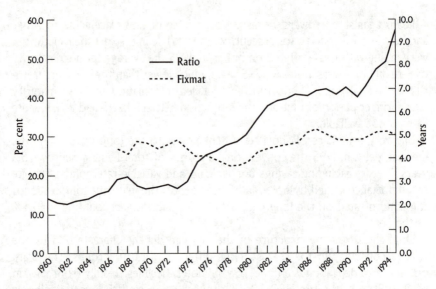

Fig. 4.9. Germany: debt ratio and debt maturity.

lack of data on loans which most likely makes the series an underestimate of the true maturity of the debt.

Maturity shows little variation over the period, confirming what resulted from the analysis of the debt structure. It first shortens from about 5 years in 1969 to just 3.8 years in 1978 and then lengthens stabilizing around 5 years from the second half of the 1980s. The impression is that of little variation and no systematic relation with the debt ratio over the whole period considered. While debt and maturity move in opposite directions until the late 1970s and in the early 1990s, they display a positive correlation over the 1980s.

Greece   Over the last two decades Greece witnessed a sharp increase in the debt ratio: from about 25% in 1980 to 107% in 1995. However, the unsustainability of the Greek fiscal policy has come to an end; because of the slow but steady improvement in the budget, the debt ratio was expected to stabilize in 1997.

Unlike in other European countries, in the 1980s, real interest payments were a minor factor in the fast accumulation of debt. Until 1987 the return on government securities is negative, owing to a highly regulated financial sector and deficit monetization. In particular, investment requirements applied on banks' deposits: in 1990 the percentage of deposits earmarked to finance the public sector was 56.5% of which two-thirds had to be invested in Treasury bills. Indeed, financial markets were liberalized later than in other European countries; the move from a system of administrative controls to market instruments was completed only between 1991 and 1993, when the obligatory investment of bank deposits in government securities was gradually abolished.

The primary market has recently been reformed and now all bonds are sold by multiple-price auctions. A secondary market for government securities, though still at an early stage, is rapidly developing and an increasing proportion of borrowing requirements is financed through securities placed with non-bank investors. In 1996 the secondary market was still organized as a double-sided auction-agency market but plans were being made to introduce a dealer system. Interestingly, bonds indexed to the price level were introduced in 1997. They are "interest indexed" bonds, i.e. they have coupons linked to the CPI and a fixed principal.

Greece stands out for the very short duration of its debt. Before 1997, when 2-year zero-coupon notes and 3-year bonds were introduced, there was no marketable instrument bearing a fixed-interest rate with a maturity longer than 1 year. Indeed, in the mid-1990s the marketable debt denominated in domestic currency was made of Treasury bills and variable-rate bonds with annual coupons indexed to the issue rate of 12-month Treasury bills. The latter, which before 1985 could only be held by banks to satisfy reserve requirements, are now issued in maturities of 3, 6 and 12 months, usually via public subscriptions. Treasury bills are mostly held by small-scale investors and those issued in physical form (now a minority) are renewable for a period equal to their initial maturity; a bill of the same nominal value is given to the holder and the interest for the new period is paid in advance.

Fixed-rate bonds with maturities of 2 and 3 years had been issued between 1987 and 1990, but the programme was suspended in 1990 because of the lack of demand. Bonds reappeared in 1992 with maturities of 2, 5 and 7 years, but this time bearing coupons indexed to the rate of 12-month Treasury bills. In the early 1990s the only fixed-rate securities with a maturity longer than 1 year were bonds with a foreign currency clause. Introduced in 1986, most of them were ECU indexed bonds with maturities between 1 and 4 years, but US dollar bonds and Deutsche Mark bonds had also been offered.

Data on the Greek debt could be found only for the period 1980–96 and its composition before 1985 has been partly estimated. However, an analysis of the debt structure for the earlier period would not be very informative given the high degree of financial regulation. Evidence on the composition and evolution of the debt by type of instrument is provided in Table 4.16. Variable-rate bonds are distinguished between those placed on the market and "Conversion bonds" arising from the abolition of mandatory investment in Treasury bills (see below). Data on the former type of bonds include a small amount of fixed-rate bonds for the year 1992, as the fixed and variable rate components could not be identified.

Table 4.16. Greece: composition by type of instrument

	1980	1983	1986	1989	1992	1995
T. Bills	55.4	43.0	43.1	50.8	35.1	29.4
Var-Bond	—	—	—	—	5.3	21.5
Var-Conver	—	—	—	—	27.3	19.2
Fix-Bond	—	—	—	6.4	n/a	—
Foreign	22.8	30.4	41.2	33.2	28.0	26.2
o/w FC-Idx	(—)	(—)	(0.8)	(4.7)	(6.3)	(5.7)
Others	21.8	26.6	15.7	9.6	4.3	3.7
PH-Ratio	22.7	34.0	48.3	60.1	84.5	106.7
CB-Held	29.5	29.2	19.0	16.1	9.0	13.1
Debt Ratio	32.2	48.0	59.6	71.6	92.9	122.8

Notes: Data refer to privately held debt. FC-Idx refers to bonds indexed to the ECU and other foreign currencies. Var-Conver refers to variable-rate "Conversion bonds." For other definitions see Table 4.8.

In 1995 Treasury bills and variable-rate bonds accounted for 70% of the debt. In fact, over the previous 20 years fixed-rate bonds denominated in the domestic currency were issued only between 1987 and 1990. In spite of having short maturities of 2 and 3 years, their share did not even reach 7%.

The large share of variable-rate bonds, 40% in 1995, not only reflects a complete reliance on such an instrument for deficit financing during the 1990s, but also institutional changes. Indeed, about half of the increase in variable-rate debt since 1991 is due to the substitution of "Conversion bonds" for Treasury bills, previously held because of mandatory investment. When investment requirements were abolished between 1991 and 1993, banks were given the option to convert their holdings of Treasury bills into (eight issues of) bonds with 3-, 5-, 6-, 7- and 8-year maturities and annual coupons linked to the rate of 12-month Treasury bills.

The debt denominated in foreign currencies, either in the form of external debt or domestic bonds indexed to foreign currencies, mainly to the ECU, is also substantial as it accounts for one-fourth of the debt. The share of foreign debt has however declined from the striking 40% it had reached in the mid-1980s. This together with the reduction of Treasury bills, which accounted for more than half of the debt in 1989, and the corresponding diffusion of variable-rate instruments fully characterize the evolution of the debt composition. Therefore, while a lengthening of the conventional average maturity of the debt has been achieved in the last 10 years, the sensitivity of the debt burden to changes in interest rates has remained very high.

High inflation can easily explain the very short duration of the Greek debt but deficit accumulation may have also played a role. In particular, by inducing fears of an impending monetization and financial instability, the debt growth may have impaired the government ability to issue fixed-rate long-term securities.

Ireland   Following a failed attempt in 1982, the Irish debt was stabilized in 1987. The effect of the fiscal consolidation has been spectacular: the debt ratio fell from 107% reached in 1987 to 78% in 1995. As for other European countries the reasons for the debt buildup from the mid-1970s to the late 1980s are in a deterioration of economic performance, generous social programs and high real interest rates.

While Ireland has attracted the economists' attention because of the very high share of foreign currency debt, long-term fixed-rate bonds have also been an important funding instrument. Bonds are now issued without call options in the maturity segments of 5, 10 and 20 years. Although the bulk of new issues is now sold through auctions, in 1997 bonds were still partly sold "on tap," as the move toward a full auction system has been gradual. A system of primary dealers in government securities was also established at the end of 1995, later than in other countries. As in Sweden, the debt is managed by an independent agency, the National Treasury Management Agency (NTMA), whose performance is evaluated by comparison to a benchmark portfolio. Established in 1990, the NTMA conducts an active policy also making use of interest-rate swaps and foreign currency swaps.

Table 4.17 presents the composition by type of instrument of the Irish debt. Ireland stands out for the large shares of foreign currency debt and fixed-rate bonds; since 1975 these two instruments alone account for more than 80% of the debt. The share of foreign currency debt, 35% in 1995, remains among the highest in the OECD area, in spite of its fast reduction from the striking 50% reached in 1983.

The use of Exchequer bills and Exchequer notes (issued since 1991) has been limited to the traditional roles of cash management and residual financing, unlike in other highly indebted countries where they have been issued to cope with structural imbalances. In effect, Exchequer bills and notes never account for more than 4% of the debt over the last two decades. [25]

The evolution of the debt structure is fully characterized by the opposite movements of fixed-rate bonds and foreign currency debt.

Until the mid-1980s changes in foreign currency debt and fixed-rate bonds are closely related to debt movements. As deficits accumulate, an increasing proportion is financed in foreign currency. When the debt declines its funding

[25] Exchequer bills are issued with a standard maturity of 3 months until 1988 and since then in maturities of 35 and 182 days. Exchequer notes are issued with maturities from 7 to 120 days and are available to all investors.

Table 4.17. Ireland: composition by type of instrument

	1960	1970	1975	1980	1983	1986	1989	1992	1995
T. Bills	6.4	10.5	5.6	1.9	1.4	2.2	3.7	0.4	3.0
Var-Bond	—	—	—	0.9	5.2	3.8	8.5	7.3	4.9
Fix-Bond	55.1	53.3	55.0	54.6	37.3	43.1	43.1	43.4	46.3
Foreign	11.9	10.3	25.2	33.4	50.5	44.5	38.0	40.5	35.4
Savings	11.8	9.1	5.0	3.1	2.0	3.5	5.2	6.6	7.8
Sav-Index	—	—	0.0	0.1	0.7	1.1	1.3	1.2	2.7
Others	14.7	16.8	9.2	6.1	2.8	1.7	0.3	0.5	0.0
PH-Ratio	49.6	51.1	56.5	67.1	87.9	105.1	94.5	83.3	77.5
CB-Held	n/a	4.7	4.5	5.7	2.9	2.1	2.0	1.5	0.6
Debt Ratio	63.2	59.9	63.9	73.5	93.5	114.3	103.2	91.2	80.8
Average maturity of marketable debt									
Convention	12.8	9.0	7.5	9.2	6.8	7.8	5.9	6.5	6.3
All-Fixed	12.8	9.0	7.5	9.3	7.3	8.1	6.5	7.3	6.7
Effective	10.7	7.9	5.5	6.1	3.2	4.2	3.4	3.5	3.7

Notes: Data refer to privately held debt which is partly estimated for 1960. Before 1974 data are for fiscal years ending in March of following year. Sav-Index refers to price-indexed savings bonds. Conventional maturity comprises Treasury bills. For other definitions see Table 4.8.

moves towards domestic currency bonds. The surge of foreign currency debt from 10% in 1970 to 50% in 1984, as the debt ratio almost doubles, is striking. A significant decline takes place after the fiscal stabilization: from 45% in 1986 to 35% in 1995. The only exception to this pattern is the early shift of the debt structure towards domestic currency bonds in the mid-1980s which anticipates the debt stabilization of 1987. In fact, the temporary increase in foreign currency debt to 41% in 1992 can be explained by both borrowing and exchange-rate devaluation related to the EMS crisis.

The significant correlation between foreign currency debt and the debt ratio (to the extent that it does not only reflect unexpected depreciation) suggests that governments may need to issue instruments which cannot be affected by surprise inflation, when the level of debt increases. The introduction of variable rate bonds in 1978 is in line with the tendency of the debt structure to move towards instruments bearing little inflation risk when the debt rises. These securities, which have coupons adjusted quarterly to the DIBOR[26] now account for 5% of the debt but their share was as high as 9% in the late 1980s.

The high share of bonds, 30% of which is held by foreign residents, accounts for the very long average term to maturity of the fixed-rate debt denominated in the domestic currency: 6.7 years in 1995. Figure 4.10 relates the debt ratio to

[26] Earlier issues paid semi-annual coupons indexed to the interest rate on Treasury bills.

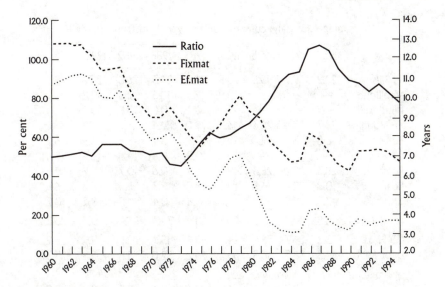

Fig. 4.10. Ireland: debt ratio and debt maturity.

the average term to maturity of fixed-rate securities denominated in domestic currency and effective maturity. Over the entire period the average maturity of fixed-rate securities falls by more than 6 years—from 12.8 to 6.7 years, while the debt increases from 54 to 78% in terms of GDP. While debt and maturity decline together until 1973, for the period 1974–85 there is some evidence of an inverse relation, since the debt accumulates while maturity shortens significantly from 9.5 to 6.7 years. However, the lengthening of maturity up to 8.1 years in 1986, at the start of fiscal stabilization, points to the absence of a systematic relation. Since the late 1980s, average maturity has remained constant around 7 years in spite of a falling debt ratio. Incidentally, the long maturity of fixed-rate bonds is against the contention that high inflation and the associated risk premium lead to a shortening of debt maturity.

When the effective maturity is considered, a strong inverse relation with the debt ratio emerges. Effective maturity shortens substantially during periods of sustained debt accumulation; it falls from 8.3 to 5.2 years between 1972 and 1976, and from 7.1 to 3.1 years between 1979 and 1985. In the following years, this inverse relation weakens; effective maturity lengthens to 4.2 years in 1986, before the debt stabilizes, and then remains roughly constant around 3.5 years in spite of a falling debt ratio. Although it cannot be found in every single period, the visual impression is still suggestive of an inverse relation between debt and effective maturity.

Italy In Italy the public debt has finally stabilized, though at a very high level: 116% of GDP in 1995. Although Italy approached the 1970s with a growing debt

Table 4.18. Italy: composition by type of instrument

	1960	1970	1975	1980	1983	1986	1989	1992	1995
T. Bills	22.2	9.7	15.5	40.5	36.9	24.3	26.8	25.6	19.7
Var-Bond	—	—	—	10.9	29.5	42.6	31.3	30.8	23.9
P-Indexed	—	—	—	—	0.3	0.1	0.1	0.1	—
Fix-Bond	28.7	33.4	28.6	16.3	9.0	12.4	18.9	20.4	32.0
Foreign	6.8	3.7	2.0	2.0	3.8	3.9	6.6	6.9	8.2
o/w ECU	—	—	—	—	(0.5)	(1.4)	(4.1)	(3.6)	(2.4)
Postal	28.3	28.2	25.3	19.1	11.9	10.6	10.7	9.7	9.9
Loans	10.8	22.2	26.8	10.2	8.0	5.7	5.3	6.2	6.1
Others	3.3	2.9	1.7	1.0	0.6	0.4	0.3	0.2	0.2
PH-Ratio	31.8	31.1	38.1	44.7	58.9	74.3	86.1	100.3	116.2
CB-Held	13.3	24.7	36.8	24.2	18.2	15.7	12.1	9.9	5.9
Debt Ratio	34.3	36.3	56.3	53.3	66.2	82.0	92.1	105.8	127.5
Average maturity of marketable debt									
Convention	11.9	7.3	4.6	1.9	1.6	3.4	2.5	2.8	3.0
All-Fixed	n/a	7.3	4.6	2.0	1.0	1.4	1.1	1.9	2.7
Effective	n/a	6.7	4.4	1.6	0.7	0.9	0.8	1.3	1.8

Notes: Data refer to privately held debt. Postal refers to Post Office certificates and savings accounts. For other definitions see Table 4.8.

ratio, the debt held by private investors increased rapidly only after 1975; from 35 to 116% in 1994. Until the mid-1970s the Bank of Italy met almost half of the borrowing requirements. The debt held by the Central Bank increased until 1976 when it reached a striking 40% of the total (see Table 4.18).

In the past a variety of instruments were used to cope with deficit accumulation. Variable-rate notes (CCTV) were introduced in 1977, earlier than in other countries. Such notes, which initially were offered with a 2-year maturity, had semi-annual coupons adjusted to the average issue yield on 6-month Treasury bills recorded in the 2 months preceding by 1 month the entitlement period of the coupon. In the following years their initial maturities have been increased up to 10 years and both annual coupons and indexation to 12-month Treasury bills have been considered. Following the French example, in 1986 options to convert variable-rate into fixed-rate notes were attached to few issues. Since 1995, variable-rate notes have been issued with 7- and 10-year maturities and have coupons indexed to the interest rate on 6-month Treasury bills recorded in the last auction preceding the entitlement period. ECU bonds and 1-year ECU bills were introduced as early as 1982. In 1983 indexation to the GDP deflator was introduced and soon abandoned, while substantial amounts of putable bonds (CTO) were issued between 1988 and 1992. This policy, which was partly motivated by the objective of favoring the household sector as the main holder of public debt, was abandoned in the late 1980s.

Fixed-rate long-term bonds became important only after the reform of the security market in 1988 when a group of primary dealers was established with the task of making an active market in government securities. Since then fixed-rate bonds have been sold through auctions and are now issued with maturities 3, 5, 10 and 30 years. Since 1990 benchmarks have also been promoted by the technique of "reopening" existing issues and trading has been supported by future contracts. In 1994 specialists in government securities were appointed with a higher status than primary dealers.

The composition of the debt by type of instrument is shown in Table 4.18. The high shares of variable-rate notes and Treasury bills, which sum to 44% in 1995, is indicative of the very short duration of the Italian debt. Treasury bills are available to personal investors and are issued in maturities of 3, 6 and 12 months. Variable-rate notes, though issued with maturities of 7 and 10 years, also bear little interest-rate and inflation risk since their coupons are indexed to the issue yield of 6- or 12-month Treasury bills.

The evolution of the debt structure is strongly characterized by the change in the funding policy. After 1976, not only monetary financing of budget deficits is abandoned, but the emphasis also shifts from non-marketable to marketable instruments, with the diffusion of Treasury bills first and then variable-rate notes. The remarkable increase in Treasury bills from 16 to 41% in the late 1970s, though instrumental for the creation of a market for government paper, points to the difficulties in issuing long-term securities when deficit monetization and regulation of the financial sector are abandoned in favor of market-oriented policies.

In the early 1980s variable-rate notes become the main financing instruments; introduced in 1977, they account for an astonishing 43% of the total in 1986. Correspondingly, issuance of fixed-rate bonds is dramatically reduced until the late 1980s; their share falls from 29% in 1975 to a mere 8% in 1984. Over the same period a comparable reduction occurs in the share of long-term loans from credit institutions.

The share of fixed-rate bonds gradually increases after the mid-1980s, but a longer maturity structure is initially achieved with bonds of maturities no longer than 3 years. Putable bonds also become a relevant instrument in this period, as their share reaches 5% in 1991.

Until the 1990s the debt buildup is thus accompanied by a shift in its structure toward instruments whose value is less affected by inflation if not toward instruments of shorter conventional maturities. Placement of fixed-rate long-term bonds proves to be difficult until the 1990s. It is only with the creation of an efficient secondary market that a true lengthening of debt maturity takes place; the share of bonds rises from 19% in 1989 up to 32% in 1995.

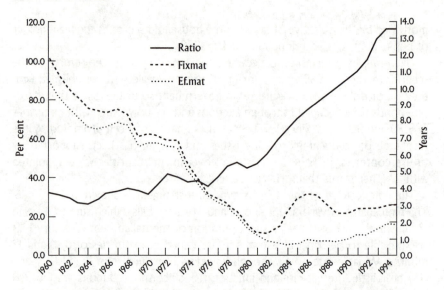

Fig. 4.11. Italy: debt ratio and debt maturity.

The increase is significant especially in the most recent period characterized by fiscal restraint.

The relation between the debt ratio and the average term to maturity is examined in Figure 4.11. Two measures of debt maturity are considered: conventionally measured maturity, which assigns the final maturity date for variable-rate notes and ECU bonds and effective maturity.[27] While over the entire period the debt has increased threefold in terms of GDP, conventional maturity has first shortened dramatically, from 11.9 to 1.6 years in 1982, and then lenghthened to 3 years in 1995. However, in the 1980s the longer maturity structure reflects the use of variable-rate notes on a large scale.

A different picture comes out when the effective maturity is considered, so as to correct for the shorter duration of variable-rate debt and for the protection against surprise inflation provided by ECU bonds and foreign currency debt. A strong inverse relation between debt and effective maturity emerges. The relation is striking until the 1990s: as the debt ratio rises from 38% in 1975 to 90% in 1990, effective maturity shortens dramatically from 4.4 to only 0.9 years. The debt and effective maturity move instead in the same direction in the most recent period as maturity lengthens to 1.8 years in 1995 while the debt reaches 116% of GDP.

Japan   The protracted recession of the early 1990s led the Japanese debt to reach 60% of GDP in 1995. After a sustained increase from the mid-1970s, the

[27] The average maturity of fixed-rate securities denominated in domestic currency is not shown here because it is almost identical to the effective maturity.

debt ratio was temporarily stabilized at 52% in 1987 and then reduced to 46% in 1991.

The Japanese security market is the second largest market in the world after the US market and a very large share of the public debt is in the form of fixed-rate long-term bonds: 61% in 1995. Although initial maturities vary between 6 and 30 years, the majority of bond issues have a typical maturity of 10 years. The choice of debt instruments with standard bullet maturities and fixed-interest rates is consistent with a debt policy which promotes marketability. In fact, there has been only one experiment with 15-year variable-rate bonds in the mid-1980s, but their share has never exceeded 3%.

The wholesale market is organized as in most OECD countries as a market-maker system run by security dealers linked by a single broker's screen. Most trading however occurs in the OTC market. The primary market (which was substantially liberalized in the mid-1980s with the admission of foreign firms to the underwriting syndicate of over 800 financial firms) presents instead peculiar features. In particular while all the other bonds are issued via auctions, the move toward an auction system for selling 10-year bonds has been gradual. Since 1990, 60% of the issues of 10-year bonds are sold by auction while the remaining 40% is underwritten by the syndicate at the average auction price.

The composition of the debt and its evolution are shown in Table 4.19. Interestingly, most of the debt is marketable since savings bonds have never been issued, and 5-year discount bonds, though being designed for personal investors, can be exchanged in an active market. This largely reflects institutional arrangements, namely, the fact that postal savings and public pension funds,

Table 4.19. Japan: composition by type of instrument

	1960	1970	1975	1980	1983	1986	1989	1992	1995
F. Bills	37.7	30.9	14.7	8.3	2.8	3.2	2.6	4.6	3.9
T. Bills	—	—	—	—	—	1.2	2.9	4.7	4.4
Notes	0	0	0	6.8	9.3	6.4	3.1	0.9	5.0
5y Bond	—	—	—	1.6	1.6	1.7	1.6	1.4	0.5
Var-Bond	—	—	—	—	1.4	2.8	2.5	2.1	1.6
Fix-Bond	37.2	53.7	66.4	69.3	71.7	71.3	72.4	67.2	60.8
Foreign	8.7	1.2	0.2	—	—	—	—	—	—
Loans	16.4	14.2	18.7	13.9	13.2	13.3	14.9	19.1	23.8
PH-Ratio	5.3	6.1	10.4	33.7	43.4	51.3	47.4	47.6	60.1
CB-Held	36.5	28.3	32.7	15.0	10.8	6.8	8.9	6.3	11.1
Debt Ratio	8.4	8.5	15.4	39.6	48.7	55.1	52.1	50.8	67.6

Notes: Data refer to privately held debt and are for fiscal years ending in March of following year. For other definitions see Table 4.8.

which ultimately are government liabilities, are invested in marketable bonds through the Trust Fund Bureau and the Postal Life Insurance Fund.

While securities have been issued in any maturity segment, since the mid-1970s until recently the share of fixed-rate long-term bonds accounts for more than two-thirds of the debt. Over the last two decades this share shows little variation oscillating in a limited range between 61% and 74% of the debt.

Financing bills with a maturity of 60 days are only used for cash management purposes and are a small component of privately held debt since most of them are held by the Central Bank. As deficits accumulation is financed by long-term bonds, the share of Financing bills falls rapidly to about 3% in the mid-1980s and then remains constant. In the period of faster debt accumulation an important role is instead played by medium-term notes. Introduced in 1978, first with a 3-year maturity and then with maturities of 2 and 4 years, medium-term notes reach a share of 9% in 1983, as the debt ratio increases from 10 to 43%.

The substitution of notes for Financing bills in the debt composition suggests that the authorities have pursued a policy of long-term funding of the rising debt. It is only after the debt stabilization in 1986 that Treasury bills are introduced and a shift towards instruments with a shorter maturity occurs. Treasury bills, which have maturities of 3 and 6 months and are used for deficit financing, replace medium-term notes in the debt composition, reaching a share of 4% in 1995. Between 1990 and 1995 the share of fixed-rate bonds also declines from 72% to 61%, as more funds are raised through non-marketable loans which now account for 24% of the debt after being roughly constant around 14% throughout the 1980s. Finally, it is worth noting that foreign currency debt has no longer been issued after being completely redeemed in the late 1970s.

In spite of the recent reduction in the share of bonds, the maturity of the Japanese debt remains among the highest in the OECD area. While data for previous years could not be found, in March 1996 the average term to maturity of all fixed-rate securities excluding Financial bills was 5.6 years and about 5 years if such bills are considered. This figure appears even more significant if one considers that the amount of bonds issued with a maturity longer than 10 years, that is, 20-year and 30-year bonds, is very limited.

In the absence of a time-series on maturity, Figure 4.12 shows the relation between the debt ratio and the share of fixed-rate long-term debt, i.e. fixed-rate notes, bonds and loans.

Netherlands   In the Netherlands the debt ratio is stable at a relatively high level: 63% in 1995. However, since the late 1980s fiscal restraint has been substantial, which explains why the debt increased rapidly only between 1978 and 1988: from 24 to 59% of GDP.

The Dutch bond market is now one of the most open and liquid markets in the world. The merit goes to reforms started in 1986, which first abolished regulations on the admissible types of debt instruments and, then, relaxed

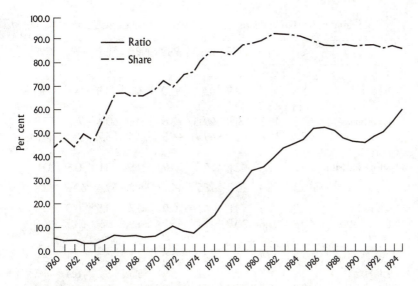

Fig. 4.12. Japan: debt maturity and share of long fixed-rate debt.

restrictions on foreign participation in the primary market. Significant deregulation has concerned the choice of debt instruments, notably their redemption features. Before 1986 all long-term bonds had sinking funds redemptions; they were repaid in yearly installments following an initial "grace" period which varied from 5 years on 10-year bonds up to 10 years on 20-year bonds. Since the bonds to be redeemed were chosen by drawings, this practice made the maturity of individual bonds uncertain. Longer-term issues were also typically callable after 10 years. The uncertainty regarding the maturity date of bonds was designed to prevent bonds with short remaining maturity from becoming more like short-term debt. The authorities held that separation between the capital and the money market could enhance their control over monetary aggregates.

The first long-term bonds with bullet maturities were issued in 1986 and soon thereafter the use of call options was discontinued. Sinking funds redemptions were abandoned after 1988. As in other European countries, this move toward simple securities, now with a typical maturity of 10 years but also with maturities of 5, 15 and 30 years, was aimed at reducing interest costs by facilitating bond pricing and attracting foreign investors. In order to improve liquidity, existing issues are often "reopened" and marketable bonds have been preferred to loans privately placed with banks and institutional investors (the Public Pension Fund, in particular).[28] The secondary market is organized as a continuous auction-agency market, since a quote-driven system was introduced and abandoned

---

[28] The last private loan was agreed in 1992.

Table 4.20. Netherlands: composition by type of instrument

	1960	1970	1975	1980	1983	1986	1989	1992	1995
T. Bills	—	—	—	—	—	—	—	—	3.1
Notes	15.3	15.6	12.9	13.7	10.0	6.3	1.5	—	—
T. Cert	6.6	3.5	0.8	0.1	—	—	—	—	—
Fix-Bond	53.3	40.5	31.8	29.0	43.6	51.6	60.6	71.3	77.9
Loans	8.3	30.6	42.4	49.9	44.5	40.6	36.7	28.2	18.1
Foreign	7.3	0.3	—	—	—	—	—	—	—
Short-NoMkt	9.2	9.4	12.1	7.3	1.9	1.5	1.1	0.5	0.9
PH-Ratio	40.3	25.4	20.7	28.7	44.7	54.2	59.6	62.6	62.7
CB-Held	2.2	5.1	1.1	1.1	0.9	0.7	1.5	1.0	0.4
Debt Ratio	40.8	25.6	20.9	29.1	45.1	54.5	60.5	63.2	63.0
Average maturity of marketable debt									
Convention	14.6	12.5	9.7	8.3	6.5	5.6	5.3	6.4	6.9
All-Fixed	11.0	9.3	7.5	6.8	5.9	5.3	5.2	6.3	6.7
Effective	10.2	9.3	7.5	6.8	5.9	5.3	5.2	6.3	6.7

Notes: Data refer to privately held debt. T. Cert denotes Treasury certificates. For other definitions see Table 4.8.

between 1990 and 1993. Interestingly, while before 1990 bonds were issued only by auctions, now auctions are coupled with an OTC "tap" issue system which is the most common system.

The maturity of the Dutch debt is one of the longest in the world; 6.7 years in 1995. The composition of the debt by type of instrument, presented in Table 4.20, shows that the share of long-term debt, bonds and loans, is remarkably large compared to other countries. Loans are privately placed with banks and financial institutions against registered "non-marketable" bonds, which can be traded without limitations despite the absence of a conventional market. Such instruments had long initial maturities ranging from 10 to 20 years, while bonds are now issued with a typical maturity of 10 years. As early as 1980 bonds and loans covered almost 80% of the debt and their share increased even further in the following years. A substitution of bonds for loans took place from the early 1980s and became significant after the market reforms; between 1986 and 1995 the share of bonds increased from 52 to 78% while that of loans fell from 41 to 18%.

The long maturity of the Dutch debt is confirmed by the low and declining share of Treasury notes; from 14% in 1980 to zero in 1992. Notes which had a typical maturity between 2 and 5 years, have not been issued since 1986. In practice, they have been replaced by Treasury bills with maturities up to 2 years following an agreement between the Government and the Netherlands Bank that the initial maturity of notes could not exceed 2 years. Treasury bills (Dutch

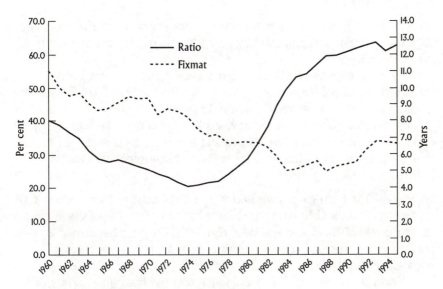

Fig. 4.13. Netherlands: debt ratio and debt maturity.

Treasury Certificates) with maturities of 3 and 12 months were reintroduced in 1993. In fact, Treasury bills had been issued until 1980 but they do not show up in yearly figures because of the legal requirement to redeem outstandings at the end of each year, since their use for deficit financing was prohibited.

The absence of foreign currency debt and the very low reliance on Central Bank financing are also noteworthy. As early as 1975 the entire debt is denominated in domestic currency and, as shown at the bottom of Table 4.20, holdings of government securities by the Netherlands Bank do not even reach 2% of total debt.

As regards to the relation between the debt ratio and its long-term component, Table 4.20 shows that the debt structure moves towards the short end when the debt declines, and lengthens as deficits accumulate. However, a different picture emerges from data on the average term to maturity reported in Figure 4.13. Maturity is estimated from the stock of both private loans and marketable securities, including notes and Treasury bills.[29]

Although debt maturity shortens from 10 to 8.2 years between 1960 and 1974, as the debt ratio is reduced to 20%, the fall in maturity is more marked in the following period; in 1988 when the debt ratio reaches 60% maturity is down to 5 years. The process reflects a continuous reduction of the maturity at issue of both long-term bonds and private loans which outweighs the effect of their increasing share. Some evidence of a negative relation between debt and

[29] Effective maturity is not reported because it coincides with conventionally measured average maturity since 1975 when the entire debt is domestic currency denominated.

debt maturity is also found in the most recent period when the stabilization of the debt ratio is accompanied by a lengthening of debt maturity up to 6.7 years in 1995.

To summarize, the relation between the debt and its average maturity is weak with minor movements in maturity since the late 1970s. The analysis also shows that maturity has remained very long especially if compared to other highly indebted countries. A tentative explanation is that, through abstention from deficit monetization, low inflation and successful pegging to the Deutsche Mark, the monetary authorities have built a stronger reputation for their anti-inflationary policy.

Portugal   The Portuguese debt (including official holdings) was 68% of GDP in 1995. In 1988 the debt ratio was stabilized at 66%, following a sharp increase since the mid-1970s when it was lower than 20%. Over the last decade the debt ratio remained roughly constant, as further fiscal consolidation was offset by slow growth in the 1990s.

In Portugal the extent of financial indexation has been impressive; in 1995, including savings bonds, almost half of the debt was indexed to short-term interest rates, the highest fraction with Greece among OECD countries, but down from the peak of 65% reached 3 years earlier. Various instruments and reference rates alternated in recent years. "Public Investment Fund" (FIP) bonds, with maturities of 7 or 8 years, issued between 1977 and 1992, had semi-annual coupons linked to a weighted average of interest rates on deposit accounts between 6 months and 1 year by the 3 institutions with largest accounts. In 1990 the reference rate was changed to the weighted average of interest rates on Treasury bills of the last 12 auctions of any maturity. Between 1986 and 1991 "Accrued Interest" bonds had also interests determined in the same fashion as FIP bonds, but paid at maturity. The interest rate on "Auctioned Credit for Public Investment" (Loan CLIP), issued in 1988 and 1989, was instead determined by auctions held at later dates. Finally, new variable-rate bonds issued since 1994 have been indexed to the 6-month LISBOR.

Increasing the duration of the government debt was certainly an objective of debt management in the late 1980s along with the modernization and reorganization of the security market. Reforms have proceded at a rapid pace with the adoption in 1988 and 1989 of multiple-yield auctions for the sale of all types of marketable debt and the establishment of specialists, i.e. primary dealers, in government securities. Following the stabilization of the debt ratio, fixed-rate bonds with a maturity of 3 years were introduced in 1988 and sold in fungible tranches, i.e. with the same coupon and maturity of existing issues. In 1993 the maturity of bonds was extended to 5, 7 and 10 years.

Table 4.21 shows the composition by instrument of the public debt. The share of fixed-rate long-term bonds is still low but increasing. In 1995 such debt accounts for no more than 21% of the total, but its increase from 4% in 1989

Table 4.21. Portugal: composition by type of instrument

	1970	1975	1980	1983	1986	1989	1992	1995
T. Bills	—	—	—	—	17.4	16.5	16.0	12.7
Var-Bond	0.0	0.0	60.4	52.8	49.8	54.3	44.4	26.5
Fix-Bond	72.3	80.7	17.8	7.1	3.5	4.0	10.3	21.2
Foreign	26.8	18.5	20.3	34.3	25.9	16.8	7.3	17.4
Savings	0.9	0.7	0.4	0.5	1.3	7.5	20.7	21.3
Other-NoMkt	0.0	0.0	1.1	5.3	2.0	1.0	1.2	0.9
Debt Ratio	18.3	23.1	35.3	51.9	57.0	63.6	58.0	68.4
Average maturity of marketable debt								
Fix-Bond	n/a	n/a	n/a	n/a	n/a	n/a	n/a	4.5
All-Fixed	n/a	n/a	n/a	n/a	n/a	n/a	n/a	3.0

Notes: Central Bank holdings are not available. For other definitions see Table 4.8.

after the debt stabilization is even more remarkable. In the 1980s no fixed-rate bonds were issued as deficit accumulation was first financed by foreign currency debt and variable-rate bonds and then by Treasury bills. Indeed, the share of fixed-rate bonds falls dramatically until 1987 when it is about to disappear with a mere 3%. Such a low share is explained by the diffusion of variable-rate marketable notes and bonds which represents about half of the debt between 1980 and 1992.

The share of foreign currency debt, 17% in 1995, is also high relative to other OECD countries. Borrowing abroad is important in the phase of faster debt accumulation; foreign currency debt rises from 20 to 36% of the total between 1980 and 1984 as the debt grows from 35 to 57% of GDP. However, in the following years such a share first declines and then rises again after 1992.

In the second half of the 1980s in the absence of a demand for instruments with longer maturities, Treasury bills of 91, 182 and 364 days become the most important financing instruments. Introduced in 1985, only 1 year later Treasury bills reach a share of 17% which will then remain roughly constant. The substitution of non-marketable savings bonds for variable-rate bonds which follows the debt stabilization is also noteworthy. However, such a substitution reflects a change in the holders of the debt but not in its duration, since Portuguese savings bonds also bear variable interest rates.[30]

The average term to maturity of fixed-rate bonds in 1995 was about 4.5 years which show a clear incidence of bonds with a 10-year maturity. The average maturity of the fixed-rate component of the debt, which consider Treasury bills, is lower, around 3 years. Although data on average maturity are not

---

[30] The main instrument, Tesouro Familiar pays quarterly interest indexed to the mean of the 3-month LISBOR over the previous 4 months.

available for a longer period, the lack of information is less important in the case of Portugal because of the large fraction of the debt at variable interest rates. In fact, since interest rates are adjusted every 6 months, the average duration on variable-rate debt is below 1 year even considering the lags in the indexation mechanism. This evidence points to a duration of the Portuguese debt which has been very short over the last two decades, though increasing since the early 1990s. An inverse relation between the debt ratio and debt maturity can be inferred from changes in the share of fixed-rate long-term debt which is shown in Figure 4.14.

Spain   The Spanish debt was 51% of GDP in 1995, a relatively low ratio if compared to other OECD countries. However, severe fiscal imbalances were experienced between 1981 and 1986 when the debt ratio rose from 10 to 35% and in the early 1990s when slow growth led to fast deficit accumulation.

   Until the 1990s the average term to maturity of the Spanish debt was one of the shortest in the OECD: in 1991 the average maturity was no longer than 18 months. Both high rates of inflation and past fiscal imbalances can explain the lack of demand for long-term securities. In fact, the low level of privately held debt not only reflects the absence of spending programs throughout the 1970s (Spain had virtually no debt before the 1980s), but also the extent to which borrowing requirements were financed by the Bank of Spain. The bottom half of Table 4.22 shows that by 1983 almost half of the debt was in the Bank's

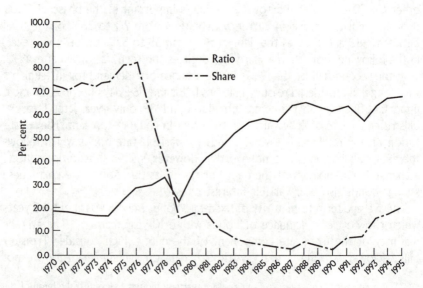

Fig. 4.14. Portugal: debt ratio and share of long fixed-rate debt.

Table 4.22. Spain: composition by type of instrument

	1962	1970	1975	1980	1983	1986	1989	1992	1995
T. Bills	—	—	—	—	17.2	49.0	61.5	47.2	32.8
Fix-Bond	87.6	34.3	22.0	22.0	19.6	24.1	30.0	35.6	53.7
Foreign	7.2	6.7	6.1	9.9	18.1	4.5	3.1	6.9	8.9
Loans	—	—	—	—	1.5	1.8	0.6	2.7	0.6
Inv.Cert	2.9	57.2	62.8	63.7	34.2	16.8	2.0	4.8	2.5
Others	2.3	1.7	9.2	4.4	9.4	3.8	2.9	2.8	1.5
PH-Ratio	15.6	12.2	9.1	9.3	15.5	34.9	32.0	37.6	51.4
CB-Held	7.6	10.3	20.6	38.7	48.0	17.3	14.7	5.6	2.2
Debt Ratio	15.6	12.4	9.2	9.8	19.5	37.5	35.0	38.3	52.2
Average maturity of marketable debt									
All-Fixed	11.8	9.6	7.3	4.2	1.7	2.0	1.2	1.9	3.1
Effective	11.8	9.6	7.3	4.2	1.3	1.9	1.2	1.7	2.8

Notes: Data refer to privately held debt. T.Bills include promissory notes "Pagarès." Inv.Cert denotes mandatory investment certificates. For other definitions see Table 4.8.

portfolio and points to the turnaround in the funding policy that occurred thereafter.[31]

Early signs of a market-oriented funding policy can be seen in the use of multiple-price auctions for the (re)introduction of bonds, "Bonos," in 1982, with a maturity of 3 years, subsequently extended to 5 years, and of long-term bonds, "Obligationes," with a maturity of 10 year in 1983. However, financial markets are liberalized and administrative controls for the conduct of monetary policy are abandoned only in the late 1980s. When this happens, market reforms take place at a rapid pace with the use of auctions for all securities since 1987 and the establishment of primary dealers in 1988. Only a subset of dealers act as market makers, are linked by an interdealer broker system, and are entiled to participate in a second-round auction.[32]

Table 4.22 shows the evolution of the composition by instrument of the Spanish debt. The table distinguishes between Loans and Investment Certificates of Indebtedness (Cedula para Inversion) with a standard 10-year maturity which were issued to commercial and savings banks under mandatory investment regulations to raise funds for public projects.

[31] In the early 1980s deficit monetization often put the Bank of Spain under pressure, as it needed to issue its own certificates to drain liquidity from the market. Such certificates are not included here, although they should be, since they are a component of privately held debt.

[32] Spanish auctions combine uniform price allocation for bids above the average price and a multiple-price system for bids below the average.

In the 1980s, as the authorities abandon the policy of deficit monetization, short-term securities emerge as the main financing instruments. The sharp increase in public debt between 1980 and 1986 is almost entirely financed with promissory notes, "Pagares del Tesoro," with initial maturities of 6 and 12 months (and 12 and 18 months since 1984). Introduced in 1981, Pagares account for an astonishing 49% of the debt in 1986. Although their diffusion is instrumental for the creation of a money market, it also testifies the difficulties in the placement of long-term securities.

The fraction of short-term debt continues to increase up to 62% in 1989 after the introduction in 1987 of "Letras", i.e. Treasury bills with a 1-year maturity (and 3 and 6 months since 1991), which replace Pagares as the main instrument. However, at the time of the fiscal stabilization in 1986, fixed-rate bonds start gaining importance. The main bulk of such securities is initially represented by "Bonos del Tesoro" which were issued in short maturities: 3, 4 and 5 years. Debt maturity lengthens significantly only in the 1990s when reliance on Treasury bills diminishes and a larger fraction of new bond issues is represented by 10-year maturity "Obligationes." The share of bonds, now with standard maturities of 3, 5, 10, 15 and 30 years, increased up to 54% in 1995 from a low 12% in 1985.

Interestingly, unlike in other countries with a low debt duration, variable-rate bonds have not been issued except for a negligible amount in 1986. The share of foreign currency debt exceeds 15% only in the early 1980s, but shows a tendency to increase during the periods of faster deficit accumulation.[33]

Figure 4.15 shows the evolution of the debt ratio and the average term to maturity of the fixed-rate debt denominated in the domestic currency.[34] Average maturity shortens dramatically from 11.8 years in 1962 to just 1.1 years in 1984 and then stabilizes in the following years. In 1990 maturity is still very low around 1 year, but it starts increasing and reaches 3.1 years in 1995. The relation between debt and maturity is weak. Maturity is on a downward trend from the mid-1960s while the debt ratio starts rising only in 1981. When this happens the shortening of maturity is not faster than in the second half of the 1970s. Although both debt and maturity stabilize in the late 1980s, debt accumulation in the following years is almost completely financed by long-term bonds.

The analysis suggests that the shortening of maturity in Spain cannot be closely related to the increase in debt but it does point to the importance of reputational aspects in the transition from substantial deficit monetization and financial regulation to market-oriented policy. If reputation is hard to

---

[33] Currency swaps are undertaken in foreign debt.

[34] Effective maturity is shown even though a comparison with the conventional definition yields negligible differences.

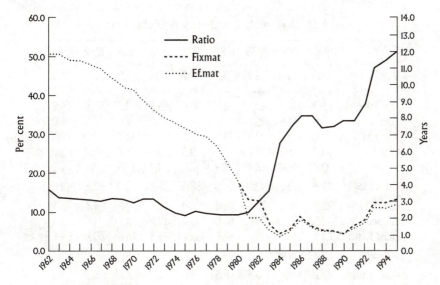

Fig. 4.15. Spain: debt ratio and debt maturity.

establish—the interest rate on long-term debt being too high—issuing short-term debt seems the only way to commit to the new policy.

Sweden Over the last two decades Sweden witnessed two phases of very rapid debt accumulation followed by equally strong fiscal corrections. The first stabilization reduced the debt ratio from 58% in 1983 to 42% in 1989. The recent debt buildup was halted by renewed fiscal efforts in the mid-1990s when the debt ratio stabilized at 81%.

The sensitivity of public finances to cyclical factors and the relatively high level of public debt stimulate discussion and raise concerns for the management of the debt (see Persson 1996). The task has been accomplished since 1789 by the "National Debt Office" (NDO), a former parliamentary agency which became an agency of the Ministry of Finance in 1989 with the objective of minimizing long-term borrowing costs. Since the early 1990s, the performance of the NDO is assessed in relation to two benchmark portfolios, one for domestic currency debt and the other for foreign currency debt. Risk taking is limited by the commitment to maintain the duration of the domestic debt within a predetermined band. A ceiling on the volume of foreign currency borrowing (decided by the government) is also in place which however does not prevent the NDO from an active management and the use of currency swaps and forward contracts.

A major initiative of the NDO was the launch of a price indexation program in 1994 (see Persson 1997). The commitment to the program is witnessed by the rapid increase in CPI indexed bonds which in 1996 accounted for more than 5% of the total debt and 10% of bonds, the second largest share in the OECD

Table **4.23.** Sweden: composition by type of instrument

	1960	1970	1975	1980	1983	1986	1989	1992	1995
T. Bills	1.0	10.8	6.9	5.6	9.7	7.3	9.5	26.7	14.3
P-Indexed	—	—	—	—	—	—	—	—	1.2
Fix-Bond	75.2	62.7	69.1	52.1	50.4	45.5	41.6	30.6	45.9
Lott-Bond	12.5	14.9	15.1	11.1	6.7	10.2	9.4	5.5	4.8
Foreign	0.0	0.0	0.3	22.1	23.5	23.8	18.3	27.0	29.3
Loans	10.9	5.6	2.2	2.1	3.5	1.8	3.8	0.9	0.0
Savings	0.4	6.0	6.4	6.9	6.1	11.4	17.3	9.3	4.5
PH-Ratio	23.4	14.6	18.0	36.0	58.4	55.7	42.0	62.6	81.1
CB-Held	25.9	30.6	26.3	9.6	16.4	14.7	0.5	4.6	3.3
CB-Sec-Ho	12.5	26.0	23.0	10.0	16.1	12.1	11.3	4.8	3.4
Debt Ratio	25.5	16.9	21.1	38.9	64.2	64.3	46.8	70.6	84.6
Average maturity of marketable debt									
Convention	n/a	n/a	6.9	5.5	4.1	4.0	3.0	2.9	4.6
All-Fixed	n/a	n/a	6.9	5.5	4.1	4.0	3.0	2.9	4.4
Effective	n/a	n/a	6.9	4.2	3.1	3.1	2.4	2.1	3.1

Notes: Data refer to privately held debt. Before 1989 foreign currency debt is evaluated at the exchange rates prevailing at the time of issue. For the year 1989 saving schemes include compulsory savings (0.3%). Price-indexed bonds are at their market value at the time of issue. Since 1986 maturity data are for June 30, and since 1988 maturity refers to the remaining period of fixed-interest rate. For other definitions see Table 4.8.

after the UK.[35] Ensuring market liquidity is also an important objective. This has been accomplished since 1987 by a quote-driven system run by primary dealers, by multiple-price auctions with "reopenings" of existing issues, and now by the use of standard maturities.

The composition of the debt by type of instrument is shown in Table 4.23. The short-term component, "T. Bills," comprises until 1982 old Treasury bills (which then disappear becoming a means of financing from the National Bank); Discount bills, that is, new Treasury bills introduced in 1982 and, since 1994, Overnight Borrowing. The long-term component, "Fix-Bond," does not distinguish between fixed-rate bonds and a small amount of revisable-rate bonds issued in 1979–80.

The evolution of the debt structure points to a strong inverse relation between debt accumulation and its fixed-rate long-term component. The shift away from long-term bonds into short-term and foreign currency debt is evident in the first period of sustained debt accumulation; between 1975 and

[35] The share of indexed bonds in 1996 is equal to 5.4% when they are evaluated at their issue price and to 7.7% if evaluated at face value, a difference explained by the fact that most of them are zero-coupon bonds.

1983 the share of bonds declines from 74 to 57% and their initial maturity is reduced. In the mid-1980s bond issues with maturities of 3 and 5 years become significant, while until then the typical maturity was 10 years. A shift towards instruments less affected by inflation during this period also shows up in the increasing importance of foreign currency debt which reaches 24% of the debt in 1983. After the stabilization of the debt ratio in the mid-1980s, the debt structure remains relatively constant, displaying minor movements such as the substitution of non-marketable savings schemes for foreign currency debt, while the initial maturity of bonds increases to 10 years in 1988. Between 1989 and 1992 the debt buildup is again accompanied by a shortening of the maturity structure; the share of Discount bills, now issued with maturities of 3, 6 and 12 months, increases from 10 to 27%.[36]

The period following the EMS crises is the only exception to this regularity, as the share of fixed-rate bonds rises from 31 to 46% with half of the increase taking place before the fiscal consolidation. However, the debt in foreign currency continues to increase, though at a diminished rate, and it now accounts for almost 30% of the debt.

The high share of foreign currency debt—the third highest share in our sample of countries—is noteworthy. Borrowing in foreign currency has been historically high for reasons related to the management of foreign-exchange reserves. The surge from 9% in 1991 to 27% in 1992 is the consequence of the Kroner devaluation and the vain attempt to defend the exchange parity by raising official reserves in the preceding months.[37]

The joint movements of the debt ratio and its average term to maturity are illustrated in Figure 4.16. Two definitions of average maturity are considered: the maturity of fixed-rate securities denominated in the domestic currency and effective maturity which assigns zero maturity to foreign currency debt and price-index-linked bonds. Movements in the average maturity of fixed-rate securities bear no relation to debt dynamics; between 1976 and 1988 debt maturity falls substantially, from almost 7 to 3 years, and then increases up to 5 years between 1992 and 1996.

On the contrary, when effective maturity is considered, there is some evidence of an inverse relation with the debt ratio. Between 1976 and 1985, as the debt more than doubles in terms of GDP, effective maturity shortens from almost 7 years to 2.8 years. When the debt ratio stabilizes this process is interrupted and effective maturity remains roughly constant at a relatively low level. In the 1990s, in spite of debt accumulation, maturity lengthens up to 3.1 years in 1996 but this increase appears very limited.

---

[36] Initially, discount bonds were issued in maturities of 6, 12, 18 and 24 months.

[37] The use of foreign debt for deficit financing was prohibited before 1992, when, in light of massive borrowing to replenish foreign exchange reserves, the "norm" was abolished.

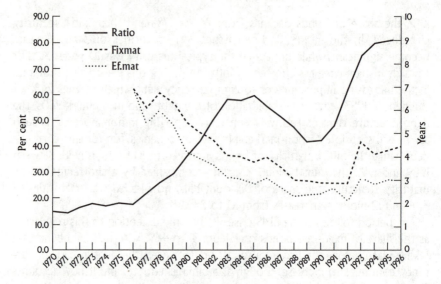

Fig. 4.16. Sweden: debt ratio and debt maturity.

United Kingdom   Although the debt has been rising since the early 1990s, the United Kingdom remains one of the least indebted OECD countries with a debt ratio equal to 48% in 1996. Fiscal policy was indeed more restrictive than anywhere else as primary surpluses were run in almost every year since the late 1970s. After being roughly constant at around 40% for more than a decade, the debt ratio eventually declined in the late 1980s to an historically low 29%, and reverse auctions were held to redeem outstanding bonds.

The UK has been among the first countries to issue price-index-linked bonds and is the country with the largest market for such bonds (see Deacon and Derry 1998). Introduced in 1981, indexed bonds have the principal adjusted to reflect changes in the Retail Price Index with an 8-month lag.[38] Indexed bonds now account for 18% of the stock of outstanding bonds and for 14% of the total debt.

The UK also stands out for the very long average maturity of fixed-rate securities—8 years including Treasury bills—the longest in the world. Unlike other countries this is not a recent phenomenon: in the mid-1980s the maturity of fixed-rate debt was 10 years. The very high share of long-term bonds, "Gilt-Edged Stock," is often explained by the high demand by insurance companies and pension funds which are the main holders of the debt. However, it is also a fact that the authorities could long rely on liquid and active secondary markets for government securities long before the mid-1980s when in most European

---

[38] The capital uplift is paid at maturity and the coupon, paid semi-annually, is calculated on the capital augmented of the inflation uplift.

countries secondary markets just began to develop. In 1986 when the Gilt-Edged market was reformed and organized as a quote-driven market run by a group of primary dealers, the GEMMs, with significant foreign participation, it was the most liquid market in Europe at the time. For instance, futures contracts had been available since 1982. Although multiple-price auctions were introduced in the early 1990s after an experiment in 1987, uniform-price auctions with a minimum price had provided since 1979 a fairly transparent method for selling bonds. The practice of selling "on tap" the unsold balance of a previous bond issue (and additional small "tranchettes" of existing bonds) has long provided a method of creating large volumes of the same bonds before the first formal "reopenings" of existing issues were tried in the late 1980s.

Although institutional aspects appear important, the low debt ratio, both historically and relative to other countries, and the historical abstention from explicit and implicit repudiation are also likely to be important factors in explaining the very long maturity of the British debt. If anything, the UK is a strong case against the contention that high inflation makes investors reluctant to hold long-term securities, since inflation in the 1970s and early 1980s was no lower than the OECD average.

Table 4.24 shows the composition of the debt by type of instrument. Fixed-rate bonds are now issued with bullet maturities of 5, 10, 15, 20 and 25 years, but the figures in the table also include (a now small amount of) "double dated" and "convertible" bonds. The former bonds are callable at any time subject to at least 3-months' notice in the last 4 or 5 years before maturity and have been issued until 1980. Convertible bonds gave holders the option to exchange them into longer maturity bonds at predetermined dates and conditions.

In 1996 the share of long-term securities in the form of fixed-rate and index-linked bonds accounts for a remarkable 73% of the debt. Savings schemes are the second largest component with a share of 15% which is high if compared to other countries. In fact, Treasury bills with typical maturities of 91 and 182 days are now mainly used for money market interventions and cash management purposes. The share of foreign currency debt is also relatively small around 5%, as such debt does not contribute to deficit financing but it is used to raise foreign-exchange reserves. Variable-rate bonds with quarterly coupons indexed to the LIBID account for a share of 2% two years after their introduction in 1994.[39]

The structure of UK debt exhibits a remarkable constancy over the last two decades. The share of total bonds, after increasing in the 1960s during the period of debt decumulation, shows little change over time as it varies in a limited range between 70 and 80%. The most significant change is the substitution of price-index-linked bonds and savings schemes for fixed-rate long-term bonds

---

[39] A previous experiment with variable-rate bonds in 1977 was abandoned in 1979 after 3 issues.

Table 4.24. United Kingdom: composition by type of instrument

	1960	1970	1975	1980	1983	1986	1989	1992	1995
T. Bills	12.6	3.9	11.6	1.3	1.1	1.2	5.8	2.2	3.2
Var-Bond	—	—	—	0.9	—	—	—	—	1.7
Fix-Bond	61.5	70.9	69.8	79.5	73.1	68.5	58.0	57.3	59.6
P-Indexed	—	—	—	1.1	5.5	8.7	11.2	12.5	13.6
Foreign	8.6	8.9	8.3	3.3	2.0	3.6	4.1	8.6	5.0
Savings	15.2	14.8	9.7	9.3	12.6	14.4	16.7	14.8	13.1
Sav-Index	—	—	0.7	3.1	3.2	1.6	1.9	2.8	2.3
Others	2.1	1.4	0.1	1.5	2.5	2.0	2.3	1.9	1.5
PH-Ratio	89.0	46.7	39.5	40.0	42.0	43.1	30.3	36.9	48.3
Off-Held	34.6	37.8	32.6	19.7	9.5	9.9	20.8	10.6	14.0
Debt Ratio	119.8	64.3	52.4	47.9	46.0	47.3	36.6	40.7	55.1
Average maturity of marketable PH debt									
Convention	13.5	13.3	12.4	12.4	10.7	10.9	10.2	10.8	10.1
All-Fixed	11.5	12.6	10.7	12.2	10.0	9.5	7.7	9.1	8.4
Effective	10.4	11.3	9.7	11.6	9.0	8.1	6.2	6.7	6.5

Notes: Data refer to privately held debt and are for fiscal years ending in March of the following year. Sav-Index denotes price-indexed savings bonds. Maturity figures for 1960 are for the year 1962. For other definitions see Table 4.8.

which occurs in the early 1980s. Three years after their introduction, indexed bonds already account for almost 6% of the debt. In the following period their share continues to rise, though at a lower rate in the 1990s. An issuing strategy relying on instruments whose value cannot be affected by inflation is also suggested by the increase from 12 to 16% of savings bonds, which have shorter initial maturities than marketable bonds and are redeemable on demand.

Since inflation and interest rates declined in the following years, issuance of price-indexed and short-term debt allowed for a substantial reduction of interests costs. By signalling the authority's unwillingness to borrow long-term at high interest rates this strategy possibly had a favorable impact on inflationary expectations, as argued by Campbell (1995) among others.

The relation between the debt ratio and its average maturity is illustrated in Figure 4.17. Two series of debt maturity are considered: the average maturity of fixed-rate marketable securities including Treasury bills, and the effective maturity. Both series suggest that there is little empirical regularity in the co-movements of debt and maturity. Until 1973 debt and maturity move in opposite directions; maturity lengthens from 11.5 years to 13.5 years while the debt ratio falls sharply from 80 to 38%. However, in the following period, while the debt ratio remains constant until 1990, its maturity shortens substantially to 7.2 years (5.6 years in the case of effective maturity). Over the last decade, as

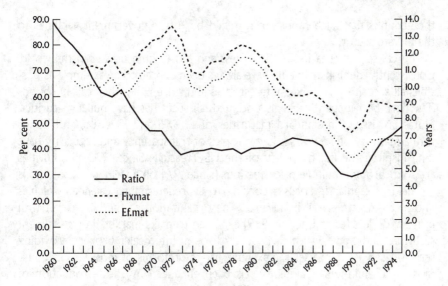

Fig. 4.17. UK: debt ratio and debt maturity.

deficit accumulation is mainly financed by long-term conventional bonds, the debt rise is accompanied by an increase in both measures of maturity: up to 8.4 and 6.5 years in 1995, respectively.

The most interesting finding is the substantial fall in maturity after 1980 which is even more evident when zero maturity is assigned to price-indexed securities. Between 1980 and 1984 effective maturity shortens considerably from 11.7 to 8.4 years. As discussed above, during this period of rapidly falling inflation the funding policy favors conventional bonds of shorter maturity and price-index-linked bonds. Whether this strategy enhanced the credibility of the anti-inflation stance, thus easing the task of monetary policy, is debatable, but it certainly reduced the possible gains from unanticipated inflation and it is a fact that inflation in the UK decreased at a faster rate than in other countries.

United States   In the United States the privately held debt was finally stabilized at 44% of GDP in 1996. The fiscal correction has halted a steady deterioration of public finances started in 1975. In that year the debt, which had fallen to a minimum of 17% of GDP, began to accumulate first slowly and then at a faster pace throughout the 1980s.

While the 44% debt ratio in 1995 appears low if compared to other countries, figures for privately held debt in the US are misleading since they exclude "Government Account Series," that is, special non-marketable paper issued to public pensions for the investment of their funds. The debt ratio attains the more familiar level of 63% when these funds are not subtracted from the debt as is customary in other countries, notably in Japan and the Netherlands, on the grounds that such funds are matched by future government liabilities to the private sector.

The US security market is the largest and most liquid market in the world. Consistently, debt instruments have always been chosen to be as simple as possible; all securities have fixed-interest rates and since 1984, when callable bonds (few have been issued) were discontinued, all securities have bullet maturities. Notes are issued in standard maturities of 2, 3, 5 and 10 years, and bonds with a maturity of 30 years. The principles of transparency and regularity have long inspired the issuing policy of the US Treasury. Since 1970 all securities are sold through multiple-price auctions (since 1974 on a yield basis). Auctions are held at regular intervals according to a predetermined calendar which is known to investors well in advance. The organization of the US market with primary dealers (established in 1939) expected to make markets in government securities and trading with each other through interdealer brokers providing screen-based assistance set the example for the reforms of most OECD countries in the mid-1980s. Liquidity has been enhanced by the introduction of bond futures contracts in the mid-1970s and by the authorization of stripping facilities in 1985.

The introduction in January 1997 of inflation-indexed notes, "TIINs," can be considered the only main innovation in the choice of instruments over the last three decades. TIINs, which are issued with maturities of 5 and 10 years, have principal and interest payments adjusted to reflect changes in the CPI with a 3-month lag. [40] The US market for price-indexed notes is becoming the second largest market after the UK, and has spurred issuance of indexed bonds by both the US private sector and other countries like Greece and Turkey.

Table 4.25 shows the composition by type of instrument of the "Privately Held debt," which is net of the Government Account Series, i.e. it does not consider the funds of public pensions invested in such series as government debt. However, the debt-to-GDP ratio is shown according to both definitions of debt, "PH-Ratio" and "PGA-Ratio."

The long maturity of the US debt is shown by the large fraction of long-term securities, notes and bonds, which stands at 70% in 1995. The other marketable debt (denoted as Tbills) is the sum of Treasury bills with standard maturities of 13, 26 and 52 weeks and Cash Management bills with flexible maturities from a few days to 6 months. Their share is now relatively low, equal to 17%, but Treasury bills were important in the past as they were used for deficit financing and accounted for one-fourth of the debt in the period 1970–83. In fact, the share of Treasury bills moves inversely with the debt ratio, first rising until the mid-1970s and then decreasing after 1983 as the debt accumulates rapidly. This

---

[40] The capital uplift is paid at maturity and the coupon, paid semi-annually, is calculated on the capital augmented of the inflation uplift.

Table 4.25. USA: composition by type of instrument

	1960	1970	1975	1980	1983	1986	1989	1992	1995
Debt excluding Government Account Series									
T. Bills	18.7	22.2	27.4	25.8	27.8	20.1	15.6	18.0	17.2
Notes	18.0	25.0	32.2	41.8	49.5	52.5	52.7	52.4	55.7
Fix-Bond	37.2	25.6	9.9	11.1	10.6	13.6	15.6	15.4	14.6
Foreign	—	0.6	0.5	1.1	—	—	—	—	—
Savings	23.2	23.6	21.6	12.3	7.1	5.5	5.8	5.4	5.5
Others	2.8	3.0	8.4	7.9	5.1	8.2	10.3	8.8	6.9
PH-Ratio	38.9	21.0	18.6	21.2	28.2	35.2	36.0	44.3	45.2
Debt including Government Account Series									
PGA-Ratio	47.8	28.5	26.3	28.0	34.9	43.4	48.2	60.5	63.4
CB-Held	9.5	16.3	16.5	13.3	10.7	8.8	7.8	6.9	7.4
Debt Ratio	53.9	35.7	32.7	32.6	39.2	48.1	52.5	65.1	68.5
Average maturity of marketable PH debt									
All-Fixed	4.3	3.7	2.7	3.8	4.1	5.3	6.0	5.9	5.3

Notes: Data refer to privately held debt and are for fiscal years ending in June of the same year until 1976 and September of the same year since 1977. PH-Ratio excludes debt in government account while PGA-Ratio includes such debt. For other definitions see Table 4.8.

suggests a positive relation between the debt and its long maturity component, i.e. notes and bonds. Finally, it is worth noting that no debt in foreign currency is outstanding and that such debt never exceeded 1.1% of the total.

The tendency of the debt structure to lengthen as the debt increases (and to shorten when the debt declines) is shown more clearly by movements in the share of long-term securities. Such a share is now 70%, but in 1974 had fallen to 41% after being almost constant at 50% until the early 1970s. Taking into account that notes have a maturity ranging from 2 to 10 years, while bonds have an initial maturity beyond 10 years, it is clear that a shortening of maturity is already taking place before the 1970s in the form of an increase in notes relative to bonds. Between the mid-1970s and the late 1980s, instead, both instruments equally contribute to the lengthening of the maturity structure. For this period the increase of long-term securities also reflects the substitution of marketable for non-marketable debt, as shown by the declining share of savings bonds; from 22% in 1975 to less than 6% since 1985. The process of maturity lengthening was interrupted temporarily in the late 1980s, to recover, though at a slower pace, in the 1990s. A substitution of notes for longer-term bonds also takes place over the most recent period.

Figure 4.18 illustrates the evolution of the debt ratio and its average term to maturity. Data on maturity refer to all marketable fixed-rate securities

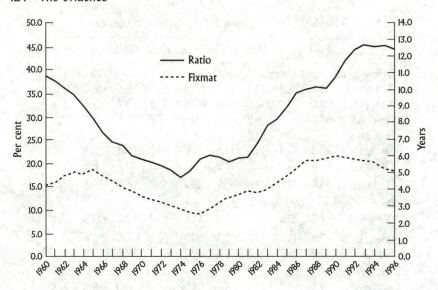

Fig. 4.18. USA: debt ratio and debt maturity.

denominated in domestic currency which are held by the private sector.[41] The figure exhibits a striking positive relation between debt and maturity. As the debt falls sharply from 39% in 1960 to 17% in 1974, maturity shortens from 4.6 to just 2.6 years in 1976. When the debt ratio increases to reach 45% in 1995, maturity first lengthens to 6.1 years in 1990 and then shortens but only slightly to 5.3 years in 1995.

Although it is tempting to attribute the cause of the shorter debt maturity of the mid-1970s to the high inflation, no such effect is at work in the early 1980s, as maturity increases steadily. In fact, institutional factors may better explain the shortening of debt maturity in the earlier period. Specifically, a 4.25% interest rate ceiling on Treasury bonds did not permit the Treasury to issue securities with maturities longer than 7 years at current market rates from 1965 to 1971. Since then, such a constraint has been gradually relaxed; a limited exception to the 4.25 ceiling was enacted by Congress in 1971, expanded in the following years and then automatically granted.

4.6   Concluding remarks

Significant differences in debt compositions by instrument and maturity emerge across OECD countries. Much of this variation is a legacy of the debt policies

[41] Effective maturity is not shown here because the correction for foreign currency debt yields negligible differences.

pursued in the 1980s. As governments relied on foreign borrowing, variable-rate bonds, non-marketable instruments and a variety of option clauses for the funding of their debts, important differences were built in the structure of their liabilities. This trend has finally reversed in the 1990s under the impulse of financial liberalization, increased foreign participation and market-oriented monetary policies.

In many European countries, during the 1980s, debt managers, operating in highly regulated markets and under the protection of capital controls, "tailored" debt instruments to the specific needs of the final holders of debt in order to save on interest costs. The choice of debt instruments often reflected the identity of the debt-holders, were they pension funds and insurance companies or commercial banks, foreign residents or the household sector. In countries where the banking sector had a role in underwriting or distributing the debt, it often negotiated terms and maturities of the securities to be issued.

In the late 1980s, European financial markets underwent profound changes as a result of significant deregulation and reforms. At the same time "demand-oriented" debt policies came to an end. The institutional changes affecting government security markets have been part of a more general strategy implying abstention from deficit monetization, the abolition of capital controls, the adoption of market-oriented monetary policies and the liberalization of financial markets. As the program of reforms continued in the 1990s, involving new countries, efficient and thick secondary markets for government securities developed in the OECD, which provide liquidity services to investors and allow governments to save on debt-servicing costs. In order to promote liquidity debt managers have relied on a mix (which differs across countries) of policy measures, such as: the promotion of quote-driven markets based on the market-making activity of primary dealers; the introduction of bond futures contracts and "repo" markets; the adoption of transparent issuing policies with multiple-price auctions held according to regular calendars; the early announcement of the type and quantity of the securities on offer; and the promotion of benchmark bonds with the use of bullet 10-year maturities and fixed-interest rates and the sale, through "reopenings," of bonds identical to the existing issues. These policies together with increasing foreign participation have produced a high degree of international integration in the markets for government securities. There has been a simplification and reduction of the security on offer and, in the process, fixed-rate long-term bonds have been favored over alternative instruments because they can be easily priced and hedged.

A convergence in the composition by instrument of public debts can thus be observed in the OECD, as a result of such events. There has been a general tendency to rely more on fixed-rate long-term bonds than on foreign currency debt and variable-rate bonds. Countries which, at the end of the 1980s, had a low share of fixed-rate long-term bonds saw it increase to the level of

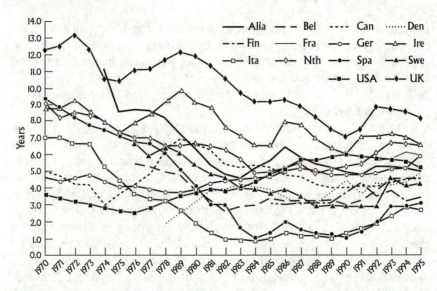

Fig. 4.19. OECD: maturity of fixed-rate domestic debt.

countries with a longer maturity structure. Figures 4.19 and 4.20 also seem to suggest that a convergence in the average term to maturity of marketable debts and of effective maturity has taken place. In fact, as shown more clearly in Table 4.26, between 1985 and 1995 most of the adjustment in the maturity of fixed-rate debt has come from a shortening of debt maturity in the UK and a lengthening of maturity in Italy and Spain while all other countries have approximately remained within the same range of maturities. The same conclusions hold true when effective maturity is considered in Table 4.27. Since 1985, with the exception of the UK, effective maturity has increased or stayed constant in all countries considered; while maturity has lengthened in Finland, Italy and Spain, the increase has been of about 1 year, not greater than in countries with a longer effective maturity.

While it is tempting to attribute differences and evolution in the funding policy of OECD countries to institutional factors, the structure of markets and the distribution of debt by type of holder cannot provide a complete explanation for the stylized facts outlined above. For instance, if it is true that efficient secondary markets make it easier to place fixed-rate long-term bonds, they do not prevent the issuance of price-index-linked bonds or variable-rate bonds, as witnessed by the recent successful introduction of such instruments in a number of countries. The decision to issue long-maturity conventional bonds remains the sole responsibility of debt managers.

The institutional view is more a description than an interpretation of events, since it offers no answer to fundamental questions such as: what did prevent

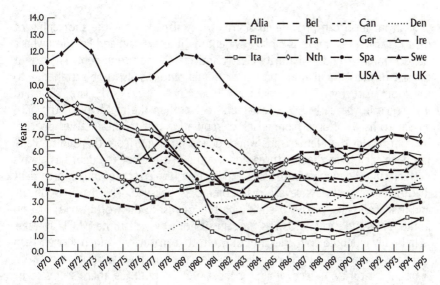

Fig. 4.20. OECD: effective maturity.

the creation of secondary markets early in the 1980s and instead made them possible a few years later? Was it the result of financial innovation or rather the consequence of important decisions regarding the objectives, the conduct and the independence of monetary policy?

Finally, the analysis points out important differences in debt composition and effective maturity across countries which cannot be related to institutional factors. In particular, there is strong evidence that effective maturity in highly indebted countries is much shorter than in less indebted countries. The maturity gap between the two groups has diminished in recent years but not vanished. In Italy the short maturity of the debt could be explained by the choice of targeting the household sector as the main holder of debt. But debt maturity fell in similar fashion in Belgium, where the banking sector was the main lender of funds to the government as well as it is in Germany, a country with a much lower debt ratio and a longer maturity. In Ireland, despite the important role played by insurance companies and pension funds, the effective maturity remained low until the 1990s, because of the large share of foreign currency debt. Although in Ireland changes in market structure have been relatively minor, the share of foreign debt fell substantially after the stabilization of the debt ratio. Until the early 1990s, effective maturity was also very short in Sweden where high levels of debt have always been a cause for concern. Effective maturity is also short in Finland, Spain and Portugal where the debt ratio is relatively lower but where severe fiscal imbalances have been experienced in the past. Finally, maturity is shortest in Greece where the debt problem is worst.

High inflation can provide an alternative explanation for the shortening of debt maturity. Its impact is mostly evident in Greece, Spain and Portugal where the downward trend in maturity clearly anticipated the rise in debt. The extent of past financial regulation and deficit monetization is also not extraneous to the short maturity of these countries. Especially in Spain in the late 1980s and in Greece in the early 1990s, attempts to lengthen the maturity of the debt appear to have suffered from a lack of reputation due to these earlier policies. By contrast, in the Netherlands where deficit financing from the Central Bank has been nihil over the last three decades the maturity of the debt has always been among the highest in the OECD. However, the effects of inflation on debt maturity are much less severe than commonly believed. The maturity of UK and Irish bonds has always been among the longest in the world while inflation in the 1970s and early 1980s was the same if not worse than the OECD average.

In highly indebted countries, not only effective maturity is much shorter than in other countries, but there is also evidence of an inverse relation between debt and maturity. Indeed, while for most OECD countries, there seems to be little systematic relation between the debt ratio and debt maturity, in Belgium, Ireland, Italy and Sweden the increase in debt has been associated with a sharp reduction in effective maturity. In Greece where the debt is greater than GDP the maturity of the debt is also very short. A positive relation between debt and maturity is found only in a few countries: in France, Germany, Japan and the US, which have a relatively low debt ratio, and in Denmark, which is significantly indebted.

Interestingly, the shortening of the effective maturity in Italy reflects the increasing use of variable-rate debt, in addition to Treasury bills. In Ireland most of the action comes from changes in the share of foreign currency debt, as the maturity of bonds denominated in domestic currency has remained very long. In Belgium and Sweden both short-term and foreign currency debt contribute to the inverse relation between debt and effective maturity. Further evidence of a positive relation between the debt ratio and instruments bearing little inflation risk comes from the introduction of indexed instruments when the debt problem emerges. Significant amounts of bonds indexed to the prevailing interest rate or to the ECU have been issued in Ireland, Italy, Greece and Portugal, while price indexation has been preferred in Sweden.

The relation between effective maturity, the debt ratio and inflation is further examined in Chapter 6 by means of simple regressions. In the same chapter the choice of debt maturity is also related to long-term interest rates in order to evaluate the impact of the cost of long-term debt on the government funding policy. The idea is that debt maturity should be sensitive to interest-rate movements and, in particular, to expectations about future rates. At this stage of the analysis there seems to be more to the choice of debt maturity than just a response to movements in interest rates.

Table 4.26. Maturity of fixed-rate domestic debt

	1970	1975	1980	1985	1990	1995
Australia	—	8.8	6.5	5.8	5.0	6.1
Austria	—	—	—	—	—	4.8
Belgium	—	5.6	4.0	3.5	3.1	4.7
Canada	5.2	3.8	6.8	5.4	4.1	4.7
Denmark	—	—	3.3	4.0	4.5	5.0
Finland	—	—	—	3.2	3.8	3.5
France	—	—	—	—	—	6.1
Germany	4.8	4.2	4.0	4.8	4.9	5.1
Ireland	9.0	7.5	9.3	6.7	6.2	6.7
Italy	7.3	4.6	2.0	1.0	1.4	2.7
Japan	—	—	—	—	—	5.0
Netherlands	9.3	7.5	6.8	5.1	5.4	6.7
Portugal	—	—	—	—	—	3.0
Spain	9.6	7.3	4.2	1.3	1.1	3.1
Sweden	—	6.9	5.5	3.8	2.9	4.4
UK	12.6	10.7	12.2	9.4	7.2	8.4
USA	3.7	2.7	3.8	4.9	6.1	5.3

Notes: Maturity measured in years. Fiscal years ending in the same year or in March of the next year. Data for Austria are for conventionally measured maturity. For Belgium and Sweden the maturity of 1976 is presented for the year 1975.

Table 4.27. Effective maturity

	1970	1975	1980	1985	1990	1995
Australia	—	7.9	4.7	4.4	4.2	5.4
Belgium	—	5.6	3.7	2.8	2.6	3.8
Canada	5.1	3.8	6.3	4.9	4.0	4.5
Denmark	—	—	2.2	3.2	3.4	4.3
Finland	—	—	—	1.4	2.1	1.9
France	—	—	—	—	—	5.6
Germany	4.5	4.1	4.0	4.8	4.8	5.0
Ireland	7.9	5.5	6.1	3.1	3.2	3.7
Italy	6.7	4.4	1.6	0.7	0.9	1.8
Japan	—	—	—	—	—	5.0
Netherlands	9.3	7.5	6.8	5.1	5.4	6.7
Spain	9.6	7.3	4.2	1.2	1.1	2.8
Sweden	—	6.9	4.2	2.8	2.5	3.1
UK	11.3	9.7	11.6	8.3	5.6	6.5
USA	3.7	2.7	3.8	4.9	6.1	5.3

Notes: Maturity measured in years. Fiscal years ending in the same year or in March of the next year.

It is true, however, that debt maturity has lengthened or stabilized since the late 1980s in countries like Belgium and the Netherlands, which have been able to tie more closely their currencies to the Deutsche Mark and, consequently, have seen a reduction in the spread between their interest rates and the German rates. Countries like Italy, Portugal and Spain have also witnessed a significant lengthening of debt maturity but only in the most recent period, when their determination to join the European Monetary Union has become clear.

5

Minimizing risk

5.1 The implicit-contingent approach

The policymaker's objective function implies a trade-off between the minimization of the expected cost of debt servicing and the minimization of budgetary risk. As shown in Chapter 3, if the expected rates of return on government securities just reflect their risk-return characteristics, the debt manager should only be concerned with risk minimization. A strategy aimed at reducing interest costs is justified only when risk premia result from: market imperfections; informational asymmetries; expectations failures; and the government's inability to credibly commit to future policy actions.

This suggests the importance of distinguishing the causes of debt-servicing costs. If they reflect the return characteristics of government securities, as determined by macroeconomic risk, high expected returns are fully consistent with efficient taxation, optimal risk-sharing and the other objectives of debt management. In the absence of imperfections, informational and credibility problems, debt managers should only minimize budgetary risk arising from macroeconomic shocks affecting interest rates, tax revenues and public spending.

The objective of minimizing risk calls for low debt returns in states where output is lower and public spending is higher than expected so as to avoid high tax rates when bad shocks to output or public spending occur. The ideal debt instrument would be negatively indexed to public spending and positively indexed to output, as shown by Lucas and Stokey (1983), King (1990), Shiller (1993), Chari, Christiano and Kehoe (1994), and Barro (1995, 1997). This design of public debt would minimize changes in labor tax rates, which would otherwise be needed to meet unexpected changes in financing needs. Good reasons for choosing this approach are the desirability of reducing tax distortions, relaxing borrowing constraints, and providing flexibility to fiscal policy.

Explicitly contingent debt of this kind is not being issued in the real world. In the case of indexation to public spending, non-existence can be easily explained by moral hazard problems on the side of the government (Calvo and Guidotti 1990 and Bohn 1990a). Instead, this argument does not apply to output-indexation; the absence of output-indexed bonds can more easily be explained by the frictions associated with the delay in recording and reporting the relevant statistics and the difficulties associated with pricing and hedging the return risk of such bonds.

Market imperfections, liquidity problems and the gains from standardization thus provides a first instance where the costs of the optimal debt design outweigh the benefits of risk minimization. Indeed, this explains why even a very "risk-averse" policymaker would prefer conventional debt instruments to output-indexed bonds. As documented in Chapter 4, no government has ever issued debt explicitly contingent on output or on output proxies despite the large use of debt indexed to interest rates, price indexes and the ECU exchange rate. As a matter of fact, governments must rely on the limited implicit contingencies offered by conventional instruments.

These considerations raise two issues. The first issue is how, and to what extent, the optimal distribution of debt returns can be obtained with conventional financial instruments. The second issue is how policy indications change when asymmetric information, expectational failures, and credibility problems are taken into consideration, in particular, whether such inefficiencies offer a motivation for a more cost-oriented debt management.

Debt policy aimed at minimizing interest costs is considered in Chapter 6. The next sections instead examine whether, in the absence of explicitly contingent debt, the strategy of minimizing budgetary risk can be carried out using conventional financial instruments: fixed-rate securities denominated in domestic currency with different maturities; variable-rate bonds; price-index-linked bonds; non-marketable loans; securities and loans denominated in foreign currency.

5.2   Price indexation and debt denomination

Unexpected financing needs may result from unanticipated public spending, unexpected falls in tax bases, high returns on government securities and interest-rate shocks. If risk minimization were the objective of debt managers, they should issue securities yielding low returns in states where financing needs are unexpectedly high.

The implicit contingent approach holds that conventional securities, being implicitly contingent on the price level, exchange rates, and interest rates of different maturities may provide substitutes for explicitly indexed debt and thus limit the need for tax adjustments. In the absence of explicitly contingent debt, shocks adversely affecting the government budget can be hedged by conventional debt instruments, to the extent that their real returns covary negatively with government financing needs. For example, if unexpected inflation were negatively correlated with output shocks, nominal debt could provide the best alternative to positive output indexation (Bohn 1990*a*). Implicit contingencies in debt returns could also be implemented by the choice of the currency of denomination (Bohn 1990*b*), and the maturity composition of public debt (Gale 1990). Long maturities could isolate the government budget from interest-rate shocks (Barro 1995, 1997).

5.2.1 Nominal versus price-indexed debt

Fixed-rate debt denominated in the domestic currency (referred to as nominal debt), is by far the most common instrument in OECD countries. Although, its use instead of price-indexed debt has long puzzled economists, nominally denominated debt, being implicitly contingent on shocks affecting the price level, could perform the shock-absorber role of explicitly contingent debt.

Nominal debt may even provide a hedge against the risk of rolling over maturing debt at higher than expected real interest rates. Refinancing risk is a familiar concern to policymakers who must roll over large debts with short and unbalanced maturity structures or service variable-rate bonds. Obviously, the government budget can be isolated from interest-rate variations by issuing long maturity debt, as in Barro (1995). However, if for any reason long-term debt cannot be issued, nominal debt provides a hedge against interest-rate risk to the extent that positive shocks to the interest rate lead to an increase in the price level. This could be the case if the money supply is constant and the money demand is interest elastic. This example has been used by Bohn (1988) to show that nominal debt may support tax smoothing better than price-indexed debt.

Bohn derives the optimal debt composition between nominal and price-indexed bonds in relation to the incidence of two types of shocks affecting consumer preferences in an OLG economy, where people must hold money in advance to purchase cash goods in the second period of their lives (credit goods are consumed in both life periods). The first type—real shocks—affects intertemporal consumption choices and, output being fixed, the real interest rate. The second type—monetary shocks—affects the choice between next-period cash and credit goods and hence the price level. In order to smooth taxes across time and states of nature, the government issues one-period nominal or price-indexed bonds, while keeping the money supply constant. The optimal share of nominal debt increases in the variance of real shocks affecting the real interest rate. Intuitively, since all the debt is renewed in each period, high real interest rates adversely affect the government budget and lead to higher taxes and tax distortions in current and/or future periods. However, when the real interest rate rises, the price level also increases to restore money-market equilibrium. This positive correlation between unexpected inflation and the real interest rate favors nominal debt over price indexation. On the other hand, as the incidence of monetary shocks increases, price-indexed debt performs better as a tax-smoothing device than nominal debt. This is because monetary shocks, affecting the real value of nominal debt, cause changes in tax needs which are unrelated to other budgetary variables.

More generally, nominal debt is a better hedge against changes in financing needs than price-indexed debt, if productivity and public spending shocks prevail over monetary disturbances and real demand shocks (other than public spending shocks). This can be easily formalized in a two-period model where the government chooses debt instruments in order to minimize the variance of tax rates across future states of the world.

5.2.2   Aggregate supply and demand shocks

Consider the choice of the debt instruments by a government which aims at smoothing tax-rates across future states of the world.[1] In the current period, say period $t-1$, taxes have already been set, while in the next period, say period t, the government raises taxes to pay for its spending and the outstanding public debt.[2] Thus, the only decision left to the government is the choice of debt instruments between: (i) fixed-rate bonds denominated in domestic currency; (ii) bonds indexed to the price level; and (iii) bonds denominated in foreign currencies. For simplicity, all types of bonds have one-period maturity so that the entire debt is financed in period $t-1$.

Though not necessary for the result, it is assumed that investors are risk-neutral so as to ensure that expected real returns are equal across all types of bonds. However, realized returns on nominal and foreign currency bonds depend on the price level and the exchange rate in the next period. Denoting the nominal interest rate as i and the inflation rate as π, the realized gross return on nominal bonds is given by $(1+i)/(1+\pi)$. The real return on price-indexed bonds is instead equal to its expected return, $(1+r)$. Finally, the real return on foreign currency bonds depends on the foreign interest rate, i^*, the rate of nominal exchange depreciation, e, and the inflation rate. The realized return on foreign currency bonds is equal to $(1+i^*)(1+e)/(1+\pi)$.

Since all the debt is repaid in period t, the government faces the following constraint:

$$\tau_t Y_t = G_t + (1+r)(1-h-h^*)D_{t-1} + \frac{(1+i_t^*)(1+e_t)}{(1+\pi_t)}h^* D_{t-1} + \frac{(1+i_t)}{(1+\pi_t)}hD_{t-1}$$

where h and h^* are the shares of nominal and foreign currency bonds in total debt, respectively, τ is the tax rate, G is public spending, Y is output and D is the value (as of time $t-1$) of the outstanding debt and where all variables are in real terms. In what follows it is assumed that the Fisher equation, $(1+i_t) = (1+r)(1+E_{t-1}\pi_t)$, and the uncovered interest parity condition, $(1+i_t) = (1+i_t^*)(1+E_{t-1}e_t)$, hold, where E_{t-1} denotes expectations conditional on the information available at period $t-1$.

These standard assumptions and a linearization of the budget constraint lead to a simple characterization of the debt-management problem. The government

---

[1] While perfect tax-smoothing may not be optimal, it is taken here as a useful simplifying assumption.

[2] Here, and in what follows, it is assumed that the government is able to fully commit to its future policy actions, so as to rule out time-consistency problems.

chooses the shares of nominal debt, h, and foreign currency debt, h^*, so as to minimize

$$Min\ Loss = E_{t-1}\tau_t^2$$
$$s.t.\ \tau_t = g_t + [1 + r - \hat{y}_t - h(\pi_t - E_{t-1}\pi_t) + h^*(q_t - E_{t-1}q_t)]d_{t-1} \quad (5.1)$$

where $\hat{y}_t$ is the rate of output growth, g_t and d_{t-1} denote the ratios of public spending and debt to GDP and q_t is the rate of exchange depreciation in terms of domestic goods, i.e. $(1 + q_t) \equiv (1 + e_t)/(1 + \pi_t)$.

The optimal shares of nominal and foreign currency debt are given by

$$h Var(\pi_t)d_{t-1} = Cov(g_t\pi_t) - Cov(\hat{y}_t\pi_t)d_{t-1} + h^* Cov(\pi_t q_t)d_{t-1} \quad (5.2)$$
$$h^* Var(q_t)d_{t-1} = Cov(\hat{y}_t q_t)d_{t-1} - Cov(g_t q_t) + h Cov(\pi_t q_t)d_{t-1} \quad (5.3)$$

where variances and covariances are conditional on the information available at the end of period $t - 1$.

Equations (5.2) and (5.3) relate the optimal choice of nominal and foreign currency debt to the covariances of their returns with the variables entering the government budget: output, government spending and interest payments on the other debt instrument. Equation (5.2) shows that the optimal share of nominal bonds is increasing in the covariance of inflation with public spending and decreasing in the covariance of inflation and output. This is because real returns on nominal bonds are inversely related to unexpected inflation. A positive covariance of inflation with public spending implies low returns on nominal bonds when tax needs are relatively high, thus making this instrument attractive for tax-smoothing. On the other hand, if output is positively correlated with inflation the return on nominal bonds is unexpectedly high at times of insufficient tax collection so that the tax rate has to increase. This can be avoided by issuing price-indexed bonds. The attractiveness of nominal bonds is also reduced by a greater variance of their returns, i.e. by a greater variance of inflation.

Although the framework is very stylized, the analysis still allows for interesting conclusions for the choice of nominal versus price-indexed debt.[3] Nominal debt is a better hedging instrument than price-indexed debt if productivity and public spending shocks prevail. The reason is that bad supply and spending shocks, i.e. shocks worsening the government budget, also lead to lower returns on nominal debt by creating unexpected inflation. In effect, unless aggregate supply is very price elastic, spending shocks induce a positive correlation between surprise inflation and financing needs. Negative supply shocks reducing output and tax revenues also lead to unexpected inflation. Put simply,

---

[3] See Bohn (1990b), Missale (1994), Goldfajn (1995). The discussion assume that it is optimal not to issue any foreign currency debt, i.e. $h^* = 0$.

both types of shocks reduce the real value of nominal bonds when financing needs are unexpectedly high.

However, if monetary disturbances and/or real shocks to aggregate demand (other than spending shocks) are more important, it may even be optimal not to issue any nominal debt: the best insurance against such shocks is offered by price-indexed debt. This is because aggregate demand disturbances induce a positive correlation between output and inflation. In particular, a negative demand shock increases the real value of nominal bonds when this is less needed, i.e. when revenues are lower than expected. Price indexation is also optimal when variations in the price level are large and unrelated to tax revenues and spending, as for purely monetary disturbances. In this case changes in the real returns of nominal bonds only add to budgetary uncertainty.

Interestingly, there is an analogy between the conditions for the optimality of public-debt indexation and those for the optimality of price indexation of nominal wages, with the notable exception that not all real shocks make nominal debt a desirable hedging instrument. Specifically, real demand shocks, other than government spending shocks, lend support to price indexation, as they induce a positive correlation between innovations in output and inflation.

5.2.3 Nominal debt and the option to inflate

The hedging role of nominal debt not only follows from it being implicitly contingent on real shocks affecting the price level under passive monetary policy. A further argument for nominal debt is that it provides an inflation tax base; it allows the government to raise state-contingent inflation taxes.[4] Fischer (1983) points out that when policy rules cannot be specified under all possible circumstances, i.e. when future contingencies cannot be covered by debt contracts, it is optimal for the government to retain some discretion over future policy actions. To quote Fischer: "The best of all possible worlds, if governments acted optimally, may be one in which the governments had the option of imposing a capital levy (by inflating) in emergencies like wars."

The idea that nominal debt allows the use of both inflation and conventional taxes, in order to distribute the cost of the adjustment to public spending shocks, is made explicit in Calvo and Guidotti (1990a). They examine the government choice between explicitly contingent, nominal and price-indexed debt in a two-period economy, where second-period spending is uncertain. The government's objective is to minimize an expected loss quadratic in both conventional taxes and inflation, i.e. to smooth taxes and inflation across states of nature. Obviously, issuing explicitly contingent debt with returns negatively indexed to government spending is ideal because it supports complete tax-smoothing and zero inflation in every state of nature. In the absence of explicitly

---

[4] Actually, within the neoclassical model, discussed in Chapter 2, contingent inflation taxes on nominal debt are not unlike contingent tax rates on capital income or contingent debt payments.

contingent debt (and insofar as the government can commit to zero average inflation), issuing only nominal debt is optimal because the government can collect state-contingent revenues with unexpected inflation when spending is high and vice versa. However, the real return on nominal debt does not fully replicate the return on explicitly contingent debt; complete tax-smoothing does not occur because inflation-smoothing is also desirable.

Using nominal debt and discretionary monetary policy for tax-smoothing obviously raises the issue of the credibility of the anti-inflationary policy. The argument that nominal debt gives rise to inflationary temptation and thus leads to higher expected inflation will be examined in Chapter 6. Other arguments in favor of price indexation are discussed by Levhari and Liviatan (1976), Fischer (1983), Barro (1995), Campbell and Shiller (1996), and the papers in Bank of England (1996) and De-Cecco, Pecchi and Piga (1997).

5.2.4 *Domestic versus foreign currency debt*

The decision to borrow in domestic versus foreign currency is tradition-ally important; in OECD countries the use of bonds and loans denominated in foreign currencies has been substantial unlike that of price-index-linked bonds whose introduction is very recent. While foreign currency financing has been reduced since the mid-1980s, in a number of countries with small open economies the share of such debt remains high (see Chapter 4).

The choice of the currency of denomination finds various explanations which are discussed in Bohn (1990*b*, 1991), de Fontaney, Milesi-Ferretti and Pill (1995), Carracedo and Dattels (1997), Watanabe (1992), among others. The choice of borrowing in foreign currency clearly interacts with the management of foreign-exchange reserves and in a number of countries is limited to that function, i.e. foreign curency debt is not used as a financing instrument. As a matter of fact, policymakers tend to avoid excessive borrowing in foreign currencies. This behavior can be fully justified from the perspective of risk minimization, insofar as foreign currency debt exposes the government bud-get to unexpected variations in the real exchange rate (in foreign inflation if "purchasing power parity" holds).

Indeed, foreign currency bonds become less attractive as the variance of their returns increases. Equation (5.3) shows that the optimal share of foreign currency bonds, h^*, decreases in the variance of the real exchange rate, $q = e - \pi$, i.e. in the variance of their real returns:

$$h^* Var(q_t)d_{t-1} = Cov(\hat{y}_t q_t)d_{t-1} - Cov(g_t q_t) + hCov(\pi_t q_t)d_{t-1}$$

Unexpected changes in the real exchange rate, if unrelated to other components of the budget, add to tax-rate variability and make it optimal to issue nominal or price-indexed bonds.

The choice of foreign currency debt also depends on the covariance of its returns with output and public spending. If unanticipated public spending leads to a depreciation of the exchange rate, the case against borrowing in foreign currency is reinforced. On the other hand, a positive covariance between output and the exchange rate suggests a tax-smoothing role for such debt, since it can be used to hedge against the risk of revenue shortfalls. This may be the case if international supply shocks, for example, oil shocks leave nominal exchange rates unaffected but induce internationally correlated inflation surprises.

The example is taken from Bohn (1990b), who considers the choice between foreign currency, nominal and price-indexed debt, in a small open economy where "purchasing power parity (PPP)" holds, so that the return on foreign bonds is equal to the negative of foreign inflation, i.e. $q = e - \pi = -\pi^*$.[5] In both the domestic and the foreign economy output is exogenous and stochastic, while aggregate demand is derived from a (standard) output-elastic money demand with velocity shocks. The government objective is to smooth tax-rate variability arising from domestic output fluctuations and monetary shocks. Within this framework, if output and hence inflation surprises are internationally correlated, foreign currency debt plays the same role as nominal debt in hedging against domestic output fluctuations. Foreign debt has the advantage over nominal debt of insulating the government budget from monetary shocks which are specific to the domestic economy. However, foreign debt increases the exposure to foreign monetary disturbances. This dependence on velocity and monetary policy shocks originating from the foreign economy casts doubts on the opportunity of borrowing in foreign currencies.

The relation between the optimal shares of nominal and foreign currency debt should also be considered. This relation is shown in Equations (5.2) and (5.3) and has been derived by Goldfajn (1995). A larger share of nominal debt is associated with a larger or smaller share of foreign currency debt depending on whether the covariance between inflation and the real exchange rate is positive or negative. Loosely speaking, if this covariance is positive, nominal and foreign currency bonds are complements in the government portfolio since their returns covary negatively.

If nominal debt can be hedged by foreign currency debt, the optimal share of nominal bonds increases with the share of foreign currency bonds and vice versa. On the contrary, when the covariance between inflation and the real exchange is negative, nominal and foreign currency bonds are close substitutes; their returns covary positively.[6] With similar risk-return characteristics and thus similar covariances with output and public spending, the choice is between

---

[5] Actually, Bohn considers the problem of a government buying insurance from abroad to insure its residents against output risk, but to recast the model in terms of tax-smoothing is straightforward.

[6] Incidentally, if the government's temptation for inflation were an issue, foreign currency debt would have an advantage as a commitment device over nominal debt and could be preferred to price-indexed debt for tax-smoothing purposes, as first shown by Bohn (1990b).

one of them and price-indexed debt.[7] If nominal debt is not useful, neither is foreign currency debt, and the government should issue only indexed bonds.[8] On the other hand, if both nominal and foreign currency debt are useful hedging instruments, the choice is mainly determined by the relative variance of their returns. To the extent that the variance of the real exchange rate is greater than the variance of inflation, foreign currency bonds are riskier than nominal bonds and should not be issued.

5.3 The implicit-contingent approach: the evidence

The implicit-contingent approach holds that debt management in conventional securities can limit costly tax adjustments in response to shocks affecting the government budget. In the absence of explicitly contingent securities, conventional instruments can be combined so as to make the real return on debt conditional on future events. While the implicit-contingent approach has been formally derived from optimal taxation principles, its policy indications are also justified by the objectives of relaxing borrowing constraints and enhancing flexibility in fiscal policy. Since the optimal debt composition depends on the type of shocks affecting the economy, finding its precise characterization can only be accomplished by empirical investigation.

In this section the relations between the variables entering the government budget, such as output and public spending, and the return on alternative debt instruments are examined for a number of OECD countries in order to estimate the debt composition which provides for each country the optimal hedge against budgetary uncertainty. The empirical analysis is based on a VAR approach to the estimation of the innovations, i.e. the unexpected components, of inflation, the real exchange rate, permanent output and permanent public spending. This approach allows the estimation of the insurance provided or the additional risk introduced into the budget by conventional debt instruments: nominal bonds, foreign currency bonds and price-indexed bonds.

Bohn (1990a), Goldfajn (1995), de Fontenay, Milesi-Ferretti and Pill (1995), Missale (1997a) and Hawkesby and Wright (1997) are the few empirical studies estimating the debt composition which minimize tax-risk. The alternative objective of minimizing deficit risk is considered by Dale, Mongiardino and Quah (1997). The tax-smoothing model with risky securities, developed by Bohn (1990a), provides the common analytical framework of the former studies. The analysis in this section also relies on Bohn's model.

---

[7] It is worth noting that such a negative covariance between inflation and real exchange rate is more likely to arise in a fixed-exchange-rate regime. As the exchange rate is fixed, foreign currency debt (or nominal debt) becomes redundant as an instrument for tax-smoothing.

[8] This assumes that lending in nominal or foreign bonds is not allowed, i.e. that h and h^* are non-negative.

5.3.1   *Minimizing risk with nominal, foreign currency and price-indexed debt*

Consider the choice of taxes and debt instruments by a government which maximizes social welfare, that is, the lifetime consumption of an infinitely lived representative individual:

$$Max \sum_{i=0}^{\infty} \beta^i E_t C_{t+i} \tag{5.4}$$

where C is consumption and β is the discount factor assumed equal to the reciprocal of the (constant) expected return: $\beta(1+r) = 1$.

Every period, the government chooses the tax rate and the shares of nominal debt, h, foreign currency debt, h^*, and price-indexed debt, $1-h-h^*$. Assume for the moment that all types of bonds have one-period maturity. Then, the unexpected component of the return on nominal debt depends on unexpected inflation, while the unexpected component of the return on foreign currency debt depends on the difference between the real exchange rate and its value as expected one period earlier.[9] These assumptions allow linearization of the government budget constraint as follows

$$D_t = G_t - \tau_t Y_t + (1+r)[1 - h\hat{\pi}_t + h^*\hat{q}_t]D_{t-1}$$

where, for the ease of notation, $\hat{\pi}$ and $\hat{q}$ denote the innovations in inflation and in the real exchange rate, i.e. $\hat{\pi}_t = (\pi_t - E_{t-1}\pi_t)$ and $\hat{q}_t = (q_t - E_{t-1}q_t)$. Taxes are distortionary so that the consumer, in addition to paying taxes, loses an amount proportional to output. Assuming that this deadweight loss is quadratic in the tax rate, the consumer budget constraint is given by

$$D_t = Y_t(1 - \tau_t - \tau_t^2) - C_t + (1+r)[1 - h\hat{\pi}_t + h^*\hat{q}_t]D_{t-1}$$

Substituting the government budget constraint into the consumer constraint, the government's problem reduces to the following minimization of tax distortions:

$$Min \ Loss = \sum_{i=0}^{\infty} \beta^i E_t[Y_{t+i}\tau_{t+i}^2]$$

$$s.t. \ D_t = G_t - \tau_t Y_t + (1+r)[1 - h\hat{\pi}_t + h^*\hat{q}_t]D_{t-1} \tag{5.5}$$

The government chooses the mix of nominal, foreign currency and indexed debt in order to smooth tax rates over time and across states of nature.

[9] It is also assumed that the government has no control over inflation so as to rule out time-consistency problems.

The timing of decisions is as follows. At the end of each period the government decides on the debt composition (to be carried to the next period) by choosing the shares h and h^* of nominal and foreign currency debt. At the beginning of the next period, inflation and the real exchange rate are observed and so are the returns on all types of bonds. Finally, the government sets the tax rate.

From the first-order conditions the following solution is derived.

$$E_t \tau_{t+1} - \tau_t = 0 \tag{5.6}$$

$$Cov_t(\tau_{t+1} \pi_{t+1}) = 0 \tag{5.7}$$

$$Cov_t(\tau_{t+1} q_{t+1}) = 0 \tag{5.8}$$

Equation (5.6) is the standard condition for tax-smoothing over time. Conditions (5.7) and (5.8) show that nominal and foreign currency debt must be chosen so as to make the conditional covariance between their returns and the tax rate equal to zero. In other words, debt returns should bear no relation to the unexpected component of the tax rate. For example, a positive covariance between the tax rate and inflation, pointing to a "too high" tax rate in states where the return on nominal debt is lower than expected, would make it optimal to issue more nominal debt in order to reduce the financing needs and, hence, the tax rate in those states. The government could improve tax-smoothing by selling nominal debt in exchange for an asset with a positive tax-return covariance. In a more complete setting with bonds of different maturities and other financial instruments the condition of zero-conditional covariance between the tax rate and debt returns should be satisfied with all the available assets. If this were not the case, the government could improve tax-smoothing by buying and selling financial instruments to the point where their returns offset the impact of output and spending shocks on tax rates.

The hypothesis of no-correlation for the US economy in the period 1954–87 is tested by Bohn (1990a), using innovations in asset returns and tax rates (revenues/GNP), as estimated by the residuals of vector autoregressions (VAR). The hypothesis is strongly rejected with all types of securities considered. However, the relevant problem for policy is to identify the debt instruments which should be issued in order to improve the extent of hedging provided by actual debt compositions. A solution to this problem is in the optimal shares, h and h^*, of nominal and foreign currency debt, which can be derived by integrating the government budget forward and imposing conditions (5.6)–(5.8).

For empirical estimation purposes it is useful to work with log-linear approximations of the budget constraint and the first-order conditions. Unlike in Bohn (1990a) and Goldfajn (1995) where linear approximations are used, the present method allows for VAR estimates in log-levels, which avoid dimensional problems and overdifferencing. The log-linearization of the dynamic budget constraint (5.5), taken in Appendix 5.1, yields

$$\rho d_t = \eta g_t - (1 - \rho + \eta)(\log \tau_t + y_t) + (r - h\hat{\pi}_t + h^*\hat{q}_t) + d_{t-1} - (1 - \rho)k \tag{5.9}$$

where lower-case letters denote logarithms. The parameter ρ is a discount factor, i.e. $\rho = exp(n - r)$ with $n < r$, where n is the growth rate of real debt, that is equal to GDP growth when tax-smoothing is operational (see Barro 1979, 1986).[10] The parameter $\eta = (\bar{G}/D)exp(-r)$ is the (discounted) ratio of government spending to public debt around which the linearization is taken, while k is an unimportant constant.[11]

Taking expectations of Equation (5.9) conditional on the information available at time t, gives a rational expectations model that can be solved forward to obtain the following intertemporal budget constraint

$$d_{t-1} = \mu + h\hat{\pi}_t - h^*\hat{q}_t + (1 - \rho + \eta) \sum_{i=0}^{\infty} \rho^i E_t(\log \tau_{t+i} + y_{t+i})$$

$$-\eta \sum_{i=0}^{\infty} \rho^i E_t g_{t+i} \tag{5.10}$$

where $\mu \equiv k - r/(1 - \rho)$ and the fact that $E_t(r - h\hat{\pi}_{t+i} + h^*\hat{q}_{t+i}) = r$ for any $i > 0$ has been used.

Substituting the log-linear approximation $E_t \log \tau_{t+i} \simeq \log \tau_t$ of the first-order conditions (5.6) into Equation (5.10) and rearranging terms yields

$$\gamma \log \tau_t = d_{t-1} - \mu - h\hat{\pi}_t + h^*\hat{q}_t - (1 - \rho + \eta) \sum_{i=0}^{\infty} \rho^i E_t y_{t+i}$$

$$+\eta \sum_{i=0}^{\infty} \rho^i E_t g_{t+i} \tag{5.11}$$

where $\gamma = (1 - \rho + \eta)/(1 - \rho) > 1$.

Implications for debt management follow from conditions (5.7) and (5.8), after substituting the linear approximation $\log \tau_t \simeq \log E_{t-1}\tau_t + (\tau_t - E_{t-1}\tau_t)/E_{t-1}\tau_t$ for $\log \tau_t$ in Equation (5.11). Multiplying all terms of Equation (5.11) by $\hat{\pi}_t$ and $\hat{q}_t$ in turn, and taking expectations conditional on the information at time $t - 1$, the following relations between the optimal shares

---

[10] Note that ρ is a number a little less than 1, as r must be greater than n to rule out Ponzi games. In the empirical analysis ρ is taken to be equal to 0.98.

[11] In the empirical analysis $\bar{G}/D$ is taken to be equal to the average of the ratio of net-of-interest spending to public debt over the estimation period.

of nominal and foreign currency debt are derived

$$h\,Var_{t-1}(\pi_t) = h^* Cov_{t-1}(\pi_t q_t) - \gamma\,Cov_{t-1}(\pi_t Y_t^p)$$
$$+(\gamma - 1)\,Cov_{t-1}(\pi_t G_t^p) \tag{5.12}$$

$$h^*\,Var_{t-1}(q_t) = h Cov_{t-1}(\pi_t q_t) + \gamma\,Cov_{t-1}(q_t Y_t^p)$$
$$-(\gamma - 1)\,Cov_{t-1}(q_t G_t^p) \tag{5.13}$$

where $Y_t^p \equiv (1 - \rho) \sum_{i=0}^{\infty} \rho^i E_t y_{t+i}$ and $G_t^p \equiv (1 - \rho) \sum_{i=0}^{\infty} \rho^i E_t g_{t+i}$ define permanent (or normal) output and permanent public spending, respectively.

These conditions are the infinite horizon counterpart of conditions (5.2) and (5.3) derived in Section 5.2.2 for the one-period problem. The difference worth noting is that the relevant innovations affecting the government budget are now those of permanent output and permanent public spending. Since the government adjusts the tax rate with the objective of maintaining it constant for all future periods, the relevant tax base is permanent output, i.e. the constant flow from the present value of output.

The optimal shares of nominal, foreign currency and indexed debt are obtained by solving equations (5.12) and (5.13) for h and h^*.

$$h = Var_{t-1}(q_t)\Omega^{-1}[(\gamma - 1)\,Cov_{t-1}(\pi_t G_t^p) - \gamma\,Cov_{t-1}(\pi_t Y_t^p)]$$
$$+ Cov_{t-1}(\pi_t q_t)\Omega^{-1}[\gamma\,Cov_{t-1}(q_t Y_t^p)$$
$$-(\gamma - 1)\,Cov_{t-1}(q_t G_t^p)] \tag{5.14}$$

$$h^* = Var_{t-1}(\pi_t)\Omega^{-1}[\gamma\,Cov_{t-1}(q_t Y_t^p) - (\gamma - 1)\,Cov_{t-1}(q_t G_t^p)]$$
$$+ Cov_{t-1}(\pi_t q_t)\Omega^{-1}[(\gamma - 1)\,Cov_{t-1}(\pi_t G_t^p)$$
$$-\gamma\,Cov_{t-1}(\pi_t Y_t^p)] \tag{5.15}$$

where $\Omega = Var_{t-1}(\pi_t)\,Var_{t-1}(q_t) - [Cov_{t-1}(\pi_t q_t)]^2 > 0$ is the determinant of the variance–covariance matrix of returns on nominal and foreign currency bonds.

The debt composition which provides the optimal hedge against macroeconomic shocks to the budget can thus be derived from the conditional covariances of permanent output and public spending with inflation and the real exchange rate and from the conditional variances of the latter variables.

5.3.2 Budgetary insurance with debt denomination and indexation: evidence from OECD countries

The composition of public debt which minimizes tax distortions depends on the conditional covariances between permanent output and public spending, inflation, the real exchange rate and the variances of the latter two variables. In this section evidence is provided on the opportunity to issue nominal, foreign currency or price-indexed bonds in the following OECD countries: Australia, Austria, Belgium, Canada, Denmark, Finland, France, Germany, Ireland, Italy, Japan, the Netherlands, Spain, Sweden, UK and US.

The analysis is based on a VAR approach to the estimation of the conditional covariances of inflation, the real exchange rate, permanent output and permanent public spending. Data are quarterly for a sample period running from the first quarter of 1970 to the fourth quarter of 1995. The VAR includes a constant, three seasonal dummies and four lags of the log-level of the following variables: (i) the seasonally adjusted real GDP; (ii) the seasonally adjusted real government consumption; (iii) the consumer price index (CPI); (iv) the real exchange rate computed as the ratio between the nominal effective exchange rate and the CPI; (v) the interest rate on 3-month Treasury bills or the 3-month interbank rate; (vi) the yield on long-term government bonds; and (vii) the M2 money supply.[12]

The conditional covariance between any two variables Y and X, i.e. $E_{t-1}[(Y_t - E_{t-1}Y_t)(X_t - E_{t-1}X_t)]$, is derived from the series of innovations, or unexpected components, $Y_t - E_{t-1}Y_t$, which are estimated as follows. A first VAR is run on the first 16 years of the sample and the vector of last residuals is taken as the estimated innovations for the first quarter of 1987. Then, a new VAR is estimated for each quarter on an updated sample which includes only the last 16 years of observations, that is, which includes the latest observation and excludes the earliest one. Each estimate in the series of innovations is thus based on 64 quarterly observations. The use of a constant window makes the estimated innovations comparable. Residuals from VARs are the empirical counterpart of the relevant economic concept of innovation. They can be thought of as unexpected components where expectations are taken relative to the restricted information set available to the econometrician, empirically, the variables included in the VAR.

The VAR residuals are also used to estimate innovations in permanent output and public spending following the procedure in Campbell and Shiller (1987) that uses the companion matrix of the VAR estimated coefficients. A more detailed description of this technique is given in Appendix 5.2.[13] Estimated innovations of permanent output and spending are also obtained by running a new VAR for each quarter. The discount factor, ρ, used to evaluate the present value of permanent output in Equation [5.11] is taken to be equal to 0.98.

In a second stage, the series of estimated innovations (residuals) are used to derive the conditional covariances which are relevant for the choice of the

[12] See the Data Appendix for detailed information on data and their sources.

[13] Alternatively, the impulse response coefficients can be used to estimate innovations in permanent output and public spending, as in Goldfajn (1995).

bonds to issue. Estimated covariances are the empirical equivalent of $E_{t-1}[(X_t - E_{t-1}X_t)(X_t - E_{t-1}X_t)]$.

Finally, the optimal shares of nominal debt, h, and foreign currency debt, h^*, are computed according to Equations (14) and (15). For this purpose $\eta = (\bar{G}/D)exp(-r)$ is taken to be equal to the 1987–95 period average of the ratio of total government outlays net of interest payments to public debt.

The shares of nominal debt and foreign currrency debt which would provide the optimal hedge against the uncertainty of government revenues and spending are shown in Table 5.1. Columns 1 and 2 report the estimates obtained when no constraint is imposed on the government portfolio, in particular when the government is allowed to hold claims on the private sector in a particular asset which are financed (and hedged) by more debt of a different type. Since these portfolios may be unfeasible or there may exist practical constraints to their implementation, it is useful to consider the shares of nominal and foreign currency debt which would be optimal if the other type of debt were not being issued. Columns 4 and 5 report for each type of debt its optimal share when the other type is in zero net supply. Constrained estimates are also interesting since they abstract from possible portfolio complementarities and substitutabilities arising from asset return correlations and point out the hedging properties of each type of instrument against changes in government revenues and spending.

Table 5.1. Debt composition providing the optimal hedge: shares of nominal debt and foreign currency debt

	Unconstrained		$V(q)/V(\pi)$	Only nominal	Only foreign
	Nominal	Foreign			
Australia	−5.11	−0.77	74.3	−3.47	−0.63
Austria	0.37	−1.84	2.6	−0.15	−1.80
Belgium	1.55	0.60	9.9	2.20	0.77
Canada	−0.77	0.11	12.2	−0.69	0.06
Denmark	2.14	−0.06	4.2	2.13	0.01
Finland	−3.30	0.34	16.6	−2.84	0.08
France	−7.71	1.07	10.8	−5.91	−0.13
Germany	4.07	3.12	14.6	4.89	3.19
Ireland	1.19	−1.10	2.9	0.47	−0.84
Italy	0.26	−0.02	38.3	0.26	−0.02
Japan	2.62	−0.02	73.5	2.59	0.03
Netherlands	−1.58	0.00	8.0	−1.58	−0.23
Spain	0.30	0.07	6.8	0.31	0.07
Sweden	1.00	0.59	8.8	0.76	0.55
UK	4.16	−0.98	43.8	2.62	−0.83
USA	−0.23	0.01	82.5	−0.23	0.01

A variety of patterns emerges across OECD economies regarding the optimal composition between nominal and price-indexed debt. The nominal debt providing insurance against budgetary uncertainty varies from about four times the level of debt in Germany to the large negative numbers of Australia and France. In the latter countries it would even be optimal for risk minimization to issue price-index bonds in amounts far exceeding the total debt (5.1 and 7.7 times respectively) and use the proceeds to lend in nominal bonds. These numbers are not uncommon in the empirical literature (see Bohn 1990*a*). In part, they reflect a degree of approximation in the linearization of the government budget constraint, but they also reflect the small variance of inflation relative to the variance of output. Since over a 3-month horizon inflation is easy to predict, the (positive or negative) stock of nominal debt must be very large to provide a significant hedge against output fluctuations and spending shocks.

From a preliminary inspection of Table 5.1 (see columns 1 and 4) the group of countries where nominal debt is a useful hedging instrument is large, thus confirming Bohn's (1988, 1990*a*) intuition and findings. Indeed, only in 6 out of the 16 countries considered nominal debt should not have been issued: Australia, Canada, Finland, France, the Netherlands and the US. In Austria the scope for nominal debt is limited to hedging against the return risk of foreign assets; when foreign currencies loans are ruled out, the share of nominal debt turns negative (see column 4). Evidence for the US is comforting from the viewpoint of policymaking, given the recent introduction of price-index-linked bonds, but is somewhat surprising since it appears to contradict the empirical findings of Bohn (1990*a*).

Bohn finds that non-indexation in the US is consistent with tax-smoothing: nominal bonds should be issued in amounts far exceeding the total debt, with the proceeds invested in price-indexed bonds. In his study, issuing nominal debt is optimal because of the negative correlation between unexpected inflation and innovations in the present value of output. A possible explanation for the difference between the present and Bohn's result is the different sample period. While the sample considered by Bohn ends in 1987, the present study uses the series of innovations for the period 1987–95. It is quite possible that during the most recent period the US economy experienced different types of shocks relative to the earlier period. For example, demand shocks could have prevailed over supply shocks. However, a closer examination reveals that the covariance between inflation and permanent output has remained negative, thus suggesting an unchanged hedging role for nominal debt against output fluctuations. Evidence in favor of price indexation comes instead from a strong negative covariance between permanent spending and inflation, which was not significant in Bohn (1990*a*).

The possibility that the type of shocks hitting OECD economies may have changed over time suggests estimating debt compositions for different periods.

This has been accomplished by dividing the horizon of the estimation in two subperiods: the period before and the period after 1991. For reason of space, results for subperiods are reported only when different from those obtained over the whole sample.

Focusing on the denomination of public debt, strong evidence is found against foreign currency debt: for most countries the optimal share of such debt is either negative or very small. Only six countries, Belgium, Canada, Finland, France, Germany and Sweden exhibit a share greater than 10%. However, in Finland and France the benefits from issuing foreign debt clearly depends on the assumption that lending in nominal debt is feasible. As this unrealistic assumption is abandoned, and a non-negativity constraint on the nominal debt is imposed, the relevant figure is the one reported in the last column of Table 5.1; it is 8% for Finland and even negative for France. In Canada the optimal share of foreign debt is also very small, around 11%.

Thus, the attitude of debt managers against borrowing in foreign currencies is strongly supported by this evidence. The poor performance of foreign currency debt as an hedging instrument is largely explained by the very high variance of the real exchange rate relative to the inflation rate (see the middle column of Table 5.1). However, even in countries where movements in the real exchange rate have been predictable, such as Austria, Denmark and Ireland, there has been no gain from issuing foreign currency debt.

This evidence is summarized by Table 5.2 which restricts the attention to countries where the optimal share of foreign currency debt is positive, either for all the period considered or for one of the two subperiods, and where France has been excluded for the reason discussed before.

Interestingly, the largest share of foreign debt is found for Germany, where it is three times as large as the whole debt. This finding is in sharp contrast with the actual composition of the German debt which show a negligible amount of foreign currency debt over the last two decades. However, foreign debt is

Table 5.2. Positive foreign currency debt

	Unconstrained		Only foreign	$V(q)/V(\pi)$	Actual
	Foreign	Nominal			
Belgium	0.60	1.55		9.9	0.11
Canada (1991–5)	0.33	−0.77	0.23	8.3	0.04
Denmark (1987–90)	1.05	1.91		2.5	0.16
Finland (1991–5)	0.80	−3.86	0.62	20.3	0.46
Germany	3.12	4.07		14.6	0.00
Spain	0.07	0.30		6.8	0.09
Sweden	0.59	1.00		8.8	0.28

outperformed as an hedging instrument by nominal debt. Column 3 shows that in Germany the optimal share of nominal debt is four times the outstanding debt. Reliance on foreign borrowing has also been very limited in Canada and Spain, but evidence for these countries suggests an optimal share around 10%, thus much lower than in Germany.

In Belgium and Sweden, and during subperiods in Denmark and Finland, a share of foreign currency debt larger than 50% seems to be optimal. However, as for Germany this result must be qualified; as indicated in column 3, in the first three countries the share of nominal debt should be twice as large as that of foreign currency debt. Interestingly, with the notable exceptions of Austria and Ireland, the group includes those countries which have been more indebted in foreign currencies. (Recall that optimal debt composition has not been estimated for Greece and Portugal.) This finding reinforces evidence in de Fontenay, Milesi-Ferretti and Pill (1995) of an hedging role for foreign currency debt in countries where its share is substantial.

Focusing on price-indexation, Table 5.3 presents countries where price-index-linked bonds are, to a first approximation, the only useful instruments to isolate the government budget from spending and output shocks. Countries where the same implication holds in only one of the two subperiods have also been reported in the bottom half of the table.

In three countries, Australia, the Netherlands and the US there is clearly no role for either nominal or foreign currency debt. In the other three, Canada Finland and France, the scope for foreign currency debt is conditional on the possibility of lending in nominal debt. As shown in column 4, when nominal

Table 5.3. Price-indexed debt

	Unconstrained		Constrained		Actual indexed
	Nominal	Foreign	Nominal	Foreign	
Australia	−5.11	−0.77	−3.47	−0.63	0.03
Austria	0.37	−1.84	−0.15		—
Canada	−0.77	0.11		0.06	0.01
Finland	−3.30	0.34		0.08	—
France	−7.71	1.07		−0.13	—
Netherlands	−1.58	0.00		−0.23	—
USA	−0.23	0.01		0.01	0.01
Positive indexed debt in subperiods					
Japan (1991–5)	−1.14	0.10		0.07	—
UK (1991–5)	−1.18	0.15		0.05	0.14

debt is constrained to be non-negative, the share of foreign currency debt falls below 10% or even becomes negative as in the case of France. On the other hand, Austria exhibits a positive share of nominal debt which turns negative if lending in foreign currency is not allowed, as shown in column 3.

When subperiods are considered it appears that two more countries, Japan and the UK, could have benefited from a large share of debt indexed to the price level. Actually, the UK in the period 1991–5 was in such a privileged situation with almost 17% of its marketable debt in price-index-linked bonds introduced in 1981. Finally, it is worth noting that for the US evidence in favor of price indexation mainly comes from the period 1987–90; a more balanced debt composition, with 20% nominal and 80% indexed, appears to perform best in the most recent period (see Table 5.5). The opposite is found for France, where price-indexed debt would have been the ideal instrument, especially since 1991. Indeed, a closer look at the French data shows that evidence against nominal debt comes from unexpected deflation coupled with lower than expected permanent output following the EMS crisis.

It is interesting that, with the exception of Sweden, all the countries where price-index-linked bonds are being issued, Australia, Canada, the UK and the US are represented in Table 5.3. Their actual share of price-indexed debt in 1995 is reported in column 5. Therefore, though admittedly informal, this evidence seems to confirm the result of Goldfajn (1995), that actual debt management is consistent with optimal taxation principles as implied by the implicit-contingent approach.

The upper part of Table 5.4 shows the optimal shares of nominal debt for the countries where such shares have been positive in both subperiods considered. In Belgium, Denmark, Germany, Ireland and Sweden the optimal share of nominal debt is equal to or greater than 100%. As shown in column 2, imposing a non-negative constraint on the share of foreign currecy debt only affects the result for Ireland where the optimal share of nominal debt falls to 50%. Nominal debt also provides insurance against permanent output shocks in Italy and Spain, though the estimated optimal shares are lower, around 30%. Thus, nominal debt appears particularly useful as a hedging instrument in highly indebted counties. Spain has a lower debt ratio but it experienced severe fiscal imbalances until the mid-1990s.

While in highly indebted countries nominal debt has consistently provided insurance against shocks to the budget, for the countries shown in the bottom half of Table 5.4 nominal debt has played such a role only over some periods. Austria, France, Japan, the UK and to a lesser extent the US exhibit remarkable changes in their optimal debt compositions between the two periods considered. Time varying debt compositions are emphasized in Table 5.5. This fact is likely to reflect a change in the types of shocks which prevailed in the two periods. This alternation of shocks is worrysome from the viewpoint

Table 5.4. Positive nominal debt

	Unconstrained		Only nominal	$V(q)/V(\pi)$	Actual nominal
	Nominal	Foreign			
Belgium	1.55	0.60		9.9	0.89
Denmark	2.13	−0.06	2.13	4.2	0.84
Germany	4.07	3.12		14.6	1.00
Ireland	1.19	−1.10	0.47	2.9	0.65
Italy	0.26	−0.02	0.26	38.3	0.93
Spain	0.30	0.07		6.8	0.91
Sweden	1.00	0.59		8.8	0.71
Positive nominal debt in subperiods					
Austria (1991–5)	4.05	−3.47	2.03	4.9	0.78
France (1987–90)	1.36	0.01		12.9	0.96
Japan (1987–90)	5.90	−0.04	5.91	37.6	1.00
UK (1987–90)	7.13	−1.36	6.23	59.0	0.81
USA (1991–5)	0.17	0.01		88.8	1.00

Table 5.5. Changes in debt compositions

	1987–90		1991–5	
	Only nominal	Only foreign	Only nominal	Only foreign
Austria	−1.08	−0.23	2.03	−2.99
France	1.38	0.27	−13.5	−0.74
Japan	5.91	−0.10	−0.85	0.07
UK	6.23	−1.28	−0.82	0.05
USA	−0.77	0.00	0.18	0.02

of policymaking; it suggests that exploiting covariances between debt returns and financing needs could be quite difficult.

Empirical research on debt management is still at an early stage. Preliminary results do suggest, however, that conventional securities can act as implicitly contingent debt and that a proper, though difficult, choice between them can help to avoid unnecessary changes in tax rates and minimize budgetary risk. If anything, there seems to be some relation between the actual composition of public debts in OECD countries and the debt compositions which would allow for hedging optimally against macroeconomic risk. This has even led Bohn (1990*a*) and Goldfajn (1995) to argue that the implicit-contingent hypothesis shows promise as a positive theory of debt management. The view that governments may use debt to limit unnecessary variations in tax rates is also supported by some of the present results, for example, by the fact that price-indexed bonds have been issued only in countries where there is no hedging role for nominal debt and by the fact that foreign currency debt appears to be useful only in the countries where its share is large.

However, differences between estimation and reality should not be overlooked. For example, Ireland which relied on foreign currency debt more than any other country in the past, should even lend in foreign currencies to implement optimal contingencies in debt returns. More importantly, the use of price-indexed debt is still very limited compared with what the evidence suggests would be optimal. However, price indexation and the currency of denomination of public debt do not exhaust the characteristics which determine contingencies in debt return: the maturity of public debt, in addition to its denomination and indexation can be designed to hedge against budgetary uncertainty.

For instance, Bohn finds some evidence in favor of a longer maturity structure of the nominal debt for the US: the conditional covariance between the present value of output and the holding-period return differential between long-term bonds and Treasury bills is positive, thus suggesting an additional hedging role for long-term nominal bonds. Before providing evidence on the relation between the return on long-term debt and the other variables entering the government budget, the next section discusses theory, focusing on refinancing risk: the main argument for long-term debt.

5.4 Refinancing risk: the role of debt maturity[14]

The maturity of conventional securities, in addition to their denomination, can partly compensate for the absence of explicitly contingent debt. As the holding-period returns on fixed-rate conventional bonds are conditional on the realization of the yields of the corresponding maturities, contingencies in debt returns can be implemented by choosing the maturity structure of the nominal debt. If macroeconomic shocks to the budget are associated with changes in the yield curve, the maturity structure can play an important hedging role and limit tax adjustments.

For expository purposes it is useful to distinguish between unexpected changes in yields to maturity (or interest rates) due to innovations in real

---

[14] This and Section 5.4.1 draw from: A. Missale, "Managing the public debt: the optimal taxation approach," published on *Journal of Economic Surveys*, 11(3), 1997.

interest rates and changes due to revisions in expected inflation. If innovations are in real interest rates, the important complication to consider is that such innovations also affect the present value of future taxes and government spending.

In a real economy the impact of unexpected changes in real interest rates on the intertemporal budget constraint depends on how the maturity structure of planned primary surpluses relates to the maturity structure of debt commitments (principals plus interests: debt for short in what follows). Unless there is a perfect matching between surpluses and maturing debt in each period, innovations in interest rates will affect the present value of surpluses and the value of debt differently. A serially uncorrelated increase in the current rate worsens the intertemporal budget if new debt is being issued, that is, if currently maturing debt exceeds the current surplus. A persistent increase in interest rates, e.g. a parallel shift in the real yield curve, adversely affects the intertemporal budget whenever the duration of the debt is shorter than that of planned surpluses. The shorter the duration of the debt, the stronger the impact. In either case tax rates must rise (in current or future periods) to satisfy the intertemporal budget constraint.

An important consideration in dealing with innovations in real rates is that the maturity structure of the debt is typically shorter than that of future surpluses. This implies that, in the absence of other shocks to the budget, unexpected rises in real interest rates must be accommodated by tax levies and vice versa. Indeed, the simplest case for long-maturity debt is made by innovations in real interest rates which are uncorrelated with other variables. Tax-smoothing suggests isolating the government budget from independent random variation in interest rates, matching surpluses to debt repayments so as to avoid having to sell new bonds (or buy back old ones) in each future period. The idea that long maturities avoid the government's exposure to the so-called "roll-over" risk is formalized by Barro (1995) in an economy where output is produced with a simple (AK) technology linear in capital and where proportional consumption taxes distort saving decisions. Since independent shocks to real interest rates on government bonds are assumed not to affect the desired consumption plan (consumption is, however, affected by the return on capital), perfect smoothing of tax rates is optimal and calls for setting the amount of debt, to be renewed in each future period, equal to zero. When consumption and public spending grow at the same rate, this can be accomplished by issuing price-indexed consols with coupons growing at this rate.

In general, however, macroeconomic shocks affecting the real interest rate also affect government revenues and spending. In this case, whether lengthening the maturity structure is desirable or not depends on the stochastic relations between the real interest rate and other variables entering the government budget. For instance, in Barro's model, consumption and therefore tax revenues are affected by serially correlated shocks to productivity.[15] As shown by Barro, when consumption is random, (long-term) debt positively indexed to consumption (or output) would allow for complete tax-smoothing. However, as suggested by Gale's model reviewed in Section 3.2, a "short" maturity structure relative to future surpluses provides an alternative solution to explicit indexation. Choosing a relatively short maturity is equivalent to indexing the public debt to interest rates. To the extent that productivity shocks are persistent, bad shocks lead to the expectation of a low return on capital in the next period and thus to a fall in the real interest rate. Since borrowing costs decrease at times of low output and consumption, a short debt maturity can also support acyclical tax rates.

The same argument for short-maturity debt holds when labor income taxation is considered, to the extent that serially correlated productivity shocks induce a positive relation between innovations in output and real interest rates. A long maturity structure is optimal instead if macroeconomic shocks induce a positive correlation between innovations in real interest rates and government financing needs. An example is provided by shocks to public spending, as they lead to an upward shift in the real yield curve.

A different picture emerges when innovations in interest rates reflect changes in expected inflation. Taxes and government spending are naturally indexed to the price level, at least at low levels of inflation, so that revisions in inflationary expectations leave the present value of future surpluses unaffected at first approximation.[16] It follows that upward revisions in expected inflation always improve the government budget by reducing the real value of the nominal debt. As long as expectations are for a sustained increase in the price level, rather than for a price jump, the effect on the debt value is increasing in debt duration.

When the focus is on changes in expected inflation, the relevant relation for the choice of nominal debt maturity is between the stochastic process for the price level and the processes for government spending and revenues (and thus output). Depending on such a relation there exists a maturity structure that implements the contingencies in debt returns needed to support efficient taxation. For instance, to the extent that the economy is hit by productivity and public spending shocks leading to serially correlated inflation, a long maturity of nominal debt can provide an even better hedge than a short maturity for the purpose of smoothing tax rates on labor income. However, the exact characterization of optimal maturity is far from straightforward, as it depends on a number of factors, such as the level of nominal debt and the relative persistence of inflation induced by the various shocks affecting the budget. For instance, if

[15] Shocks to productivity and to the rate of capital depreciation are the only sources of uncertainty in the model.

[16] Actually, real taxes are increasing and real spending decreasing in the inflation rate because of various nominalistic features of tax systems.

productivity and spending shocks were as important as monetary disturbances but generated more persistence in inflation, then long-maturity debt would perform better as a shock absorber.

So far, there has been little research formalizing implications of debt maturity for efficient taxation. An exception is provided by Calvo and Guidotti (1990*a*), who stress that long-maturity debt enlarges the inflation tax base on an intertemporal dimension. It allows the government to collect (the same amount of) state-contingent inflation taxes over a longer horizon and, thus, to smooth the inflation rate over time. They formalize this argument by extending the model, reviewed in Section 5.2.3, to three periods. Issuing two-period nominal debt is preferable than rolling over one-period nominal debt. This is because one-period debt provides an inflation tax base only in the second period. As uncertainty about government spending is then resolved, the government cannot raise contingent inflation taxes on the part of the debt which is rolled over to the third period. By contrast, since its nominal return is predetermined, two-period debt provides a tax-base for state-contingent inflation in both the second and the third period. As inflation taxes and hence inflation can be smoothed over time, the cost of using state-contingent inflation is reduced. Then more contingencies in debt returns can be implemented in order to reduce variations in conventional taxes.

Important results on the implications of debt maturity for risk minimization have been derived in the literature on confidence crises reviewed in the next section.

5.4.1 Confidence crises and debt maturity

A "too short" maturity of either nominal or indexed debt (relative to current and future surpluses) exposes the intertemporal government budget to interest-rate risk. Even in the absence of exogenous uncertainty, this exposure may generate by itself endogenous uncertainty about the interest rate. As shown in Calvo (1988), the inability of the government to commit not to inflate or repudiate the debt and of private investors to coordinate on a low-interest rate create a potential for multiple equilibria. If raising conventional taxes is increasingly costly, the government incentive to inflate or levy taxes on debt is increasing in real interest payments. Thus, investors' expectations that a government, facing a high-interest rate, will not increase taxes but will resort to some form of implicit or explicit repudiation can be self-fulfilling. Although the role of debt maturity is not examined by Calvo, for repudiation to be an issue the amount of debt to be rolled over must be substantial, that is, the level of debt must be considerably high and its maturity considerably short.

Alesina, Prati and Tabellini (1990) show that a short and unbalanced maturity structure exposes the government to the risk of a funding crisis in an infinite horizon model with no exogenous uncertainty. In their model the government is willing to service the debt by raising conventional taxes, as long as their convex cost is lower than a fixed cost of full repudiation resulting from disruption of financial markets, lost reputation, undesirable redistribution, etc. In a good equilibrium the government rolls over the outstanding debt at world interest rates and meets interest payments by raising conventional taxes. However, if the maturity structure of the debt is short and unbalanced, so that the amount of debt maturing at certain dates is substantial, debt default is also an equilibrium. If investors asked for repayment of maturing obligations, the welfare cost of raising distorting taxes would exceed the cost of repudiation. Then the market for debt disappears as each investor realizes that in the next period the government will be unwilling to service the debt by increasing taxes in the event that everyone else will ask for repayment. A long and balanced maturity structure rules out the crisis equilibrium since it reduces the amount of debt maturing at each date and thus the taxes to be levied in order to resist a crisis.

Although full repudiation of domestic debt almost never occurred (Eichengreen 1990), in the interwar period some governments did halt "debt runs" by suspending principal repayments and converting short-term into long-term debt. However, Alesina, De Broeck, Prati and Tabellini (1992) find no significant impact of the average term to maturity of public debt on the interest rate differential between public and private securities for highly indebted OECD countries. Indeed, monetization seems a more realistic option facing a government with temporary financing problems. While this may not eliminate the problem, implications for the choice of the maturity of nominal debt change, unless there is a once-and-for-all increase in the price level, so that the inflation tax does not discriminate between securities of different maturities.

The case of a currency crisis leading to an exchange-rate devaluation followed by repegging and thus to a discrete jump in the price level is examined in Giavazzi and Pagano (1990). In their model the government weighs the convex cost of distortionary taxes against a fixed cost of currency devaluation with a relative weight which is not publicly known. In a good equilibrium there is no speculative attack and new debt issues are financed at world interest rates while taxes are raised to repay interests. However, a crisis equilibrium characterized by high domestic interest rates which incorporate a devaluation premium is possible when a large share of debt must be renewed. Then, a rise in interest rates (needed to support the exchange-rate parity) worsens the intertemporal government budget, increasing the probability that the government will opt for monetization and currency devaluation, thus validating investors' expectations. A long and balanced maturity structure rules out the crisis equilibrium by reducing the fraction of debt to be renewed on unfavorable terms and therefore, the cost of resisting the speculative attack.

The debt crisis argument makes a strong case for long-maturity debt, in that it shows how changes in interest rates with potentially minor consequences may degenerate into costly roll-over crises in highly indebted countries. In models of currency crises, issuing debt denominated in foreign currency may also provide a solution because it removes the temptation for exchange-rate depreciation and can be issued at no premium during a speculative attack. This role is however questionable; if crises occur for reasons unrelated to debt management, their consequences can be even worse with foreign currency debt than they would be with conventional debt (see Obstfeld 1994). For instance, in the event of devaluation the debt burden will be higher and the tax base for inflation lower. Expectations may even react negatively to the issuance of foreign debt, since such debt leads to higher taxes and a higher rate of devaluation if the fixed parity is abandoned.

While a satisfactory formalization of the role of debt maturity is still to come, empirical evidence on the relation between long debt returns, permanent output and public spending can shed light on the hedging properties of long-maturity debt.

5.4.2   Budgetary insurance with debt maturity: evidence from OECD countries

The maturity composition of the nominal debt is, traditionally, the most important decision of debt management but empirical evidence on the role of debt maturity in minimizing the risk of tax adjustments is scarce.

Implications for the choice of debt maturity can be derived from an extention of Bohn's model presented in Section 5.3.1 which considers long-term nominal debt along with short-term nominal, indexed and foreign currency debt. The government problem is to choose from this enlarged set of instruments the composition of the debt which minimizes tax distortions:

$$Min \ Loss = \sum_{i=0}^{\infty} \beta^i E_t[Y_{t+i}\tau_{t+i}^2]$$

$$s.t. \ D_t = G_t - \tau_t Y_t + (1+r)[1 - s\hat{\pi}_t + l\hat{R}_t + h^*\hat{q}_t]D_{t-1} \qquad (5.16)$$

where s defines the share of short-term nominal debt and l the share of long-term nominal debt (possibly a vector of bond shares of various maturities). $\hat{R}_t = R_t - E_{t-1}R_t$ denotes the unexpected component of the holding-period return, R_t, on long-term nominal debt.[17] With a quarter as the unit period, the innovation in inflation, $\hat{\pi}_t$, is precisely the unanticipated component of the real return on a 3-month fixed-rate security, say, a 3-month Treasury bill. The innovation in the real exchange rate, $\hat{q}_t$, is the unanticipated component of the return on a 3-month bond denominated in foreign currency. At the

---

[17] Formally, $\hat{R}_t$ should be the vector of unexpected returns (per quarterly holding period) on public securities of all existing maturities longer than three months and l should be the vector of their shares in total debt.

end of each period the government chooses the share of each type of debt. Then at the beginning of the next period, inflation, bond prices and the real exchange rate are observed and so are the returns on all types of debt. Finally, the government sets the tax rate.

The solution of this problem is the same as in Equations (5.6)–(5.8), supplemented by the condition of zero conditional covariance between the tax rate and the return on long-term nominal bonds.

$$E_t \tau_{t+1} - \tau_t = 0 \tag{5.17}$$
$$Cov_t(\tau_{t+1}\pi_{t+1}) = 0 \tag{5.18}$$
$$Cov_t(\tau_{t+1}q_{t+1}) = 0 \tag{5.19}$$
$$Cov_t(\tau_{t+1}R_{t+1}) = 0 \tag{5.20}$$

In principle, the conditional covariance in (5.20) should be satisfied with nominal bonds of all existing maturities. If this were not the case, the government could improve tax-smoothing by selling maturities with returns positively correlated with the tax rate in exchange for maturities with a negative return correlation, to the point where the return on the debt portfolio would offset the impact of output and spending shocks on tax rates.

An explicit solution in terms of the optimal shares, s, l and h^*, can be derived by integrating the government budget forward and imposing conditions (5.17)–(5.20). Following the same steps (and notation) as in Section 5.3.1 gives the log-linear approximation of the intertemporal budget constraint (cf. Equation (5.11)):

$$\gamma \log \tau_t = d_{t-1} - \mu - s\hat{\pi}_t + l\hat{R}_t + h^*\hat{q}_t$$
$$-(1 - \rho + \eta)\sum_{i=0}^{\infty} \rho^i E_t y_{t+i} + \eta \sum_{i=0}^{\infty} \rho^i E_t g_{t+i} \tag{5.21}$$

where the fact that $E_t R_{t+i} = r$ for any $i > 0$ has been used.

Conditions (5.18) to (5.20) can be imposed after replacing $\log \tau_t$ with its linear approximation $\log \tau_t \simeq \log E_{t-1}\tau_t + (\tau_t - E_{t-1}\tau_t)/E_{t-1}\tau_t$, and multiplying all terms of Equation (5.21) by $\hat{\pi}_t$, $\hat{R}_t$ and $\hat{q}_t$ in turn. Taking expectations conditional on the information at time $t - 1$, yields the following relations between the optimal shares of nominal and foreign currency debt

$$s \, Var_{t-1}(\pi_t) = h^* Cov_{t-1}(\pi_t q_t) + l Cov_{t-1}(\pi_t R_t) - \gamma \, Cov_{t-1}(\pi_t Y_t^p)$$
$$+(\gamma - 1)Cov_{t-1}(\pi_t G_t^p)$$
$$h^* \, Var_{t-1}(q_t) = s Cov_{t-1}(\pi_t q_t) - l Cov_{t-1}(q_t R_t) + \gamma \, Cov_{t-1}(q_t Y_t^p)$$
$$-(\gamma - 1)Cov_{t-1}(q_t G_t^p)$$
$$l \, Var_{t-1}(R_t) = s Cov_{t-1}(R_t \pi_t) - h^* Cov_{t-1}(R_t q_t) + \gamma \, Cov_{t-1}(R_t Y_t^p)$$
$$-(\gamma - 1)Cov_{t-1}(R_t G_t^p)$$

$$\tag{5.22}$$

These conditions extend conditions (5.12) and (5.13) derived in Section 5.3.1 to the more general case when the government can rely on long-term bonds to minimize the risk of tax adjustments. Shocks to permanent output and public spending can be hedged by long-term bonds if their real returns are relatively lower when permanent output is unexpectedly low and permanent spending is unexpectedly high. In these instances the government experiences a capital gain on the outstanding debt which reduces the need for a tax-rate increase.

Since the real interest rate, r, is assumed to be constant the role of long-term debt in avoiding the risk of refinancing cannot be addressed within the present framework. The consideration of roll-over risk provides an argument in favor of long-term debt in addition to its possible role in hedging output shocks. For instance the role for long-term debt would be reinforced if holding returns and permanent output were positively correlated. Since holding returns are inversely related to yields to maturity and thus to the cost of refinancing maturing debt, interest rates and the cost of borrowing would be unexpectedly high when permanent output is unexpectedly low. On the other hand, "some" long-term debt may still be optimal, as opposed to negative long-term debt, in order to avoid refinancing risk even if holding returns are negatively correlated with permanent output. As the present model does not consider roll-over risk, it will tend to bias empirical findings against long-term nominal or indexed debt.

The optimal share of long-term nominal debt also depends on the shares of the other instruments in the government portfolio and on the covariance of their returns, loosely speaking, on the substitutability or complementarity of long-term nominal bonds with other types of debt. For the same reason, the choice of the currency composition and indexation of the debt depends on the availability of long-term nominal debt. Since the entire variance-covariance matrix of existing asset returns should be considered, the results of the present analysis must be regarded as preliminary.

Empirically, the optimal shares of short-term and long-term nominal debt, foreign currency and indexed debt (obtained by solving Equations (5.22)) can be estimated from the conditional covariances of their returns with permanent output and public spending, inflation and the real exchange rate. A first approach to the problem is to combine financial data on unexpected holding-period returns to innovations in the above variables as estimated by the VAR described in Section 5.2.2. This approach has been followed by Bohn (1990*a*) at the cost of disregarding the covariances between asset returns. However, since series of holding-period returns for the sample period 1970–95 are available only for a few countries, it has been decided to use data on the yields to maturity of long-term bonds.

Yields to maturity can be related to holding-period returns as follows. Consider a long-term bond maturing $(m+1)$ periods from now and denote its price at time $t-1$ by P_{t-1}^{m+1}. Suppose, for a moment, that the bond is a zero-coupon bond. Then the return on holding the bond for one period depends on the price of such bond one period from now and thus on the realization of the corresponding yield to maturity. Since after one period the remaining term to maturity of the bond is reduced to m, its price will then be equal to P_t^m which implies a holding-period return equal to P_t^m / P_{t-1}^{m+1} and a real return equal to

$$1 + R_t^m = \frac{P_t^m}{P_{t-1}^{m+1}(1 + \pi_t)}$$

Taking logarithms on both sides, the return is approximated by:

$$R_t^m \simeq \log P_t^m - \log P_{t-1}^{m+1} - \pi_t$$

Then, holding returns can be related to yields to maturity, simply noting that $\log P_t^m = -m i_t^m$, where i_t^m denotes the yield to maturity, as of time t, of a zero-coupon bond with a term to maturity equal to m. It follows that the real return is approximately equal to (see Campbell 1995)

$$R_t^m \simeq -(m)i_t^m + (m+1)i_{t-1}^{m+1} - \pi_t \tag{5.23}$$

Taking expectations and subtracting the resulting expression from Equation (5.23), gives the unexpected component of the return as

$$R_t^m - E_{t-1}R_t^m \simeq -m[i_t^m - E_{t-1}i_t^m] - [\pi_t - E_{t-1}\pi_t] \tag{5.24}$$

Therefore, the real return on a zero-coupon bond of a $m+1$ remaining maturity is equal to the real return on a bond of one-period maturity, $-[\pi_t - E_{t-1}\pi_t]$, minus the unexpected component of the m-period yield to maturity multiplied by the maturity (minus one), m, of the bond.

Equation (5.24) also holds as an approximation for coupon bonds selling at par, with the only difference that m must be replaced by Macaulay's duration since for coupon bonds duration and remaining term to maturity are no longer the same (see Section 4.4). In fact, denoting with $m_d + 1$ its Macaulay's duration, the linear approximation of the holding return on a coupon bond selling at par is equal to[18]

$$R_t^m \simeq -(m_d)i_t^m + (m_d + 1)i_{t-1}^{m+1} - \pi_t$$

which is equal to Equation (5.23) and from which Equation (5.24) can be derived.

[18] For a derivation see Shiller (1990: 640–4, table 18.1) and Shiller, Campbell and Schoenholtz (1983).

Equation (5.24) shows that whether the long duration of a bond provides a hedge against budgetary risk, in addition or in spite of it being nominally denominated, depends on the unanticipated component of the yield of the corresponding maturity. The relation between unexpected returns and yields to maturity allows an estimation of the optimal share of long-term debt using the innovations in yields to maturity (and inflation) as estimated by the residuals in the corresponding equation of the VAR. Formally, the estimated share corresponds to nominal bonds with the same maturity as the yield used in the VAR. Such a maturity varies across countries depending on the benchmark yield considered in the OECD statistics; it is 20 years long in the case of the UK but it is as short as 3 years for Italy. To take into account that yields are from coupon bonds, the duration of the representative bonds instead of their maturity has been used for m. The duration has been estimated assuming that bonds have been trading at par, and bearing a coupon equal to the sample average of the yields.

The optimal shares of long-term nominal, short-term nominal and foreign currency debt are shown in the first three columns of Table 5.6. Column 4 indicates the duration in years of the long-term nominal bond whose yields have been used in the estimation. Columns 5 to 7 report optimal shares for

Table 5.6. Hedging properties of debt instruments: shares of long and short nominal debt and foreign currency debt

	Unconstrained			Duration in years	Only long	Only short	Only foreign
	Long	Short	Foreign				
Australia	0.27	−5.12	−0.76	6.6	0.32	−3.47	−0.63
Austria	2.10	−1.99	−1.12	2.8	1.76	−0.15	−1.80
Belgium	0.19	1.33	0.62	5.4	0.26	2.20	0.77
Canada	−0.02	−0.75	0.08	6.8	−0.03	−0.69	0.06
Denmark	0.24	1.05	0.05	6.2	0.30	2.13	0.01
Finland	−0.01	−3.27	0.35	4.1	−0.26	−2.84	0.08
France	0.16	−8.31	1.14	6.6	−0.16	−5.91	−0.13
Germany	0.84	1.33	3.02	7.3	1.04	4.89	3.19
Ireland	0.20	0.78	−1.04	5.1	0.28	0.47	−0.84
Italy	−0.05	0.37	−0.03	2.6	0.00	0.26	−0.02
Japan	0.48	2.06	0.17	7.6	0.42	2.59	0.03
Netherlands	0.15	−1.89	0.07	5.6	0.08	−1.58	−0.23
Spain	0.02	0.28	0.07	2.6	0.06	0.31	0.07
Sweden	−0.19	1.42	0.63	6.7	−0.10	0.76	0.55
UK	−0.21	5.31	−1.10	8.8	0.21	2.62	−0.83
USA	0.20	−0.81	−0.07	7.1	0.15	−0.23	0.01

each instrument when the other two instruments are in zero net supply. For short-term debt and foreign currency debt such shares are the same as in Table 5.1 and recalled here for convenience.

The optimal debt compositions by maturity and currency denomination varies considerably across OECD countries. For most countries the optimal share of long-term nominal debt is positive suggesting that such debt can provide insurance against unexpected changes in tax needs which arise from output shocks. Indeed, evidence in favor of long-term debt comes more from a negative correlation of nominal yields to maturity with permanent output than from a positive correlation with innovations in permanent public spending.

This role for long-maturity debt is highlighted in column 5, which does not consider indirect effects arising from the other types of debt in the government portfolio. Even when the interactions with the other instruments are allowed for, long-term debt maintains a role in minimizing budgetary risk. The optimal share of long-maturity debt is particulary large in Austria, Germany and Japan, it is important in Australia and accounts for a 20% of the debt in Belgium, Ireland and the US. Only in four countries, Canada, Finland, Italy and Sweden there appears to be no role for long-term nominal bonds. For the UK evidence on long-term debt is mixed; it depends on whether holding a large share of foreign assets is feasible or not. As this practical constraint is taken into account, long-term debt fares better, as column 5 points out. On the other hand, the same column shows that long-term debt has no hedging role in France; its share is positive only if one allows for short-term lending to the private sector.

The consideration of long-term debt possibly led to changes in the optimal debt composition by currency denomination and indexation derived in the previous section, because of the complementarity or substitutability of the different instruments in the government portfolio. However, the impact is minor, as can be seen by comparing Table 5.6 to Table 5.1. In particular, the optimal share of foreign currency debt is barely affected by the introduction of long-term bonds; only in Austria and Japan such share rises by more than 10 percentage points. The increase is qualitatively significant for Japan where foreign currency debt turns positive (and equal to 0.17%), but not for Austria where its share remains negative and large in size. The reason for the denomination of the debt to be invariant to the maturity of the debt instruments is either the low conditional correlation between changes in the real exchange rate and in yields to maturity or (when such a correlation is stronger) the absence of foreign currency debt in the optimal portfolio.

In a few countries the composition between nominal and price-indexed debt seems to depend on the availability of long-term debt. Since the share of foreign currency debt is unchanged, differences in optimal indexation are traced out by changes in the sum of fixed-rate short- and long-term debt. The share of

Table 5.7. Price-indexed debt

	Unconstrained			Constrained			Actual indexed
	Long	Short	Foreign	Long	Short	Foreign	
Australia	0.27	−5.12	−0.76	0.32			0.03
Austria	2.10	−1.99	−1.12	1.76			—
Canada	−0.02	−0.75	0.08			0.06	0.01
Finland	−0.01	−3.27	0.35			0.08	—
France	0.16	−8.31	1.14	−0.16		−0.11	—
Netherlands	0.15	−1.89	0.07	0.08		−0.22	—
USA	0.20	−0.81	−0.07	0.15			0.01
Positive indexed debt in subperiods							
Japan (1991–5)	0.09	−1.27	0.13	0.06		0.09	—
UK (1991–5)	0.04	−1.38	0.15	−0.04		0.06	0.14

fixed-rate debt is considerably lower than in Section 5.2 for Denmark, Germany and the UK.[19] This can be easily explained by the close substitutability between long- and short-term debt and by the additional hedging properties of long-term debt. Since the insurance that the government obtains with nominal debt is increased by the yield sensitivity of long-term bonds, a lower share of debt has to be contingent on inflation. However, in all the three countries considered the optimal share of fixed-rate debt denominated in the domestic currency is still so high that there is no scope for price indexation. In the case of France the composition between nominal and indexed debt is also qualitatively the same; the total share of nominal debt increases but remains negative.

Table 5.7 focuses on countries where price-index-linked bonds appear the main instruments to isolate the government budget from spending and output shocks. The selection is made depending on whether the shares of the unconstrained estimation sum up to a negative or a positive number. Columns 1 to 3 report unconstrained estimates, while columns 4 to 6 take non-negativity constraints into consideration and show the share of each type of debt when the other instruments exhibiting a negative unconstrained share are set equal to zero. Evidence for countries where the same implication holds in only one of the two subperiods are reported in the bottom half of the table.

The list looks very much the same as in Section 5.2; the same countries where price-indexed debt outperformed any other instrument are still represented in

---

[19] For the UK this conclusion follows from imposing a non-negativity constraint on foreign currency debt.

Table 5.7. However, a new fact emerges: in most countries long-term debt is a useful hedge against permanent output fluctuations with the notable exceptions of Canada and Finland. In order to ensure that the hedging role for long-term debt does not depend on the possibility of short-term lending, it is worth looking at the estimates which consider non-negativity constraints. Columns 4 to 5 show that four countries, Australia, Austria, the Netherlands and the US still benefit from long-term nominal debt besides price indexation. The share of such debt in the optimal portfolio is 32% in the case of Australia and a modest 15 and 8% for the US and the Netherlands, respectively, while it is larger than total debt in Austria.

This evidence suggests that long-term nominal debt, being contingent on long yields, can still provide budgetary insurance in countries where short-term nominal debt does not. Indeed, in these countries long yields display a negative correlation with permanent output (and in the US also positive correlation with permanent spending), which more than offset the effects of inflation on the correlation of their return with permanent output. This positive relation between output and prices, coupled with the negative relation between output and interest rates, can possibly arise from monetary shocks or be induced by monetary policy.

No doubt, the optimal maturity structure of the nominal debt, more precisely, its composition between short- and long-term bonds, is the most interesting issue which can be addressed by introducing long-term bonds. Table 5.8

Table 5.8. Positive nominal debt in any period

	Unconstrained			Constrained			Long/ short ratio
	Long	Short	Foreign	Long	Short	Foreign	
Belgium	0.19	1.33	0.62				0.14
Denmark	0.24	1.05	0.05				0.23
Germany	0.84	1.33	3.02				0.63
Ireland	0.20	0.78	−1.04	0.28	0.00		0.26
Italy	−0.05	0.37	−0.03		0.26		0.00
Spain	0.02	0.28	0.07				0.07
Sweden	−0.19	1.42	0.63		1.00	0.59	0.00
Positive nominal debt in subperiods							
Austria (1991–5)	2.36	1.56	−2.36	3.11	−0.40		1.51
France (1987–90)	0.09	0.90	0.13				0.10
Japan (1987–90)	1.13	5.10	0.59				0.22
UK (1987–90)	−0.56	9.95	−1.79	0.14	5.58		0.00

shows the optimal shares of long- and short-maturity debt for the countries where the share of fixed-rate debt denominated in the domestic currency has been positive in at least one of the two periods 1987–90 and 1993–5. Unconstrained estimates are reported in columns 1 to 3 while estimates resulting from setting equal to zero the instruments which show a negative share in the unconstrained estimates are in column 4 to 6.

Most countries exhibit a positive share of long-term nominal debt which increases when the interaction between the returns on the various assets is disregarded, as shown above. Evidence that both long- and short-term nominal debt are part of the optimal portfolio suggests that long-term debt has hedging properties in addition to being contingent on current inflation. However, the estimated maturity structure clearly points to short-term debt as the best instrument. With the exceptions of Germany, Ireland and Austria in the period 1991–5, the share of long-term debt does not even reach one-fourth of short-term debt. In fact, evidence is mixed for Ireland, since the relative proportion between long- and short-term debt depends on whether lending in foreign currency is feasible or not.[20] The general impression is that, if nominal debt is optimal, most of the insurance against unexpected financing needs can be secured by short-term securities. This conclusion holds exactly for Italy and Sweden where the share of long-term debt is even negative.

The picture which emerges from the analysis is one of little contribution of long-term debt to tax-smoothing, when the relevant contingencies in debt returns are provided by current inflation, and one of more contributions when contingencies from current inflation should be avoided. A possible explanation for the unsatisfactory performance of long-term debt is the volatility of the holding returns on the benchmark bonds for which data on interest rates are collected. These are usually 10-year bonds with a duration between 6 and 7 years (see column 4 in Table 5.6). It follows that, even though long-term bonds provide an alternative form of insurance, when inflation contingencies are effective short-term debt is preferred because the volatility of current inflation is lower than that of holding returns.

This evidence must however be interpreted with caution for a number of reasons. A main problem is the sensitivity of the optimal shares of long-term debt to the duration of the debt instruments for which data on yields to maturity are reported. For instance a duration of 3.5 instead of 7.1 years would lead to an increase in the share of long-term bonds from 20 to 40% in the US. Since issuance of long-duration bonds typically corresponds to a much shorter

---

[20] The explanation is that the returns on all types of debt are fairly correlated, and while fixed-rate nominal instruments provide hedges against permanent output and spending shocks, foreign currency debt enhances such uncertainty. If holdings of foreign currency assets are constrained, this also reduces the nominal debt which is optimal to issue, such that only the best hedging instrument, long-term nominal debt, finds space in the optimal portfolio.

average duration of long-term debt, if innovations in the yields to maturity were similar across maturities, one could conclude in favor of long-term bonds. It is unfortunate that research on tax-smoothing has not so far relied on the entire term structure of interest rates.[21]

A second problem is that refinancing risk is not properly modelled in the present framework, since the real interest rate on price-indexed bonds is constant and, although unexpected changes in yield to maturity are assumed to affect the value of the outstanding debt, their effects on the cost of financing maturing issues and new deficits are not taken into account. This implies that the benefits of long-term bonds in isolating the budget from interest-rate risk are underestimated. This consideration applies to price-indexed bonds and, to a greater extent, to nominal bonds when such debt provides a hedge against permanent output and spending shocks.

5.5 Concluding remarks

Conventional financial instruments can be used to minimize the risk of tax-rate adjustments in response to shocks adversely affecting the government budget. The choice of debt instruments depends on the types of shocks hitting the economy and on their persistence. Fixed-rate conventional bonds, being contingent on inflation, provide insurance against supply shocks leading to lower than expected tax revenues and higher than expected inflation. If demand shocks (apart from public spending shocks) prevail, price-index-linked bonds should be issued in order to avoid high real returns when income falls below expectations. Long-term debt denominated in foreign currency can be an alternative to price-indexed debt for domestic demand shocks, but it exposes the government budget to foreign monetary disturbances and to exchange-rate risk if PPP does not hold. Foreign currency debt may also provide a hedge against output shocks if such shocks are internationally correlated, while it is a risky instrument in fixed-exchange regimes if exchange parity realignments are more closely related to fiscal imbalances than to excess demand growth.

While tax-smoothing implications for the choices of indexation and currency denomination of public debt have been studied at length, the role of the maturity structure in minimizing the risk of tax adjustments has been formalized only recently (see Barro 1995). Lack of interest is surprising in light of policymakers' concern for refinancing risk. The role of long-term bonds in minimizing the debt which is rolled over and thus the risk of refinancing at higher than expected interest rates was discussed in Section 5.4. Risk, and thus the role for long-maturity debt, are enhanced when the unexpected rise in yields to maturity is associated with a fall in permanent output and a rise in permanent

---

[21] Dale, Mongiardino and Quah (1997) use holding returns from a large sample of bonds but consider deficit-smoothing rather than tax-smoothing as the objective of the government.

spending. On the other hand, if interest rates are procyclical, short-term debt is not so much a concern, since indexing the cost of borrowing to economic activity, that is, to the source of government revenues, is desirable. It is often argued that if movements in nominal interest rates reflect anticipated payment for future inflation, then short-term debt as well as price-index-linked bonds should be issued to hedge the "inflation risk." However, this point can be made only if changes in expected inflation are unrelated to real variables. If upward revisions in inflationary expectations and yields to maturity are associated with a worsening of economic prospects, long-term nominal debt can still be effective as a hedge against the forthcoming fall in tax revenues.

The hedging properties of the various instruments also depend on the persistence of the different shocks affecting the economy and on the fiscal and monetary policy responses to such shocks. Shock persistence has important implications for the choice of debt maturity, but also matters for price indexation. For instance, as argued by Hawkesby and Wright (1997), if supply shocks were more persistent than demand shocks, their impact on permanent output would be stronger, thus suggesting the need for a larger share of fixed-rate conventional debt. The monetary regime, i.e. the choice of the monetary policy targets, has also implications for debt management, since it helps to determine the co-movements and persistence of inflation, output and interest rates. For instance, fixed-rate conventional bonds should be preferred to price-index-linked bonds, to the extent that monetary policy tends to react more to demand shocks than to supply shocks. Leaving time-consistency issues aside, the interactions between debt management and monetary policy remain largely unexplored and represent a potentially fruitful direction for future research.

Evidence on the conditional covariances of inflation, exchange rates, yields to maturity, permanent output and public spending has been used to estimate the debt composition which provides the optimal hedge against budgetary risk for a number of OECD countries. The analysis, which relies on innovations in the above variables as estimated by vector autoregressions, builds on and extends Bohn's (1990*a*) seminal work for the US. Since the analysis relies on a number of simplifying assumptions, it is best viewed as a preliminary step toward a better understanding of the relationships between shocks affecting the government budget and debt returns.

Differences in sign and relative strength of the relevant covariances across countries, allow for only few general conclusions. Interestingly, evidence against foreign currency denominated debt is strong for almost all countries considered. Overall, there seems to be more scope for price-indexation than is contemplated by actual arrangements, and has been found in previous analysis (see Bohn 1990*a*, Goldfajn 1995). Even in the UK price-indexed debt falls short of the estimated optimal share. However, evidence on whether price-indexed bonds should be issued instead of fixed-rate bonds varies across countries reflecting the type of shocks that each country experiences. In a number of countries nominal debt appears to have consistently provided a hedge against output fluctuations. Nominal debt benefits Germany and a group of highly indebted countries: Belgium, Ireland, Italy, Spain and Sweden. Long-term nominal debt should also be issued in such countries, because of the negative correlation between holding-period returns and permanent output innovations. The optimal maturity structure is however heavily concentrated on the short end. In fact, long-term nominal debt provides insurance against permanent output uncertainty, but its optimal share is small due to the large volatility of holding returns, possibly because of returns being unprecisely estimated from yields to maturity.

This evidence should be regarded as far from being conclusive. Confidence can be attached more to the direction of the detected relations than to the precise estimates of debt shares. For instance, the problems associated with estimating the share of long-term debt and the fact that such estimates do not account for the protection that long-term debt offers against unexpected changes in the real cost of borrowing, prevent a proper assessment of the hedging role of such debt. Nevertheless, it is fair to say that the present results do not support the view of a strong hedging role for long-term nominal debt which has been conjectured in previous works (see Goldfajn 1995 and Missale 1997*b*).

Finally, a word should be said on the policy relevance of these results. As much as debt composition varies across countries, changes in debt composition may also occur over time for each single country, when different shocks prevail in different periods. This is the case, for example, in France, the UK, Japan and Austria. While expected, such changes suggest a limited relevance of the present analysis for policymaking. Relying on past evidence for the choice of debt instruments could be misleading since the relevant covariances may change depending on the future shocks which the economy will experience. The problem would be severe if the relationships between the relevant variables were going to change as could be the case, say, for a change in the monetary policy regime. This consideration suggests the need for more structural analysis and for a comparison across forecasting methods in future research.

Appendix 5.I: Derivation of log-linear approximations

Consider the government budget constraint of Equation (5.5):

$$D_t = G_t - T_t + (1 + R_t)D_{t-1}$$

where $T_t = \tau_t Y_t$ are taxes and $(1 + R_t) = (1 + r)(1 - m\hat{\pi}_t + m^*\hat{q}_t)$ is the real (gross) return on public debt.

The first step to derive the log-linear approximation of the budget constraint is to divide Equation (5.5) by D_{t-1} and take logarithms. Denoting logarithms with lower-case letters, we have

$$log(1 + R_t) = log[exp(d_t - d_{t-1}) - exp(g_t - d_{t-1}) + exp(t_t - d_{t-1})]$$

The right-hand side of this equation is a non-linear function of the growth rate of debt, $d_t - d_{t-1}$, the logarithm of the spending/debt ratio, $g_t - d_{t-1}$, and the logarithm of the revenue/debt ratio, $t_t - d_{t-1}$. The next step is to take a first-order Taylor expansion of this function around the means of such variables, say, the points: $d_t - d_{t-1} = n$; $g_t - d_{t-1} = z$ and; $t_t - d_{t-1} = x = log(exp(r) - exp(n) + exp(z))$. (In the empirical analysis the point z is taken to be the sample average of the corresponding variable.)

The resulting approximation is

$$log[exp(d_t - d_{t-1}) - exp(g_t - d_{t-1}) + exp(t_t - d_{t-1})]$$
$$\simeq (1 - \rho)k + \rho(d_t - d_{t-1}) - \eta(g_t - d_{t-1}) + (1 - \rho + \eta)(t_t - d_{t-1})$$

where $(1 - \rho)k = r - n + (1 - \rho)(n - x) + \eta(z - x)$ is an unimportant constant, and $\eta = exp(z - r)$ is equal to the discounted mean of the spending/debt ratio, i.e. $\eta = (\bar{G}/D)exp(-r)$. The parameter $\rho = exp(n - r)$ is a discount factor, i.e. ρ is a number a little less than 1, since $r > n$ is needed to satisfy the No-Ponzi games condition. (Note that n is equal to the growth rate of GDP under tax-smoothing.)

Finally, Equation (5.9) in the main text is obtained by approximating $log(1 + R_t)$ with $r - m\hat{\pi}_t + m^*\hat{q}_t$:

$$r - m\hat{\pi}_t + m^*\hat{q}_t = (1 - \rho)k + \rho d_t - d_{t-1} - \eta g_t + (1 - \rho + \eta)(log\,\tau_t + y_t)$$

where $log\,\tau_t + y_t = t_t$.

Consider the first-order condition (5.6):

$$E_t\tau_{t+i} = \tau_t \qquad \text{for } i > 0$$

The log-linear approximation of this condition is derived from the following first-order Taylor expansion of $log\,\tau_{t+i}$ around its conditional expectation $E_t\tau_{t+i}$:

$$log\,\tau_{t+i} \simeq log(E_t\tau_{t+i}) + \frac{\tau_{t+i} - E_t\tau_{t+i}}{E_t\tau_{t+i}}$$

Taking conditional expectations and using the first-order condition, $E_t\tau_{t+i} = \tau_t$, yields the following approximation:

$$E_t log\,\tau_{t+i} \simeq log\,\tau_t$$

Appendix 5.2: Innovations in permanent output and public spending

The expectational revisions in permanent output and permanent public spending can be estimated as follows. Consider a VAR representation for output, y_t, public spending, g_t, and a third variable x_t (that stands for the additional five variables used in the empirical estimation), with their means and seasonals removed:

$$\begin{bmatrix} y_t \\ g_t \\ x_t \end{bmatrix} = \begin{bmatrix} a(L) & b(L) & c(L) \\ d(L) & e(L) & f(L) \\ k(L) & l(L) & s(L) \end{bmatrix} \cdot \begin{bmatrix} y_{t-1} \\ g_{t-1} \\ x_{t-1} \end{bmatrix} + \begin{bmatrix} u_{1t} \\ u_{2t} \\ u_{3t} \end{bmatrix}$$

where the polynomials in the lag operator $a(L), b(L), \ldots, s(L)$ are all of order p (where $p = 12$ with monthly data, and $p = 4$ with quarterly data). This VAR can be used for multiperiod forecasting of y_t and g_t and thus, for estimating the annuity values of output and public spending, i.e. permanent output and permanent public spending.

To simplify notation, the VAR can be stacked into the following first-order system:

$$\begin{bmatrix} y_t \\ y_{t-1} \\ \vdots \\ y_{t-p+1} \\ g_t \\ g_{t-1} \\ \vdots \\ g_{t-p+1} \\ x_t \\ x_{t-1} \\ \vdots \\ x_{t-p+1} \end{bmatrix} = \begin{bmatrix} a_1 \cdots a_p & b_1 \cdots b_p & c_1 \cdots c_p \\ 1 & & \\ & \ddots & \\ & 1 & \\ d_1 \cdots d_p & e_1 \cdots e_p & f_1 \cdots f_p \\ & 1 & \\ & & \ddots \\ & & 1 \\ k_1 \cdots k_p & l_1 \cdots l_p & s_1 \cdots s_p \\ & & 1 \\ & & \ddots \ 1 \end{bmatrix} \cdot \begin{bmatrix} y_{t-1} \\ y_{t-2} \\ \vdots \\ y_{t-p} \\ g_{t-1} \\ g_{t-2} \\ \vdots \\ g_{t-p} \\ x_{t-1} \\ x_{t-2} \\ \vdots \\ x_{t-p} \end{bmatrix} + \begin{bmatrix} u_{1t} \\ 0 \\ \vdots \\ 0 \\ u_{2t} \\ 0 \\ \vdots \\ 0 \\ u_{3t} \\ 0 \\ \vdots \\ 0 \end{bmatrix}$$

where blank elements are zero. This system can be written more succinctly as $z_t = Az_{t-1} + v_t$. The matrix A is called the companion matrix of the VAR. For all i, $E(z_{t+i} \mid H_t) = A^i z_t$ where H_t is the limited information set containing current and lagged values of z_t. (Conditional expectations are taken to be linear projections on informations.)

Recall that permanent output is defined as

$$Y_t^p = (1 - \rho) \sum_{i=0}^{\infty} \rho^i E_t y_{t+i}$$

Then, projecting Y_t^p on the limited information set H_t, an estimate of permanent output is given by

$$E(Y_t^p \mid H_t) = (1 - \rho) \sum_{i=0}^{\infty} \rho^i E(y_{t+i} \mid H_t)$$

which, using the definition of z_t and the companion matrix, can be written as

$$E(Y_t^p \mid H_t) = (1 - \rho) \sum_{i=0}^{\infty} \rho^i j' E(z_{t+i} \mid H_t) = (1 - \rho) \sum_{i=0}^{\infty} \rho^i j' A^i z_t \qquad (5.25)$$

Similarly, an estimate of permanent public spending is given by

$$E(G_t^p \mid H_t) = (1 - \rho) \sum_{i=0}^{\infty} \rho^i w' A^i z_t \qquad (5.26)$$

where j' and w' are row vectors with $3p$ elements, all of which are zero except for the first element of j' and the $p + 1$ element of w', which are unity.

Assuming that the infinite sum on the right-hand side of Equation (5.26) converges (i.e. that the eigenvalues of the matrix $[I - \rho A]$ lie outside the unit circle), the estimate of permanent output reduces to

$$E(Y_t^p \mid H_t) = (1 - \rho) \sum_{i=0}^{\infty} \rho^i j' A^i z_t = (1 - \rho) j' [I - \rho A]^{-1} z_t \qquad (5.27)$$

Finally, the innovation in permanent output is derived by subtracting from Equation (5.27) the expectation of permanent output as of period $t - 1$; more precisely, the expectation conditional on the information set H_{t-1}:

$$E(Y_t^p \mid H_t) - E(Y_t^p \mid H_{t-1}) = (1 - \rho) j' [I - \rho A]^{-1} (z_t - A z_{t-1}) = (1 - \rho) j' [I - \rho A]^{-1} v_t$$

where v_t is the column vector of the error terms, $v_t' = [u_{1t}, 0, \ldots, 0, u_{2t}, 0, \ldots, 0, u_{3t}, 0, \ldots, 0]$. The innovation in permanent spending is derived in similar fashion and is equal to the formula for permanent output, after substituting vector w' for vector j'.

In the empirical analysis the vector of latest residuals of the VAR is taken as the estimate of vector v_t. A new VAR and hence a new vector of error terms, v_t, is estimated for each period t.

6

Minimizing cost

6.1 Minimizing the expected cost of debt servicing

A realistic representation of the policymaker's objective function implies a trade-off between the minimization of the expected cost of debt servicing and the minimization of budgetary risk. Implications of the implicit-contingent approach reviewed in Chapter 5 follow from a specification of this trade-off which gives all the weight to risk minimization. Indeed, issuing securities which yield low returns in low-output states reduces budgetary risk but increases the expected cost of debt servicing. High-interest costs have to be paid for a policy which insures the government against the risk of having to adjust tax rates in response to macroeconomic shocks affecting its budget. Risk-averse investors will ask for a premium in order to hold securities with returns positively correlated to their income.

Could a policy which increases borrowing costs ever be optimal? Is the objective of minimizing risk always justified or should some consideration be given to a cost-oriented debt management? These questions arise quite naturally, given that minimizing the costs of debt servicing is officially or informally stated as the main goal of debt management in all OECD countries.

A first answer to this question has already been given at the end of Chapter 3: a policy which does not reduce interest costs is optimal if the expected returns on government securities reflect their risk-return characteristics (resulting from macroeconomic uncertainty), that is, if they result from properly called risk-premia. In this case, securities which yield low returns in low-output states may increase the expected cost of debt servicing and the expected level of taxes, but this debt design is optimal since it supports non-distortionary taxation, relaxes liquidity constraints, and provides flexibility to fiscal policy.

On the contrary, the objective of minimizing the expected cost of debt servicing can be justified when risk-premia follow from: (i) market imperfections; (ii) informational asymmetries between the government and private agents; (iii) systematic mistakes made by private agents in forming expectations; and (iv) the government's inability to commit to future policy actions.

The absence of informational and credibility problems, expectational failures and market imperfections has been an important assumption of the analysis so far. In this chapter various arguments for minimizing the expected costs of debt servicing are examined, such as informational advantages on the side of the government, failure of the expectations theory of the term structure of interest rates, market inefficiencies, and credibility problems.

6.2   Informational problems

6.2.1   *Taking views on interest rates*

Should debt managers try to outperform the market so as to save on the cost of debt servicing? While the subject is one that remains largely unexplored in the literature, there are at least two reasons why discretionary debt management deserves attention. A first reason, explored in what follows, is that debt managers may have superior or even private information on the evolution of interest rates. The second reason, examined in the next section, is that the expectations theory of the term structure may fail, either because investors are systematically wrong in their expectations of future interest rates or because of time-varying term-premia.

If the government has better information than the private sector on the likelihood of future events, for example, on the evolution of future interest rates, in principle, such information could be used to achieve important reductions in borrowing costs. In particular, informational advantages on the part of the government may suggest the adoption of discretionary debt policy: to issue short-term debt when interest rates are expected to fall and long-term debt when interest rates are expected to rise. Arguments in favor of "beat the market" strategies have been made from Tobin (1963) to Campbell (1995).

An "active" debt management, led by "views" about future interest rates, inflation and exchange rates, raises however both issues of feasibility and effectiveness. A main problem is why policymakers should be better at predicting interest rates than market participants. Indeed, it is doubtful that debt managers have superior information about the future path for interest rates or a better understanding of forthcoming events than market participants, except for the case where they have control of (short) interest rates or are informed about monetary policy. Thus, the relevant exception is when debt managers are central bank officials, as was the case in many OECD countries in the past, or they are informed by the monetary authority about future policy actions.

However, even if debt managers had private information, whether or not asymmetric information is an argument for discretionary debt management can be disputed. A first problem is that an active debt policy which tries to anticipate future movements in interest rates would inevitably end up signaling the intentions of the monetary authority. At times, this may create problems for the conduct of both monetary policy and debt management. For instance, a government which wants to issue long-term debt for reasons different from interest-rate expectations, might find itself unable to borrow long term since such a decision would be interpreted as a sign of an impending rise in interest rates. There is however one relevant exception when the government may want to use debt management to convey information to the private sector: when interest rates are "unfairly high" because of investors' lack of confidence in the government resolution to carry out its announcements, that is, when the credibility of the government is at stake. Credibility problems will be examined in the following sections.

The reputational costs of opportunistic behavior are a second and even more relevant problem for discretionary debt management. As debt managers attempt to exploit their informational advantage to the expense of private investors, a risk premium will be asked to hold government securities. Since placement of public debt is a repeated event, the gains from surprising investors can be short-lived while the costs of a lost reputation long-lasting. Giovannini (1997) provides a number of arguments against an active debt management. Piga (1998) examines the problem of opportunistic behavior on the part of the central bank and/or the government, concluding in favor of an independent agency in charge of debt management.

If anything, the cost of discretion appears to be well understood in real economies: the transparency of government financial operations, time regularity of auctions, and early announcement of the amounts on issue are distinguishing features of the issuing policies of most OECD countries. As documented in Chapter 4, most countries emphasize the transparency and regularity of the issuing policy, and now set a regular auction calendar with the types and amounts of new bond issues specified in advance. A predictable issuing process is valuable to security dealers, usually primary dealers participating in the auctions, who are willing to pay a premium for the reduced uncertainty.

6.2.2 The term structure of interest rates

The second argument for a discretionary debt management which aims at reducing the cost of debt servicing points to the possible failure of the expectations theory of the term structure of interest rates. The theory implies apart from the existence of constant term-premia, that long-term interest rates simply reflect the expected path for future short-term interest rates: long interest rates should be high relative to short rates when interest rates are expected to rise. By contrast, for the period 1952–91, Campbell (1995) documents that in the United States "when long rates are high relative to short rates ... long rates tend to fall contrary to the expectations hypothesis."

Campbell's tentative explanation is that term-premia, far from being constant, increase with the yield spread between long and short rates. The reason is that the risk of investing in long-term bonds increases when interest rates are expected to rise, so that the greater the yield spread the higher is the required excess returns on long-term bonds, that is, the term premium. This evidence seems to suggest that on average substantial savings on interest payments could be made by following the simple rule of issuing short-term bonds when the yield curve is particularly steep and long-term bonds when short interest rates are high relative to long rates. This consideration does not, however, extend to other OECD countries where evidence is found in favor of the expectations hypothesis of the term structure (see e.g. Hardouvelis (1994) and Gerlach and Smets (1997)).

Even in the US, the success of discretionary debt management may depend on whether the expectations hypothesis fails because of time-varying term-premia or because of expectations. In the latter case, as for any policy that tries to exploit an expectations failure, the success will depend on how fast people learn and revise their expectations in response to changes in debt management. If debt managers can save on interest payments by surprising the market, a debt policy which systematically attempts to do so will soon become ineffective. In general, instead, Lucas's (1976) critique does not apply to the case of time-varying term-premia.

However, exploiting time-varying term-premia is not necessarily optimal as it depends on the nature of the perceived risk. If the high term-premia, observed when interest rates are expected to rise, reflect the correct perception of a true risk of investing in long-term securities, then there is no reason for the government to incur such risk by issuing short-term debt, that is, by borrowing short-term to lend long-term. The correct argument for cost reduction would have to be based on the relation between such risk and other variables entering the government budget. Alternatively, it should be argued that the risk, which leads to changes in required excess returns, is misperceived or reflects the uncertainty that investors have about future monetary policy. While such uncertainty may not be shared by the debt managers, exploiting the informational advantage gives rise to the same problems as those discussed in the previous section.

6.3   Market imperfections: promoting liquidity

The liquidity of government securities can be as important as their return characteristics. Since liquidity and marketability are valued, interest costs can be considerably reduced by promoting "benchmark bonds," namely, by increasing the size of bond issues with the same risk-return characteristics, in practice, with the same coupon and maturity. Likewise, there can be costs when "new" public assets are introduced. Indeed, arguments in favor of "standardization" have long been made, at least since the work of Friedman (1959).

A variety of policies regarding the organization of primary and secondary markets for government securities exists, which can enhance the efficiency and the liquidity of security markets. These policies are documented in Chapter 4, and in greater detail in Broker (1993) and Sundararajan, Dattels and

Blommestein (1997). They comprise: the use of multiple-price auctions as the main method for selling bonds; the organization of multiple-quotation markets for large volume transactions; the establishment of a system of primary dealers expected to make markets in government securities; and the introduction of futures contracts and repurchase agreement markets in government securities.

As attention is restricted to the choice of debt instruments and their relative amounts, liquid markets make a strong argument for large volumes of bonds with the same risk-return characteristics and thus for standard debt instruments issued in large quantities. Since liquidity and standardization are consistent with alternative risk-return characteristics of government securities, in principle, these goals should leave governments with enough degrees of freedom in the choice of the type of instruments; the objective of improving liquidity should only limit the diversification in the menu of public assets. In practice, however, the cost of financial innovation tends to favor the status quo, that is, conventional financial instruments. Furthermore, among conventional instruments, fixed-rate securities are likely to enjoy a cost advantage; they are favored by security dealers because of their simplicity which proves to be an advantage for fast pricing and hedging strategies. The risk of this policy is therefore to shape the characteristics of debt instruments on the trading needs of security dealers and, more generally, on the preferences of market participants.

Focusing on fixed-rate securities, thick and efficient markets can be obtained by issuing significant amounts of bonds with the same coupon and maturity date. While, in the past this was accomplished by the use of consols, nowadays, most OECD countries issue fungible bonds, that is, bonds with the same coupon and maturity date of the outstanding bonds, though sold through auctions held at later dates, i.e. by "reopenings" of existing issues.[1] The promotion of benchmark bonds has, at first approximation, no adverse consequences for budgetary risk and taxation. The important exception is that this policy may expose the government budget to interest-rate shocks at the time when large volumes of debt have to be rolled over.

Debt policies which improves the efficiency of secondary markets for government securities may also have a positive effect on social welfare. Efficient and liquid markets for standard government securities not only reduce the expected cost of debt servicing, but also help investors to cope with the risk of idiosyncratic shocks, like taste or liquidity shocks. Indeed, the consideration of idiosyncratic risk makes a welfare argument for such policies; efficient secondary markets for government securities can provide liquidity and information which private security markets cannot offer because of imperfections

---

[1] In few countries, notably in Denmark and, until recently, in Ireland this objective is and was achieved by selling bonds "on tap" (see Section 4.2).

and/or externalities. For example, government securities can be held to avoid the "risk of early liquidations" of private assets. This role is important especially when, due to risk heterogeneity of private borrowers, thin security markets for private debt and informational asymmetries involve high costs from unexpected sales (see Pagano 1989).[2] If setting up a market to meet liquidity needs is costly or benefits cannot be internalized, a well-functioning secondary market for government securities may fill this role.

This should be contrasted with implications for debt management following from the consideration of macroeconomic risk. For instance, securities which provide explicit insurance against income risk, say, which yield high returns in states where output is lower than expected, are not always desirable, since the implied tax redistribution must also be taken into consideration. On the contrary, there is substantial merit in improving the efficiency of government security markets.

6.4   Asymmetric information

Expected return on government securities can be high, not only because of risk premia reflecting particular risk-return characteristics, or perceived to be high by policymakers because of different views on future interest rates, but also because of the lack of credibility of policy announcements due to informational asymmetries.

For instance, if the government's determination at carrying out a stabilization program is not known to the private sector, interest rates, both short- and long-term rates, will remain high until the time when uncertainty as to the outcome of the stabilization is resolved. In this situation, as Campbell (1995) points out, a government fully committed to fiscal restraint and price stability can reduce the cost of debt servicing by issuing short-term debt. The reason is that, short-term debt will be refinanced after tax levies and spending cuts are observed, and thus at a lower interest rate. Furthermore, such a policy may bring additional benefits to the extent that it signals the government's resolution (see also Drudi and Prati 1997).

Under the same circumstances, when high-interest rates reflect "too high" expected inflation, the role of short-term debt can be played by price-indexed debt. Debt management during the Thatcher government's stabilization provides the clearest example where a policy, aimed at reducing the costs of debt servicing, was successful and possibly conveyed a positive signal about the government's intentions. In the UK, in the early 1980s interest rates were high: long rates were high reflecting investors' fears that the inflation inherited from the pre-Thatcher years would continue; short rates were high because

---

[2] In most European countries private debt is not securitized which strengthens the argument for public debt.

of tight monetary policy aimed at reducing inflation. In such a situation the decision by the British government of issuing price-index-linked bonds led to substantial savings in interest costs as inflation rapidly decreased in the following years.

The importance of credibility in determining the choice of debt maturity at the start of fiscal and monetary stabilizations is confirmed by empirical evidence. Missale, Giavazzi and Benigno (1997) examine the choice of debt maturity during the first two years of 62 episodes of fiscal stabilization in OECD countries over the 1975–95 period.[3] They find strong evidence of policymakers reducing the share of fixed-rate long-term debt denominated in the domestic currency the higher are long-term interest rates at beginning of the stabilization attempt and the lower is the gain in credibility as measured by the fall in the long rate differential with German rates in the first year of the program.

These facts can be interpreted as evidence that when governments tend to reduce the share of long-term debt the lower is their initial reputation and the less credible is the program. This policy can be justified and an argument for interest-cost reduction can be made, if information between the government and private investors is asymmetric, as is usually the case at the outset of a stabilization attempt when private investors may lack full confidence in the announced budget cuts.

Credibility problems also arise because of opportunistic behavior on the side of the government. High-interest rates may reflect investors' lack of confidence that the government will abstain from inflationary financing in the presence of fixed-rate long-term nominal debt. Then, in order to maintain the credibility of the anti-inflation stance, governments may need to issue price-indexed debt, foreign currency debt and short-term nominal debt. The problem of the time inconsistency of fiscal and monetary policy is examined in the next sections.

6.5 Time consistency: nominal debt

The final argument for minimizing the expected cost of debt servicing is that particular types of debt or particular debt structures create an incentive for the government to reduce the return on debt either through inflation, or changes in interest rates or even outright taxation. As investors realize the government's temptation, they ask for interest rates higher than they would be if the government could credibly commit to abstain from such actions. Thus, when it borrows in particular instruments, a committed government may face interest costs that are not justified on the basis of the risk-return characteristics of such instruments.

---

[3] An episode of fiscal stabilization is defined as a period during which the structural primary surplus improved by at least 1% of GDP.

This rationale for cost reductions is the one that has most attracted the economists' attention since the temptation to alter debt returns naturally arises in the presence of tax distortions and most of the literature on debt management stems from optimal taxation analysis. The idea is that the *ex ante* optimal policy of announcing no taxes on public debt or no inflation, ex-post is no longer optimal: once the debt has been issued it is supplied inelastically. *Ex post*, the least distortionary policy is to levy taxes on debt or to reduce its real value through unanticipated inflation instead of raising distorting taxes on labor income. This problem is known as the time inconsistency of the optimal plan.

In theory, choosing instruments which provide incentives for consistent behavior and thus minimize interest costs is fully justified as a welfare-maximizing policy; it obtains as the time-consistent solution to the problem of minimizing tax distortions. In practice it may be difficult to distinguish whether interest rates are "high" because they reflect the government's lack of commitment to policy announcements or, more simply, the investors' assessment of the probability of future events.

The role of debt management in containing the costs of time consistency is also limited to the violation of implicit commitments. The choice of debt instruments can do very little against the temptation to explicitly repudiate the debt, except for specific assumptions about the type and cost of repudiation (see Section 5.4.1 and De Broeck 1997).[4] However, such actions are rare events and it is sensible to assume that the social cost of breaking explicit commitments, such as repaying the debt, is much higher than the cost of violating an implicit commitment such as maintaining the real value of currency.

As we focus on the temptation to reduce the real value of nominal debt by surprise inflation, the role of debt management is clear: the incentive to inflate can be eliminated by issuing price-indexed debt or foreign currency debt. The problem has long been recognized; historically, inflating the debt away has been the preferred form of repudiation and recommendations to issue price-indexed bonds, in order to remove inflationary temptations, have been made since the work of Back and Musgrave (1941).

Lucas and Stokey (1983) show that, in the absence of precommitment, nominal debt could not even be issued if only anticipated inflation were costly, as in a purely neoclassical framework. This is because, once the nominal debt had been issued, optimal taxation would call for a price-level jump so as to wipe out the entire debt instead of raising distorting taxes on labor income. The same problem arises with money. Persson, Persson and Svensson (1987) show

---

[4] The distribution by type of holder determines the cost of outright taxation. Insofar as the choice of debt instruments is related to debt ownership implications for debt management may also emerge. De Broeck shows that debt accumulation in highly indebted countries is significantly related to changes in the distribution of debt by type of holder.

that a solution requires that each government leave to its successor net nominal claims on the private sector with a value equal to the money stock. This solution rules out any incentive for unexpected inflation or deflation but it is clearly counterfactual and has led the following research to assume that actual, and not only anticipated, inflation is costly.

When actual inflation is costly, government borrowing in nominal debt is possible but may give rise to inflationary expectations and lead to high-interest rates and inflation. The reason is that, realizing the government incentive to inflate, investors ask for interest rates—reflecting anticipated inflation—so high that the government is unwilling to trade further inflation costs for lower tax distortions. In this way the government cannot expect to obtain any revenue from surprise inflation, and nominal debt leads to an inflationary bias, that is, to a "too high" inflation equilibrium.[5]

Time-consistency problems may also arise because of the temptation to reduce the value of debt and future spending commitments by altering the path for interest rates. To the extent that the government can affect real interest rates a problem emerges even if debt liabilities are fully indexed to the price level or, even better, fully honored commitments to real payments. As shown by Lucas and Stokey (1983), a time-consistent solution requires that the maturity structure of, say, price-indexed debt be properly designed so as to remove any devaluation incentive. In their model (see Chapter 2), the optimal tax plan is time inconsistent, since the government can affect real interest rates and thus the value of future debt payments and spending commitments. In fact, in a closed economy without capital, real rates (literally, intertemporal marginal rates of substitution) depend on labor and consumption choices which can be affected by the government choice of labor income-tax rates. As new debt is issued or old debt is bought back, each successive government faces different debt payments from its predecessor and, generally, would want to change the path for real interest rates. However, since the effects of changes in interest rates on the debt value also depend on its maturity structure, the latter can be redesigned in each period to remove any incentive for debt devaluation. Specific policy implications for the choice of debt maturity cannot be easily derived, as they depend on the future path for taxes and spending, but some intuition can be gained from special cases. For example, if spending is constant so that each government raises constant taxes to meet spending and interest payments, then a time-consistent solution is ensured by consols paying the same coupon in every period. In fact, only if no new debt is ever issued or redeemed, can changes in interest rates leave the intertemporal budget constraint unaffected, which rules out any incentive to deviate from the optimal tax plan. The analogy

[5] Inflationary temptations are stronger if domestic currency debt is held by foreign residents as stressed by Bohn (1991). An alternative solution to price indexation is to issue foreign currency debt (see also Watanabe 1992).

with the problem of insuring the budget against interest-rate risk, discussed in Section 5.4.1 is clear, and may further help the intuition: in the Lucas–Stokey's solution it is as if the budget were insulated from government-induced changes in interest rates.

However, the introduction of uncertainty raises the issue of how time-consistency problems relate to the minimization of budgetary risk. This issue is examined in the next section.

6.5.1 Implicit-contingent approach and time consistency

As discussed in Section 5.4, and shown by Barro (1995, 1997), if uncertainty only concerns government bond prices—i.e. interest rates—then full price indexation and an insulating maturity structure (such as Lucas and Stokey's maturity) provide an ideal solution to the minimization of tax uncertainty. For other sources of risk and shocks hitting the economy, explicitly contingent debt would instead be needed for unexpected variations in the tax-base or in government spending to be hedged optimally.

If moral hazard explains the absence of explicitly contingent debt, then nominal debt is likely to suffer from the same problem and, as Barro (1997) suggests, price-indexed debt, with an insulating maturity structure à la Lucas–Stokey, is again the optimal choice. If instead, as argued in Section 4.1, contingent securities like output-indexed bonds are not issued because of market imperfections and the frictions and delay associated with reporting the relevant statistics, then price-indexed debt does not necessarily provide the best solution to the problem of minimizing inflation and tax distortions. Nominal debt could be a valuable hedge against budgetary risk, in which case the costs of time inconsistency would have to be weighed against the desirability of either absorbing shocks affecting the government budget or maintaining flexibility in responding to situations which are not covered by explicit contracts. As the two motivations are jointly taken into account, the choice of debt indexation and denomination should consider how to implement relevant contingencies in debt returns as well as incentives for consistent behavior.

Bohn (1988) shows that, insofar as nominal debt provides a hedge against real shocks affecting the government budget, issuing some nominal debt is optimal even in the presence of time-consistency problems. In Calvo and Guidotti (1990a) the inflationary bias calls for indexing only a share of the debt to the price level. Some nominal debt is desirable since state-contingent inflation can be used to smooth the impact of spending shocks on conventional tax rates.

The literature combining anti-temptation and implicit-contingent aspects suggests both incentive and insurance considerations as important determinants of debt management. This view is appealing in that it points to a recurrent theme of economics: that providing insurance relaxes the incentives for consistent behavior, while incentive problems limit the scope for insurance. The important insight is that the optimal debt composition between price-indexed and nominal bonds should hinge on the trade-off between controlling inflationary expectations with incentives for consistent behavior and losing insurance or flexibility to cope with shocks adversely affecting the budget.

6.6 Nominal debt maturity and opportunistic behavior

While general conclusions have been reached on how insurance and incentive considerations interact in determining the denomination of government liabilities, research on the maturity structure of nominal debt combining both aspects is still at an early stage. A long maturity can be used to implement more contingencies in debt returns or to insulate the government budget from refinancing risk. Debt maturity also affects inflation incentives; since it is unlikely that governments are able or willing to engineer a once-and-for-all jump in the price level, the maturity of nominal debt determines the impact of inflation on the real value of the debt.

Incentive problems have been studied by Calvo and Guidotti (1990*a*, 1990*b*, 1992, 1993) and by Missale and Blanchard (1994). Because of the different assumptions on how people form expectations about government behavior, this research has led to conflicting results. Calvo and Guidotti assume that private agents do not take into account past government actions in forming expectations, so that the government acts opportunistically in every period. Missale and Blanchard consider instead the possibility of reputational equilibria where agents take into consideration the entire history of government decisions.

When the government acts opportunistically the role of nominal debt maturity in ensuring the time consistency of tax and inflation policy depends on whether governments can issue price-indexed and foreign currency debt to control inflationary expectations. Calvo and Guidotti (1992) consider the government choice between taxes and inflation to finance public spending and nominal debt of various maturities in an infinite-horizon deterministic model.[6] Both inflation and conventional taxes are increasingly costly and only nominal debt can be issued. The inflationary bias induced by nominal debt leads to "debt aversion": taxes are raised early to reduce the nominal debt over time, as opposed to the precommitment policy of constant taxes and debt. The reason is that a current debt reduction implies a lower inflation tax-base in all future periods which leads to a reduction in expected and equilibrium inflation forever after. Along the optimal path taxes and inflation are decreasing while over time the debt is reduced to zero, rising temporarily when government spending exceeds its permanent level.

---

[6] See also Calvo and Guidotti's (1990*b*) three-period version of the model.

The important result is that the average term to maturity of the debt should be reduced as the level of debt decreases in order to make the optimal plan time consistent. Debt maturity matters even if along the optimal plan inflation is so high that there is no incentive—within each period—to trade further inflation costs for lower tax distortions. Still maturity matters because, as in Lucas and Stokey (1983), successive governments can engage in debt devaluations by altering the path for interest rates through revisions of the inflation (and tax) plan. Deviations from the optimal plan can be thought of as inflation-induced "twists" in the yield curve. Intuitively, a "too long" maturity (relative to the announced plan of tax repayments and inflation) gives rise to the temptation to raise long interest rates (future inflation), while a "too short" maturity introduces the temptation to raise short interest rates (current inflation).

To understand the role of debt maturity, consider the incentive effects of a "too long" and a "too short" maturity respectively. As the nominal return on long maturity debt is predetermined over a long future period, the government has no incentive to redeem it early: it can devalue the debt by inflating more than announced in future periods. Hence, a too long maturity sets an incentive to delay tax repayments, in order to exploit nominal debt as an inflation tax-base over a longer horizon. If, instead, debt maturity is too short, for example if the whole debt is maturing at the end of the current period, only current surprise inflation is effective. Deviations from announced inflation for future periods would be offset by revisions in interest rates.[7] Finally, when current inflation is high the government meets a high present value of inflation distortions and consequently has an incentive for anticipating debt repayment. Hence, a too short maturity sets an incentive to inflate in the current period and to anticipate debt repayments.

The reason why the level of debt and its average maturity display a positive relation in a time-consistent solution is that inflation and thus the incentive for early debt repayment are increasing in the level of debt and decreasing in average maturity. At high levels of debt there is no need to provide additional incentives for early repayment because inflation and inflation distortions are already high. It follows that a (relatively) long maturity can be in place. As the nominal debt is reduced over time, each successive government faces a lower inflation distortion and thus a lower incentive for anticipating debt repayments. Then the maturity of the debt must be shortened to set incentives for (inflation and) faster debt repayment.[8]

---

[7] For instance, if the real value of debt were reduced by current inflation, future period inflation would be lower than announced, but this surprise deflation would come at no cost for the government; it would be reflected in lower interest rates at which the debt is rolled over.

[8] The maturity structure displays a negative co-movement with permanent government spending. An increase in spending raises taxes and thus leads to higher inflation. However, while it is optimal to accelerate debt repayment, there is no effect on inflation tax-bases (as opposed to the case of high debt levels) and a shorter maturity structure is needed to provide the right incentive for fast debt repayment.

The indication to shorten the maturity of nominal debt as the debt decreases hinges critically on the government's inability to issue price-indexed or foreign currency debt. Implications for nominal debt maturity change if the government can issue securities whose value cannot be affected by surprise inflation. Such instruments allow control over the inflation tax-base, and thus provide a more efficient way of dealing with inflationary expectations than early debt repayments.

In Calvo and Guidotti (1990a) (see Section 5.2.3), issuing only two-period nominal bonds is optimal, since the optimal dimension of the inflation tax-base and hence, the optimal insurance-incentive trade-off is obtained by indexing part of the debt to the price level. In this case the government is free to choose long nominal debt to equalize inflation tax-bases and to smooth inflation over time, as in the case of precommitment discussed earlier.

High interest rates incorporating the expectation of inflationary financing provide a clear instance when the objective of minimizing costs is fully justified and where a trade-off may emerge with the ojective of minimizing budgetary risk. Time consistency makes a strong theoretical argument for price-indexed debt and for what can be referred to as an insulating maturity structure. However, empirically, identifying time-consistency problems is quite difficult. For instance, there is no doubt that early introduction of price-index-linked bonds in the UK led to substantial savings in real interest payments throughout the early 1990s (Bank of England 1996 and Deacon and Derry 1998), but it is difficult to ascertain whether expected inflation has been high because the government stand against inflation was not credible, because of an inflation-risk premium, or just because of pessimistic expectations which simply turned out to be wrong (see Breedon and Chadha 1998). It was likewise difficult in the years preceding the 1992 EMS crisis to understand whether the substantial interest spreads between borrowing in domestic versus foreign currencies (observed in weak currency countries) reflected a perceived lack of commitment to the fixed parity or the existence of important differences between exchange rates and their expected values as implied by economic "fundamentals."

In order to shed light on the relevance of credibility issues, new evidence on the relation between the average term to maturity, the level of debt and inflation and interet rates is provided in the next section.

6.7 Debt and debt maturity: the evidence

It is commonly held that large nominal debts reduce the government determination to adopt anti-inflationary policies, and thus make their stand against inflation less credible. However, and contrary to the main predictions of the theory, the incentive for inflation created by nominal debt does not lead to high inflation. Indeed, for OECD countries there is no evidence of a relation between inflation and the level of nominal debt over time and little evidence of a relation across countries (see e.g. Masson and Mussa 1995). Unless one is willing to believe that governments which accumulate more debt do so because of their reputation for being tough on inflation, the hypothesis that a high level of nominal debt leads to high inflation must be considered wrong.

This evidence suggests that in actual economies incentive problems are dealt with successfully and raises the issue of whether any debt management is needed. In fact, governments might have the ability to precommit to low inflation, also by subtracting the monetary authority from their influence. In effect, increasingly independent central banks have probably been a main factor in the recent experience of decreasing inflation and rising debts. However, the absence of a relation between debt and inflation over the last 40 years suggests that, by behaving consistently, OECD governments may have built a reputation for low inflation.

Indeed, it is unrealistic to imagine that governments act by choosing the short-run optimal policy every time, since reputational considerations may also be important in the way people form expectations about government behavior. As shown by Barro and Gordon (1983), when expectations depend on the history of past government decisions—on reputational aspects—there exist better time-consistent equilibria than the high-debt–high-inflation equilibrium.

Although high levels of debt do not lead to high inflation, credibility problems seem to matter for the choice of debt instruments: evidence on the composition and maturity of OECD countries' debts suggests that the low-inflation outcome may have required the governments of highly indebted countries to reduce the maturity of the debt as the debt increased. The analysis in Chapter 4 informally showed that, while for most countries there has been little systematic relation between the level of debt and its maturity, in Belgium, Ireland, Italy and Sweden, the accumulation of debt has been associated with either a shortening of the average term to maturity of nominal debt or with an increase in the share of debt denominated in foreign currency or with indexation to a short-term interest rate.[9] Maturity is also very short in Spain which has recently experienced severe fiscal imbalances and it is probably shortest in Greece, a country whose debt has reached a level higher than GDP.

The relation between debt, maturity, inflation and interest rates is investigated in the next section to evaluate whether this inverse relation is significant and robust to the consideration of other variables possibly affecting the choice of debt maturity.

[9] De Broeck (1997) also finds evidence of a significant relation between the debt ratio and shifts in its ownership. Further evidence of a negative relation between debt and debt maturity, when the debt ratio rises, is presented by De-Haan, Sikken and Hilder (1995). Calvo, Guidotti and Leiderman (1991) investigate the effect of debt and public spending on debt maturity. Finally, Miller (1997) finds a negative relation across countries between the share of fixed-rate long-term debt and political instability and polarization and a positive relation with the degree of central bank independence.

6.7.1　Evidence from OECD countries

In this section the relation between the maturity of public debt, the level of debt, inflation and long-term interest rates is examined for OECD countries over the period 1961–95. The choice of maturity, indexation and denomination of public debt is related to variables which determine the burden of taxation and the cost of long-term conventional bonds. The idea to be explored is that the "effective maturity" must shorten when the debt increases for the anti-inflationary policy to remain credible.

The effective maturity is taken as the best proxy for the duration of the debt relative to inflation, namely, the elasticity of the debt value to a permanent change in the inflation rate. The latter is the relevant concept for the theory which is developed in the next section. The rationale for effective maturity and details on its construction are extensively discussed in Section 4.4. The effective maturity series is constructed using the average remaining term to maturity as a proxy for the duration of fixed-rate securities denominated in the domesting currency while it is based on the following assumptions for other types of debt. The inflation elasticity of price-indexed debt is naturally set to zero. Zero maturity is also assigned to foreign currency (and ECU) denominated debt, thus assuming implicitly that inflation would be reflected one for one in currency depreciation. As shown in Table 4.1 (see Section 4.3) this makes a substantial difference for countries like Austria, Belgium, Denmark, Finland, Ireland, Greece, Portugal and Sweden. A correction is also needed for variable-rate debt, a substantial amount of which has been issued in Austria, Greece, Italy and Portugal (see Table 4.4 in Section 4.3). For such debt, the average time interval between coupon adjustments, increased by the eventual indexation lag, is taken as the relevant duration for purposes of computing effective maturity. Ideally, one would like to compute effective maturity for privately held debt (or market holdings of debt) rather than for total debt; time-series evidence on the average maturity of the debt in market hands is however available only for few countries: Australia, UK and the US. For all other countries the effective maturity is for total debt. For countries where data on maturity are not available, or are available for a period that is too short for estimation purposes, the share of fixed-rate long-term debt denominated in the domestic currency is used in place of effective maturity.

The debt burden is measured by privately held debt—that part of the government debt held by the public rather than by the central bank or government agencies—as a proportion of GDP. Privately held debt, rather than total debt, is the relevant tax-base for unexpected inflation. The difference between market holdings and total debt is sometimes substantial; in Italy, central bank holdings were equal to 13% of total debt in 1960, going up to 40% in 1976 (through monetization of the deficit), and back down to 6% in 1995. However, for Austria, France and Portugal the total debt is used because of unavailability of data on central bank holdings.

Finally, the series of inflation and long-term interest rates are taken from the OECD Economic Outlook. (Sources for the series and details of construction are given in the appendix at the end of this volume.)

Figures 4.1 to 4.18 show the evolution of debt and effective maturity since 1960 for the sample of OECD countries considered. The evolution of the average term to maturity of the fixed-rate component of the debt is also shown in the same figures. In cases where the average and effective maturity are not available or are available over a short period, the share of fixed-rate long-term debt is presented.

For most countries over the last 30 years, there has been little systematic relation between the level of debt and both its average term to maturity and effective maturity. One set of countries stands however in clear exception to this general statement. In highly indebted countries like Belgium, Ireland, Italy, Sweden and, to a lesser extent, Spain debt accumulation has been associated with either a shortening of the average maturity of the nominal debt or with an increase in the share of debt denominated in foreign currency or with indexation to prevailing interest rates. Indeed, at high levels of debt a significant inverse relation emerges between the level of debt and "effective maturity." Moreover, in these countries effective maturity is considerably shorter than in other less indebted economies, as shown in Table 4.20. In highly indebted countries, the effective maturity decreased by half or more from the mid-1970s to the late 1980s. Although maturity lengthened in the early 1990s, in 1995 it was still very low standing at 1.8 years for Italy, 2.8 years for Spain and 3.1 years for Sweden compared, for example, to 5.6 years for France or 6.5 years for the UK. Effective maturity has instead increased up to 3.7 in Ireland, which had experienced a spectacular fiscal consolidation since the late 1980s, and it has lengthened to 3.8 years in Belgium, a country which had successfully tied its currency to the Deutsche Mark.

Table 6.1 reports the results from simple regressions of the log of effective maturity on a constant, the log of the debt/GDP ratio and the inflation rate for the period 1961–95. For countries, denoted with the superscript b, the dependent variable is instead the share of fixed-rate long-term debt, since maturity is not available for the whole sample. In the highly indebted countries, Belgium, Ireland, Italy, Spain and Sweden, the coefficient of the debt ratio is negative and highly significant, confirming the visual impression. The debt ratio is also significant in the case of Finland and Portugal, which have a relatively lower debt but experienced important fiscal imbalances. The debt ratio is also significant, but enters with a positive sign, in the case of Denmark, a country with a relatively high debt ratio. Likewise the debt is positive and significant in France, Japan and the US, and positive but less significant in Germany and

Table 6.1. Regressions of maturity on debt and inflation

Country	Const	log(D/Y)	π	R^2	DW	t-statistic
Australia[a]	1.05	0.10	0.04	0.25	0.37	−1.5[−3.8]
(1974–95)		(0.3)	(2.6)			
Austria[b]	0.47	−0.02	−0.01	0.04	0.56	−2.2[−3.7]
(1969–95)		(−0.8)	(−0.1)			
Belgium[b]	0.55	−0.22	−0.01	0.64	0.28	−1.7[−3.6]
(1961–95)		(−6.8)	(−0.2)			
Canada[a]	2.99	−0.33	−0.04	0.17	0.23	−2.1[−3.6]
(1961–95)		(−2.5)	(−2.9)			−3.4 ADF2
Denmark[b]	0.57	0.07	−0.01	0.50	0.62	−2.0[−3.7]
(1969–95)		(4.5)	(−0.2)			
Finland[b]	0.29	−0.14	−0.02	0.52	0.86	−2.7[−3.7]
(1970–95)		(−5.2)	(−3.6)			
France[b]	−3.05	0.62	0.01	0.87	0.58	−2.6[−3.7]
(1971–95)		(8.3)	(1.5)			
Germany[a]	0.13	0.14	−0.01	0.29	0.50	−2.8[−3.7]
(1967–95)		(3.1)	(−0.7)			−2.6 ADF3
Ireland[a]	8.59	−1.59	−0.02	0.82	0.53	−2.5[−3.6]
(1961–95)		(−12.5)	(−3.4)			
Italy[a]	8.13	−1.71	−0.05	0.75	0.20	−1.3[−3.6]
(1961–95)		(−9.8)	(−3.9)			−1.9 ADF2
Japan[b]	0.63	0.15	0.01	0.90	0.77	−1.9[−3.6]
(1961–95)		(16.0)	(4.3)			
Netherlands[a]	3.78	−0.48	−0.02	0.47	0.17	−1.8[−3.6]
(1961–95)		(−4.5)	(−1.4)			
Portugal[b]	−3.68	−0.52	−0.01	0.76	0.83	−2.9[−3.7]
(1970–95)		(−9.0)	(−1.3)			−3.3 ADF2
Spain[a]	6.72	−1.56	−0.09	0.59	0.43	−1.9[−3.6]
(1962–95)		(−7.0)	(−3.5)			
Sweden[b]	0.36	−0.27	0.00	0.86	0.55	−1.8[−3.6]
(1961–95)		(−14.5)	(0.1)			−3.3 ADF3
UK[a]	−0.33	0.61	0.03	0.45	0.66	−2.6[−3.6]
(1962–95)		(4.6)	(4.5)			
USA[a]	−0.99	0.69	−0.01	0.74	0.36	−2.7[−3.6]
(1961–95)		(7.5)	(−0.9)			

Notes: The sample period is 1961–95 unless indicated otherwise. The last column reports the *t*-statistic of the coefficient on the lagged residual, in a regression of the first difference of the residual on the lagged level and the lagged first difference. The values in brackets are the critical values, at the 10% significance level, of the test of the hypothesis of no co-integration (from Table 1 in Mackinnon (1991)). Augmented Dickey-Fuller (ADFn) with *n* lags are shown, when relevant, on the second row. Numbers in parentheses are *t*-statistics.
[a] dependent variable: log(maturity).
[b] dependent variable: share of long-term debt.

the US, countries with less severe or smaller fiscal problems and a long debt maturity.

A second interesting finding is the lack of explanatory power of the inflation rate. It has long been argued that high inflation is associated with higher inflation uncertainty, leading to higher risk-premia on long-term nominal debt, and thus leading governments to stop issuing long-term debt. Indeed, when inflation is very high, long nominal assets, private or public, disappear. But the regressions show that inflation significantly decreases maturity only in few cases: Finland, Ireland, Italy and Spain. However, in all four, the debt ratio dominates inflation, both quantitatively and statistically. For other countries inflation is not significant or even with a positive sign as for Japan and the UK. The basic reason why regressions favor the debt ratio in highly indebted countries comes from the evidence at the end of the sample. Since the late 1980s inflation has slowed down, while the debt ratio has stabilized; and, like the debt ratio, effective maturity has stabilized rather than increasing back to earlier levels.

The regressions provide however an important caveat. The low Durbin–Watson statistics indicate that the series may not be co-integrated and that the strong estimated relation between debt and maturity may be spurious. The tests of co-integration in the last column indeed indicate that the hypothesis of no co-integration cannot be rejected at the 10% confidence level, so that part of the relation may indeed be spurious. Evidence in favor of an effect of the debt ratio appears strong, but the caveat must be made.

The lack of explanatory power of inflation is surprising and may reflect a weak link between current inflation and the cost of long-term borrowing. Indeed, inflation is a rough approximation (or an indirect measure) of term-premia and thus of the relative cost of issuing long-term debt instead of short-term or variable-rate or foreign currency debt. By substituting the long-term interest rate for inflation in the above regression a fairer comparison obtains between the idea that the effective maturity must shorten when the debt increases for the anti-inflationary policy to remain credible and the simple relative-cost hypothesis according to which the supply of long-term debt is negatively related to its yield to maturity. To the extent that high levels of debt tend to be associated with high interest rates, these two variables are expected to be fairly correlated and the impact of the debt ratio on debt maturity to disappear when the interest rate is introduced in the regression. On the contrary, if the hypothesis is correct, that a shorter maturity is needed to maintain the credibility of the anti-inflationary policy when the debt rises, then effective maturity should react to an increase in the debt ratio while the long-term interest rate should remain relatively constant.

Simple OLS regressions of the log of effective maturity on a constant, the log of the debt ratio and the long-term interest rate, provide an informal test of the

Table 6.2. Regressions of maturity on debt and long rate

Country	Const	log(D/Y)	Rate	R^2	DW	t-statistic
Australia[a]	1.02	0.52	−0.08	0.42	0.51	−2.2[−3.8]
(1974–95)		(1.9)	(−3.9)			
Austria[b]	0.52	−0.02	−0.01	0.06	0.51	−2.1[−3.7]
(1969–95)		(−1.2)	(−0.8)			
Belgium[b]	0.64	−0.21	−0.01	0.68	0.24	−1.7[−3.6]
(1961–95)		(−7.9)	(−2.0)			
Canada[a]	2.26	−0.06	−0.04	0.16	0.20	−2.0[−3.6]
(1961–95)		(−0.6)	(−2.8)			−3.5 $_{ADF3}$
Denmark[b]	0.55	0.08	0.00	0.51	0.65	−2.1[−3.7]
(1969–95)		(5.3)	(0.5)			
Finland[b]	0.44	−0.06	−0.01	0.29	0.49	−2.8[−3.7]
(1970–95)		(−3.4)	(−1.1)			
France[b]	−2.58	0.54	0.00	0.86	0.59	−2.8[−3.7]
(1971–95)		(11.2)	(0.6)			
Germany[a]	−0.02	0.15	0.00	0.28	0.49	−2.6[−3.7]
(1967–95)		(3.5)	(0.1)			−2.5 $_{ADF3}$
Ireland[a]	7.84	−1.36	−0.04	0.83	0.48	−2.5[−3.6]
(1961–95)		(−11.1)	(−3.8)			
Italy[a]	6.33	−1.02	−0.13	0.88	0.26	−1.4[−3.6]
(1961–95)		(−7.0)	(−8.0)			−3.2 $_{ADF4}$
Japan[b]	0.58	0.11	0.02	0.94	1.30	−2.7[−3.6]
(1967–94)		(20.0)	(6.6)			−4.2 $_{ADF4}$
Netherlands[a]	3.95	−0.41	−0.07	0.68	0.46	−2.7[−3.6]
(1961–95)		(−7.7)	(−5.5)			
Portugal[b]	−1.61	−0.29	−0.02	0.86	0.94	−3.1[−3.7]
(1970–95)		(−4.5)	(−4.3)			−4.0 $_{ADF2}$
Spain[a]	6.36	−0.89	−0.21	0.93	1.29	−2.3[−3.6]
(1966–95)		(−12.8)	(−13.8)			
Sweden[b]	0.44	−0.26	−0.01	0.85	0.51	−1.8[−3.6]
(1960–95)		(−9.2)	(−0.9)			−3.4 $_{ADF3}$
UK[a]	−1.73	0.87	0.06	0.39	0.45	−2.0[−3.6]
(1962–95)		(4.8)	(3.9)			
USA[a]	−1.25	0.74	0.01	0.72	0.27	−2.7[−3.6]
(1961–95)		(9.5)	(0.7)			

Notes: see Notes to Table 6.1.

two hypotheses. The results from such regressions are reported in Table 6.2. Contrary to what was expected, for most of the countries considered, the long-term interest rate does not perform better than inflation. In all the countries displaying a positive relation between debt and effective maturity, as for inflation, the coefficient of the interest rate is not statistically different from zero at any reasonable confidence level. The only exceptions are Japan and the UK where the long rate puzzlingly enters with a positive sign (as well as inflation). The long-term rate has also no impact on the share of fixed-rate long-term debt in Austria, Finland and Sweden, thus confirming the previous result with inflation. In Belgium and Ireland, the long rate performs no better than inflation and much worse than the debt ratio which remains highly significant.

However, the long interest rate does impact on effective maturity in a few countries. The choice of debt maturity appears to reflect interest-rate movements in Australia and in Canada, though the evidence for the latter country is very weak, while the debt ratio has no role in both countries. More interestingly, the long-term interest rate is highly significant in Italy, Portugal and Spain, for which a strong inverse relation was detected between effective maturity and the debt ratio, but not with inflation. The interest rate is also significant along with the debt ratio for the Netherlands, where evidence of a negative impact of the debt ratio was weak in the inflation regression. However, for this group of countries, though significant, the interest rate does not outperform the debt ratio: the debt ratio does as good as the interest rate. Therefore, there seems to be important information in the evolution of the debt ratio which can explain the behavior of effective maturity in addition to changes in the cost of long-term nominal debt.

The third regression examines whether the effects of the debt ratio and the interest rate are robust to the introduction of a time trend. For the sake of exposition countries have been divided between those where the debt ratio is positively related to maturity and those where it is negatively related to maturity. On this ground evidence is not presented for Australia, Austria and Canada.[10]

Table 6.3 reports the results from regressions of the log of effective maturity (or the share of long-term debt) on a constant, the log of the debt ratio, the long-term interest rate and a time trend for the group of countries where a positive relation between maturity and debt was detected. The results vary across the six countries. In France, Germany and the UK the coefficient of the debt ratio is not significantly different from zero; no variable, except for the time trend, helps to explain movements in effective maturity. Evidence of a positive relation between debt and maturity in Denmark, Japan and the US is instead unaffected by the introduction of the time trend. In all three countries deficit accumulation has been financed with fixed-rate long-term securities.

Table 6.4 reports the results from the same regression for the group of countries where a negative relation between maturity and debt was detected. Results from regressions where inflation replaces the long-term interest rates

---

[10]   In Australia the result of a significant negative effect of the interest rate is confirmed by the introduction of a time trend while in the case of Canada the coefficient of the debt ratio turns positive.

Table 6.3. Positive debt effect

Country	Const	log(D/Y)	Rate	Time	R^2	DW	t-statistic
Denmark[b]	1.29	0.20	−0.01	−0.02	0.68	0.96	−1.8[−4.2]
(1969–95)		(5.9)	(−2.2)	(−3.8)			
France[b]	−0.52	0.09	−0.01	0.02	0.93	0.83	−3.5[−4.2]
(1971–95)		(0.9)	(−1.7)	(5.1)			
Germany[a]	3.57	−0.23	−0.01	0.02	0.47	0.52	−2.8[−4.2]
(1967–95)		(−1.8)	(−0.7)	(3.2)			
Japan[b]	0.55	0.10	0.02	0.001	0.94	1.32	−2.6[−4.2]
(1967–94)		(6.5)	(5.9)	(0.8)			−3.9 $_{ADF4}$
UK[a]	−1.74	0.12	0.04	−0.02	0.73	0.45	−4.4[−4.1]
(1962–95)		(0.7)	(3.6)	(−6.2)			
USA[a]	−1.75	0.88	0.02	−0.01	0.73	0.30	−3.0[−4.1]
(1961–95)		(7.4)	(1.6)	(−1.5)			

Notes: see Notes to Table 6.1.

are also reported in the few cases where the relevant specification is uncertain. Results vary across countries. For the Netherlands and Portugal the time trend clearly dominates the debt ratio which becomes not significant at any reasonable confidence level. The time trend performs as well as debt ratio in Ireland and Sweden but strong evidence remains of an inverse relation between debt and effective maturity. In Belgium, where the debt and the share of fixed-rate long-term debt have behaved very differently from smooth trends, the time trend does poorly in comparison to the debt ratio. Finally, there is no evidence of a time trend in the case of Finland, Italy and Spain; clearly, for these countries the correct specification does not include a trend (and the relevant regression is that in Table 6.2). Again, with the exception of Ireland, co-integration tests cannot reject the hypothesis of no co-integration.

To summarize, in six countries, Belgium, Finland, Ireland, Italy, Spain and Sweden, the debt ratio and effective maturity have moved in opposite directions over the last 35 years; and in all six countries, the relation largely remains when one controls either for inflation, or for the long-term interest rate or for an otherwise unexplained time trend. Interestingly, these countries are, or have been until recently, the countries with the highest debt ratio or countries like Finland and Spain which suffered from severe fiscal imbalances. This evidence is also consistent with the disappearence of fixed-rate long-term debt in Greece, a country with a debt ratio above 100% (for which data could not be obtained for the period before 1980). On the contrary there is no evidence of a relation between debt and maturity for Canada where the debt ratio is approaching that level.

Indeed, at high levels of debt a significant inverse relation emerges between the level of debt and "effective maturity"; more precisely, the elasticity of the

Table 6.4. Negative debt effect

Country	Const	log(D/Y)	Rate	π	Time	R^2	DW	t-statistic
Belgium[b]	0.55	−0.37	−0.02		0.01	0.92	0.73	−3.2[−4.1]
(1961–95)		(−18.6)	(−9.7)		(10.6)			
Belgium[b]	0.40	−0.39		−0.01	0.01	0.75	0.39	−1.8[−4.1]
(1961–95)		(−7.5)		(−2.4)	(3.8)			
Finland[b]	0.42	−0.07	−0.01		0.001	0.26	0.48	−2.8[−4.2]
(1970–95)		(−1.6)	(−0.9)		[0.2]			
Finland[b]	0.25	−0.15		−0.02	0.00	0.50	0.84	−2.6[−4.2]
(1970–95)		(−3.6)		(−3.4)	[0.3]			
Ireland[a]	4.81	−0.55	−0.02		−0.03	0.92	0.76	−4.3[−4.1]
(1961–95)		(−3.6)	(−3.7)		(−6.2)			−4.5 ADF2
Ireland[a]	5.29	−0.69		−0.01	−0.03	0.92	0.83	−3.9[−4.1]
(1961–95)		(−4.3)		(−3.7)	(−6.4)			−4.4 ADF2
Italy[a]	7.15	−1.28	−0.13		0.01	0.87	0.28	−1.5[−4.1]
(1961–95)		(−2.2)	(−5.6)		[0.4]			−3.1 ADF4
Netherlands[a]	2.96	−0.16	−0.03		−0.01	0.74	0.33	−1.8[−4.1]
(1961–95)		(−1.7)	(−1.4)		(−2.9)			
Portugal[b]	0.97	−0.02	−0.03		−0.02	0.87	0.64	−3.2[−4.2]
(1970–95)		(−0.2)	(−4.9)		(−1.9)			−4.2 ADF2
Spain[a]	6.57	−0.97	−0.22		0.01	0.93	1.40	−2.6[−4.2]
(1966–95)		(−6.2)	(−9.6)		[0.6]			
Sweden[b]	0.63	−0.15	0.01		−0.01	0.91	0.80	−1.7[−4.1]
(1961–95)		(−4.7)	(0.9)		(−4.4)			−3.0 ADF3

Notes: see Notes to Table 6.1.

value of the debt to unexpected inflation. Moreover, in these countries effective maturity is considerably shorter than in other less indebted OECD economies.

These are the stylized facts which motivate the model presented in the next section.

6.8 Maturity, debt and reputation[ll]

A tentative explanation for the facts of the previous section—the existence of an inverse relation between debt and effective maturity at high levels of debt and the absence of a relation between debt and inflation—can be based on the idea of a reputation equilibrium.

By consistently adopting anti-inflationary policies a government can build a reputation for "low" inflation. However, at high levels of debt, investors may still perceive the debt burden as a strong incentive for inflation and the government must decrease the effective maturity of the debt as the debt increases

---

[ll] This section is based on the paper by A. Missale and O. J. Blanchard, "The debt burden and debt maturity," published in *American Economic Review*, 84(1), March 1994.

in order to maintain the credibility of its anti-inflationary policy. The argument is based on a simple observation: inflation is effective as a way of reducing the debt only if government securities have a long term to maturity, are non-indexed and are denominated in domestic currency. To sustain a reputation equilibrium the incentive to reduce the value of the debt by unexpected infla-tion must not exceed the cost of lost reputation. As the incentive to inflate increases in both the level of debt and its effective maturity, the government will maintain its no-inflation pledge credible by reducing effective maturity as the debt increases.

The model proposed in this section shows the mechanisms at work and the role of debt maturity. It captures two aspects of the problem faced by the government. The first is that, other things equal, a higher level of nominal debt leads to a stronger temptation to inflate. The second is that the longer the effective maturity of the debt, the larger is the decrease in the market value of the debt associated with a given unexpected increase in inflation. The relation between debt, maturity and inflation is formalized by the following accumulation equation:

$$D_t = (1 + r)[1 - m_{t-1}(\pi_t - E_{t-1}\pi_t)]D_{t-1} + G_t - T_t \qquad (6.1)$$

where G_t and T_t denote government spending and taxes during period t, while D_t is the real value of debt at the beginning of period $t + 1$. Finally, r is the real interest rate, which is assumed constant.

The important assumption is in the formalization of the relation between maturity, unexpected inflation and the value of debt. Maturity is formalized by an index m, which gives the effect of a given unexpected rate of inflation on the value of the debt. A strict interpretation of this assumption is that the government can choose to issue a combination of price-indexed debt—zero maturity nominal debt—and one-period maturity nominal debt. If the government issues only indexed debt, m is then equal to zero: there is no effect of unexpected inflation on the value of the debt. If the government issues only one-period nominal debt, then m is equal to 1. However, a more general interpretation is used informally in what follows, in which m stands for the duration of the debt, conceptually allowing debt to be of maturity longer than one period. The reason why that interpretation is more questionable is that, when the maturity of the debt exceeds one period, the sequence of unexpected inflation over the life of the bonds should appear in Equation (6.1). This sequence is not introduced to preserve analytical tractability.

Finally, it is assumed that taxes are set in the current period so as to remain at the same level in all future periods and equal to the current level, once the effect of unexpected inflation has been taken into account:

$$T_t = G_t^P + r[1 - m_{t-1}(\pi_t - E_{t-1}\pi_{t-1})]D_{t-1} \qquad (6.2)$$

where G_t^P denotes "permanent" (or normal) spending, i.e. the annuity value of current and future spending, discounted at the interest rate r:

$$G_t^P \equiv (r/(1+r)) \sum_{i=0}^{\infty} (1+r)^{-i} G_{t+i} \qquad (6.3)$$

where G_t varies over time, following an arbitrary but deterministic process.

As shown in Missale and Blanchard (1991) this apparently ad hoc rule for taxes is indeed the optimal tax-smoothing rule which can be derived within the same model when a quadratic term in taxes is introduced in the government loss function. This rule has been derived in Section 5.3.1. Replacing the expression (6.2) for taxes in the budget constraint (6.1) yields

$$D_t = G_t - G_t^P + [1 - m_{t-1}(\pi_t - E_{t-1}\pi_t)]D_{t-1} \qquad (6.4)$$

Thus, under this tax-smoothing rule and in the absence of unexpected inflation, the debt increases when current spending exceeds permanent spending, that is when current spending is unusually high in comparison to spending in the future. The effect of unexpected inflation is to decrease the value of the debt, and the strength of the effect depends on the effective maturity, m_{t-1}.

The government's objective is to minimize the expected present discounted value, V_t, of current and future values of the one-period loss function, L_t. For simplicity the discount rate is assumed to be equal to the real interest rate, r. The one-period loss function is the sum of three terms:

$$L_t = (1/2)\pi_t^2 + (b/2)[k - (\pi_t - E_{t-1}\pi_t)]^2 + cT_t \qquad (6.5)$$

The first term reflects the costs of inflation, the second the benefits of unexpected inflation through output effects, where k is the difference between the optimal level of output in the absence of labor market distortions and normal output. The third term reflects the cost of taxation. The assumption that the loss is linear rather than quadratic in taxes is theoretically unappealing, but does not affect the qualitative results. Replacing the expression for taxes (6.2), in Equation (6.5) gives:

$$L_t = (1/2)\pi_t^2 + (b/2)[k - (\pi_t - E_{t-1}\pi_t)]^2 + cG_t^P \qquad (6.6)$$
$$+ cr[1 - m_{t-1}(\pi_t - E_{t-1}\pi_t)]D_{t-1}$$

The timing of decisions is the following. At the end of period $t - 1$, the government inherits D_{t-1}, whose equation of motion is given by (6.4), and decides on its maturity, m_{t-1}, for period t. This maturity is known to people when they form their (rational) expectations. Then, at the beginning of period t, the government chooses the rate of inflation, π_t.

Except for the complications introduced by the dynamics of debt and the ability to choose maturity, the problem is standard. Clearly the best outcome is zero inflation. But, in the absence of reputational effects, the no-inflation outcome is time inconsistent, and the result is positive rather than zero inflation. In what follows the existence and characteristics of a reputational equilibrium are examined.

The equilibrium is sustained by the expectations that the government will not inflate as long as it did not in the past. In other words, so long as the government does not use inflation, people assume that it will not do so in the future. If the government relies on unexpected inflation, people then assume that it will act opportunistically every period, choosing inflation so as to minimize V_t given people's expectations.

Solving for the reputational equilibrium requires the derivation of the value of the loss function under reputation, and thus zero inflation, and under cheating and the subsequent loss of reputation.

In the reputational equilibrium, the government does not attempt to inflate the debt away, and both actual and expected inflation are equal to zero. Thus, the value of the loss function, $V_{R,t}$ (R for reputation) is given by:

$$V_{R,t} = (1+1/r)L_{R,t} = (1+1/r)\left[cG_t^P + crD_{t-1} + bk^2/2\right] \qquad (6.7)$$

The loss comes from the taxation required to finance permanent public spending and to service the debt inherited from the past, D_{t-1}. As taxes are constant over time, at the level $\bar{T} = G_t^P + rD_{t-1}$, the loss, V_R, is also constant over time.

To characterize the value of the loss function when the government inflates in the current period, the model must be solved backwards, starting in period $t+1$, after the government has used unexpected inflation to reduce the debt burden. Once the government has inflated and lost its reputation, it will want to choose a level of maturity equal to zero. The reason is simple: the higher the maturity of the debt, the higher is the incentive to inflate. Given the loss of reputation, this only leads people to anticipate higher inflation, leading in turn to higher actual and expected inflation and an increased value of the loss function. When the maturity of debt is equal to zero, debt is unaffected by inflation and, under the assumption (6.2), taxes remain constant forever at $T^* = T_{t+1} = G_{t+1}^P + rD_t$. The minimization problem faced by the government is therefore the same every period. For example, in period $t+1$ the government minimizes

$$L_{C,t+1} = (1/2)\pi_{t+1}^2 + (b/2)[k - (\pi_{t+1} - E_t\pi_{t+1})]^2 + c(G_{t+1}^P + rD_t)$$

where maturity, m_t, has been set equal to zero.

The rate of inflation—actual and expected—is given by

$$\pi_{t+1} = E_t \pi_{t+1} = bk$$

implying that the present value of the loss function from next period on is equal to

$$V_{C,t+1} = (1+1/r)L_{C,t+1} = (1+1/r)[(1+b)bk^2/2 + c(G^P_{t+1} + rD_t)] \quad (6.8)$$

Using the relation $G^P_{t+1} = G^P_t + r(G^P_t - G_t)$, which obtains from the definition of G^P_t, in the debt accumulation Equation (6.4), taxes for time $t+1$ (and for all future periods) are equal to

$$T_{t+1} = G^P_{t+1} + rD_t = G^P_t + r[1 - m_{t-1}\pi_t]D_{t-1}$$

and thus equal to current taxes, T_t.

In other words, when the government inflates, it sets taxes at the same level as the level it intends to maintain them in all future periods. This level depends on the value of the debt after the government has inflated. Using this result in Equation (6.8), yields

$$V_{C,t+1} = (1+1/r)L_{C,t+1} = (1+1/r) \; [(1+b)bk^2/2 + cG^P_t$$
$$+ cr(1 - m_{t-1}\pi_t)D_{t-1}] \quad (6.9)$$

Equation (6.9) shows that the burden of taxation and thus the value of the loss function is reduced—for all future periods—to the extent that inflation in the current period reduces the real value of debt, i.e. reduces D_t below D_{t-1}. The returns to inflating the debt away can therefore be substantial. Moreover, because the government can set maturity equal to zero, it can substantially reduce the equilibrium rate of inflation.

Consider now the minimization problem faced by the government in the current period. For the moment, take the decision about maturity, m_{t-1}, as given. Since people's expectations of inflation are equal to zero, the government chooses inflation to minimize

$$V_{C,t} = (1/2)\pi_t^2 + (b/2)[k - \pi_t]^2 + c[G^P_t + (1 - m_{t-1}\pi_t)rD_{t-1}]$$
$$+ (1/(1+r))V_{C,t+1}$$
$$= (1/2)\pi_t^2 + (b/2)[k - \pi_t]^2 + (1+1/r)c[G^P_t + (1 - m_{t-1}\pi_t)rD_{t-1}]$$
$$+ (1+b)bk^2/2r$$

where, for the second equality, $V_{C,t+1}$ has been replaced by its value from Equation (6.9). Solving for the inflation rate gives

$$\pi_t = [bk + (1+r)cm_{t-1}D_{t-1}]/(1+b) \quad (6.10)$$

The inflation rate is an increasing function of k, the difference between normal output and optimal output in the absence of labor market distortions, and of

c, the weight given to the debt burden in the loss function. More interestingly, the inflation rate is an increasing function of maturity and of the level of the debt. Replacing π_t by its value from (6.10) in the the loss function, $V_{C,t}$, gives

$$V_{C,t} = (1 + 1/r)c[G_t^P + rD_{t-1}] + (1 + b + r)bk^2/2r$$
$$-[bk + c(1+r)m_{t-1}D_{t-1}]^2/2(1+b) \qquad (6.11)$$

The maximum value of effective maturity consistent with zero inflation can then be derived from the condition for a reputation equilibrium. The government will choose not to inflate if the resulting loss, V_R, is no greater than V_C, the loss when it inflates. Using Equations (6.7) and (6.11), and rearranging terms gives the following condition

$$c(1+r)m_{t-1}D_{t-1} \leq (bk/\sqrt{r})(\sqrt{1+b} - \sqrt{r})$$

This condition can be solved for the maximum value of m consistent with zero inflation being an equilibrium:

$$\bar{m}_{t-1} = \frac{bk(\sqrt{1+b} - \sqrt{r})}{c\sqrt{r}(1+r)D_{t-1}} \qquad (6.12)$$

where $\bar{m}_{t-1}$ defines the *maximum* effective maturity.

For reputation to remain an equilibrium when the debt increases, the maximum effective maturity has to decrease, since the incentive to inflate is proportional to the product of m_{t-1} and D_{t-1}. As long as the coefficient b, which reflects the incentive to inflate for other reasons than debt reduction, is positive, $\bar{m}$ is positive: there is always a maturity short enough to sustain the zero inflation equilibrium.[12] Therefore, if the government wants to maintain the credibility of its anti-inflationary policy, the maximum maturity of the debt will be a decreasing function of the level of debt. Using this result and Equation (6.4), the model implies the following dynamics of debt and maximum maturity:

$$D_t - D_{t-1} = G_t - G_t^P = G_t + rD_{t-1} - \bar{T}$$
$$\bar{m}_{t-1} = \lambda/D_{t-1}$$

where $\bar{T} = rD_{t-1} + G_t^P$ denotes the constant level of taxes and where $\lambda \equiv bk(\sqrt{1+b} - \sqrt{r})/[c\sqrt{r}(1+r)]$ is a decreasing function of the real interest rate and the cost of tax distortions.

In equilibrium, while taxes remain constant, permanent spending, debt and maturity change over time: a sustained period of unusually high spending leads to a sustained increase in debt and a sustained decrease in maximum maturity.

---

[12] Note that if b or k are equal to zero, so that the only incentive to inflate is to reduce the debt, then there exists no positive maturity which can sustain the reputation equilibrium; this is because in that case, the government can, by choosing zero maturity after having cheated, fully avoid being punished in the future.

6.9   The trade-off between risk and credibility

As shown in the previous section, the incentive to reduce the value of the debt by unexpected inflation must not exceed the cost of a lost reputation for low inflation to be sustained as a reputation equilibrium. As the incentive to inflate increases with both the level of debt and its effective maturity, the government will maintain the credibility of its anti-inflationary policy by reducing effective maturity as the debt increases.[13]

This explanation can account for both the shortening of the effective maturity observed in highly indebted countries and the absence of an inflationary bias. However, what has been derived is a theory of maximum maturity not of maturity itself. In the absence of uncertainty, the government is indifferent to choosing any maturity below the maximum maturity, $\bar{m}$, and, thus, it could well choose zero effective maturity all the time, either in the form of very short-term debt or in the form of variable-rate or price-indexed debt.

In this section uncertainty is introduced to show that a theory of debt maturity can be derived from the interaction of reputation and risk-hedging considerations. In an uncertain environment where shocks affect tax revenues and debt returns, the government has a preference for a specific effective maturity. As suggested by the implicit-contingent approach, there is an optimal elasticity of debt to unexpected inflation and, thus, a preferred effective maturity, achieved through a combination of nominal debt of various maturities, indexed debt and foreign currency debt. Then, as long as debt is not too high, actual maturity is equal to that preferred maturity but at higher levels of debt the maximum maturity consistent with reputation becomes a binding constraint. This line of explanation can potentially account for both the lack of a relation at low levels of debt as well as the emergence of an inverse relation at higher levels.

Consider a simple economy where uncertainty is introduced via supply and demand shocks. The supply side of the economy is described by the following output process:

$$y_t = y_{t-1} + u_t \tag{6.13}$$

where y_t denotes the log of output and u_t is a productivity shock. Output is stochastic and, except for the effects of inflation which are not explicitly modeled, follows a random walk. Therefore, productivity shocks, u_t, have a permanent effect on output and thus on the tax-base that is relevant for tax-smoothing (see Section 5.3.1). Output shocks are assumed to be i.i.d. with mean

---

[13] More precisely, as shown in Missale and Blanchard (1991), when the timing of taxation is endogenous the reputational constraint binds only at high levels of debt. Only when debt exceeds a threshold level will there be a maximum effective maturity that is consistent with reputation being an equilibrium and is decreasing in debt.

zero and variance σ_u

$$E_t u_{t+1} = 0 \qquad E_t u_{t+1}^2 = \sigma_u$$

The demand side of the economy is derived from an income-elastic money demand

$$\pi_t = x_t - (y_t - y_{t-1}) + v_t$$

where x_t is the rate of money growth and v_t is a demand disturbance, say, a velocity shock. Demand shocks are i.i.d. with mean zero and variance σ_v

$$E_{t-1} v_t = 0 \qquad E_{t-1} v_t^2 = \sigma_v \qquad Cov_{t-1}(v_t u_t) = 0$$

Combining supply and demand gives the inflation rate as a function of monetary policy and of the shocks hitting the economy

$$\pi_t = x_t - u_t + v_t \tag{6.14}$$

The growth rate of money supply, x_t, is chosen before productivity and velocity shocks realize, so that there is no role for monetary policy to offset their inflationary consequences. This implies that the government decides "planned" inflation by choosing the growth rate of money supply but it cannot control realized inflation. Since the choices of planned inflation, π_t^p, and money growth are equivalent, the government is viewed as directly setting planned inflation. Then, realized inflation is given by

$$\pi_t = \pi_t^p - u_t + v_t \tag{6.15}$$

and differs from planned inflation because of supply and demand shocks.

Monetary policy is perfectly observable and has no role in offsetting or dampening the effects of inflation shocks, since they occur after the money supply has been set and vanish after one period. Since the costs of such shocks cannot be avoided, it is sensible to modify the loss function and to define the inflation costs over planned inflation instead of realized inflation.[14] The one-period loss becomes:

$$L_t = (1/2)(\pi_t^p)^2 + (b/2)[k - (\pi_t^p - E_{t-1}\pi_t)]^2 + (c/2)\tau_t^2 \tag{6.16}$$

Inflation surprises, $\pi_t^p - E_{t-1}\pi_t$, continue to display desirable output effects, though such effects are not explicitly modeled in Equation (6.13). Introducing inflation surprises in Equation (6.13) is straightforward but irrelevant for

[14] The consideration of such costs would make cheating more costly than reputation since the marginal cost of inflation increases with the inflation rate.

tax-smoothing because they have transitory effects, and thus no impact on permanent output, the relevant tax-base for tax-smoothing. To simplify the analysis output effects are assumed to derive from inflation surprises which are planned by the government and not from inflation shocks.

Finally, the loss function differs from that in the previous section; instead of being linear in taxes the loss is now quadratic in the tax rate, τ_t. This assumption allows examination of the government's choice of taxes. Tax revenues depend on the uncertain path for output as shown by the dynamic budget constraint

$$D_t = (1+r)[1 - m_{t-1}(\pi_t^P - E_{t-1}\pi_t + v_t - u_t)]D_{t-1} - \tau_t Y_t \qquad [6.17]$$

where Y_t is the level of output and government spending, G_t, has been assumed constant and equal to zero.

There are three unexpected components of the return on debt. The first corresponds to the inflation surprise as planned by the government which has been the focus of the previous section. The second and third components correspond to the random effects on inflation of demand and supply shocks. Positive demand shocks lead to unexpected inflation and low debt returns, while positive productivity shocks lead to unexpected deflation and to higher than expected returns on (long-term) nominal debt.

To the extent that the debt is nominal and long term, demand shocks, v_t, affect debt returns and thus taxation. As effective maturity is set to zero, for example, by issuing price-indexed bonds, velocity shocks are fully neutralized. In this way, debt returns would also be insulated from productivity shocks, u_t, that is, by the other source of unexpected inflation. However, making the real return on debt completely "safe" may increase rather than reduce the variability of the debt ratio because output grows at the uncertain rate, u_t. This is made clear by dividing the budget constraint by Y_t and using Equation [6.13]. Linearizing the resulting expression around a zero growth for output, $u_t \simeq E_{t-1}u_t = 0$, yields

$$d_t = (1+r)[1 - m_{t-1}(\pi_t^P - E_{t-1}\pi_t) - m_{t-1}(v_t - u_t) - u_t]d_{t-1} - \tau_t \qquad [6.18]$$

where d_t denotes the debt/GDP ratio. If all the debt is indexed to the price level, i.e. if $m = 0$, the debt ratio grows at the same rate of output, u_t, so that any permanent fall in output, by u_t, calls for a substantial increase in the tax rate. This tax adjustment can be avoided if the real return on debt is correspondingly reduced so as to leave the debt ratio unaffected at the initial level of the tax rate. In particular, in the absence of demand shocks, output shocks can optimally be hedged by setting $m = 1$, that is, by issuing only (long-term) nominal debt. The choice of debt maturity is examined in the next section.

6.9.1 Optimal hedging with precommitment

Suppose that the government can commit to zero planned inflation independently from the debt level and from the choice of debt maturity. If there were no uncertainty, the effective maturity of public debt would be irrelevant. As supply and demand shocks affect both debt returns and tax revenues, debt maturity may play an important hedging role: there is an optimal effective maturity which minimizes variations in tax rates and it depends on the relative importance of demand and supply shocks.

To derive the optimal effective maturity, the government solves the following tax-smoothing problem

$$Min \ (c/2) \sum_{i=0}^{\infty} (1+r)^{-i} E_t \tau_{t+i}^2$$

$$s.t. \ d_t = (1+r)[1 - m_{t-1}(v_t - u_t) - u_t]d_{t-1} - \tau_t \qquad (6.19)$$

where expected and planned inflation have been set equal to zero, i.e. at their optimal levels, when the government is able to precommit.

The solution to this problem implies the first-order conditions

$$E_t \tau_{t+1} - \tau_t = 0 \qquad (6.20)$$

$$E_{t-1}(\tau_t - E_{t-1}\tau_t)(v_t - u_t) = 0 \qquad (6.21)$$

Equation (6.20) is the familiar condition for tax-smoothing over time, while Equation (6.21) is the condition of zero conditional covariance between the tax rate and the return on nominal debt which has been discussed in Section 5.3.1. A positive conditional covariance suggests "too low" a share of fixed-rate debt; a larger share would avoid tax rates being higher than expected in states where nominal-debt returns are unexpectedly low.

A closed form solution for the tax rate is derived by adopting the linearization proposed by Bohn (1990a). The budget constraint is linearized around the value of the debt ratio which is expected to prevail in future periods under tax-smoothing. Since there is no government spending, the expected debt ratio is equal to the current debt ratio. The shocks v_t and u_t are linearized around their expected values.

$$d_{t-1} \simeq \bar{d}_R \equiv E_{t-1}d_{t+i} = d_{t-1}$$

$$u_t \simeq E_{t-1}u_t = 0 \qquad v_t \simeq E_{t-1}v_t = 0$$

The linearized budget constraint is equal to

$$d_t = (1+r)d_{t-1} - (1+r)[m_{t-1}(v_t - u_t) - u_t]\bar{d}_R - \tau_t \qquad (6.22)$$

Integrating Equation (6.22) forward, taking expectations and imposing the condition (6.20) yields

$$\tau_t = rd_{t-1} - r\bar{d_R}m_{t-1}(v_t - u_t) - r\bar{d_R}\sum_{i=0}^{\infty}(1+r)^{-i}E_t u_{t+i} \qquad (6.23)$$

where the fact has been used that $E_t(v_{t+i} - u_{t+i}) = 0$ for any $i > 0$, i.e. that future debt returns are expected to be equal to 'r'.

Since taxes are levied to pay for the interests on debt, and tax rates are planned to be constant, they are immediately adjusted as unexpected inflation reduces the debt value. The last term captures the effect of innovations in permanent output. Since output shocks are serially uncorrelated and $E_t u_{t+i} = 0$, such term simplifies to $r\bar{d_R}u_t$, but it has been written explicitly to show that the current tax rate is lower than interest payments whenever output is expected to grow so as to reach a permanently higher level.

In order to derive the optimal maturity at period t, the unexpected change in the tax rate is computed leading Equation (6.23) by one period and subtracting from the resulting expression its value as expected one period earlier. This yields

$$\tau_{t+1} - E_t\tau_{t+1} = -r\bar{d_R}[m_t v_{t+1} + (1 - m_t)u_{t+1}] \qquad (6.24)$$

Equation (6.24) shows how demand and supply shocks leads to unexpected changes in the tax rate. As debt maturity, m_t, determines the relative impact of demand and supply shocks, a proper choice of maturity can limit budgetary risk, i.e. the risk of tax adjustments.

If the economy were only hit by demand shocks, then issuing price-indexed debt—i.e. setting $m = 0$—would eliminate any variability in debt returns and thus any uncertainty affecting the government budget. On the contrary, if tax-rate adjustments were caused by output shocks, the optimal policy would be to issue only (long-term) nominal debt—i.e. to set $m = 1$—since bad ouput shocks lead to unexpected inflation. With $m = 1$, the return on nominal debt would be as if it were fully indexed to the rate of output growth, thus implying a constant debt ratio and a constant tax rate.

While with only one type of shock a single debt instrument is sufficient to eliminate any variation in tax rates, with both types of shocks explicitly contingent debt is needed to maintain constant tax rates. In the absence of contingent debt, there is an optimal mix between nominal and price-indexed debt which minimizes tax adjustments. Multiplying Equation (6.24) by the unexpected component of nominal debt returns $(v_{t+1} - u_{t+1})$ and imposing condition (6.21) yields the maturity, m^*, which is optimal in the absence of credibility problems

$$m^* = \frac{\sigma_u}{\sigma_v + \sigma_u}$$

The optimal hedging maturity does not depend on the debt ratio and increases with the variance of supply relative to demand shocks. As the variance of supply shocks increases, the share of fixed-rate long-term debt tends to 1, while it goes to zero as the volatility of aggregate demand grows infinitely large.

The fact that the optimal hedging maturity is between zero and 1 is not surprising, since a strict interpretation of the budget constraints implies that the government can choose between price-indexed debt and one-period maturity nominal debt. However, the more general interpretation adopted in the previous section is used informally in what follows, in which m stands for the effective maturity of the debt. Alternatively, m can be thought as the share of fixed-rate long-term debt, that is, the share of debt which can be inflated away.

To conclude, if aggregate demand disturbances are the only source of uncertainty in the economy, there is no constraint on the choice of effective maturity that can be set equal to zero in every period. When the economy is affected by supply shocks in addition to demand shocks, the maturity which limits variations in tax rates becomes positive and a trade-off may emerge between the objective of minimizing the risk of tax adjustments and the objective of reducing the costs of credibility. This trade-off is examined in the next section.

6.9.2 The trade-off between insurance and reputation

In a reputation equilibrium, at the beginning of each period the government chooses money growth so as to plan for zero inflation and it is expected to do so as long as it behaves non-opportunistically. The government's choice of planned inflation is public knowledge and is made before the realization of the shocks, v_t and u_t, i.e. the government has no informational advantage.

Since inflation and expected inflation are equal to zero, the government's problem almost reduces to the tax-smoothing problem (6.19), examined in the previous section. However, unlike in the case of precommitment, the intertemporal choice of tax rates interacts with the choice of debt maturity. Since the commitment to zero inflation is not fully credible, there may exist a *maximum* effective maturity, $\bar{m}$, that cannot be exceeded for the government's anti-inflationary policy to be credible. This introduces an additional constraint on the government's choice. Thus, the government minimizes the expected loss

$$V_{R,t} = (1 + 1/r)(b/2)k^2 + (c/2)\sum_{i=0}^{\infty}(1 + r)^{-i}E_t\tau_{t+i}^2 \qquad [6.25]$$

subject to

$$d_t = (1+r)d_{t-1} - (1+r)[m_{t-1}(v_t - u_t) - u_t]\bar{d}_R - \tau_t$$

and the constraints

$$m_{t+i} \leq \bar{m}_{t+i}(d_{t+i}) \qquad for\ i = 0,1,2\ldots\infty$$

where $\bar{m}_{t+i}(d_{t+i})$ indicates that the maximum maturity is a function of the debt ratio. The first-order conditions are equal to

$$c\tau_t = cE_t\tau_{t+1} + (1+r)^{-1}\lambda_t(\partial\bar{m}_t/\partial d_t)$$

$$\lambda_t = (1+r)\bar{d}\,cE_t\tau_{t+1}(u_{t+1} - v_{t+1})$$

where λ_t is the Lagrange multiplier associated with the constraint $m_t \leq \bar{m}_t$, i.e. the marginal cost of reducing debt maturity.

If the constraint is binding, $\lambda_t > 0$, the marginal relief from tax distortions, $c\tau_t$, from increasing the debt in the current period is equal to the expected marginal cost of redeeming the additional debt in the next period, $cE_t\tau_{t+1}$, plus the marginal cost of tightening the constraint, $m_t = \bar{m}_t(d_t)$, because of the increase in debt. Such a cost is related to the positive covariance between the tax rate and the real return on debt which follows from not fully exploiting the hedging property of nominal debt (see condition (6.21)). Thus, when the constraint is binding the government raises taxes in the current period in order to relax the constraint. Indeed, if credibility problems prevent optimal hedging across states of nature, the government may want to change the intertemporal choice of tax rates, so as to distribute tax distortions both across time and states of nature.

On the other hand, if the optimal hedging maturity m^*, i.e. the maturity that the government would choose if it were able to precommit, is shorter than the maximum maturity, $\bar{m}$, consistent with reputation, then the constraint on maturity is not binding, $\lambda_t = 0$, and the first-order conditions are the same as (6.20) and (6.21) in the case of precommitment.

In what follows, the expected tax rates are assumed to remain constant at the current level, as if the constraints on debt maturity were not binding. The maximum maturity consistent with reputation being an equilibrium is first derived conditional on this hypothesis. Then, the hypothesis is relaxed to examine the implications for the evolution of debt and effective maturity.

In a reputation equilibrium the government sets planned inflation equal to zero and it is expected to do so. Provided that the maximum maturity is not binding, the tax rates are equal to

$$\tau_{t+i} = rd_{t+i-1} - r\bar{d}_R[m_{t+i-1}v_{t+i} + (1 - m_{t+i-1})u_{t+i}] \qquad (6.26)$$

which, using the linear budget constraint in (6.22), imply the following dynamics for the debt ratio

$$d_{t+i} = d_{t-1+i} - \bar{d}_R[m_{t-1+i}v_{t+i} + (1 - m_{t+i-1})u_{t+i}] \tag{6.27}$$

Finally, the value of the loss under reputation is obtained substituting the optimal tax rates following in the loss function (6.25):

$$\tau_{t+i} = r\bar{d}_R[1 - \sum_{j=0}^{i}(m_{t-1+j}v_{t+j} + (1 - m_{t-1+j})u_{t+j})] \tag{6.28}$$

which are derived (for any future period $t+i$) from Equations (6.26) and (6.27) through recursive substitutions.

In Equation (6.28) the future path for the effective maturity has not been specified. In fact, the government may need to choose an effective maturity lower than $\bar{m}$ in order to sustain the reputation equilibrium. How does this consideration affect the loss that the government experiences? Two cases can be distinguished.

In a first case the maximum effective maturity consistent with reputation is not binding, i.e. $m^* < \bar{m}$, and the government chooses the maturity, $m^* = \sigma_u/(\sigma_v + \sigma_u)$ which provides the best hedge against supply and demand shocks. The government will continue to do so as long as the debt ratio remains below the level at which the maximum maturity becomes binding, that is, until a series of adverse output and demand shocks occur. If debt maturity is constant at its optimal value, then an explicit solution for the loss (6.25) follows. Noting that v_t and u_t are uncorrelated through time and $m_{t+i} = m^*$, the loss—as expected at time $t - 1$, before the shocks v_t and u_t realize—is equal to

$$V_{R,t} = (1/2)(1+1/r)\left\{bk^2 + c(r\bar{d})^2[1 + (1+1/r)(m^{*2}\sigma_v + (1 - m^*)^2\sigma_u)]\right\}$$

In a second case the maximum effective maturity consistent with reputation is lower than the optimal hedging maturity, i.e. $\bar{m} \leq m^*$, and the government must choose the maximum maturity in order to maintain its non-inflation pledge credible. This case will be relevant at high levels of debt. To characterize the expected loss is difficult, in this case, because the maximum maturity will vary inversely with the debt ratio. Since, under reputation the debt ratio follows a random walk, the maximum maturity follows the same process: all its changes are permanent and unpredictable on the basis of the current information. Nevertheless, innovations in debt maturity, $\bar{m}_{t+i} - E_{t-1}\bar{m}_{t+i} = \bar{m}_{t+i} - \bar{m}_{t-1}$, depend on the debt ratio and thus on the accumulated series of shocks occurring between time $t + i$ and the current period.

Since the exact specification of the expected loss is of little interest for the following discussion, such loss is indicated using the compact notation

$$V_{R,t} = (1/2)(1+1/r)\left\{ bk^2 + c(r\bar{d})^2[1 + (1+1/r)(m_R^2\sigma_v + (1-m_R)^2\sigma_v)] \right\}$$

(6.29)

where $m_R \le \bar{m}_{t-1}$ is the constant maturity equivalent to the path for m_{t+i} in Equation (6.28).

6.9.3   From optimal to maximum maturity

For zero inflation to be an equilibrium, the reputational loss from inflating the debt away, i.e. the loss from higher inflation forever after, must be greater than the gains from permanently lower tax distortions. Since the effect of a given inflation rate on the value of the debt increases with debt maturity, a no-inflation outcome may require a short effective maturity.

To derive the loss that the government would experience if it were ever to deviate from equilibrium, first consider the choice of taxes after the government has inflated. At the end of period t the government faces the same taxation problem as in the reputation equilibrium, except for the lower debt ratio which results from having inflated at the beginning of period t. Since the tax rate, τ_t, is set after the shocks v_t and u_t realize, it is as if the government entered period t with the lower debt ratio $[1 - m_{t-1}(\pi_t^P + v_t - u_t) + u_t]d_{t-1}$. It would be natural to take this level of debt as the point around which the budget constraint is linearized. However, since the impact of the shocks v_t and u_t on the debt ratio is minor compared to the effect of unexpected inflation, a simplifying assumption is to set period-t shocks equal to zero—i.e. $v_t = u_t = 0$—and to take the inflated level of debt as the point around which the budget constraint is linearized, that is[15]

$$d_t \simeq \bar{d}_C \equiv E_t d_{t+i} = (1 - m_{t-1}\pi_t^P)d_{t-1}$$

Taking zero as the point of linearization for unexpected inflation and output growth, the linear budget constraint is equal to

$$d_{t+1} = (1+r)d_t - (1+r)[m_t(\pi_{t+1}^P - E_t\pi_{t+1})$$
$$+ m_t(v_{t+1} - u_{t+1}) + u_{t+1}]\bar{d}_C - \tau_{t+1}$$
$$d_t = (1+r)[1 - m_t\pi_{t+1}^P]d_{t-1} - \tau_t$$

(6.30)

[15] Alternatively, the approximation $[m_{t-1}v_t + (1 - m_{t-1})u_t]\pi_t^P = 0$ can be used.

Thus, after inflating in period t, the government chooses taxes for period t and taxes and inflation for all future periods so as to minimize

$$V_{C,t} = Z + (c/2)\tau_t^2 + (1/2)\sum_{i=1}^{\infty}(1+r)^{-i}$$
$$\times E_t\left\{(\pi_{t+i}^p)^2 + b[k - (\pi_{t+i}^p - E_t\pi_{t+i})]^2 + c\tau_{t+i}^2\right\} \qquad [6.31]$$

subject to the constraints [6.30] and where $Z = (1/2)(\pi_t^p)^2 + (b/2)(k - \pi_t^p)^2$ is predetermined at the time the current tax rate, τ_t, is chosen.

As in the reputation equilibrium the government sets the tax rate in period t at the same level as the level it expects to maintain tax rates in all future periods, $\tau_t = E_t\tau_{t+i}$.[16] Taking expectations, and integrating the budget constraint forward, tax rates are shown to be set so as to finance the flow of interest payments from the lower level of debt, $\bar{d}_C = (1 - m_{t-1}\pi_t^p)d_{t-1}$:

$$\tau_{t+i} = rd_{t+i-1} - [m_{t-1+i}v_{t+i} + (1 - m_{t-1+i})u_{t+i}]r\bar{d}_C \qquad [6.32]$$
$$\tau_t = r(1 - m_{t-1}\pi_t)d_{t-1}$$

This choice of taxes implies the following debt dynamics

$$d_{t+i} = d_{t-1+i} - [m_{t-1+i}(\pi_{t+i}^p - E_t\pi_{t+i} + v_{t+i} - u_{t+i}) + u_{t+i}]\bar{d}_C$$

Consider now the choice of planned inflation and debt maturity for time $t+1$ and all future periods. Once the government has lost its reputation, people form expectations on the hypothesis that the government acts opportunistically every period. Expected inflation is such that the marginal cost of inflation equals the benefits of surprise inflation. Since such benefits depend on the output effect and increase with the debt ratio and the maturity of the debt, in equilibrium planned and expected inflation are equal to

$$\pi_{t+1}^p = E_t\pi_{t+1} = bk + cE_t\tau_{t+1}(1+r)m_t\bar{d}_C \qquad [6.33]$$

Since a "long" effective maturity—a high m—leads to high expected and equilibrium inflation, the government may want to reduce maturity. In the absence of uncertainty, the government would set maturity equal to zero since there would be no cost in doing so. In general, this is no longer true under uncertainty.

When tax revenues are uncertain because of output shocks, long-term nominal debt has a hedging role whose benefits must be weighed against the inflation costs of a long maturity. Debt maturity is set equal to zero only if the output

---

[16] This result hinges, however, on the linearization being taken. In general, the inflation tax-base would not be constant at $\bar{d}_C$ and the government would have an incentive for early debt repayments in order to reduce inflation as in Calvo and Guidotti (1992).

incentives for surprise inflation are stronger than insurance motivations. It can be shown that the condition for this to happen is $bk > \sigma_u$. Intuitively, if the marginal cost of increasing debt maturity when maturity is zero, bk, is greater than the marginal benefit of doing so, σ_u, the government would choose zero maturity as in the deterministic case. Planned and expected inflation for time $t + 1$, and in all future periods, would then be equal to bk.

If instead the variance of output growth is high relative to the output benefits of surprise inflation, the government chooses a positive debt maturity in order to contain the risk of tax adjustments. As a result, inflation and debt maturity vary with the debt ratio. Equation (6.33) shows that such a relation arises from the expected marginal cost $cE_t\tau_{t+1}$ of taxation which increases with the tax rate and thus with the debt ratio. As the debt ratio increases, say, because of adverse output shocks, so does the temptation for inflationary financing and thus expected and planned inflation. As the government attempts to control expected inflation by reducing debt maturity when the debt increases, a negative relationship between the debt ratio and debt maturity may also emerge when it loses its reputation.

The net effect of a rising debt on expected and planned inflation can be considerably dampened by the choice of debt maturity. Since an analytical solution for the inflation path and for the dynamics of debt maturity cannot be derived, in what follows it is assumed that expected and planned inflation are constant and equal to

$$\pi^p_{t+i} = E_t\pi_{t+i} = \Pi_2 \geq bk$$

This assumption (which is correct for $bk > \sigma_u$), preserves analytical tractability at the cost of losing a precise characterization of the costs that the government incurs when reputation is lost.

Substituting the constant inflation rate and the value of tax rates from Equation (6.32) in Equation (6.31) gives the value of the loss function at period t when the government inflates:

$$V_{C,t} = (1/2)(\pi^p_t)^2 + (b/2)(k - \pi^p_t)^2 + (1/2r)(\Pi^2_2 + bk^2)$$
$$+(c/2)(1+1/r)[(1 - m_{t-1}\pi^p_t)rd_{t-1}]^2(1 + H_C) \qquad (6.34)$$

where $H_C \equiv (1/r)(m^2_C\sigma_v + (1 - m_C)^2\sigma_u)]$ and m_C is the constant maturity which makes $r\sum_{i=1}^{\infty}(1 + r)^{-i-1}E_{t-1}[\sum_{j=1}^{i}(m_{t-1+j}v_{t+j} + (1 - m_{t-1+j})u_{t+j})]^2$ equal to H_C.

Therefore, if the government inflates, it chooses planned inflation as

$$\pi^p_t = \frac{bk + c(1 + r)rd_{t-1}m_{t-1}d_{t-1}(1 + H_C)}{1 + b + c(1 + r)r(m_{t-1}d_{t-1})^2(1 + H_C)} \qquad (6.35)$$

The inflation rate is greater than it would be in the absence of uncertainty because of the term H_C which captures the additional distortions due to tax uncertainty.[17] Since the cost of tax uncertainty increases with the level of the tax rate and thus with the debt ratio, reducing such a cost provides an additional incentive to inflate in the current period. The lower the maturity m_C which will prevail in future periods, the higher is the cost H_C and thus current inflation.

Substituting Equation (6.35) for the inflation rate in (6.34), yields the expected loss under cheating, V_C, as a function of the debt ratio, debt maturity in period $t-1$, and future inflation, Π_2. The maximum maturity consistent with reputation can then be derived as the maximum maturity for which the expected loss under cheating, V_C, is greater than the expected loss under reputation, V_R. Consider the difference between V_C and V_R for a given value of m_{t-1}.[18] This difference is proportional to:

$$
\begin{aligned}
V_{C,t} - V_{R,t} \propto (1+b)[\Pi_2^2 &+ c(1+r)(E_{t-1}\tau_R)^2(H_C - H_R)] - r(bk)^2 \\
&- 2rc(1+r)bk(E_{t-1}\tau_R)(1+H_C)(m_{t-1}d_{t-1}) \\
&- rc(1+r)(1+H_C)[c(1+r)(E_{t-1}\tau_R)^2(1+H_R) \\
&- \Pi_2^2](m_{t-1}d_{t-1})^2
\end{aligned}
\tag{6.36}
$$

where $E_{t-1}\tau_R = E_{t-1}\tau_{t+i} = rd_{t-1}$ denotes the tax rate which, at the beginning of period t, is expected to prevail in the current and all future periods under reputation.

The first term in brackets is the expected future loss differential between inflating and maintaining reputation, evaluated at $E_{t-1}\tau_R$ and thus at the same debt ratio. The expected loss under cheating differs from the loss under reputation not only because of future inflation, but also because of differences in debt maturity and thus in the costs of tax uncertainty. As discussed earlier, if the variance of supply shocks is negligible compared to demand shocks, then the optimal hedging maturity is close to zero and it can be attained at no cost by the government. In that case $H_C = H_R = 0$ and $\Pi_2 = bk$, and the loss differential (6.36) is the same as in the deterministic case but the maximum maturity consistent with reputation is not binding.

On the contrary, if supply shocks are important, a short maturity is costly but may be needed to sustain a no-inflation outcome. If this is the case, budgetary uncertainty is not optimally hedged, which adds to the costs of both maintaining a credible anti-inflationary policy and inflating the debt away. Since the choice of m_R is unrelated to m_C, the net effect on the loss differential and thus on the likelihood of a no-inflation outcome is ambiguous. If $bk > \sigma_u$ and thus the government sets maturity equal to zero after inflating, then $H_R < H_C$, i.e. budgetary uncertainty helps to sustain an equilibrium with zero inflation. If

---

[17] The inflation rate is increasing in H_C for $(1+b) > mbk$ which is always verified since $(1 - m\pi_t^p) = 1 - m(bk/(1+b))$ must be positive.

[18] Both V_C and V_R are computed for shocks v_t and u_t equal to zero in period t.

instead $bk < \sigma_u$, the government finds it optimal to accept higher inflation in exchange for a longer maturity, so that H_C may be lower than H_R. Interestingly, unlike in the deterministic case, future inflation is positive and reputation can be an equilibrium even with $b = 0$, since it is no longer optimal for the government to choose zero maturity after inflating. However, for low enough bk and high σ_u the second-order polynomial in (6.36) could be negative for $m = 0$ and thus a reputation equilibrium could not exist even for very short maturity. In what follows it is assumed that this is not the case.

The maximum value of debt maturity consistent with reputation being an equilibrium, $\bar{m}$, is found as the maximum maturity for which the loss differential (6.36) is non-negative. Assuming $m^* > 0$ and noting that the expression is a second-degree polynomial in the product $m_{t-1}d_{t-1}$, it is easy to show the following.

For low enough values of the initial debt ratio, d_{t-1}, and thus of the expected tax rate $E_{t-1}\tau_R$, reputation is an equilibrium independently of the maturity of the debt. The condition for this to happen is that the determinant of the second-degree polynomial on the right-hand side of (6.36) be negative when maturity is set at its optimal level m^*, i.e. the condition is

$$(E_{t-1}\tau_R)^2 \le \frac{(1+b)\Pi_2^2 - r(bk)^2}{(1+b)c(1+r)(1+H_R)} \tag{6.37}$$

where H_R is evaluated at its minimizing maturity m^*.

When this is the case, maturity can be set equal to the optimal hedging maturity $m^* = \sigma_u/(\sigma_v + \sigma_u)$, which minimizes the risk of tax adjustments. Its value depends on the stochastic structure of the economy; it increases with the variance of supply shocks relative to demand shocks.

For higher values of the debt ratio, and thus of the expected tax rate $E_{t-1}\tau_R$, condition (6.37) does not hold and there is a maximum maturity consistent with reputation being an equilibrium. In Appendix 6.1 it is shown that values of $m_{t-1}d_{t-1}$ less than Λ_{t-1} are required to sustain this equilibrium, where Λ_{t-1} is the relevant root which solves the polynomial on the right-hand side of (6.36). The maximum maturity consistent with reputation is thus equal to

$$\bar{m}_{t-1} = \Lambda_{t-1}(E_{t-1}\tau_R; H_R; H_C)/d_{t-1}$$

where Λ_{t-1} is a function of $E_{t-1}\tau_R$, H_C and H_R. The root Λ_{t-1} and thus the maximum maturity, $\bar{m}_{t-1}$, can be shown to increase with H_C (and Π_2) and decrease with H_R. More importantly the maximum maturity is a decreasing function of the expected tax rate. While in a deterministic framework the tax rate is constant, in the presence of shocks affecting the government budget the expected tax rate changes with the debt ratio. Bad shocks to permanent output and unexpected deflation increase the debt ratio and, hence, the current and expected tax rate, $E_{t-1}\tau_R$. Thus, a sustained period of unexpectedly low growth and deflation leads to a sustained increase in the debt ratio and in the tax rate. The maximum maturity consistent with reputation shortens, directly because of the rise in the debt ratio d_{t-1} and indirectly because of the fall of Λ_{t-1} when the tax rate increases.

To summarize, as long as the maximum maturity, $\bar{m}_{t-1}$, is greater than the optimal hedging maturity $m^* = \sigma_u/(\sigma_v + \sigma_u)$, then the maturity $\bar{m}$ is not binding and the government can choose the maturity m^*. In this case, the anti-inflationary policy can be maintained without constraints on debt maturity.

However, at higher levels of debt, the maximum maturity consistent with reputation is binding and the government must choose a shorter maturity than the optimal hedging maturity m^*. This is because the optimal maturity is constant while the maximum maturity is decreasing with the debt ratio. In other words, there is always a high enough debt ratio at which the government must choose the maturity, $\bar{m}_{t-1}$, in order to maintain the credibility of its anti-inflationary stance. This level of debt depends on the variance of supply relative to demand shocks since it is implicitly defined by

$$\frac{d_{t-1}}{\Lambda_{t-1}(E_{t-1}\tau_R; H_R; H_C)} \geq \frac{\sigma_u}{\sigma_v + \sigma_u}$$

When this level is reached, a further increase in the debt ratio leads to a decrease in maximum and actual maturity.

This result must, however, be qualified. In deriving the optimal solution for the tax rate under reputation it was noted that the tax-smoothing solution is exact only if the maximum maturity is not binding. When instead the maximum maturity is binding, $\bar{m}_{t-1} \leq m^*$, the government raises current taxes above the level which would be optimal for smoothing tax rates over time. The government increases taxes in order to contain the debt accumulation and the corresponding fall in maximum maturity $\bar{m}_{t-1}$. In other words, the government reduces the expected loss from tax distortions by forgoing intertemporal tax smoothing in exchange for more smoothing across future states of the world. Since cost minimization implies that the cost be shared between intertemporal deviations and across-state deviations from the optimal tax plan, both the debt ratio rises and maturity shortens when bad shocks occur. However, movements in the debt ratio and debt maturity are less pronounced relative to the solution that has been shown above.

A theory of debt maturity has been derived. When supply and demand shocks are considered, the government is no longer indifferent to the choice of debt maturity. The government has a preference for a specific maturity which depends on the type of shocks hitting the economy. Supply shocks favor long maturity debt as the optimal choice while demand shocks call for short maturity or price-indexed debt. At low levels of debt, the government can choose this optimal hedging maturity without impairing the credibility of its anti-inflationary policy. At high levels of debt, low inflation may require that the effective maturity be shorter than the optimal maturity. Thus, the government chooses the maximum maturity consistent with reputation and an inverse relation emerges between the debt ratio and debt maturity. The critical level of the debt ratio which triggers such a relation varies across countries, as it depends on the relative importance of the shocks affecting their economies.

6.10 Concluding remarks

There are two approaches to cost minimization. A first approach aims to reduce the liquidity premium and the risk premium due to the uncertainty regarding the primary issuing policy and trading activities in government securities, that is, to types of risk which do not depend on macroeconomic events. Interest costs can be reduced by enhancing the transparency and predictability of the issuing policy, by increasing the liquidity and efficiency of the secondary market, by promoting benchmark bonds and introducing futures contracts and "repo" markets. These policies allow to save on the risk premium which would otherwise be required by the investors to hold illiquid assets. This approach implies a regular, predictable issuing strategy which relies on the same set of instruments irrespective of market conditions. The downside of this approach is the risk of shaping the characteristics of debt instruments on the trading needs of security dealers and, more generally, on the preferences of market participants.

A second approach to cost minimization is to issue and trade debt instruments whenever their prices do not reflect the views and information of debt managers. It is based on the idea that debt managers should better predict the evolution of interest rates, inflation and exchange rates, perhaps, because of the informational advantages which arise as a by-product of policymaking, early access to government statistics and coordination with the monetary authority. This approach implies an "active" policy with a choice of debt instruments conditional on market prices and led by "views" and private information about policy and future events; it is not much different from private speculating activity.[19] Debt management may also save on interest costs by exploiting arbitrage opportunities which arise because of market imperfections, by filling the gaps in the maturity structure or by satisfying the market demand for specific debt instruments.

Many arguments have been put forward against the adoption of discretionary debt management. An "active" policy is bound to be ineffective in the long run, since debt managers are unlikely to systematically outperform the market and if they do so because of informational advantages the gains from opportunistic

---

[19] The scope for "activism" has been much increased by the possibility to use interest rate and foreign currency swaps. "Activism" is also encouraged by the adoption of benchmark portfolios against which the cost performance of the debt manager is measured.

behavior will be short-lived. In the long run a policy which saves on interest costs by exploiting private information and surprising investors will imply higher servicing cost as investors will require a premium to hold government securities for the uncertainty and losses that they experience. As suggested by Giovannini (1997), a premium may also arise if "activism generates volatility or signals higher volatility to come."

The idea that "active" debt management would convey valuable information and move asset prices in the direction consistent with government's information is also ill-conceived. As Giovannini points out there are more efficient ways to disclose information. If anything, the cost advantages of such policies should be minor as people would soon revise their expectations as the debt manager tried to exploit its private information. More importantly, anticipating the behavior of interest rates or signaling the government intentions may create instability and problems for the conduct of debt and monetary policy. Since disclosing information is not always convenient for the government, investors would be lured into guessing monetary policy changes from debt decisions. As a result, true signals would not be believed, while uninformative decisions would be interpreted as signals of impending changes in interest rates.

Discretion should only be used under exceptional circumstances, that is, when the interest rates on debt are "unfair" in the sense that they result from the lack of confidence in the government resolution to carry out its announcements, i.e. when the credibility of the government is at stake. This may happen, for instance, at the outset of a stabilization attempt when issuing long-term debt can be particularly costly because long-term interest rates do not incorporate the expectations of the lower rates which will prevail as a result of future fiscal and monetary restraint.

Costs may be high also because investors perceive a government incentive to undertake actions which reduce the return on debt instruments, say, to inflate and alter interest rates. Indeed, much of the literature on debt management has been concerned with the adverse incentive effects created by conventional debt instruments and "unbalanced" maturity structures. Fixed-rate nominal debt, in particular, has been deemed to lead to inflationary temptations undermining the credibility of the government anti-inflationary stance. In effect, nominal debt may imply high costs from deflationary policy when such policy is not anticipated and make the government unwilling to act firmly. These considerations make an argument for issuing price-indexed debt since such debt increases the commitment to low inflation and thus the credibility of the anti-inflationary policy. If a problem exists, interest costs could be substantially reduced by an indexation program, perhaps, also because interest rates on conventional debt would fall.

Is there a credibility problem? The issue arises because there is no relation between nominal debt and inflation. If anything, as documented by Masson and

Mussa (1995), debt accumulation is partly a consequence of disinflation. In this chapter new evidence has been produced which shows that, at high levels of debt, a credibility problem indeed emerges. For highly indebted countries or for countries with important fiscal imbalances there is strong evidence of an inverse relationship between the level of debt and the elasticity of the debt value to unexpected inflation. Debt accumulation does not imply an inflationary bias, as most models would predict but, rather, leads governments to reduce the duration of the debt (which is relevant for the effect of inflation) as the level of debt increases in order to reduce the possible gains from surprise inflation. In highly indebted OECD countries governments issued, or were forced to issue, short-term conventional debt, variable-rate and foreign currency debt to maintain the credibility of their anti-inflationary policies and thus avoid high interest rates. Only in the 1990s, and especially after the Maastrich Treaty, fixed-rate long-term debt has been issued in these countries, despite constant or rising debt ratios. This lengthening of nominal debt maturity is consistent with the view that credibility problems have found a solution with the establishment of independent central banks and the slow but significant buildup of a reputation for low inflation.

When the analysis of incentive effects is coupled with risk-hedging considerations a clear policy indication emerges: governments may and should buy insurance from the private sector, to the extent that this policy is not perceived as creating a temptation for opportunistic financing. For instance, fixed-rate long-term debt may well be the optimal instrument even if it implies higher expected servicing costs, when such costs reflect properly called risk premia. It is not optimal when interest rates are high because of the lack of credibility of the anti-inflationary policy.

Appendix 6.1

In this Appendix it is shown that for values of $E_{t-1}\tau_R$ such that condition (6.37) does not hold, values of $m_{t-1}d_{t-1}$ lower than Λ_{t-1} are required to sustain a reputation equilibrium where Λ_{t-1} is the relevant root which solves the polynomial on the right-hand side of (6.36).

If condition (6.37) does not hold, the determinant of the polynomial in (6.36) is positive. Therefore, there are two roots, and two cases to consider, depending on the sign of the coefficient of $(m_{t-1}d_{t-1})^2$. This coefficient is positive if

$$c(1+r)(E_{t-1}\tau_R)^2(1+H_R) - \Pi_2^2 < 0$$

which may hold even if the determinant is positive. In this case the polynomial is convex and has two positive real roots. It follows that the relevant root—call it Λ_{t-1}—is the lowest, and values of $m_{t-1}d_{t-1}$ less than Λ_{t-1} are required to sustain a reputation equilibrium. Note that, as the polynomial is positive for values of md less than Λ_{t-1} and greater than the other root—call it Λ_2—, reputation would appear to hold both for values of $m_{t-1}d_{t-1}$ less than Λ_{t-1} and for values greater than Λ_2. Using (6.35) however, it can be shown that values of $m_{t-1}d_{t-1}$ greater than Λ_2 imply a negative terminal value of debt, i.e. a negative value of $(1 - m_{t-1}\pi_t)d_{t-1}$, and thus are unacceptable. The coefficient of $(m_{t-1}d_{t-1})^2$ is instead negative if

$$c(1+r)(E_{t-1}\tau_R)^2(1+H_R) - \Pi_2^2 > 0$$

which holds for levels of the debt ratio and the expected tax rate higher than those considered in the first case. Then, the polynomial is concave in $m_{t-1}d_{t-1}$ and has one negative and one positive root. The polynomial is positive for values of $m_{t-1}d_{t-1}$ between zero and the positive root which is equal to Λ_{t-1}.

7

Policy conclusions

7.1 Policy conclusions

Public debt management has important welfare effects. The choice of debt instruments determines the distribution of debt returns and the allocation of taxes across future states of the world with important implications for the distribution of risk and the efficiency of taxation.

In this book two general strategies have been distinguished depending on the implied positive or negative relation of debt returns with output shocks and their welfare merits have been evaluated. Evidence has been presented on the composition and maturity structure of government debt across OECD countries and new facts have emerged regarding their funding policies. Finally, the goals of minimizing budgetary risk and the cost of debt servicing have been discussed emphasizing their policy implications. Two questions naturally arise: (i) did we get any closer to "optimal debt management" or to the basic principles which should guide the choice of policymakers?; (ii) do these principles lead to practical policy measures? Hopefully, the answer to these questions is yes! The answers are made explicit in these conclusions.

At several stages of the analysis it was stressed that the policymakers' approach to debt management implies a trade-off between cost and risk minimization. More precisely, the attitude of policymakers can be better defined as the minimization of borrowing costs "without taking too much risk." This book argues for a change of priorities: debt management should aim at minimizing budgetary risk to the extent that this does not lead to unjustified, excessive costs.

The shift of emphasis from cost to risk does not mean that debt-servicing costs are not important or should be ignored. In the previous chapter it has been stressed that cost minimization is justified by market imperfections, credibility problems and, in general, when cost reduction is attained without redistributing macroeconomic risk.

As regards market imperfections and informational failures the main point is that only one cost-minimizing strategy is warranted and its implementation should marginally interfere with risk minimization. Interest costs can and should be reduced by enhancing the transparency and predictability of the issuing policy, by increasing the liquidity and efficiency of secondary markets, by promoting benchmark bonds and introducing borrowing and risk-hedging facilities. A regular issuing strategy which relies on the same set of instruments irrespective of market conditions and increases the issue size of government securities allows saving on risk premia which would otherwise be required for the uncertainty of sales and the illiquidity of government securities. This policy approach is also beneficial in that it helps to reduce idiosyncratic risk. Its downside is the risk of shaping the characteristics of government securities on the trading needs of security dealers or, more generally, on the preferences of market participants. Debt managers may be tempted to rely on funding instruments which are in high demand but increase the exposure of the government budget to macroeconomic risk. For example, the preference of primary dealers for fixed-rate securities should not prevent the government from issuing price-index-linked bonds when the indexation program is suggested by risk-hedging considerations.

On the contrary, strong arguments have been made against directional trade, that is against "active" debt management led by views and information about future events, say, future interest rates, inflation and exchange rates. If debt managers and private investors share the same information, then activism is going to be ineffective if not generating more volatility and higher risk premia. Active debt management can work, in the short run, only if debt managers are better informed about future policy actions. However, since placement of public debt is a repeated event, exploiting private information to the expense of private investors would lead to higher costs in the long run. Because of the loss of reputation from opportunistic behavior, a higher risk premium will be asked by investors to hold government securities. Discretion should only be used under exceptional circumstances, that is, when the interest rates on debt are "unfair" in that they result from the lack of confidence in the government resolution to carry out its announcements, i.e. when the credibility of the government is at stake.

Finally, debt-servicing costs should not be reduced by issuing instruments which satisfy the demand by particular investors and thus bear lower risk premia. For example, saving on the inflation-risk premium should not be an argument for issuing price-index-linked bonds. The fact that such a policy not only minimizes costs but also provides insurance to debt-holders is not sufficient to conclude that it is socially optimal. To the extent that insurance premia originate from macroeconomic risk, such policies are likely to have a negative effect on welfare. The reason is simple: macroeconomic risk cannot be eliminated; it can only be shared or, better, redistributed. A policy, which minimizes costs by insuring investors, shifts the risk to taxpayer or, if taxes are postponed, to future generations. It is hard to see the reason why taxpayers and future generations should be in a better position than investors to cope with macroeconomic risk.[1] The fact that taxation is compulsory, while investing in public

---

[1] The risk-sharing argument for indexation should be based on the need of public innovation to create a market for private indexed debt.

debt is not, suggests buying insurance from investors as a better policy than forcing taxpayers to supply insurance to investors. It is surprising that these simple arguments are hardly recognized in practical policy discussions. While it is conceivable that people ignore the link between debt returns and tax risk, there is no excuse for debt managers to disregard the tax effects of their decisions.

Why buying insurance from the private sector against macroeconomic risk is the optimal policy? Which risk should be minimized? Most policymakers confine their attention to interest-rate risk, that is to the risk of refinancing a large share of debt at higher than expected interest rates or to the possibility of roll-over crises. Often, no distinction is made between real and nominal interest rates. No doubt, refinancing risk is relevant, but the uncertainty of public spending and tax bases is also important.

This book argues for an extended definition of risk; it argues that the uncertainty of tax revenues and public spending should also matter. As a private investor takes labor income into account in deciding her portfolio, a debt manager should be concerned not only with financial liabilities but also with the net income from the real activity of the government: revenues and spending. This implies that unexpected changes in the tax-base, mainly due to output fluctuations, should be hedged by debt instruments as much as interest-rate variations and exchange-rate risk should be avoided.

Output-indexed bonds with a long maturity would be the ideal instruments to cope with tax-base uncertainty, while avoiding interest-rate risk. Output bonds, unlike bonds indexed to public spending, would not suffer from moral hazard problems, and would provide an almost perfect stabilizer of deficit fluctuations over the cycle. This design of public debt would reduce the need for tax adjustments when bad shocks to output occur, thus minimizing tax distortions. It would also provide valuable flexibility to the conduct of fiscal policy and help to relax borrowing constraints by allowing for lower tax rates in states where output is low and constraints are binding.

However, output bonds neither exist nor is their introduction advocated in this book. Issuing such bonds is difficult and costly because of the frictions associated with the delay in recording and reporting the relevant indexation parameter. Because of the difficulties in pricing and hedging the return risk of such bonds, the costs of the innovation would certainly outweigh its benefits.

In the real world the distribution of debt returns, which minimize budgetary risk, has to be obtained by the choice of conventional instruments. The debt manager is left with the limited but at times important contingencies offered by conventional financial instruments: nominal debt, foreign currency debt, price-indexed debt and variable-rate debt, with various maturities, coupons and indexation clauses. Such instruments can be combined so as to provide the optimal hedge against budgetary uncertainty, that is, low debt returns at times when output and thus tax revenues are lower than expected. To the skeptical policymaker it is helpful to remind the insurance that fixed-rate conventional debt has historically provided during wars, that is, at times of high public spending and inflation. Nobody would deny the shock-absorber role of such debt at the time of the first oil shock and the lasting benefits for countries like the UK, which happened to have it in long maturities. It is likewise useful to remember the impact of the EMS crisis on the financial position of European countries which had a large share of their debt denominated in foreign currencies.

The optimal composition of public debt, by denomination, price indexation and maturity, depends on the shocks hitting the economy, on their persistence and on the monetary policy response to such shocks. For example, monetary and real shocks to aggregate demand lend support to price-indexation policies, while supply and public spending shocks favor nominal debt as the optimal choice. The risk-minimizing composition of public debt will also depend on the monetary regime and it is likely to vary across countries depending on the stochastic structures of their economies.

What type of debt should governments issue to minimize budgetary risk? Should they issue nominal debt or price-indexed debt? Should the debt be denominated in domestic or in foreign currency? Should the debt have a short or long maturity? Specific policy indications can be derived from an empirical investigation of how unexpected components of security returns relate to innovations in permanent output and public spending. New evidence for OECD countries is provided in this book. It shows that foreign currency debt should not be issued in almost all countries considered. Such debt is not only risky because of the high volatility of exchange rates but also because it increases the budget exposure to bad spending and output shocks. This is an important result for policymaking which is shared by other studies in the field.

The case for conventional versus price-indexed debt varies across countries. In Belgium, Denmark, Germany, Ireland, Italy, Spain and Sweden, nominal debt seems to have consistently provided a valuable hedge against unexpected financing needs due to permanent output shortfalls. On the contrary, price indexation appears to benefit Australia, Canada, Finland, France, Japan, the Netherlands, the UK and the US. Some price-indexed debt could also be issued in the former countries. Overall, the case against price-indexed debt is much weaker than in previous research. A possible explanation is in the larger set of variables used to predict future movements in output, public spending and inflation. With regards to the choice of debt maturity, long-term nominal debt appears to provide some budgetary insurance for most of the countries considered, since innovations in long-term interest rates and output are negatively correlated but, consistently with previous studies, the role of long-maturity debt is limited.

These findings are important but not yet policy indications. Indeed, more research is needed to draw reliable conclusions for policymaking. The sensitivity of the results to the variables used in the estimation is one problem, but there are others, perhaps, more relevant. For instance, the results are biased in favor of short-maturity debt, since most models fail to capture the risk of refinancing, which is a main motivation for long-term bonds. The approach used in this book is not immune from this problem. Another problem is that the role of debt instruments which are useful to cope with rare but important events, such as an oil shock or a currency crisis, will be downplayed if the sample period does not include such events. Evidence of a role of long-maturity debt in preventing a roll-over crisis may not even exist precisely because such debt was there to avoid the crisis. Finally, for a number of countries, the sensitivity of the results to the period considered points to a common but relevant problem for the use of past information for policymaking: nothing ensures that shocks which happened in the past will again take place in the future.

These considerations suggest the need for more empirical and theoretical work; by no means should it be concluded that this research is an intellectual curiosity that policymakers can disregard. No policymaker is indifferent to the role of money supply even if there is no conclusive evidence on its real effects and thousands of articles have been written on the subject while there are just few empirical studies on the risk-minimizing composition of public debt. Indeed, very little is known on the hedging properties of debt instruments and a lot more is to be learned from this research. It is true, however, that the empirical analysis will have to move away from reduced-form techniques to adopt a structural approach. Theoretical research will have to consider how the relations between output, spending and debt returns are generated by specific characteristics of the economy. A particular attention should be given to the interaction between monetary policy and debt management. In fact, depending on the monetary regime, say, on whether the authority targets inflation or the nominal exchange rate, different co-movements should be expected between the returns on debt instruments and macroeconomic variables affecting the government budget. There is no doubt that precise answers on the hedging role of debt instruments will come as more effort will be devoted to this analysis.

The risk-minimizing composition of public debt can and should be identified and debt managers should aim to achieve it unless unjustified costs must be sustained. The objective of minimizing budgetary risk should indeed be weighed against the objective of containing funding costs. The main point is that only two types of costs should be considered: the costs of market imperfections such as those leading to liquidity premia and the costs due to credibility problems, arising either from the uncertainty about the government's announcements or because of the incentives for opportunistic financing created by particular types of debt. Costs arising from properly called risk-premia should instead be diregarded unless redistribution were actively pursued in favor of debt-holders.

From the viewpoint of policymaking, the suggested approach implies, starting from the current debt composition, to move toward the optimal risk-hedging portfolio until a trade-off with cost minimization emerges and the burden of liquidity and credibility costs outweighs the benefits of risk minimization. For instance, governments should buy insurance from the private sector to the extent that this policy is not perceived as creating a temptation for inflationary financing. This may happen if risk-hedging consideration suggests fixed-rate long-term bonds as the optimal instruments. Issuing such debt can no longer be optimal when it leads to high interest rates reflecting a lack of credibility in the government resolution not to inflate. To the other extreme, the minimization of budgetary risk may require the introduction of price-index-linked bonds but the debt manager may find the costs of setting up a market for such debt unsustainable.

Obviously, a trade-off may not exist or can be met only as the outstanding amount of the optimal hedging instrument increases. For instance, in the UK price-index-linked bonds have provided both valuable insurance against the uncertain financing needs generated by output fluctuations and a cheap source of financing because of a positive inflation premium. The fact that a larger share of indexed debt is not outstanding suggests that a trade-off emerges as more indexed debt is issued. Indeed, the costs of placing index-linked bonds outside the portfolios of institutional investors are substantial because of the illiquidity of the market.

For other countries, in particular, for Belgium, Ireland, Italy, Spain and Sweden, fixed-rate conventional debt appears to provide the best solution to risk minimization. Perhaps, nominal debt should be issued in long maturities in order to insulate the government budget from interest-rate shocks or unanticipated changes in interest rates induced by monetary restraint. Lengthening the maturity of conventional debt in these countries may indeed be optimal and this task has been made easier as liquid markets for long-term fixed-rate securities have developed. For the past there is instead strong evidence that foreign currency debt, variable-rate debt and short-term nominal debt had to be issued, as the debt rose, in order to avoid inflationary temptations. This suggests the existence of a trade-off, at high levels of debt, between the extent of budgetary insurance or flexibility that can be obtained with long-term nominal debt and the higher interest costs due to credibility problems.

The establishment of increasingly independent central banks and the Maastricht Treaty have strongly contributed to the credibility of the anti-inflationary policy in these countries and clearly reduced the costs of long-term funding. The participation in the European Monetary Union with the full delegation of monetary policy will make the problem soon disappear. Hopefully, it will also make debt managers' lives easier.

Appendix: Data and data sources

Data for GDP, governmment spending (consumption) and their deflators are from *National Accounts*, OECD. Quarterly data on interest rates and consumer price indexes are from *Main Economic Indicators*, OECD and from *International Financial Statistics*, IMF. Portuguese interest rates are from *Statistical Bulletin*, Banco de Portugal. When quarterly series starting in 1970 were not available from international statistics, they were obtained from national sources. Yearly series of interest rates starting in 1960 were obtained from the *OECD Economic Outlook: Historical Statistics*, OECD. Data on debt composition and debt maturity were obtained from national sources and the relevant series were constructed as explained in what follows for each country separately.

Australia   Data on the composition and maturity of central government debt were obtained from the monthly *Reserve Bank of Australia Bulletin*, Reserve Bank of Australia. The same publication provides data on the distribution by holder.

"Debt" refers to central government debt and excludes Internal Treasury Bills. Privately held debt is net of Treasury notes and bonds held by the Reserve Bank of Australia and by the government. Government holdings refer to debt held by the "Loan Consolidation and Investment Reserve" (LCIR). Privately held debt and its composition in Table 4.8 also excludes Public Treasury bills since a large fraction of such instruments was held by the Reserve Bank in the period 1974–9 and completely held by the bank in the period 1980–2, though precise data on the composition of bank holdings between bills and bonds could not be found. Since 1982 Treasury bills have no longer been issued.

The series of average maturity were constructed from the published series of "conventional" average term to maturity which refers to privately held (or market holdings) of Treasury notes and bonds. The maturity of the fixed-rate component was obtained by correcting the published series for the presence of price-index-linked bonds and variable-rate bonds. The effective maturity series was constructed by assigning zero maturity to indexed bonds and foreign currency debt and the average time interval between quarterly coupon adjustments for variable-rate bonds: 1.5 months.

The data-set in Table A.1 is organized as follows (initial maturities in parenthesis): TBILL = Public Treasury bills; TNOTE = Treasury notes, i.e. "new" Treasury bills (5, 13 and 26 weeks); P-INDEX = price-index-linked bonds (10 and 20 years); VAR.BOND = variable-rate bonds (3.5 and 5 years); FIX.BOND = fixed-rate bonds (from 3 to 30 years, mostly 3 and 10 years); SAVING = savings bonds; OTH.NMK = other non-marketable debt; FOR.CUR = foreign currency debt; CB.NOTE = Treasury notes held by the Reserve Bank; CB.BILL = Treasury bills held by the Reserve Bank; CB.BOND = fixed-rate bonds held by the Reserve Bank. For the period 1974–9 it includes Treasury bills held by the Reserve Bank. For 1995 it includes $200 million and $20 million of variable-rate bonds and price-index-linked bonds, respectively; GV.BOND = fixed-rate bonds held by the LCIR. For the period 1974–9 it includes bonds held by the Reserve Bank; CON.MAT = conventional average maturity of privately held notes and bonds; FIX.MAT = average maturity of fixed-rate bonds and notes; EF.MAT = effective maturity.

Austria Data were obtained from the *Federal Debt Report*, Oesterreichische Postsparkasse that was provided by Economic Studies Division of the Oesterreichische Nationalbank.

"Debt" refers to central government debt. The debt composition shown in Table 4.9 refers to debt net of Central Bank credit to the government but is gross of official holdings, since data on security holdings by the Central Bank and the government could not be found.

Data on average remaining term to maturity could not be found. A survey by the Swedish National Debt Office among representatives of OECD countries reports for the Austrian debt a conventionally measured maturity equal to 6.7 years in 1992 and 4.8 years in 1994. The share of fixed-rate long-term debt considers fixed-rate notes, bonds and loans.

The data-set in Table A.2 is organized as follows (initial maturity in parenthesis): TBILL = standard fixed-rate Treasury bills (up to 1 year). Until recently short-term promissory notes. It includes variable-rate Treasury bills (TB.VAR) for the period before 1987; TB.VAR = variable-rate Treasury bills, "Primarmarkt-Orientiert Bundesschatzscheine," extended TBILL up to 10 years; VAR.NOTE = floating-rate notes, "Bundesschatzscheine Floater"; VAR.BOND = variable-rate bonds (10-year); NOTES = fixed-rate long-term notes, "Bundesobligationen" (currently 10 years); FIX.BOND = fixed-rate bonds, "Anleihen" (from 2 to 30 years, mostly 5 and 10 years). It includes NOTES until 1974; INSURAN FIX.LOAN = Insurance fixed-rate loans. Until 1977 it includes INSURAN VAR.LOAN, OTH.FIX and OTH.VAR; INSURAN VAR.LOAN = Insurance variable-rate loans. For the period 1978–9 it includes OTH.VAR (since 1978 the Federal Debt Report distinguishes between fixed-rate and variable-rate loans); BANK FIX.LOAN = fixed-rate loans from banks: BANK VAR.LOAN = variable-rate loans from banks; OTH.FIX = other non-marketable fixed-rate debt, OTH.VAR = other non-marketable variable-rate debt; CB.BOR = Central Bank credit to the government; FOR.CUR = foreign currency debt.

Belgium Data on public debt and its maturity were obtained from *Situation Generale du Tresor Public*, Chambre des Representants, and from *Annuaire Statistique de la Belgique*, Institut National de Statistique, Ministère des Affaires Economiques. Further information and official maturity series were obtained from the *Annual Report on Public Debt*, Ministère des Finances, Trésorerie. Data on Central Bank holdings and Central Bank advances to the "Fonds des Rentes" were obtained from *Bulletin de la Banque Nationale de Belgique*, Bank Nationale de Belgique. Information on interest-rate indexation and "put options" were provided by the Ministère des Finances, Trésorerie.

"Debt" corresponds broadly to central government debt; it excludes guaranteed debt and includes "Indirect Debt," i.e. bonds issued by public agencies, such as the "Fonds des Routes" and the "Office de la Navigation," which are similar for characteristics and backing to bonds issued directly by the Treasury.

Privately held debt was derived by deducting debt held by the Central Bank and Central Bank advances to the "Fonds des Rentes (FdR)," the institution performing open market operations until the reform of the money market in January 1991. Until 1991 the FdR financed its operations both issuing its own short-term certificates and by borrowing from the Central Bank, so that only the latter component has been considered.

It has been deducted from short-term certificates (TBILL below), since most of the assets in the FdR's portfolio were in such form. Although, this procedure underestimates privately held short-term debt, more detailed data could not be found.

The average remaining maturity of fixed-rate securities denominated in domestic currency was constructed from data on the year of maturity of each fixed-rate bond and OLO line, assigning a maturity date of 30 June for that year. This procedure leads to an overestimate of the true maturity since the government redeemed bonds, issued in the period 1975–89, through a combination of annual repurchases up to 5% of the issue amount in the secondary market, and a large lump-sum payment at final maturity. Treasury bills and short-term certificates were given the average remaining maturity corresponding to their initial maturity, which is currently 3, 6 and 12 months (it was 1, 2, 3, 6, 9 and 12 months for "Certificats de Trésorerie"). The same criterium was applied to medium-term debt. The earliest redemption date was used for bonds with a put option, the latest redemption date for bonds with a call option. The effective maturity was computed by assigning zero maturity to foreign currency debt. The time before the next adjustment of the coupon was used as the maturity of variable-rate and revisable-rate bonds (direct debt) issued in the period 1994–5. No correction was instead made for variable-rate and revisable-rate bonds outstanding before 1994 because information on indexation features could not be found. Such debt, mostly debt assumed by the government, accounts for a share no greater than 2%. The share of fixed-rate long-term debt was defined as the share of fixed-rate securities denominated in the domestic currency with an initial maturity longer than 4 years, i.e. it excludes medium-term debt.

The data-set in Table A.3 is organized as follows (initial maturity in parenthesis): TBILL = Treasury bills (3, 6 and 12 months). Past data refer to short-term certificates and other short-term debt with initial maturity no longer than 1 year. MEDIUM = debt with initial maturity shorter than 4 years and longer than 1 year; FIX.BOND DIRECTE = OLO bonds (from 4 to 20 years, mostly 10 years) and other fixed-rate bonds issued directly by the Central Government; FIX.BOND INDIR = fixed-rate bonds with initial maturity longer than 4 years issued by public agencies; VAR.BOND DIRECTE = revisable-rate bonds (10 years) and variable-rate bonds (5 years) issued by the central government; VAR.BOND INDIR = revisable-rate and variable-rate bonds issued by public agencies; FOR.CUR = foreign currency debt; POSTAL DEPOSIT = savings accounts with the Post Office; FdR.ADV = Central Bank advances to the "Fonds des Rentes"; CB.BILL = Treasury bills held by the Central Bank; CB.BOR = short-term borrowing from the Central Bank; CB.BOND = long-term bonds held by the Central Bank; CON.TOT = Conventional average maturity of total debt, including postal deposits and foreign currency debt; FIX.MAT = average maturity of fixed-rate debt; EF.MAT = effective maturity.

Canada Data on public debt were obtained from *Bank of Canada Review*, Bank of Canada, and from *Public Accounts*, Department of Finance. Data on debt maturity and the composition of debt holdings by the Central Bank were obtained from *Bank of Canada Review*. Detailed information on the amounts and indexation characteristics of price-index-linked bonds were provided by the Financial Market Department of the Bank of Canada.

"Debt" refers to national debt which broadly corresponds to central government debt. It considers all financial and non-financial liabilities but excludes guaranteed debt. The debt composition in Table 4.11 refers to financial "unmatured debt", i.e. to outstanding securities, loans and savings bonds. This definition excludes (not yet repaid but) matured debt and other liabilities, since the latter, mainly "Superannuation Accounts," are a roughly constant fraction of GDP and thus their evolution is not informative about changes in the debt structure.

Privately held debt is net of the securities held by the Central Bank but it is gross of government holdings of marketable debt, as information on the latter was not available for all the periods considered. Their share does not however exceed 0.5% between 1974 and 1991. Privately held debt also includes government non-marketable debt held in government accounts for a share lower than 1.3% since the mid-1970s. In fact, whether this is considered as privately held debt depends on the debt definition (see the discussion for the US).

The Bank of Canada publishes two series of the average remaining term to maturity of marketable securities, including both Treasury bills and securities denominated in foreign currency. One considers all marketable securities while the other refers to the stock held by the general public, i.e. it excludes the securities held by the Central Bank, the government and the chartered banks.

The maturity of all outstanding securities was used to compute the average maturity of fixed-rate securities and the effective maturity. The estimated average maturity of fixed-rate securities corrects the published maturity series for the presence of price-index-linked bonds but not for foreign currency debt. The effective maturity series was constructed on the assumption that the securities denominated in the domestic currency and those denominated in foreign currency have the same average maturity. Zero maturity was assigned to price-indexed debt and foreign currency debt.

The data-set in Table A.4 is organized as follows (initial maturity in parentheses): TBILL = cash management bills (from 1 to 41 days) and Treasury bills (3, 6 and 12 months); FIX.BOND = fixed-rate bonds (2, 3, 5, 10 and 30 years); P-INDEX = price-index-linked bonds (30 years); FC.US.BIL = US-Canada bills denominated in US dollars; FC.MKT = marketable foreign currency debt; FC.NMK = other non-marketable foreign currency debt; SAVING = savings bonds; MATUR = matured marketable debt; GV.NMK = non-marketable bonds issued to the Canada Pension Plan Investment Fund, i.e. debt held in government accounts; OTH.LIAB = other (non-financial) liabilities. Liabilities arise from government borrowing funds which it administers: superannuation accounts; Canada Pension Plan Account, Government Annuities Account, etc.; CB.BILL = Treasury bills held by the Central Bank; CB.BOND = bonds held by the Central Bank; CON.MAT = conventional average maturity of marketable debt (see above); CON.GP = conventional average maturity of marketable debt held by the general public (see above); FIX.MAT = average maturity of fixed-rate marketable debt, including foreign currency debt; EF.MAT = effective maturity.

Denmark   Data on public debt and debt maturity were obtained from *Danish Government Securities*, Danmarks Nationalbank. For the period 1969–82 data on debt are from *Statistisk Månedsoversigt*, and *Danmarks Nationalbank Annual Report*, Danmarks Nationalbank.

"Debt" refers to central government debt. The debt composition shown in Table 4.12 refers to debt net of government holdings but gross of securities held by the Central Bank, since such information could not be obtained for all the period considered. In the 1980s the share of securities held in the bank's portfolio was however small, not exceeding 2%. The positive balance of the credit account of Treasury at the National Bank is not subtracted from gross debt. The Danish Treasury held net claims against the bank, resulting from the difference between the amount held in the "consolidated account" (on the liability side of the bank's balance sheet) and the borrowings from the current account, which was used for cash management by the government.

The published series of average remaining maturity considers all securities denominated in the domestic currency, i.e. Treasury bills, notes, bonds and lottery bonds. Two series of debt duration, one excluding and the other correcting for variable-rate bonds, are also published. The average maturity of fixed-rate securities denominated in the domestic currency was obtained for the period 1990–5 by correcting the published series of maturity for the presence of variable-rate debt, while the average maturity of fixed-rate securities was available for the earlier period.

The effective maturity was computed as follows. Foreign currency debt was assigned zero maturity. Variable-rate bonds were assigned the average time remaining before the adjustment of their quarterly coupon: 1.5 months. To take into account the imperfection of the indexation mechanism the maturity of 1.5 months was augmented by the lag— 4.8 months—between the determination of the reference rate and the beginning of the entitlement period.

The data-set in Table A.5 is organized as follows (initial maturity in parentheses): TBILLS = Treasury bills (3, 6 and 9 months); TNOTE = Treasury notes (2 years and 50 days and currently 2.5 years); VAR.BOND = variable-rate bonds (5 and 10 years); FIX.BOND = fixed-rate long-term bonds (mostly 5 and 10 years, also 30 years); ECU.BOND = ECU bonds; FOR.CUR = foreign currency debt; LOT.BOND = lottery bonds with returns determined by drawings. For the years 1970 and 1971 it includes a small amount of savings bonds; COMP = compulsory savings; CB.BOR government net account at the Central Bank (a minus sign indicates that the government is a creditor); GV.SEC = marketable securities held by the government; GV.ECU = ECU bonds held by the government; GV.FOR = foreign currency debt held by the government; CB.SEC = marketable securities held by the Central Bank; CON.MAT = conventional average maturity. The method of calculation has changed in 1990; FIX.MAT = average maturity of fixed-rate debt; EF.MAT = effective maturity; FIX.DUR = duration of fixed-rate debt; TOT.DUR = duration of fixed-rate and variable-rate debt. It assigns a duration of 3 months to variable-rate bonds.

Finland   For the period 1985–96 data on debt composition were obtained from *Markka-Denominated Borrowing by the Finnish Central Government* and for the period 1970–84 from the *Statistical Yearbook*. The link between the two series, further details on debt composition, and data on average maturity were provided by the Financing Unit of the Ministry of Finance. Central Bank holdings of debt are from the *Annual Report*, Bank of Finland.

"Debt" refers to central government debt. Privately held debt excludes debt held by the Central Bank and, for the period 1990–4, it excludes a small amount of "Debt to the Pension Fund."

The average remaining term to maturity provided by the Financing Unit of the Ministry of Finance refers to all marketable securities denominated in the domestic currency, including Treasury bills. Effective maturity was obtained by assigning zero maturity to the debt denominated in foreign currency.

The data-set in Table A.6 is organized as follows (initial maturity in parentheses): TBILL = Treasury bills. It comprises old Treasury bills (from 1 to 18 months), new Treasury bills (1, 3, 6 and 12 months) and HF bills for the years 1991 and 1992; YIELD = yield bonds for personal investors (from 2 to 4 years but up to 8 years); NEW.BOND = new fixed-rate bonds, housing bonds and serial bonds (from 3 to 10 years, mostly 5 and 10 years); OLD.BOND = old fixed-rate publicly issued bonds; REG.BOND = old fixed-rate "registered bonds," i.e. non-marketable privately placed bonds; PRO.NOTE = long-term promissory notes; SH.LOAN = short-term loans; LG.LOAN = long-term loans; FOR.CUR = foreign currency debt; CB.TBILL = Treasury bills held by the Central Bank; CB.BOND = fixed-rate bonds held by the Central Bank; CB.PRO = promissory notes held by the Central Bank; FIX.MAT = average maturity of marketable fixed-rate debt (same as conventional maturity); EF.MAT = effective maturity.

France   Data on debt and debt maturity were obtained from *French Government Securities, Annual Report 1995*, and *French Government Securities, Monthly Bulletin*, Ministère de l'Èconomie et des Finances (internet address: www.tresor.finances.fr/oat/). For the period 1970–85, data on debt composition and information on debt instruments were provided by the Ministère de l'Èconomie et des Finances. Data were also obtained from the *Bulletin de la Banque de France: Supplément Statistiques (Trimestrelle)*, Banque de France.

"Debt" refers to Central Government debt. Debt figures are gross of the Treasury credit balance with the Bank of France and of debt held by the Central Bank, since data on bank holdings could not be found. Data on debt are net of "Revalorisation du 7%" and debt due to international organizations, i.e. the IMF. The debt composition in Table 4.14, distinguishes fixed-rate bonds with the option to exchange them into variable-rate bonds while variable-rate bonds with the option to exchange them into fixed-rate bonds are considered as variable-rate debt. Bonds for which the exchange option had been exercised were considered as the type of debt in which they were converted. As an exchange option expired, bonds were considered as standard bonds with no option. Fixed-rate bonds include renewable bonds. Bonds indexed to the price of gold and to the European Unit of Account could not be distinguished from fixed-rate bonds because detailed information on their amounts could not be found. In the mid-1970s such bonds approximately account for 10% of total debt while their share is negligible in the 1980s.

Data on debt maturity are not available before 1990. The average remaining term to maturity of fixed-rate component of the debt denominated in domestic currency was constructed from data on the year of maturity of each fixed-rate note and fixed-rate bond assigning a maturity date of 30 June for that year. Bonds with an exchange option from fixed to variable coupons were also considered. Treasury bills were given their published average maturity. Effective maturity was estimated assigning zero maturity to ECU notes and bonds and the average time before the adjustment of the coupon for variable-rate bonds. As most variable-rate bonds pay annual coupons, a tentative average time to adjustment of 6 months was assumed. The share of fixed-rate long-term debt considers fixed-rate notes, bonds, and long-term loans denominated in the domestic currency and excludes fixed-rate bonds exchangeable into variable-rate bonds. Such share also includes bonds indexed to the price of gold and to the European Unit of Account because data on their amount could not be found.

The data-set in Table A.7 is organized as follows (initial maturity in parentheses): TBILL BTF = Treasury bills BTF (13, 26 and 52 weeks). Past data refer to "Bons en Compte Courant"; NOTES BTAN = Treasury notes (2 and 5 years); ECU.NOTE BTAN = ECU denominated Treasury notes; VAR.BOND = variable-rate OAT bonds; ECU.BOND OAT = ECU denominated Treasury bonds; FIX.BOND OAT = fixed-rate long-term bonds (10, 15, 20, 30 years); OPTION VAR-FIX = variable-rate bonds with an option for the holder to exchange them into fixed-rate bonds; NO CONV Stay VAR = bonds which remained at variable-rate as the exchange option expired without being exercised; OPTION FIX-VAR = fixed-rate bonds with an option for the holder to exchange them into variable-rate bonds. CONV into VAR = fixed-rate bond converted into variable-rate bonds; RENEW ORT = renewable bonds bearing the option for an exchange into later issues; OTH.BOND = other long-term bonds. It includes fixed-rate bonds and bonds indexed to the price of gold and to the European Unit of Account. Until 1979 it includes non-marketable long-term debt; NMK LONG = non-marketable long-term debt; NMK SHORT = non-marketable short-term debt; SAVING = savings bonds; POSTAL DEPOSIT = deposits with the Post Office. It includes Treasury currency; CB.BOR = Treasury account at the Central Bank (a minus sign indicates that the Treasury is a creditor); FOR.CUR = foreign currency debt; FOR.FSC = foreign currency debt issued to provide funds to the "Fonds de Stabilisation des Changes"; CON.MAT = conventional average maturity; FIX.BOND = average maturity of fixed-rate long-term bonds; FIX.MAT = average maturity of fixed-rate marketable debt; EF.MAT = effective maturity.

Germany Data on public debt were obtained from *Monthly Report of the Deutsche Bundesbank*, Deutsche Bundesbank. Data on debt maturity were obtained from *Statistische Beihefte zu den Monatsberichten der Deutschen Bundesbank-Reihe 2; Wertpapier Statistik*, Deutsche Bundesbank. Information on interest-rate indexation was provided by the Bunderministerium der Finanzen.

"Debt" refers to general government debt. Official debt data are consolidated across the various levels of government and are net of government holdings. Privately held debt was derived by deducting Central Bank holdings. In constructing Table 4.15 "old debts" tax certificates and "East-German debt" were not considered to better understand the evolution of the debt structure. These old debts comprise equalization claims, covering claims, commutation and compensation debt and (new) debt arising from the Investment Assistance Levy.

The average remaining maturity of the debt denominated in domestic currency, which is roughly equal to the effective maturity due to the low share of foreign currency debt, was estimated in two steps. First, the average remaining maturity of medium- and long-term government paper outstanding—excluding variable-rate bonds—was computed from their distribution by class of remaining maturity, which is published by the Bundesbank. Government paper includes marketable securities and savings bonds issued by the Federal Government, the States (Landers), the Federal Post Office, and the Federal Railway. Second, Treasury discount notes and Treasury financing paper were assigned an estimated average remaining maturity of 1.25 years: Treasury discount notes are issued with maturities ranging from 6 months to 2 years, Treasury financing paper with maturities between 1 and 2 years. Because of the inclusion of saving bonds (6- and 7-year initial maturity) and Treasury financing paper the series is not directly comparable to those of other countries, but the low share of savings bonds makes this a minor problem.

The data-set in Table A.8 is organized as follows (initial maturity in parentheses): TBILL = Treasury bills; TDISC = Treasury discount notes (from 6 months to 2 years) and non-marketable Federal financing paper (from 1 to 2 years); Notes = Treasury notes (4 years, in the past from 2 to 6 years); 5Y.BOND = special federal bonds (5 years); VAR.BOND = variable-rate bonds (10 years); FIX.BOND = fixed-rate long-term bonds (mostly 10 years but up to 30 years); BK.LOAN = loans from banks (against borrowers' notes, i.e. negotiable privately placed notes); SS.LOAN = loans from social security funds (...); OTH.LOAN = other loans (...); FOR.CUR = foreign currency denominated debt; SAVING = savings bonds; TAX.CER = short-term tax certificates; OLD.DEBT = old debts (see above). It includes debt arising from the Investment Assistance Levy; CB.BOR = borrowing from the Central Bank; CB.SP.CR = special credit from the Central Bank; EAST.GE = East German debts; CB.TDIS = Treasury discount notes held by the Central Bank; CB.BOND = long-term bonds held by the Central Bank; CB.OLD = equalization claims (old debts) held by the Central Bank; CON.LONG = conventional average maturity of medium- and long-term marketable debt, savings bonds, bonds issued by the Post Office and Federal Railways. It excludes Treasury discount notes and Treasury financing paper; FIX.MAT = average maturity of fixed-rate debt including Treasury discount notes and Treasury financing paper; EF.MAT = effective maturity.

Greece Data on public debt for the period 1980–95 were obtained from *OECD Economic Surveys*, OECD various issues and *Annual Report*, Bank of Greece. Data on debt holdings of the Bank of Greece are from *Monthly Statistical Bulletin*, Bank of Greece, Economic Research Division.

"Debt" refers to general government debt. Data on debt composition have been partly estimated for the period 1980–6. Privately held debt was obtained by deducting Central Bank holdings of Treasury bills and bonds (from Treasury bills) and loans from the Central Bank. The composition of the debt in Table 4.16 distinguishes between variable-rate bonds placed on the market and "conversion bonds" arising from the abolition of mandatory investment in Treasury bills. Data on the former type of bonds include a small amount of fixed-rate bonds for the year 1992, as the fixed- and variable-rate components could not be identified. Foreign currency debt includes bonds with a foreign currency clause, i.e. domestic bonds indexed to foreign currencies, mainly to the ECU.

The data-set in Table A.9 is organized as follows (initial maturity in parentheses): TBILL = Treasury bills (3, 6 and 12 months); BONDS FIX + VAR = fixed-rate bonds (2 and 3 years) for the period 1987–91. Fixed-rate and variable-rate bonds (2, 5 and 7 years) in 1992. Variable-rate bonds since 1993; VAR.BOND CONVER = variable-rate "conversion bonds" (see above); ECU.BOND = bonds indexed to foreign currencies, mainly to the ECU; CB.LOAN = loans from the Central Bank; OTH.VAR = other non-marketable variable-rate debt; FOR.CUR = foreign currency debt; CB.SEC = Treasury bills and bonds held by the Central Bank.

Ireland Data on public debt and its maturity for the period 1991–5 were obtained from *Report and Accounts for the year ended 31 December* (various years), National Treasury Management Agency. The source of data for the earlier period was *Finance Accounts* and the *Statistical Yearbook*, Department of Finance, Stationery Office. Data on debt held by government departments and by the Central Bank were obtained from *Central Bank of Ireland Quarterly Bulletin*, Central Bank of Ireland.

"Debt" refers to national debt which corresponds broadly to central government debt and excludes guaranteed debt. The reported debt figures have been corrected to avoid double counting, i.e. they are net of liabilities of the Exchequer to itself: "capitalized liabilities," reflecting loans raised by local authorities from the Local Loans Fund which in turn raised the finance from general Exchequer borrowing.

Privately held debt in Table 4.17 was derived by deducting Central Bank and government holdings. Government holdings includes ways and means advances and bonds held by government departments. The latter, as well as bonds in Central Bank portfolio were estimated for the period 1960–8 because of unavailability of data. It should be noted that full deduction of the stock of bonds held in government department accounts yields an underestimate of privately held debt as part of these bonds represents investments of Post Office Savings Bank deposits and hence a liability towards the private sector. A deduction was also made in respect of the change in deposits held by the Exchequer overseas (foreign indebtedness under section 4 of the Appropriation Act 1965). These deposits do not represent net new borrowing, as they have a direct counterpart in the Statement of Capital Assets held by the Exchequer.

The series of maturity were computed as follows. Bonds were given a maturity date of 30 June in the year of maturity. Treasury bills were given the average remaining maturity corresponding to their initial maturity. Exchequer bills are issued with a 91-day maturity and since 1988 with a 35-day and 182-day maturity. Exchequer notes issued since 1991 have maturities from 7 to 120 days. The final maturity date was assigned to bonds with call options (double-dated bonds) in the calculation of all series of maturity.

The effective maturity was computed assigning to variable-rate bonds the average term remaining before the adjustment of their coupon. Variable-rate bonds have been issued in two forms. The coupon on earlier issues was adjusted semi-annually to the interest rate of Treasury bills, while recent issues bear coupons adjusted quarterly to the 3-month DIBOR. The coupon is derived as the average of the reference rate for the 10 business days immediately preceding the second business day before the entitlement date. The average time before the next coupon adjustment was considered to be equal to 0.2 years.

The data-set in Table A.10 is organized as follows (initial maturity in parentheses): TBILLS = Treasury bills, i.e. Exchequer bills (91 and 182 days) and Exchequer notes (from 7 to 120 days); M.NOTE = medium-term notes; VAR.BOND = variable-rate bonds; FIX.BOND = fixed-rate bonds (mostly 5, 10 and 20 years); FOR.CUR = foreign currency debt; SAVING = non-marketable savings schemes, excluding price-index-linked savings bonds; IDX.SAV = price-index-linked savings bonds; OTHER = other short-term debt; GV.WAYS = ways and means advances, i.e. borrowing from a number of funds under the control of the Ministry of Finance, such as Post Office Savings Bank Funds, National Loans Sinking Funds, Social Insurance Investment Funds; CB.BOR = borrowing from the Central Bank. It includes the overdraft at the Central Bank; GV.BILL = Treasury bills held in government accounts; GV.BOND = bonds held in government accounts; GV.FOR = foreign currency debt held in government accounts (see above); CB.BILL = Treasury bills held by the Central Bank; CB.BOND = bonds held by the Central Bank; CON.BOND = conventional average maturity of fixed-rate and variable-rate bonds; CON.MAT = conventional average maturity of marketable debt including Treasury bills; FIX.BOND = average maturity of fixed-rate bonds; FIX.MAT = average maturity of fixed-rate marketable debt including Treasury bills; EF.MAT = effective maturity.

Italy   Data on public debt for the period 1970–92 were obtained from *Bollettino Statistico*, Banca d'Italia, Servizio Studi. For the period 1960–9 the source was Morcaldo and Salvemini, "Il Debito Pubblico; Analisi dell'Evoluzione nel Periodo 1960–83 e Prospettive," *Rivista di Politica Economica*, 1984. Data on the average remaining maturity of marketable securities were provided by the Research Department of the Bank of Italy.

"Debt" refers to public sector debt. Published data distinguish between privately held debt and total debt.

The published series of (conventional) average maturity refers to all marketable securities denominated in domestic currency, including Treasury bills and ECU indexed bills and bonds payable in Italian Lire. It assigns the final maturity date to variable-rate bonds, price-index-linked bonds and putable bonds. The series of average maturity of the fixed-rate component of the debt was derived by purging the conventionally measured maturity by variable-rate bonds, ECU bills and bonds, price-index-linked bonds and assigning the earlier redemption date to putable bonds.

The effective maturity was computed assigning zero maturity to foreign currency debt, ECU bonds and bills and price-index-linked bonds. The weights in privately held debt were used for the purpose of computing maturity instead of total debt for the period before 1970, since data on Central Bank holdings of bonds for that period are not available. The earlier redemption date was used for putable bonds. Variable-rate bonds were assigned the average time remaining before the coupon adjustment. Variable-rate bonds bear annual or semi-annual coupons. To take into account the imperfection of the indexation mechanism the maturity computed above was augmented by the lag— 2.25 months—(1-month since 1995) between the determination of the reference rate and the beginning of the entitlement period.

The data-set in Table A.11 is organized as follows (initial maturity in parentheses). Data are for privately held debt, i.e. they exclude debt held by the Central Bank and in government accounts.

TBILL = Treasury bills (3, 6 and 12 months); CRBILL = Treasury bills held by banks in fulfillment of legal reserve requirement; VAR.BOND = variable-rate bonds (7 and 10 years). It includes variable-rate discount certificates (CTS) and a small amount of variable-rate bonds with the option to be exchanged in fixed-rate bonds;

P-INDEX = price-index-linked bonds (10 years); FIX.BOND BTP = fixed-rate bonds (3, 5, 10 and 30 years); FIX.BOND COT = fixed-rate bonds. It includes putable bonds and lire 47,217 bn. of two-year discount bonds in 1995; OTH.BOND = old fixed-rate bonds issued by the central government and fixed-rate public sector bonds. It includes FIX.BOND BTP until 1964 and FIX.BOND COT until 1968; ECU.BILL = ECU indexed bills (1 year); ECU.BOND = ECU indexed bonds (4, 7 and 8 years); FOR.COR = foreign currency debt; POSTAL = Post Office savings certificates and Post Office savings accounts; LOAN = loans from banks; OTHER = other non-marketable debt; PH.DEBT = total privately held debt; CB.BILL = Treasury bills held by the Central Bank; CB.VAR = variable-rate bonds held by the Central Bank; CB.BTP = fixed-rate bonds BTP held by the Central Bank; CB.COT = fixed-rate bonds COT held by the Central Bank; CB.OTH BOND = other fixed-rate bonds held by the Central Bank; CB.BTE = ECU bills held by the Central Bank; CB.ECU = ECU bonds held by the Central Bank; CB.BOR = government account at the Central Bank, i.e. borrowing from Central Bank; CB.TOT = total debt held by the Central Bank; CON.MAT = conventional average maturity (see above); FIX.MAT = average maturity of fixed-rate marketable debt; MAT.COR VAR.BON = average maturity of marketable debt considering the average time before coupon adjustments for variable-rate debt; EF.MAT = effective maturity.

Japan   Data on debt composition were obtained from *Economic Statistics Annual*, Research and Statistics Department, Bank of Japan. Data on variable-rate debt and maturity were provided by the Ministry of Finance, Financial Bureau, Government Debt Division.

"Debt" refers to central government debt. Privately held debt was derived by deducting Central Bank holdings of financing bills and marketable securities. Securities, i.e. Treasury bills and bonds, held by the Central Bank were considered as being long-term bonds.

Data on average remaining term to maturity are available only for March 1996 when the maturity of fixed-rate marketable debt, i.e. financing and Treasury bills, notes and all types of bonds, was 4.9 years and effective maturity was 4.8 years.

The share of fixed-rate long-term debt denominated in the domestic currency comprises fixed-rate notes, 5-year special bonds, long-term bonds and loans.

The data-set in Table A.12 is organized as follows (initial maturity in parentheses): FBILL = Financing bills (60 days); TBILL = Treasury bills (3 and 6 months): VAR.BOND = variable-rate bonds (15 years); M.NOTES = medium-term notes (2 and 4 years); 5Y.BOND = 5-year discount bonds (5 years); LG.BOND = fixed-rate long-term bonds (from 6 to 30 years, mostly 10 years); OTH.BOND = other fixed-rate bonds. It includes long-term bonds for the period 1961–5; FOR.CUR = foreign currency debt; LOAN = non-marketable loans; CB.FBILL = financing bills held by the Central Bank; CB.SEC = Treasury bills and bonds held by the Central Bank.

Netherlands   Data on debt composition and debt maturity were obtained from *1995 Annual Report*, Agency of the Ministry of Finance and from the *Quarterly Review*, Agency of the Ministry of Finance. Data on debt composition are also published in the *Annual Report De Nederlandesche Bank*, De Nederlandesche Bank. The same publication and the *De Nederlandesche Bank Quarterly Bulletin*, De Nederlandesche Bank, provide data on the holdings of debt by the Central Bank.

"Debt" refers to central government debt. The composition between bonds and Treasury notes has been partly estimated for the period 1988–91 to eliminate the break in the official series that arises because of a change in official statistics: notes with an initial term to maturity of 2 years or longer are classified as bonds. This determines an increase in the official bond series amounting to 5,834 m. of guilders as of January 1988. Privately held debt was obtained by deducting Central Bank holdings.

The average remaining term to maturity of fixed-rate debt denominated in domestic currency, was estimated in two steps. First, the average remaining maturity of long-term bonds, private loans and Treasury certificates was computed from their distribution by class of remaining maturity. Since bonds with sinking funds redemption (in equal yearly installments) are considered as having a remaining maturity equal to: remaining grace period + (1 + number of remaining redemption years)/2, the average maturity accounts for amortization practices in use before 1986. Callable bonds are classified according to the last redemption date. (Since 1989 data on Conventional maturity are official.) In the second step, Treasury notes were assigned an estimated average remaining maturity equal to 2 years until 1987 and 1 year since 1988; in the earlier period Teasury notes were issued with maturities ranging from 2 to 5 years and since 1987 with maturities ranging from 1 to 2 years. Treasury bills with maturities between 6 and 9 months were assigned an average maturity of 0.5 years.

The data-set in Table A.13 is organized as follows (initial maturity in parentheses): TBILL = Treasury bills (Dutch Treasury Certificates) (mostly 3 and 9 months); Notes = Treasury notes (between 2 and 5 years). It is estimated for the years 1988 and 1989 for which official data report 6,752 m. and 3,282 m. guilders, respectively; FIX.BOND = fixed-rate bonds (mostly 10 years and up to 30 years); LOAN = privately-placed loans against registered "non-marketable" bonds which can however be traded without limitations (from 10 to 20 years); T.CER = long-term Treasury certificates; FOR.CUR = foreign currency debt; PRESUB = presubscription account of the General Public Service Pension Fund (short-term non-marketable debt); LOCAL = short-term non-marketable debt to local authorities; OTH.SH = other short-term non-marketable debt. It is net of Central Bank advances of guilders 143 m. for the year 1989. It includes Treasury currency; CB.NP = Treasury notes and certificates purchased by the Central Bank; TOTAL = total debt. It includes a negligible amount of tax certificates for the period 1960–6; CB.ND = Treasury notes and certificates discounted by the Central Bank; CB.BOND = bonds held by the Central Bank; CB.LOAN = privately placed loans held by the Central Bank; CON.MAT = conventional average maturity of Treasury certificates, bonds and private loans. It excludes notes; FIX.MAT = average maturity of fixed-rate debt, including notes and Treasury bills; EF.MAT = effective maturity.

Portugal   For the period 1980–95 data on debt composition and information on debt instruments were provided by the Direcção-Geral da Junta do Crédito Público and by the Banco de Portugal. Further information was obtained from *Mercado da Dívida Pública*, Instituto de Gestão do Crédito Público (IGCP), Ministéiro das Finaças (internet address: www.igcp.pt) and in the *Annual Report* of the Banco de Portugal. For the period 1970–80 data on debt composition (official values from Conta Geral do Estado) were provided by the Instituto de Gestão do Crédito Público. The composition between variable and fixed-rate debt for this period was partly estimated, since the distinction between these two types of debt is not available for the "Dívida Interna a cargo da Direcçã-Geral do Tesouro."

"Debt" refers to public debt, and is gross of the debt held by the Central Bank since data on bank holdings could not be found. There is a discontinuity in the series of "other marketable fixed-rate debt" because of the different data sources for the periods 1970–9 and 1980–95. Furthermore, data on "other non-marketable variable-rate debt" are not available for the earlier period.

The average term to maturity of fixed-rate bonds in 1995 was about 4.5 years. The average maturity of the fixed-rate component of the debt, which consider Treasury bills, was equal to 3.0 years while conventional maturity including variable-rate bonds was 2.7 years.

The share of fixed-rate long-term debt includes fixed-rate bonds and other fixed-rate long-term debt denominated in domestic currency.

The data-set in Table A.14 is organized as follows (initial maturity in parentheses). TBILL = Treasury bills (91, 182 and 364 days); VAR.BOND CLIP = variable-rate bonds, "Auctioned Credit for Public Investment"; VAR.BOND FIP = variable-rate bonds, "Public Investment Fund bonds" (7 and 8 years); VAR.BOND OTRV = new variable-rate bonds; VAR.BOND OCA = variable-rate "Accrued Interest" bonds; SP.CERT OCA.INT = fixed-rate special certificates arising from the interests accrued on OCA bonds and paid at maturity; OTH.VAR = other variable-rate debt; FIX.BOND OT = fixed-rate long-term bonds (3, 5, 7 and 10 years); OTH.FIX = other marketable fixed-rate debt (see above); FOR.CUR = foreign currency debt; SAVING = variable-rate savings schemes; OTH.NMK VAR = other non-marketable variable-rate debt.

Spain Data on public debt for the period 1981–95, and data on its average remaining maturity for the period 1962–95 were obtained from *Boletín Estadístico*, Banco de Espanã. A longer series for public debt, as well as data on Central Bank holdings, were provided by the Banco de Espanã.

"Debt" refers to central government debt. Privately held debt was obtained by deducting Central Bank holdings.

Data on the average term to maturity of marketable fixed-rate securities, including Treasury bills (Pagares and Letras), denominated in domestic currency are published for the period 1980–95. A longer series was derived from the distribution by class of remaining maturity of the same group of securities. Conventional average maturity is equal to the average maturity of fixed-rate marketable debt. The effective maturity was computed by assigning zero maturity to foreign currency debt.

The data-set in Table A.15 is organized as follows (initial maturity in parentheses). TBILL = Treasury bills, "Letras," with (3, 6 and 12 months); P.NOTE = promissory notes, "Pagares del Tesoro," (6, 12 and 18 months); FIX.BOND = fixed-rate long-term bonds (3, 5, 10 and 15 years). It includes a negligible amount of variable-rate bonds (one issue in 1986); FOR.CUR = foreign currency debt; INV.CERT = Investment Certificates of Indebtedness issued to commercial and savings banks under mandatory investment regulations to raise funds for public projects (10 years); LOAN = non-marketable loans; CURR = Treasury currency; CAJA = deposits at "Caja General de Depósitos"; OTHER = other debt; CB.LOAN = Central Bank loans; CB.BILL = Treasury bills held by the Central Bank; CB.BOND = bonds held by the Central Bank; CB.INV = Investment Certificates held by the Central Bank; FIX.MAT = average maturity of fixed-rate marketable debt; EF.MAT = effective maturity.

Sweden Data on public debt and its maturity were obtained from *Annual Report*, the Swedish National Debt Office (SNDO), [internet address: www.sndo.se] and from *Statistisk Arsbok*, Sveriges Riksbank [Quarterly Bulletin of the Central Bank of Sweden]. Data on debt holdings were obtained from *Statistiska Meddelanden*, Statistiska centralbyrán and from *Statistisk Arsbok*, Sveriges Riksbank. Further information on debt maturity and price-index-linked debt was provided by the SNDO.

"Debt" refers to central government debt. Privately held debt was obtained by deducting Central Bank holdings. Price-index-linked bonds are evaluated at their issue price instead of their face value. (The difference between the issue price and the face value is substantial since the first indexed bonds were zero coupon bonds.) Until 1988 foreign currency debt is evaluated at the exchange rates of the time of issue; since 1989 at current exchange rates.

Data on the average term to maturity are published in the "Annual Report," for the period since 1988, for both total domestic currency debt [CON.TOT below] and marketable debt, i.e. Treasury discount bills and bonds [CON.MAT below]. A series which excludes price-index-linked bonds is also published and was used to compute the maturity of marketable fixed-rate debt [MAT.FIX below]. Data are for 30 June of each year and since 1988 maturity is defined as "remaining period of fixed interest rate," which coincides with the remaining term to maturity, since almost all Swedish bonds are fixed-rate bonds. The average maturity of marketable fixed-rate debt for the period 1985–7 and the years 1976 and 1980 was provided by the SNDO, while for the other years it was estimated as follows. The average maturity of all types of bonds was derived from data on their gross issues and redemptions. Then the average maturity of the debt was computed as the weighted average of the series so derived and a maturity of 6 months for Treasury discount bills. (The estimates are roughly equal to the official figures for the years when the latter exists.) The effective maturity was computed by assigning zero maturity to foreign currency debt and to indexed debt. No correction was made for the small amount of old revisable-rate debt.

The data-set in Table A.16 is organized as follows (initial maturity in parentheses): Old.BILL = until 1988 old Treasury bills (since 1983 entirely held by the Central Bank). Since 1989 borrowing from the Central Bank (credit line with the Central Bank). Since 1994 it includes overnight borrowing; TBILL = Treasury discount bills, i.e. new Treasury bills (3, 6 and 12 months); P-INDEX = price-index-linked bonds evaluated at their market price when issued; FIX.BOND = fixed-rate long-term bonds (2, 3, 5, 10 and 15 years). It includes a small amount of revisable-rate bonds issued in 1979–80; T.BOND = other fixed-rate long-term Treasury bonds; LOT.BON = lottery bonds; FOR.CUR = foreign currency debt, until 1988 evaluated at the exchange rates prevailing at the time of issue; SAVING = savings bonds; NAT.SAV = National Savings Account, i.e. savings via the bank system guaranteed by the State; DEBT.ACC = National Debt Account, i.e. an account for saving in bonds at fixed- or variable-rates; BK.LOAN = loans from banks; SS.LOAN = loans from State institutions and funds; COMPUL = compulsory savings; CB.Old.BILL = until 1989 old Treasury bills held by the Central Bank. Since 1989 borrowing from the Central Bank (credit line with the Central Bank); CB.BILL = Treasury discount bills held by the Central Bank; CB.BOND = fixed-rate bonds held by the Central Bank; CB.TBON = other fixed-rate bonds held by the Central Bank; IDX.FACE = price-index-linked bonds evaluated at face value; CON.TOT = conventional average maturity of total domestic currency debt, including saving schemes; CON.MAT = conventional average maturity of marketable debt, including price-indexed debt; MAT.FIX = average maturity of fixed-rate marketable debt; EF.MAT = effective maturity.

United Kingdom   Data on public debt and its maturity were obtained from *Bank of England Quarterly Bulletin*, Economics Division, Bank of England. Further information was obtained from the *Gilt-Edged Market Review*, and *British Government Securities*, Bank of England (internet address: www.bankofengland.co.uk).

"Debt" refers to national debt which corresponds broadly to Central Government debt. It includes guaranteed marketable securities and excludes interest-free notes due to the IMF. Since 1971 published data distinguish between market holdings , i.e. privately held debt and official holdings of debt, the latter including debt held by government departments and the Bank of England. For the period 1966–70 privately held bonds have been partly estimated. The composition of non-marketable debt has also been estimated for the period 1960–5.

Data on average remaining term to maturity refer to "market holdings" (privately held debt) of marketable bonds denominated in domestic currency, issued or guaranteed by the government. Various series of maturity are available. The two series reported here (MAT.BOND and MAT.FX.B) use the earliest conversion date for convertible bonds and the latest redemption date for callable bonds. The two series differ depending on whether price-index-linked bonds are included (MAT.BOND) or excluded (MAT.FX.B) from the computation.

The series which excludes indexed bonds was used to compute the average maturity of fixed-rate securities denominated in domestic currency. To this end Treasury bills were given an average remaining maturity corresponding to their initial maturity; 0.15 years until 1987 and 0.2 years since 1988. (Treasury bills have an initial maturity of 91 days and after 1987 of 91 and 182 days.) The effective maturity is computed by assigning zero maturity to foreign currency debt and price-index-linked bonds. No correction was made for the small component of variable-rate bonds: 2% in 1997.

The data-set in Table A.17 is organized as follows (initial maturity in parentheses): TBILL = Treasury bills (91 and 182 days); VAR.BOND = variable-rate bonds (5 years); FIX.BOND = fixed-rate long-term bonds, "Gilt-Edged Stock" (5, 10, 15, 20 and 25 years). It includes a now small amounts of "double-dated" callable bonds and of "convertible" bonds giving the holder the option to exchange them into longer maturity bonds; P-INDEX = price-index-linked bonds (up to 40 years). The value of price-index-linked bonds comprises the capital uplift; FOR.CUR = foreign currency debt; SAVING = savings schemes; IDX.SAV = price-index-linked savings bonds; TAX.CER = tax certificates; OTHER = other debt; PH.DEBT = total privately held debt; OFF.HELD = official holdings, i.e. debt held by government departments and by the Central Bank; MAT.BOND = average maturity of marketable bonds; MAT.FX.B = average maturity of marketable fixed-rate bonds, i.e. it excludes indexed bonds; CON.MAT = average maturity of marketable bonds and Treasury bills; FIX.MAT = average maturity of marketable fixed-rate bonds and Treasury bills; EF.MAT = effective maturity.

United States Data on public debt and its maturity were obtained from *Treasury Bulletin*, Office of the Secretary Department of the Treasury. Data on the composition of the debt held by the Federal Reserve were obtained from *Federal Reserve Bulletin*, Board of Governors of the Federal Reserve System.

"Debt" refers to Federal government debt and excludes guaranteed debt. Published data on debt distinguish between privately held debt, debt held by the Federal Reserve, and debt held in government accounts. Figures for privately held debt exclude "Government Account Series," that is, special non-marketable paper issued to public pensions for the investment of their funds. This practice causes an asymmetry with other countries, notably with Japan and the Netherlands, where such debts are not considered among official holdings on the basis that they are matched by future government liabilities to the private sector. Table 4.25 shows the composition by type of instrument of privately held debt net of the Government Account Series. The latter can be obtained in terms of GDP as the difference between "PGA-Ratio" and "PH-Ratio" in the same table. The composition of government holdings between Treasury bills, notes and bonds could not be found and was estimated assuming that holdings of such debts reflect their shares in the outstanding stock.

The published series of the average term to maturity refers to privately held debt. It considers all marketable fixed-rate securities denominated in domestic currency, including Treasury bills. Effective maturity is not reported as the correction for foreign currency debt is negligible. In practice, conventional maturity, average maturity of fixed-rate securities and effective maturity coincide.

The data-set in Table A.17 is organized as follows (initial maturity in parentheses): TBILL = Treasury bills (13, 26, and 52 weeks) and cash management bills (from few days to 6 months); T.CERT = short-term Treasury certificates; Notes = fixed-rate long-term notes (2, 3, 5 and 10 years); FIX.BOND = fixed-rate long-term bonds (30 years); FOR.CUR = foreign currency debt; SAVING = savings bonds; OTH.MKT = other marketable debt, i.e. Federal Financing Bank securities; OTH.NMK = other non-marketable debt, mainly State and local government series; GV.ACC = non-marketable government account series (see above); MATUR = matured debt and debt bearing no interest; GV.MKT = marketable securities held in government accounts; GV.OTH = other non-marketable debt held in government accounts; CB.BILL = Treasury bills held by the Federal Reserve; CB.CERT = Treasury certificates held by the Federal Reserve; CB.NOTE = notes held by the Federal Reserve; CB.BOND = bonds held by the Federal Reserve; FIX.MAT = average maturity of marketable fixed-rate debt held by the private sector (see above).

A.1 Australia [Million dollars]

	TBILL	TNOTE	P-INDEX	VAR.BOND	FIX.BOND	SAVING	OTH.NMK	FOR.CUR
1974.2	931	387	0	0	11479	998	480	1031
1975.2	1010	2076	0	0	12056	965	481	1182
1976.2	2017	456	0	0	13946	2097	496	1326
1977.2	1300	370	0	0	15283	2473	503	1870
1978.2	1500	363	0	0	16135	2891	543	3635
1979.2	2000	1410	0	0	16930	3174	648	5256
1980.2	2500	1615	0	0	17380	3359	721	5397
1981.2	1900	3527	0	0	17568	3039	793	4652
1982.2	1400	3680	0	0	18637	2318	838	5352
1983.2	0	3636	0	0	21772	4709	880	6919
1984.2	0	2073	0	0	29426	6652	966	7084
1985.2	0	2895	0	0	35653	5976	994	9793
1986.2	0	6854	225.4	0	37986.6	3971	978	13831
1987.2	0	8140	529.1	0	39798.9	3461	921	15065
1988.2	0	7850	730.7	0	37627.3	3496	869	12691
1989.2	0	9533	730.7	0	34022.3	2746	816	9388
1990.2	0	8207	730.7	0	32648.3	876	805	6953
1991.2	0	11897	730.7	0	31174.3	538	798	4957
1992.2	0	13874	730.7	0	39353.3	382	777	5038
1993.2	0	15600	1482.7	0	53577.3	182	730	5898
1994.2	0	16185	2582.7	0	67431.3	107	827	4577
1995.2	0	14163	3127.4	3700	81129.6	0	766	3319

A.1 Australia [Million dollars] (continued)

	TOTAL	CB.NOTE	CB.BILL	CB.BOND	GV.BOND	CON.MAT	FIX.MAT	EF.MAT
1974.2	15306	0	n/a	1443	2977	11.4	11.4	10.2
1975.2	17770	22	n/a	1254	3198	8.8	8.8	7.9
1976.2	20338	14	n/a	2724	3091	8.9	8.9	8.0
1977.2	21799	194	n/a	4105	3735	8.8	8.8	7.6
1978.2	25067	162	n/a	4230	3821	8.4	8.4	6.5
1979.2	29418	415	n/a	4782	4007	7.4	7.4	5.4
1980.2	30972	385	2500	2319	1653	6.5	6.5	4.7
1981.2	31479	678	1900	2196	1290	5.5	5.5	4.3
1982.2	32225	1164	1400	2299	1166	4.9	4.9	3.8
1983.2	37916	1304	0	2321	845	4.7	4.7	3.5
1984.2	46201	791	0	2166	764	5.3	5.3	4.2
1985.2	55311	870	0	5686	890	5.8	5.8	4.4
1986.2	63846	3227	0	6441	757	6.7	6.6	4.7
1987.2	67915	1171	0	611	743	6.1	6.0	4.3
1988.2	63264	780	0	2903	450	5.8	5.6	4.2
1989.2	57236	526	0	2915	255	5.5	5.4	4.3
1990.2	50220	387	0	1617	1668	5.2	5.0	4.2
1991.2	50095	104	0	2432	1221	5.0	4.9	4.3
1992.2	60155	593	0	7260	1153	5.5	5.4	4.8
1993.2	77470	2655	0	10717	797	5.6	5.4	4.7
1994.2	91710	2777	0	9692	680	5.6	5.3	4.8
1995.2	106205	954	0	13931	594	6.3	6.1	5.4

A.2 Austria [Million schilling]

	TBILL	TB.VAR	VAR.NOTE	VAR.BOND	NOTES	FIX.BOND	INSURAN FIX.LOAN	INSURAN VAR.LOAN
1969	6764	n/a	0	0	n/a	16565	1301	n/a
1970	8252	n/a	0	0	n/a	17111	1522	n/a
1971	10138	n/a	0	0	n/a	17686	1786	n/a
1972	10802	n/a	0	0	n/a	20758	2181	n/a
1973	16072	n/a	0	0	n/a	22812	2365	n/a
1974	16940	n/a	0	0	n/a	22137	2360	n/a
1975	22747	n/a	0	0	10326	25129	2128	n/a
1976	24919	n/a	0	0	24274	32696	4095	n/a
1977	23336	n/a	0	0	33334	39333	5556	n/a
1978	24160	n/a	0	0	42007	47749	5534	974
1979	25013	n/a	0	0	50508	57765	7459	1002
1980	30992	n/a	0	0	52600	70182	8588	797
1981	32140	n/a	0	0	53948	74024	4985	5223
1982	41670	n/a	0	0	57884	82109	4257	6588
1983	47135	n/a	0	0	69888	97320	3601	12853
1984	49181	n/a	0	0	72242	103964	2919	20767
1985	50291	n/a	0	0	77186	114436	2273	28382
1986	51416	n/a	2050	0	94520	125160	1974	38263
1987	16550	36456	8050	0	116673	137931	1579	45422
1988	13050	36356	21810	0	127103	151496	3606	48207
1989	17860	35456	37960	1447	120342	182290	9619	48440
1990	19300	35456	60910	1447	115087	212255	13939	48027
1991	21250	34756	66500	1447	106964	265617	19021	51987
1992	23150	34656	50000	1447	98263	315517	24900	55302
1993	34640	34656	51810	1447	85621	394779	27379	55966
1994	31380	32676	57310	0	74688	474395	38933	58145

	BANK FIX.LOAN	BANK VAR.LOAN	OTH.FIX	OTH.VAR	CB.BOR	FOR.CUR	TOTAL
1969	1013	0	n/a	n/a	5199	12762	43604
1970	1626	0	n/a	n/a	5073	13489	47072
1971	2020	0	n/a	n/a	3086	12132	46847
1972	2631	0	n/a	n/a	3183	10304	49858
1973	2453	0	n/a	n/a	3532	9019	56252
1974	2322	0	n/a	n/a	4097	13540	61395
1975	3956	0	n/a	n/a	4020	32062	100367
1976	8995	0	n/a	n/a	3846	34958	133782
1977	11003	0	921	n/a	3672	47427	164581
1978	14365	0	846	n/a	3507	60026	199167
1979	21442	0	745	n/a	3131	63655	230719
1980	21957	0	629	95	2700	72641	261181
1981	2002	25376	822	150	2044	94565	295278
1982	2517	35081	766	129	2231	108351	341581
1983	2000	54457	668	107	2573	125590	416192
1984	10917	87291	431	298	2820	118958	469788
1985	19952	111676	409	199	2093	118718	525616
1986	38929	138373	338	43	1200	124605	616870
1987	50573	158689	263	22	580	124739	697526
1988	62847	150792	194	0	410	130802	746673
1989	69535	150889	126	0	371	125834	800168
1990	65814	153495	78	0	443	135359	861608
1991	64322	156891	73	0	458	148458	957745
1992	62901	153144	68	0	504	172141	991993
1993	59467	149853	64	0	506	212857	1109046
1994	44374	153731	1205	0	597	260941	1228374
1995	51155	152335	53	0	0	296630	1350357

A.3 Belgium (Billion francs)

	TBILL	MEDIUM	FIX.BOND DIRECT	FIX.BOND INDIR	VAR.BOND DIRECT	VAR.BOND INDIR	FOR.CUR
1960	68.6	18.1	211.6	19.4	0	0	46.1
1961	70.9	17.4	217.4	24.0	0	0	48.5
1962	50.1	20.9	251.6	26.0	0	0	38.5
1963	55.1	13.7	261.6	27.8	0	0	48.0
1964	51.2	6.3	276.9	31.8	0	0	49.7
1965	58.6	6.8	293.6	32.4	0	0	46.9
1966	59.9	7.8	305.6	29.5	0	0	51.3
1967	57.8	8.5	317.1	38.8	0	0	57.3
1968	66.2	9.1	335.0	45.6	0	0	56.9
1969	67.3	13.9	347.7	50.9	0	0	63.1
1970	78.1	12.5	359.6	59.7	0	0	52.3
1971	66.9	13.4	426.5	54.8	0	0	24.1
1972	57.7	17.7	494.9	63.8	0	0	10.1
1973	56.6	15.9	559.4	61.4	0	0	7.0
1974	57.7	19.7	613.7	58.0	0	0	5.8
1975	71.0	17.3	681.9	84.2	0	0	4.6

1976	116.6	13.0	752.5	95.9	0	0	3.7
1977	156.0	6.3	864.6	118.5	0	0	3.3
1978	195.6	6.0	976.6	150.2	0	0	15.0
1979	242.2	5.8	1064.9	188.0	0	0	57.3
1980	390.7	5.7	1116.3	205.1	1	0	153.6
1981	608.6	5.7	1123.2	221.6	4.3	0	388.4
1982	843.3	3.4	1177.9	325.3	6.3	0	642.4
1983	953.0	45.4	1395.4	407.3	7.3	0	823.9
1984	1062.9	142.8	1552.6	409.1	9.3	0	1018.3
1985	1151.5	156.0	1932.0	498.5	102.7	0	990.4
1986	1430.0	98.8	2119.4	547.1	108.6	0	1020.3
1987	1537.6	80.1	2428.9	589.9	101.6	0	1046.0
1988	1570.8	51.5	2826.4	638.8	98.4	0	1087.5
1989	1724.9	35.4	3150.6	543.5	96.8	0.8	1131.1
1990	1827.1	19.3	3522.9	530.6	92.5	21.3	1111.7
1991	1821.8	1.1	4248.1	355.9	79.2	47.3	1107.0
1992	1841.3	0.9	4837.8	378.6	66.4	71.3	1010.5
1993	1626.0	0.9	5311.0	327.4	59.0	153.1	1520.0
1994	2115.9	0.6	5090.6	121.8	461.6	121.4	1349.5
1995	1657.3	0.5	5628.0	122.4	842.2	112.8	1085.3

A.3 Belgium (Billion francs) [*continued*]

	POSTAL DEPOSIT	TOTAL	FdR.ADV	CB.BOR	CB.TBILL	CB.BOND	CON.TOT	FIX.MAT	EF.MAT
1960	32.4	396.2	0	6.0	0	36.5	n/a	n/a	n/a
1961	32.8	411.0	0	6.5	0	36.6	n/a	n/a	n/a
1962	36.1	423.2	0	5.1	0	36.6	n/a	n/a	n/a
1963	39.8	446.0	0	9.3	0	36.7	n/a	n/a	n/a
1964	46.2	462.1	0	9.8	0	36.8	n/a	n/a	n/a
1965	46.3	484.6	0	9.0	0	36.9	n/a	n/a	n/a
1966	49.4	503.5	0	9.6	0	37.2	n/a	n/a	n/a
1967	45.9	525.4	0	2.7	0	37.4	n/a	n/a	n/a
1968	54.5	567.3	0	14.7	0	37.5	n/a	n/a	n/a
1969	52.9	595.8	0	15.5	0	37.6	n/a	n/a	n/a
1970	57.3	619.5	0	13.3	0	37.7	n/a	n/a	n/a
1971	57.2	642.9	0	4.9	0	37.8	n/a	n/a	n/a
1972	66.0	710.2	0	1.1	0	38.1	n/a	n/a	n/a
1973	63.4	763.7	0	3.2	0	38.3	n/a	n/a	n/a
1974	65.7	820.6	0	6.0	0	38.8	n/a	n/a	n/a
1975	69.4	928.4	0	5.0	0	39.3	n/a	n/a	n/a
1976	76.8	1058.5	0	21.2	0	39.5	6.9	5.6	5.6

1977	79.9	1228.6	3.0	37.4	0	40.1	6.3	5.4	5.4
1978	83.6	1427.0	16.0	37.0	0	40.5	5.6	5.1	5.0
1979	80.9	1639.1	52.5	37.0	0	41.2	5.1	4.9	4.7
1980	84.4	1956.8	77.1	37.0	0	42.0	4.5	4.0	3.7
1981	87.4	2439.2	149.5	37.0	0	42.9	3.7	3.3	2.7
1982	86.4	3085.0	181.1	37.0	0	44.1	3.3	2.7	2.1
1983	83.7	3716.0	188.4	37.0	0	45.6	3.5	3.0	2.3
1984	69.9	4264.9	200.6	37.0	0	46.8	3.7	3.1	2.3
1985	83.5	4914.6	182.2	37.0	0	48.3	4.2	3.5	2.8
1986	94.0	5418.2	209.4	37.0	0	50.1	3.8	3.3	2.6
1987	88.4	5872.5	127.6	37.0	0	53.2	3.6	3.3	2.7
1988	88.9	6362.3	106.6	37.0	0	56.8	3.5	3.3	2.7
1989	105.1	6788.2	66.5	37.0	0	60.1	3.4	3.3	2.7
1990	99.2	7224.6	36.7	37.0	0	64.6	3.1	3.1	2.6
1991	90.5	7750.9	0	0.0	17.7	34.2	3.4	3.3	2.8
1992	81.8	8288.6	0	0.2	17.4	37.2	3.9	3.9	3.4
1993	75.6	9073.0	0	0	32.4	40.4	4.2	4.6	3.8
1994	74.4	9335.8	0	0	17.9	43.8	4.4	4.6	3.8
1995	81.1	9529.6	0	0	23.9	46.7	4.7	4.7	3.8

A.4 Canada [Million dollars]

	TBILL	P-INDEX	FIX.BOND	FC.US.BIL	FC.MKT	FC.NMK	SAVING	GV.NMK	MATUR
1960.1	2125	0	10427	0	202	0	3137	0	12
1961.1	1935	0	10447	0	130	0	3556	0	16
1962.1	1885	0	10813	0	130	0	4055	63	29
1963.1	2165	0	10792	0	411	0	4582	12	16
1964.1	2230	0	11042	0	376	0	5092	0	19
1965.1	2140	0	10867	0	376	0	5552	43	14
1966.1	2150	0	10712	0	371	0	5733	144	15
1967.1	2310	0	10986	0	366	0	6016	262	20
1968.1	2480	0	11542	0	160	0	6097	302	14
1969.1	2840	0	12264	0	442	0	6168	387	14
1970.1	2895	0	12248	0	447	0	6579	468	13
1971.1	3735	0	12990	0	336	0	7805	336	11
1972.1	3830	0	13353	0	336	0	9712	27	11
1973.1	4290	0	13392	0	333	0	10989	35	24
1974.1	4905	0	13560	0	258	0	10406	42	17
1975.1	5630	0	14292	0	198	0	12915	52	13
1976.1	6495	0	15457	0	166	0	15517	62	13

1977.1	0	8255	17724	0	164	0	16304	72	13
1978.1	0	11295	21147	0	180	850	18011	84	13
1979.1	0	13535	26497	0	2976	4240	19247	96	9
1980.1	0	16325	32900	0	2990	1712	18081	113	12
1981.1	0	21770	40795	0	2929	1707	15812	136	13
1982.1	0	19375	43429	0	3295	1122	24977	154	11
1983.1	0	29125	48303	0	3409	1825	32641	171	16
1984.1	0	41700	56811	0	2183	3923	38204	189	33
1985.1	0	52300	69256	0	2117	6959	41959	205	22
1986.1	0	61950	81067	0	5890	7920	44245	445	30
1987.1	0	76950	94426	1045	5868	5096	44310	1796	18
1988.1	0	81050	103899	1045	6323	3926	53323	2492	36
1989.1	0	102700	115748	1131	5373	1911	47756	3006	30
1990.1	0	118550	127682	1446	4129	177	40929	3072	29
1991.1	0	139150	143600	1008	3555	0	34444	3492	53
1992.1	1200	152300	156862	0	3535	0	35598	3501	29
1993.1	1525	162050	176940	2552	2926	0	34369	3505	27
1994.1	2725	166000	200720	5649	5019	0	31331	3497	29
1995.1	4475	164450	221038	9046	7875	0	30756	3488	41
1996.1	5825	166100	246586	6986	9514	0	30801	3478	31

A.4 Canada [Million dollars] (continued)

	OTH.LIAB	TOTAL	CB.BILL	CB.BOND	CON.MAT	CON.GP	FIX.MAT	EF.MAT
1960.1	3518	19421	402	2196	9.4	10.6	9.4	9.3
1961.1	4052	20136	306	2356	9.3	11.3	9.3	9.2
1962.1	5023	21998	233	2579	8.0	10.4	8.0	7.9
1963.1	5371	23349	373	2460	8.4	10.9	8.4	8.1
1964.1	6387	25146	479	2534	7.8	10.6	7.8	7.6
1965.1	7269	26261	486	2528	7.9	10.3	7.9	7.7
1966.1	7836	26961	516	2850	7.7	10.0	7.7	7.5
1967.1	8547	28507	398	3095	7.4	9.9	7.4	7.2
1968.1	9531	30126	206	3027	6.8	8.7	6.8	6.7
1969.1	10306	32421	358	3476	6.2	8.5	6.2	6.0
1970.1	11091	33741	408	3523	5.7	7.7	5.7	5.5
1971.1	12248	37461	679	3743	5.2	7.9	5.2	5.1
1972.1	13938	41207	915	4144	4.9	7.0	4.9	4.8
1973.1	15689	44752	1032	4688	4.4	6.6	4.4	4.3
1974.1	18471	47659	1176	5060	4.3	6.8	4.3	4.2
1975.1	19889	52989	1776	5435	3.1	6.1	3.1	3.1
1976.1	22064	59774	2149	5727	3.8	6.4	3.8	3.8

1977.1	24965	67497	1921	6744	4.4	6.8	4.4	4.4
1978.1	28494	80074	2968	7956	5.0	7.4	5.0	4.8
1979.1	30608	97208	4024	8766	6.4	9.3	6.4	5.4
1980.1	33069	105202	4630	9951	7.2	9.4	7.2	6.6
1981.1	37648	120810	4076	11274	6.8	8.2	6.8	6.3
1982.1	45628	137991	4984	12011	6.5	7.8	6.5	6.1
1983.1	51049	166539	2270	12979	5.6	6.2	5.6	5.2
1984.1	57010	200053	2543	14514	5.4	5.8	5.4	5.1
1985.1	64782	237600	3049	13655	5.5	6.0	5.5	5.1
1986.1	68502	270049	4065	10355	5.4	5.2	5.4	4.9
1987.1	75930	305439	6882	10555	4.9	5.0	4.9	4.6
1988.1	85204	337298	10026	10483	4.8	4.5	4.8	4.5
1989.1	97246	374901	9083	10631	4.3	4.0	4.3	4.1
1990.1	103474	399488	12007	9967	4.1	4.0	4.1	4.0
1991.1	110029	435331	12386	9725	4.1	4.5	4.1	4.0
1992.1	114794	467819	14871	8922	4.3	4.5	4.2	4.1
1993.1	120906	504800	13358	7724	4.3	4.4	4.2	4.1
1994.1	133151	548121	20036	6367	4.6	4.8	4.4	4.3
1995.1	141694	582863	16291	5597	4.8	5.0	4.5	4.3
1996.1	153475	622796	19524	5113	5.0		4.7	4.5

A.5 Denmark [Million kroner]

	TBILL	TNOTE	FIX.BOND	VAR.BOND	ECU.BOND	FOR.CUR	LOT.BOND	COMP	CB.BOR
1970.1	0	0	2680	0	0	3191	657	0	-2949
1971.1	0	0	2531	0	0	3699	639	0	-6368
1972.1	0	0	2383	0	0	5292	533	0	-8295
1973.1	0	0	2234	0	0	6106	500	0	-11203
1974.1	0	0	2089	0	0	6517	500	0	-15355
1975.1	0	0	1947	0	0	7243	500	0	-12986
1976.1	0	0	7805	0	0	10429	500	0	-8937
1977.1	0	5000	12446	0	0	18979	500	0	-15855
1977.4	0	6803	19282	0	0	24410	1000	0	-14143
1978.4	0	13050	31071	0	0	29139	1000	0	-17686
1979.4	0	16950	44392	0	0	35744	1000	0	-12383
1980.4	0	21350	68207	0	0	45346	1200	0	-10117
1981.4	0	33250	100926	0	0	57521	1200	0	-2626
1982.4	0	36150	166618	0	0	79142	1200	0	-5235
1983.4	0	40700	230592	0	0	102514	1200	0	-15907
1984.4	0	37800	288959	3400	0	98534	1200	0	-9273
1985.4	0	28760	302749	27125	0	92930	1200	1404	-13184
1986.4	0	27500	282451	39935	0	119913	1200	1497	-48424
1987.4	0	43675	243212	56935	0	127637	1200	1464	-55819
1988.4	0	54085	215492	82785	0	124333	1200	1425	-45321
1989.4	0	64550	221592	88410	0	116031	1200	1375	-32215
1990.4	21350	68850	229221	85010	0	119101	1200	864	-38405
1991.4	49250	74050	252481	85010	0	92339	1200	392	-11425
1992.4	55485	71150	316690	57147	9827	104633	1200	0	-31269
1993.4	58339	94200	357346	41241	9824	165612	1200	0	-89568
1994.4	56238	111705	409565	30345	9698	131565	1200	0	-56910
1995.4	58385	102497	466608	20722	9244	111653	1200	0	-35444

A.5 Denmark [Million kroner] *(continued)*

	TOTAL	GV.SEC	GV.ECU	GV.FOR	CB.BOR	CB.SEC	CON.MAT	FIX.MAT	EF.MAT	FIX.DUR	TOT.DUR
1970.1	3579	n/a	0	n/a	−2949	n/a	n/a	n/a	n/a	n/a	n/a
1971.1	501	n/a	0	n/a	−6368	n/a	n/a	n/a	n/a	n/a	n/a
1972.1	−87	n/a	0	n/a	−8295	n/a	n/a	n/a	n/a	n/a	n/a
1973.1	−2363	n/a	0	n/a	−11203	n/a	n/a	n/a	n/a	n/a	n/a
1974.1	−6249	n/a	0	n/a	−15355	n/a	n/a	n/a	n/a	n/a	n/a
1975.1	−3296	n/a	0	n/a	−12986	n/a	n/a	n/a	n/a	n/a	n/a
1976.1	9797	n/a	0	n/a	−8937	n/a	n/a	n/a	n/a	n/a	n/a
1977.1	21070	n/a	0	n/a	−15855	n/a	n/a	n/a	n/a	n/a	n/a
1977.4	37352	n/a	0	n/a	−14143	n/a	n/a	n/a	n/a	n/a	n/a
1978.4	56574	n/a	0	n/a	−17686	1664	1.9	1.9	1.2	n/a	n/a
1979.4	85703	n/a	0	n/a	−12383	n/a	2.6	2.6	1.7	n/a	n/a
1980.4	125986	n/a	0	n/a	−10117	n/a	3.3	3.3	2.2	n/a	n/a
1981.4	190271	n/a	0	n/a	−2626	751	4.0	4.0	2.8	2.4	2.4
1982.4	277875	n/a	0	n/a	−5235	1846	4.1	4.0	2.9	2.4	2.4
1983.4	359099	n/a	0	n/a	−15907	1966	4.3	4.3	3.1	3.0	3.0
1984.4	420620	50	0	328	−9273	3107	4.3	4.2	3.2	2.8	2.8
1985.4	440984	41	0	545	−13184	2575	4.2	4.0	3.2	3.0	2.8
1986.4	424072	30	0	2463	−48424	4777	4.0	3.5	2.6	2.9	2.6
1987.4	418304	21	0	1516	−55819	3272	3.6	3.1	2.2	2.4	2.1
1988.4	433999	18	0	1569	−45321	4047	3.6	3.1	2.2	2.5	2.0
1989.4	460943	11	0	1574	−32215	4232	4.0	3.8	2.8	2.8	2.2
1990.4	487191	5	0	1126	−38405	4640	4.4	4.5	3.4	3.1	2.4
1991.4	543297	1	0	1374	−11425	n/a	3.6	3.7	3.1	2.8	2.3
1992.4	584863	0	0	1151	−31269	n/a	4.2	4.3	3.5	3.2	2.8
1993.4	638194	0	0	1338	−89568	n/a	4.2	4.2	3.2	3.5	3.3
1994.4	693406	0	970	1784	−56910	n/a	4.4	4.4	3.6	3.4	3.3
1995.4	734575	0	1138	5516	−35444	n/a	5.0	5.0	4.3	4.0	3.9

A.6 Finland [Million markkas]

	TBILL	YIELD	NEW.BOND	OLD.BOND	REG.BOND	PRO.NOTE	SH.LOAN	LG.LOAN	FOR.CUR	TOTAL	CB.TBILL	CB.BOND	CB.PRO	FIX.MAT	EF.MAT
1970	0	0	0	1238	1151	51	204	0	1557	4201	0	64	0	n/a	n/a
1971	0	0	0	1225	1202	43	0	0	1523	3993	0	38	0	n/a	n/a
1972	0	0	0	1130	1136	4	0	0	1517	3787	0	47	0	n/a	n/a
1973	0	0	0	776	981	2	0	0	1395	3154	0	53	0	n/a	n/a
1974	0	0	0	596	931	1	0	0	1152	2680	0	71	0	n/a	n/a
1975	0	0	0	811	834	1	289	0	1609	3544	0	70	0	n/a	n/a
1976	0	0	0	1323	844	8	200	0	2248	4623	0	74	0	n/a	n/a
1977	0	0	0	1909	1026	29	110	0	3679	6753	0	59	0	n/a	n/a
1978	0	0	0	2959	1072	576	229	0	7360	12196	0	93	188	n/a	n/a
1979	0	0	0	3956	1228	867	174	0	8964	15189	0	145	346	n/a	n/a
1980	0	0	0	5325	1555	705	40	0	10341	17966	0	288	512	n/a	n/a
1981	0	0	0	6303	1744	715	9	0	13331	22102	0	386	354	n/a	n/a
1982	0	0	0	7635	2896	847	63	0	18807	30248	0	435	0	n/a	n/a
1983	0	0	0	9503	4864	2013	18	0	21723	38121	0	449	1000	n/a	n/a
1984	0	0	0	12037	5367	1653	266	0	24946	44269	0	124	1000	n/a	n/a
1985	1571	0	0	14994	3781	526	432	0	25677	46981	0	118	0	3.2	1.4
1986	2063	0	0	18059	4031	449	411	0	26981	51994	0	59	0	3.1	1.5
1987	3018	0	0	22121	4397	295	0	0	28680	58511	0	4	0	3.2	1.6
1988	2290	0	0	24244	4904	368	0	0	26279	58085	88	20	0	3.2	1.7
1989	250	895	1530	21702	5401	349	0	0	22786	52913	0	8	0	3.2	1.8
1990	0	1867	4800	17315	4832	3431	0	0	24793	57038	0	0	0	3.8	2.1
1991	5180	4029	13533	13456	4177	8031	0	0	43646	92052	0	3	0	4.4	2.3
1992	14762	5924	24423	10231	3430	10125	0	0	106387	175282	0	0	0	3.6	1.4
1993	22824	8442	55918	6722	2602	13458	0	0	155577	265543	0	0	0	3.9	1.6
1994	33153	9670	78554	4784	1863	15237	0	0	176562	319823	0	0	0	3.3	1.5
1995	37864	18442	120788	3089	1229	16263	0	1629	172301	371605	0	0	0	3.5	1.9
1996	36820	30914	145059	1728	1718	15469	0	1071	175008	407787	0	0	0		

A.7 France [Million French francs]

	TBILL BTF	NOTES BTAN	ECU.NOTE BTAN	VAR.BOND OAT	ECU.BOND OAT	FIX.BOND OAT	OPTION VAR-FIX	NO CONV Stay VAR	OPTION FIX-VAR	CONV into VAR	RENEW ORT	OTH.BOND LONG
1971	31040	0	0	0	0	0	0	0	0	0	0	16050
1972	20200	0	0	0	0	0	0	0	0	0	0	15180
1973	4130	0	0	0	0	0	0	0	0	0	0	30360
1974	3623	0	0	0	0	0	0	0	0	0	0	44090
1975	43928	0	0	0	0	0	0	0	0	0	0	36330
1976	52259	0	0	0	0	0	0	0	0	0	0	31330
1977	58079	0	0	0	0	0	0	0	0	0	0	38880
1978	80820	0	0	0	0	0	0	0	0	0	0	48560
1979	88932	0	0	0	0	0	0	0	0	0	0	70950
1980	82983	0	0	0	0	0	0	0	0	0	0	111030
1981	139731	0	0	0	0	0	0	0	0	0	0	134480
1982	225414	0	0	0	0	0	0	0	0	0	0	154120
1983	266647	0	0	0	0	0	0	0	17940	0	1010	181220
1984	315409	0	0	0	0	0	25082	0	25760	0	31710	195630
1985	337070	0	0	2550	0	40450	44752	0	45156	4	39210	193792
1986	269342	101000	0	18400	0	88375	32479	629	116535	69	39199	184338
1987	222200	212200	0	45901	0	145204	14597	629	114662	98	36174	169124
1988	173600	276400	0	86167	11376	229310	4137	3596	114538	115	31563	149874
1989	168000	352000	0	113028	38451	324848	0	4043	114513	128	13421	131743
1990	143300	406600	0	125295	52994	423155	0	4043	114485	139	2180	109852
1991	139360	417710	0	125449	65139	519345	0	4043	114325	146	9	93199
1992	258485	456224	0	114987	80736	733996	0	2722	100998	98	7	38499
1993	188877	581951	12177	84733	86736	959122	0	2722	99564	101	7	124760
1994	239729	659209	27377	84738	86736	1194064	0	2722	99553	106	0	91306
1995	291627	724122	36302	84743	84810	1406154	0	2722	92941	39	0	89956

A.7 France [Million French francs] (continued)

	NMK LONG	NMK SHORT	SAVING	POSTAL DEPOSIT	CB.BOR	FOR.CUR	FOR.FSC	TOTAL	CON.MAT	FIX.BON	FIX.MAT	EE.MAT
1971	n/a	0	33780	75290	6500	2450	0	165110	n/a	n/a	n/a	n/a
1972	n/a	0	35690	85430	5700	2100	0	164300	n/a	n/a	n/a	n/a
1973	n/a	0	36550	95610	1200	1570	0	169420	n/a	n/a	n/a	n/a
1974	n/a	0	33160	105030	4400	1278	0	191581	n/a	n/a	n/a	n/a
1975	n/a	0	33680	107930	−800	893	0	221961	n/a	n/a	n/a	n/a
1976	n/a	1518	39180	117130	11500	663	0	253580	n/a	n/a	n/a	n/a
1977	n/a	1728	43060	129250	7000	436	0	278433	n/a	n/a	n/a	n/a
1978	n/a	1833	45040	142840	−15300	261	0	304054	n/a	n/a	n/a	n/a
1979	n/a	1828	47630	151130	−8900	199	0	351769	n/a	n/a	n/a	n/a
1980	5990	1820	48620	165520	−18060	85	0	397988	n/a	n/a	n/a	n/a
1981	9660	760	46740	178480	−31450	105	0	478506	n/a	n/a	n/a	n/a
1982	48410	270	44340	200450	−81650	115	20170	611639	n/a	n/a	n/a	n/a
1983	46150	13640	41300	214870	−41980	139	63230	804166	n/a	n/a	n/a	n/a

1984	42741	14198	38460	250602	−56069	141	71820	955484	n/a	n/a	n/a	n/a
1985	44505	14328	36242	287648	−55141	144	44773	1075483	n/a	n/a	n/a	n/a
1986	39983	907	34640	275358	−38551	163	7082	1169948	n/a	n/a	n/a	n/a
1987	35277	723	34227	308797	−91533	179	3667	1252126	n/a	n/a	n/a	n/a
1988	69700	700	33700	308200	−43400	179	2600	1440979	n/a	n/a	n/a	n/a
1989	82300	600	32000	320200	−86400	173	2500	1584473	n/a	n/a	n/a	n/a
1990	79640	600	30270	339900	−73980	0	200	1744130	5.5	n/a	n/a	n/a
1991	71480	600	24570	329740	−63070	0	0	1829900	5.9	n/a	n/a	n/a
1992	50160	600	19060	318130	−108040	0	0	2051065	6.4	10.0	5.8	5.2
1993	77590	600	15180	339220	−161720	0	0	2405620	6.5	9.4	5.8	5.3
1994	74890	600	12610	375520	−101480	0	0	2847680	6.5	9.5	6.3	5.7
1995	68450	600	10190	396510	−108480	0	0	3180686	6.3	9.3	6.1	5.6

A.8 Germany [Million Deutsche Marks]

	TDISC	TFINAN	NOTES	5Y.BOND	VAR.BOND	FIX.BOND	BK.LOAN	SS.LOAN
1960	986	0	820	0	0	3528	10600	2667
1961	441	0	822	0	0	4810	11693	4687
1962	480	0	735	0	0	5700	13227	4880
1963	401	0	626	0	0	7712	15582	5066
1964	547	0	1088	0	0	8974	19656	5657
1965	1328	0	1168	0	0	11195	24749	6591
1966	3643	0	1259	0	0	12092	29519	7245
1967	7882	0	3189	0	0	14230	35113	8387
1968	8753	0	4044	0	0	16074	43782	6957
1969	2360	0	3659	0	0	15986	51813	6101
1970	1700	0	3210	0	0	16916	59523	5725
1971	1700	0	2570	0	0	18695	70665	6511
1972	1400	0	2414	0	0	20780	81874	7374
1973	1025	0	1812	0	0	24378	92077	14392
1974	5299	0	1978	0	0	26215	107755	16954
1975	12123	123	6401	0	0	30878	150102	18426
1976	7437	972	11194	0	0	37627	180908	12953

1977	7322	1232	20005	0	0	41542	195206	10342
1978	6933	1637	25266	0	0	45179	227075	10144
1979	5697	2425	21277	592	0	54197	262087	10125
1980	3145	2818	18499	8641	0	54707	305724	10570
1981	5978	3128	12231	20050	0	55513	378817	10691
1982	11403	4646	12204	34298	0	66322	417144	10690
1983	12013	3483	19743	47255	0	77303	437908	10527
1984	7249	2931	21946	61244	0	90661	456268	9809
1985	6352	3525	25723	71955	0	109911	464921	9088
1986	5572	2653	33279	80105	0	143362	456259	8223
1987	3749	1747	46939	84417	0	171873	461882	7502
1988	3974	1475	51164	89705	0	200756	477457	7171
1989	4324	7830	50448	93870	0	225063	472947	6743
1990	20100	18213	50080	123014	5000	271251	494059	6364
1991	16060	18649	6159	133663	5000	328202	527630	6998
1992	12367	23819	109733	153825	5000	357230	539235	7021
1993	7685	22904	150138	188767	5000	397073	578352	6076
1994	5928	14578	169181	181737	15000	450408	646855	5329
1995	2851	5221	219864	170719	15000	592224	767253	4971

A.8 Germany [Million Deutsche Marks] (*continued*)

	OTH.LOA	FOR.CUR	SAVING	TAX.CER	OLD.DEBT	CB.BOR	CB.SP.CR	EAST.GE
1960	2604	7104	0	164	23572	78	30	0
1961	2811	3754	0	100	23451	163	3807	0
1962	3235	3683	0	53	23495	739	3732	0
1963	4399	3488	0	51	23964	1749	3624	0
1964	5121	3416	0	51	24377	1212	2982	0
1965	6339	3309	0	51	24530	1408	2314	0
1966	7868	2376	0	51	24571	1164	2505	0
1967	8690	2296	0	51	24539	2220	1578	0
1968	9221	1951	0	47	24159	1344	783	0
1969	9884	1473	280	47	23605	1974	722	0
1970	11104	1351	575	50	23015	2334	387	0
1971	12592	1289	1554	50	22384	2349	41	0
1972	14667	1071	4191	38	21813	440	0	0
1973	6222	814	3001	39	21143	2851	0	0
1974	6969	726	4725	38	20492	1232	0	0
1975	7638	717	9802	31	19788	361	0	0
1976	9581	581	14474	11	19117	1795	0	0

Year							
1977	10925	503	21956	0	18547	905	0
1978	1118	536	24734	0	18035	156	0
1979	12517	495	26625	0	17588	309	0
1980	20801	15	24080	0	17174	2437	0
1981	23835	12	13841	0	16777	4745	0
1982	26798	5	13508	0	16405	1395	0
1983	30085	4	15906	0	16582	901	0
1984	27581	4	21101	0	16287	2440	0
1985	27173	3	25921	0	15442	179	0
1986	25351	3	28128	0	15082	2950	0
1987	24042	1	31128	0	14727	808	0
1988	21045	1	34895	0	14362	1010	0
1989	19208	1	33366	0	13983	1053	0
1990	20181	1	30892	0	13592	742	0
1991	21762	1	34696	0	13375	189	1481
1992	18053	1	35415	0	77535	4542	1451
1993	19187	1	46093	0	86455	0	1421
1994	25047	1	59334	0	87360	0	1391
1995	36954	1	78456	0	87355	0	15106

A.8 Germany [Million Deutsche Marks] *(continued)*

	TOTAL	CB.DIS	CB.BOND	CB.BOR	CB.SP.CR	CB.OLD	CON.LONG	FIX.MAT	EF.MAT
1960	52153	0	10	78	30	8764	n/a	n/a	n/a
1961	56539	0	10	163	3807	8724	n/a	n/a	n/a
1962	59959	0	10	739	3732	8727	n/a	n/a	n/a
1963	66662	100	10	1749	3624	8680	n/a	n/a	n/a
1964	73081	200	11	1212	2982	8680	n/a	n/a	n/a
1965	82982	10	13	1408	2314	8681	n/a	n/a	n/a
1966	92293	409	10	1164	2505	8682	n/a	n/a	n/a
1967	108175	0	591	2220	1578	8682	6.0	4.5	4.1
1968	117115	5	348	1344	783	8683	5.6	4.3	4.0
1969	117904	395	199	1974	722	8683	5.3	4.9	4.6
1970	125890	0	175	2334	387	8683	5.1	4.8	4.5
1971	140400	0	67	2349	41	8683	4.8	4.5	4.3
1972	156062	0	20	440	0	8683	4.9	4.7	4.6
1973	167754	0	6	2851	0	8683	5.1	4.9	4.8
1974	192383	0	289	1232	0	8683	5.0	4.5	4.4
1975	256390	0	3926	361	0	8683	5.0	4.2	4.1
1976	296650	0	709	1795	0	8683	4.6	4.2	4.2
1977	328485	0	359	905	0	8683	4.3	4.0	4.0

1978	370813	0	2341	156	0	8683	4.1	3.8	3.8
1979	413934	0	1054	309	0	8683	4.0	3.8	3.8
1980	468611	0	2280	2437	0	8683	4.1	4.0	4.0
1981	545618	0	2310	4745	0	8683	4.6	4.4	4.4
1982	614818	0	3813	1395	0	8683	5.0	4.6	4.6
1983	671710	0	5806	901	0	8683	5.0	4.6	4.6
1984	717521	0	2937	2440	0	8683	4.9	4.7	4.7
1985	760193	0	2766	179	0	8683	4.9	4.8	4.8
1986	800967	0	3668	2950	0	8683	5.3	5.2	5.2
1987	848815	0	3151	808	0	8683	5.4	5.3	5.3
1988	903015	0	3593	1010	0	8683	5.2	5.1	5.1
1989	928836	0	3150	1053	0	8683	5.0	4.9	4.9
1990	1053489	0	3300	742	0	8683	5.2	4.9	4.8
1991	1173864	0	4132	189	0	8683	5.1	4.9	4.8
1992	1345224	0	5733	4542	0	8683	5.2	5.0	4.9
1993	1509150	0	4398	0	0	8683	5.4	5.2	5.2
1994	1662150	0	2931	0	0	8683	5.4	5.2	5.1
1995	1995974	0	822	0	0	8683	5.1	5.1	5.0

A.9 Greece (Billion drachmae)

	TBILL	BONDS FIX+VAR	VAR.BOND CONVER	ECU.BOND	CB.LOAN	OTH.VAR	FOREIGN	TOTAL	CB.SEC	CB.LOAN
1980	258	0	0	0	195	101	106	660	0	195
1981	300	0	0	0	344	204	160	1008	0	344
1982	358	0	0	0	606	331	n/a	n/a	0	606
1983	542	0	0	0	517	334	382	1775	2	517
1984	748	0	0	0	652	503	n/a	n/a	0	652
1985	1121	0	0	0	709	516	1035	3381	4	709
1986	1388	0	0	25	739	502	1290	3944	11	739

Year										
1987	1850	72	0	57	825	534	1472	4810	65	825
1988	2766	237	0	57	847	626	1686	6219	137	847
1989	3504	414	0	305	1043	626	1856	7748	202	1043
1990	4833	429	626	849	1090	422	2079	10328	188	1090
1991	4974	330	2766	939	1214	484	2766	13473	161	1214
1992	5601	821	4220	976	1347	665	3339	16969	188	1347
1993	5766	2452	5397	1702	3444	835	4482	24078	337	3444
1994	7533	3380	5179	1879	3622	929	5388	27910	308	3622
1995	8422	5939	5291	1574	3866	1017	5672	31781	303	3866
1996	9810	9772	4737	239	3902	957	6378	35795	233	3902

A.10 Ireland [Million Irish pounds]

	TBILL	M.NOTE	VAR.BOND	FIX.BOND	FOR.CUR	SAVING	IDX.SAV	OTHER	GV.WAYS	CB.BOR	TOTAL	GV.BILL	GV.BOND
1960.1	15.8	0	0	188.9	43.1	38.7	0	47.7	59.9	0	394.1	0	n/a
1961.1	23.0	0	0	197.4	42.5	42.3	0	52.8	61.4	0	419.4	0	n/a
1962.1	31.5	0	0	214.5	41.9	46.2	0	56.2	65.5	0	455.8	0	n/a
1963.1	26.5	0	0	250.9	40.9	49.7	0	62.8	66.7	0	497.5	0	n/a
1964.1	35.5	0	0	272.1	40.0	54.3	0	71.5	66.5	0	539.9	0	n/a
1965.1	49.0	0	0	290.9	39.1	61.2	0	82.8	72.8	0	595.8	0	n/a
1966.1	59.3	0	0	340.4	52.9	65.4	0	98.7	54.7	0	671.4	0	n/a
1967.1	50.0	22.0	0	358.8	61.3	72.0	0	86.5	54.8	17.4	722.8	0	n/a
1968.1	75.0	20.8	0	387.2	51.9	75.9	0	98.4	48.6	17.4	775.2	0	n/a
1969.1	82.0	19.5	0	458.3	54.8	78.1	0	99.8	28.3	31.6	852.4	7.4	64.3
1970.1	82.0	18.1	0	528.9	69.6	78.1	0	125.6	29.5	7.4	939.2	11.7	58.4
1971.1	102.0	16.7	0	543.7	89.9	79.3	0	146.1	43.4	6.6	1027.7	9.3	60.7
1972.1	117.0	15.1	0	659.8	107.6	90.5	0	154.9	14.8	3.2	1162.9	10.2	97.8
1973.1	117.0	13.3	0	753.8	126.4	98.8	0	172.9	33.8	3.2	1319.2	10.0	110.6
1974.1	117.0	11.5	0	847.2	167.3	100.8	0	224.9	68.3	3.9	1540.9	0	95.0
1974.4	117.0	9.5	0	1006.0	312.0	103.6	0	191.5	48.9	18.1	1806.6	1.7	130.9
1975.4	118.0	7.4	0	1457.5	567.2	112.1	0.4	208.1	76.4	3.9	2551.0	0	114.7
1976.4	120.0	5.1	0	1749.9	1039.6	124.3	1.4	228.9	73.2	5.5	3347.9	0	118.7

1977.4	120.0	2.7	0	2283.1	1038.8	143.3	3.0	263.3	41.8	5.5	3901.5	0	184.6
1978.4	120.0	0	20.0	2867.2	1063.9	173.1	4.1	309.7	199.4	5.5	4762.9	0	87.7
1979.4	120.0	0	50.0	3675.8	1542.4	188.8	4.5	354.7	110.0	8.9	6055.1	0	353.2
1980.4	150.0	0	60.0	4091.5	2206.8	202.4	6.9	400.3	116.1	69.3	7303.3	23.3	156.5
1981.4	205.0	0	345.0	4219.4	3793.9	223.2	31.8	400.1	226.3	9.1	9453.8	13.5	193.4
1982.4	195.0	0	635.0	4827.7	5290.3	242.7	55.5	393.4	180.3	57.1	11877.0	64.8	189.8
1983.4	195.0	0	710.0	5652.7	7017.5	278.2	97.8	384.7	193.4	88.1	14617.4	0	231.7
1984.4	428.3	0	805.0	6875.3	7926.2	340.8	145.2	379.0	168.1	68.6	17136.5	0	494.2
1985.4	270.7	0	936.0	7664.2	8441.2	544.4	131.5	365.2	379.8	118.2	18851.2	0	252.8
1986.4	470.0	0	791.0	10085.0	9753.5	729.6	227.0	354.2	115.8	121.9	22648.0	0	857.3
1987.4	885.0	0	868.4	11641.5	9692.6	790.3	243.6	53.5	169.4	124.3	24468.6	0	1276.8
1988.4	942.9	0	1646.3	10650.5	9498.4	1045.6	292.4	117.6	1553.1	126.1	25872.9	0	225.8
1989.4	1167.2	0	2047.9	10632.8	9167.5	1249.0	302.2	60.6	1614.3	128.3	26369.8	0	202.9
1990.4	950.0	0	2500.4	10698.4	8848.1	1341.9	285.6	131.9	1547.6	130.2	26434.1	0	232.6
1991.4	544.9	0	2328.2	11492.5	9127.9	1496.6	299.8	118.9	1705.5	131.2	27245.6	0	257.7
1992.4	109.9	0	1822.7	11524.7	10855.7	1639.9	308.2	129.8	955.4	131.7	27478.0	0	441.6
1993.4	448.2	0	1631.0	12615.5	12274.9	1885.0	332.1	150.8	472.1	131.7	29941.3	0	262.9
1994.4	662.1	0	1512.8	13030.0	11530.7	2168.8	506.1	25.9	517.0	131.7	30085.1	0	104.0
1995.4	892.3	0	1447.3	13949.8	10915.3	2316.8	802.5	7.3	769.9	131.7	31232.9	0	106.2

A.10 Ireland [Million Irish pounds] [*continued*]

	GV.WAYS	GV.FOR	CB.BILL	CB.BOND	CB.BOR	CON.BOND	CON.MAT	FIX.BOND	FIX.MAT	EF.MAT
1960.1	59.9	0	0	n/a	0	14.2	13.1	14.2	13.1	10.8
1961.1	61.4	0	0	n/a	0	14.3	12.8	14.3	12.8	10.7
1962.1	65.5	0	0.5	n/a	0	14.7	12.8	14.7	12.8	11.0
1963.1	66.7	0	0	n/a	0	14.2	12.8	14.2	12.8	11.2
1964.1	66.5	0	0	n/a	0	14.3	12.7	14.3	12.7	11.2
1965.1	72.8	0	2.9	n/a	0	14.2	12.2	14.2	12.2	11.0
1966.1	54.7	0	0	n/a	0	13.4	11.4	13.4	11.4	10.1
1967.1	54.8	0	0	n/a	17.4	13.1	11.5	13.1	11.5	10.0
1968.1	48.6	0	0	n/a	17.4	13.8	11.6	13.8	11.6	10.4
1969.1	28.3	0	3.6	21.2	31.6	12.1	10.3	12.1	10.3	9.3
1970.1	29.5	0	17.8	17.4	7.4	11.1	9.6	11.1	9.6	8.7
1971.1	43.4	0	17.7	18.9	6.6	10.6	9.0	10.6	9.0	7.9
1972.1	14.8	0	0	23.1	3.2	10.6	9.0	10.6	9.0	7.9
1973.1	33.8	0	59.5	24.0	3.2	10.9	9.5	10.9	9.5	8.3
1974.1	68.3	0	44.9	51.2	3.9	10.0	8.8	10.0	8.8	7.5
1974.4	48.9	0	0.9	52.2	18.1	9.0	8.1	9.0	8.1	6.3
1975.4	76.4	0	0	102.4	3.9	8.1	7.5	8.1	7.5	5.5
1976.4	73.2	0	1.0	91.9	5.5	8.7	8.1	8.7	8.1	5.2

1977.4	41.8	0	1.5	97.2	5.5	9.1	8.6	9.1	8.6	6.0
1978.4	199.4	0	28.1	103.8	5.5	9.7	9.4	9.8	9.4	6.9
1979.4	110.0	0	69.9	199.4	8.9	10.3	10.0	10.4	10.1	7.1
1980.4	116.1	0	2.9	330.2	69.3	9.5	9.2	9.6	9.3	6.1
1981.4	226.3	56.2	2.6	322.7	9.1	8.9	8.5	9.4	9.0	4.7
1982.4	180.3	42.2	14.1	326.9	57.1	7.4	7.2	8.1	7.8	3.6
1983.4	193.4	118.0	2.6	320.9	88.1	7.0	6.8	7.6	7.3	3.2
1984.4	168.1	16.4	89.1	355.4	68.6	6.6	6.2	7.1	6.7	3.1
1985.4	379.8	327.4	9.5	326.4	118.2	6.5	6.3	6.9	6.7	3.1
1986.4	115.8	533.9	5.3	315.3	121.9	8.1	7.8	8.5	8.1	4.2
1987.4	169.4	0	115.4	249.7	124.3	8.1	7.5	8.5	7.9	4.3
1988.4	1553.1	0	335.5	16.7	126.1	7.1	6.6	7.7	7.1	3.7
1989.4	1614.3	44.9	285.3	79.4	128.3	6.4	5.9	7.2	6.5	3.4
1990.4	1547.6	0	357.7	0	130.2	5.9	5.5	6.7	6.2	3.2
1991.4	1705.5	269.3	0	240.0	131.2	6.6	6.4	7.5	7.2	3.8
1992.4	955.4	733.4	0	240.0	131.7	6.6	6.5	7.3	7.3	3.5
1993.4	472.1	889.0	0	180.0	131.7	6.9	6.7	7.6	7.3	3.6
1994.4	517.0	552.8	0	120.0	131.7	6.9	6.6	7.5	7.2	3.7
1995.4	769.9	351.9	0	50.0	131.7	6.7	6.3	7.1	6.7	3.7

A.ll Italy (Billion lire)

	TBILL	CR.BILL	VAR.BOND	P-INDEX	FIX.BOND BTP	FIX.BOND COT	OTH.BOND	ECU.BILL	ECU.BOND	FOR.CUR	POSTAL	LOAN	OTHER	PH.DEBT
1960	429	1312	0	0	n/a		2256	0	0	533	2222	847	259	7858
1961	342	1499	0	0	n/a		2366	0	0	545	2494	902	269	8417
1962	347	1522	0	0	n/a		2375	0	0	568	2865	1031	329	9037
1963	230	1508	0	0	n/a		2194	0	0	579	3286	1288	326	9411
1964	328	1482	0	0	n/a		2229	0	0	609	3607	1576	339	10170
1965	350	1669	0	0	1837		1054	0	0	685	4013	1915	353	11876
1966	344	1765	0	0	2477		1849	0	0	707	4448	2304	408	14302
1967	362	1735	0	0	2472		2694	0	0	706	4904	2766	457	16096
1968	326	1844	0	0	2694		3671	0	0	724	5252	3460	506	18477
1969	111	1914	0	0	2927	168	3670	0	0	763	5627	3904	546	19630
1970	125	1897	0	0	2425	151	4387	0	0	761	5865	4616	607	20834
1971	723	2277	0	0	2511	127	6048	0	0	776	6999	6004	660	26125
1972	799	3390	0	0	2616	113	7588	0	0	739	8713	8604	693	33055
1973	880	3809	0	0	2613	88	8456	0	0	915	10245	10791	745	38542
1974	2509	4061	0	0	2585	62	10668	0	0	996	11074	12639	819	45413
1975	7544	652	0	0	4540	31	10558	0	0	1061	13387	14184	921	52877
1976	9620	0	0	0	5862	13	10531	0	0	1474	16023	16890	1032	61444

1977	24709	0	3583	0	6245	7	15086	0	0	1616	19234	14362	1170	86012
1978	33979	0	10635	0	12425	7	16430	0	0	1941	24105	14322	1404	115248
1979	43905	0	20651	0	16040	7	15310	0	0	2392	30853	17002	1563	147723
1980	70123	0	18959	0	14368	7	13875	0	0	3433	33048	17746	1699	173257
1981	97036	0	23054	0	16420	827	15501	0	0	6578	35639	18781	1779	215614
1982	127904	0	46312	0	16638	813	13829	0	1236	9567	39322	24056	1938	281615
1983	137682	0	110274	1000	19369	745	13609	0	1984	12181	44261	29800	2147	373052
1984	152457	0	166347	1000	23716	18	13207	0	3489	16068	50626	38630	2379	467936
1985	152469	0	237912	1000	28840	7588	15624	0	7096	17924	59693	36418	2437	567002
1986	162319	0	284852	1000	60172	7092	15666	0	9365	16951	70960	37948	2461	668786
1987	190701	0	318974	1000	72394	12112	15756	2323	12313	21160	83877	41376	2606	774592
1988	232013	0	302953	1000	131265	12752	15365	8033	24122	25038	94873	46085	2743	896241
1989	275741	0	321503	1000	155418	27031	11411	11305	30864	25784	110237	54620	2844	1027757
1990	315259	0	390062	1000	138744	52273	13281	7345	38996	33874	122954	61888	3032	1178708
1991	333435	0	408197	1000	214107	72995	12310	4997	40146	39830	134700	80715	3205	1345656
1992	386349	0	465538	1000	227125	69603	11231	7672	46790	50090	146115	93398	3458	1508369
1993	392322	0	480654	0	356853	70524	11499	7256	49578	76295	159937	111520	3599	1719835
1994	397292	0	515445	0	453865	64736	17816	0	55196	94527	184436	120070	3632	1907014
1995	407457	0	494164	0	541572	102092	17802	0	48785	119664	204648	126480	3844	2066507

A.II Italy (Billion lire)

	CB.BILL	CB.VAR	CB.BTP	CB.COT	CR.OTH BOND	CB.BTE	CB.ECU	CB.BOR	CB.TOT	CON.MAT	FIX.MAT	MAT.COR VAR. BON	EF.MAT
1960	n/a	0	n/a	n/a	n/a	0	0	n/a	1203	11.9	11.9	11.9	10.5
1961	n/a	0	n/a	n/a	n/a	0	0	n/a	1076	10.8	10.8	10.8	9.6
1962	136	0	n/a	n/a	n/a	0	0	n/a	1271	10.0	10.0	10.0	8.8
1963	82	0	n/a	n/a	n/a	0	0	n/a	2036	9.4	9.4	9.4	8.2
1964	242	0	n/a	n/a	n/a	0	0	n/a	2479	8.8	8.8	8.8	7.6
1965	108	0	n/a	n/a	n/a	0	0	n/a	2755	8.6	8.6	8.6	7.5
1966	142	0	n/a	n/a	382	0	0	n/a	2690	8.5	8.5	8.5	7.7
1967	153	0	n/a	n/a	694	0	0	n/a	2544	8.7	8.7	8.7	7.9
1968	255	0	n/a	n/a	883	0	0	n/a	3050	8.4	8.4	8.4	7.7
1969	512	0	n/a	143	2411	0	0	n/a	4363	7.1	7.1	7.1	6.5
1970	0	0	486	452	2554	0	0	3334	6826	7.3	7.3	7.3	6.7
1971	50	0	392	565	3324	0	0	3595	7926	7.2	7.2	7.2	6.7
1972	0	0	287	1092	4115	0	0	4064	9558	6.9	6.9	6.9	6.5
1973	1468	0	323	990	6786	0	0	5137	14704	6.8	6.8	6.8	6.5
1974	6290	0	384	882	8053	0	0	5513	21122	5.4	5.4	5.4	5.1
1975	11654	0	338	1238	12012	0	0	5532	30774	4.6	4.6	4.6	4.4
1976	18028	0	522	2357	13201	0	0	6885	40993	3.7	3.7	3.7	3.5

1977	7588	1910.0	1255	8201	13517	0	0	5556	38027	3.3	3.4	3.4	3.3	3.1
1978	3987	4508.4	4746	9393	12124	0	0	8395	43153	3.1	3.4	2.9	2.9	2.9
1979	3657	4696.9	2780	9033	11249	0	0	11839	43255	2.6	2.8	2.4	2.4	2.4
1980	2641	9130.9	2734	8297	10418	0	0	22076	55297	1.9	2.0	2.0	1.7	1.6
1981	9420	7928.1	4606	7574	9540	0	0	28809	67877	1.3	1.4	1.4	1.2	1.2
1982	11577	12705.6	2716	6662	8680	0	359	37693	80392	1.3	1.0	1.0	0.9	0.8
1983	12760	15811.0	3740	5811	7806	0	485	36567	82980	1.6	1.0	1.0	0.8	0.7
1984	6875	16355.8	8062	4826	6814	0	763	49856	93553	2.5	0.9	0.9	0.7	0.6
1985	20003	24187.4	7163	4025	5875	0	1244	53545	116042	3.4	1.0	1.0	0.8	0.7
1986	19924	30036.9	10589	3085	4912	0	1032	55218	124798	3.7	1.4	1.4	1.0	0.9
1987	16955	34876.8	11517	2201	4040	0	920	65442	135951	3.6	1.2	1.2	0.9	0.8
1988	12545	40327.2	12485	1599	3187	0	284	69146	139571	3.0	1.2	1.2	0.9	0.9
1989	8220	42144.6	16371	1600	2351	1	445	70981	142112	2.5	1.1	1.1	0.9	0.8
1990	13194	27239.5	21098	3023	1460	1	284	73792	140091	2.5	1.4	1.4	1.0	0.9
1991	9482	18706.4	32287	4072	863	0	89	76264	141763	2.7	1.7	1.7	1.2	1.1
1992	173	20970.3	55241	5560	453	0	201	83380	165979	2.8	1.9	1.9	1.4	1.3
1993	412	25708.3	64611	4446	139	160	140	48868	144484	2.8	2.4	2.4	1.7	1.6
1994	14306	25830.7	78950	5204	76245	0	103	−62852	137787	2.9	2.9	2.9	2.1	1.9
1995	3327	22941.2	92262	5204	77411	0	24	−71291	129877	3.0	2.7	2.7	2.0	1.8

A. 12 Japan [100 Million yen]

	FBILL	TBILL	VAR.BOND	M.NOTES	S.Y.BOND	LG.BOND	OTH.BOND	FOR.CUR	LOAN	TOTAL	CB.FBILL	CB.SEC
1961.1	6796	0	0	0	0	n/a	4468	740	1397	13401	3588	1307
1962.1	5811	0	0	0	0	n/a	4363	563	1490	12227	3700	206
1963.1	6671	0	0	0	0	n/a	4136	481	1516	12804	3362	334
1964.1	5516	0	0	0	0	n/a	4245	463	1620	11844	3509	566
1965.1	6555	0	0	0	0	n/a	4332	607	1995	13489	2010	2071
1966.1	7185	0	0	0	0	4438	2445	573	3023	17664	857	2075
1967.1	8234	0	0	0	0	11155	3063	542	3627	26621	1157	1005
1968.1	12056	0	0	0	0	18355	3195	584	3992	38182	6558	3903
1969.1	15845	0	0	0	0	22893	3855	579	4684	47856	6812	8001
1970.1	18254	0	0	0	0	26934	3841	579	5184	54792	7901	11297
1971.1	19414	0	0	0	0	30385	5589	541	6332	62261	5616	12034
1972.1	20631	0	0	0	0	41656	5229	474	8095	76085	10627	2427
1973.1	35410	0	0	0	0	60108	4976	435	16112	117041	9294	11859
1974.1	32567	0	0	0	0	77340	5331	397	15909	131544	20879	16705
1975.1	38205	0	0	0	0	97992	6802	362	13731	157092	24734	31236
1976.1	41230	0	0	0	0	150855	6909	330	28626	227950	18628	55919

1977.1	50888	0	0	0	989	220706	7561	296	46338	326778	23809	62547
1978.1	73250	0	0	0	3901	315729	8237	273	59587	460977	16392	64656
1979.1	106585	0	0	13017	6805	406623	9726	163	80478	623397	10024	85488
1980.1	98619	0	0	35173	9928	517698	10045	163	103911	775537	47989	90871
1981.1	118594	0	0	55297	13071	637016	13675	151	112313	950117	51638	90773
1982.1	115646	0	0	70129	14975	737847	13347	119	116256	1068319	81588	81888
1983.1	97673	0	3000	95516	16387	850135	13474	112	137091	1213388	71038	85427
1984.1	96077	0	17450	113510	19166	947038	17856	38	161304	1372439	61662	86729
1985.1	98232	0	32450	122550	22980	1038974	21009	31	165187	1501393	79872	69792
1986.1	102612	10236	47450	118605	26595	1141427	21793	7	166986	1635711	79358	44423
1987.1	144620	20226	47450	110945	30080	1242564	21994	6	229005	1846890	88389	36346
1988.1	190040	20007	47450	90934	31961	1327740	23042	4	254944	1986122	111970	58169
1989.1	204754	24014	47450	77087	33072	1386178	23150	0	266350	2062055	143252	32894
1990.1	166160	55028	47450	58332	30268	1418021	21881	0	283193	2080333	117099	68045
1991.1	163560	82116	47450	46084	26619	1461110	22093	0	317708	2166740	114089	88294
1992.1	158020	91819	47450	38336	23234	1515634	20098	0	351318	2245909	74498	84673
1993.1	155930	106545	47450	32271	19817	1577596	25371	0	428528	2393508	54679	95080
1994.1	222210	111144	47450	64444	15679	1686677	25960	0	505223	2678787	171243	133268
1995.1	229880	117760	47450	99927	14232	1786677	27597	0	593685	2917208	156977	165701
1996.1	293620	127835	47450	145317	13630	1917615	27906	0	690154	3263527	181503	179782
1997.1	306390	131186	47450	178104	13185	2076656	28042	0	770672	3551685	188102	262386

A.13 Netherlands [Million guilder]

	TBILL	NOTES	FIX.BOND	FIX.LOAN	T.CER	FOR.CUR	PRESUB	LOCAL	OTH.SH
1960	0	2894	9808	1514	1200	1321	537	220	917
1961	0	2873	10064	1480	1200	1010	990	114	990
1962	0	2833	9964	1785	1200	770	1218	353	1117
1963	0	2677	10557	2331	1200	463	986	310	1145
1964	0	2860	10751	2455	1200	419	1465	239	981
1965	0	2951	10716	3098	1200	367	1663	99	1141
1966	0	3126	10686	4217	1200	345	1628	0	1185
1967	0	4059	11002	5826	1200	345	1330	10	1376
1968	0	4620	11255	7330	1200	108	836	13	1553
1969	0	4809	12115	7989	1150	108	1429	11	2070
1970	0	5049	12780	9582	1100	98	1072	2	1877
1971	0	5605	13515	10033	1050	74	2091	5	1907
1972	0	4477	13603	12048	1000	60	2200	0	3160
1973	0	4287	13466	13565	558	39	2704	312	3943
1974	0	4974	13461	15971	448	23	2617	0	3807
1975	0	6400	14760	19628	348	12	2002	0	3585
1976	0	8372	16616	24118	249	0	1986	0	3655

Year									
1977	0	8772	18129	28700	199	0	2606	0	3297
1978	0	9182	20166	34864	149	0	2128	215	5824
1979	0	10855	22909	41078	99	0	2010	0	7443
1980	0	14223	28847	49194	50	0	1334	0	5871
1981	0	16488	38220	58610	0	0	1545	0	3594
1982	0	18543	54800	67977	0	0	1575	0	1758
1983	0	18288	76111	77151	0	0	2175	224	846
1984	0	17401	99003	84309	0	0	1705	16	682
1985	0	17083	114733	93751	0	0	1842	373	501
1986	0	15655	123164	96302	0	0	1612	1301	701
1987	0	13485	136612	97862	0	0	1468	827	903
1988	0	10252	157082	103367	0	0	1225	947	1600
1989	0	4852	179010	106395	0	0	932	0	2330
1990	0	1575	202531	109577	0	0	630	563	2790
1991	0	0	228264	106719	0	0	290	369	2892
1992	0	0	256029	100106	0	0	4	309	1559
1993	3000	0	275678	89898	0	0	0	29	2605
1994	7556	0	281054	79198	0	0	0	1538	5299
1995	12500	0	311701	72182	0	0	0	187	3255

A.13 Netherlands [Million guilder] (*continued*)

	CB.NP	TOTAL	CB.NP	CB.ND	CB.BOND	CB.LOA	CON.MAT	FIX.MAT	EF.MAT
1960	184	18600	184	115	110	0	14.6	11.0	10.2
1961	519	19244	519	76	109	0	13.8	10.0	9.5
1962	311	19555	311	299	109	0	13.2	9.5	9.1
1963	523	20194	523	221	108	0	13.1	9.7	9.5
1964	346	20717	346	13	99	0	12.3	9.1	8.9
1965	704	21940	704	84	87	0	11.9	8.6	8.5
1966	1139	23527	1139	157	87	0	12.1	8.8	8.6
1967	894	26042	894	274	91	0	12.4	9.1	9.0
1968	1613	28528	1613	250	101	0	13.1	9.5	9.5
1969	1043	30724	1043	595	116	0	13.0	9.4	9.4
1970	1388	32948	1388	167	118	0	12.5	9.3	9.3
1971	839	35119	839	842	118	0	11.5	8.4	8.4
1972	0	36548	0	329	112	0	11.6	8.8	8.8
1973	0	38774	0	221	86	0	11.7	8.6	8.6
1974	0	41301	0	51	61	0	10.9	8.2	8.2
1975	0	46735	0	422	72	0	9.7	7.5	7.5
1976	0	54996	0	76	96	0	9.1	7.2	7.2

1977	0	61703	0	62	195	0	9.0	7.2	7.2
1978	0	72528	0	275	193	20	8.4	6.7	6.7
1979	0	84394	0	464	190	65	8.4	6.7	6.7
1980	0	99519	0	692	273	95	8.3	6.8	6.8
1981	0	118457	0	250	301	95	7.8	6.7	6.7
1982	0	144653	0	380	383	95	7.3	6.4	6.4
1983	0	174795	0	913	603	95	6.5	5.9	5.9
1984	0	203116	0	1756	725	95	5.4	5.1	5.1
1985	0	228283	0	1881	791	95	5.4	5.1	5.1
1986	0	238735	0	664	895	95	5.6	5.3	5.3
1987	0	251157	0	350	986	95	5.9	5.6	5.6
1988	180	274473	180	559	1954	95	5.2	5.0	5.0
1989	0	293699	0	507	3671	164	5.3	5.3	5.3
1990	0	317666	0	57	3349	132	5.5	5.4	5.4
1991	0	338534	0	46	3624	131	5.7	5.6	5.6
1992	0	358007	0	69	3384	130	6.4	6.2	6.2
1993	0	371210	0	31	1545	0	6.8	6.8	6.8
1994	0	374645	0	23	1499	0	6.9	6.8	6.8
1995	0	399825	0	10	1527	0	6.9	6.7	6.7

A.14 Portugal [Billion escudos]

	TBILL	VAR.BOND CLIP	VAR.BOND FIP	VAR.BOND OTRV	VAR.BOND OCA	SP.CERT OCA.INT	OTH.VAR OT	FIX.BOND OT	OTH.FIX	FOR.CUR	SAVING	OTH.NMK VAR	TOTAL
1970	0	0	0	0	0	0	0	0	26.7	9.9	0.3	n/a	36.9
1971	0	0	0	0	0	0	0	0	28.9	11.8	0.4	n/a	41.1
1972	0	0	0	0	0	0	0	0	33.0	11.4	0.5	n/a	45.0
1973	0	0	0	0	0	0	0	0	37.8	13.9	0.6	n/a	52.3
1974	0	0	0	0	0	0	0	0	45.7	15.3	0.6	n/a	61.6
1975	0	0	0	0	0	0	0	0	80.2	18.4	0.7	n/a	99.3
1976	0	0	0	0	0	0	0	0	123.9	25.8	0.8	n/a	150.4
1977	0	0	13.2	0	0	0	42.0	0	121.4	32.2	1.0	n/a	209.9
1978	0	0	20.5	0	0	0	87.0	0	118.7	68.7	1.3	n/a	296.3
1979	0	0	35.5	0	0	0	93.7	0	38.3	85.9	1.7	n/a	255.1
1980	0	0	36.2	0	0	0	267.7	0	89.8	102.1	2.2	5.5	503.5

1981	0	0	51.9	0	0	0	363.2	0	122.5	154.6	3.4	15.3	710.9
1982	0	0	58.8	0	0	0	491.6	0	100.6	257.3	4.9	46.0	959.2
1983	0	0	68.1	0	0	0	648.8	0	97.0	465.7	7.4	71.6	1358.6
1984	0	0	76.5	0	0	0	880.6	0	97.6	664.6	10.6	100.0	1829.9
1985	150.0	0	159.3	0	0	0	1129.4	0	100.0	737.3	16.2	52.4	2344.6
1986	500.0	0	199.5	0	19.0	0	1206.9	0	101.1	743.7	37.7	58.7	2866.6
1987	800.0	200.0	256.3	0	18.2	0	1636.6	0	102.2	790.3	109.4	46.4	3759.4
1988	832.2	429.0	282.8	0	15.5	0	1771.2	139.8	112.5	888.2	217.4	69.4	4529.0
1989	853.3	429.0	636.9	0	145.9	0	1598.2	121.2	84.4	871.4	388.0	50.9	5179.2
1990	1086.2	429.0	1042.8	0	320.3	35.7	1439.6	75.4	69.1	673.3	662.2	102.0	5935.6
1991	1543.8	429.0	1836.0	0	380.4	95.5	518.9	513.2	51.6	534.8	980.8	298.8	7182.8
1992	1193.0	320.0	1878.0	0	366.6	166.9	737.3	559.6	43.6	542.8	1540.0	86.3	7434.1
1993	975.5	320.0	1748.5	0	366.6	239.7	686.5	1334.8	40.2	992.1	1846.5	99.8	8650.2
1994	1325.2	320.0	1638.5	200.0	238.2	175.8	606.7	1691.9	32.8	1371.4	1995.3	107.9	9703.7
1995	1340.1	82.0	1525.1	711.5	59.0	43.6	424.3	2187.1	29.1	1837.7	2256.4	90.3	10586.2

A.15 Spain [Billion pesetas]

	TBILL	P.NOTE	FIX.BOND	FOR.CUR	INV.CERT	LOAN	CURR	OTHER
1962	0	0	125.2	10.3	4.1	0	0	3.3
1963	0	0	123.2	11.9	9.5	0	0	4.0
1964	1	0	121.2	13.2	24.5	0	0	5.5
1965	0	0	119.2	14.0	51.0	0	0	3.2
1966	0	0	117.0	15.8	75.4	0	0	5.6
1967	0	0	114.8	18.6	103.3	0	0	1.1
1968	0	0	117.5	20.8	137.8	0	0	5.6
1969	0	0	116.6	21.3	168.4	0	0	4.9
1970	0	0	114.6	21.6	185.3	0	0	5.6
1971	0	0	132.1	22.3	228.6	0	13.3	7.3
1972	0	0	143.5	24.9	260.0	0	14.7	21.5
1973	0	0	138.0	24.1	272.1	0	15.7	22.4
1974	0	0	132.1	30.2	296.0	0	17.6	25.0
1975	0	0	124.4	33.4	347.8	0	20.6	29.9
1976	0	0	117.0	70.4	464.7	0	29.9	57.4
1977	0	0	129.5	191.5	561.0	0	26.1	54.1

Year								
1978	0	0	161.9	141.2	686.1	0	30.0	41.8
1979	0	0	249.2	135.7	838.1	0	39.6	34.0
1980	0	0	316.9	140.1	970.4	0	47.5	14.4
1981	0	30.0	403.2	222.4	1092.6	0	58.6	12.5
1982	0	115.0	630.4	383.9	1220.7	0	74.5	146.4
1983	0	1310.0	729.7	631.4	1352.0	54.1	110.7	216.9
1984	0	3675.4	827.5	793.3	1963.3	61.0	125.7	250.6
1985	0	5100.3	1124.4	761.3	2055.5	160.7	143.3	250.7
1986	0	5962.8	2977.2	513.1	2033.5	202.3	154.5	272.1
1987	2538.0	5331.9	3311.4	463.3	1873.8	218.5	180.6	219.9
1988	3657.9	5051.3	4301.0	459.0	312.1	280.0	234.5	218.3
1989	5403.7	4570.9	4552.9	442.9	284.5	87.1	272.6	141.9
1990	7382.0	3708.1	5140.0	621.6	254.3	242.4	292.0	119.7
1991	7712.0	2629.0	7177.7	839.9	406.4	474.5	309.8	139.4
1992	9789.0	732.4	8296.2	1544.2	1061.2	594.0	324.5	290.2
1993	10723.4	0	14594.2	2391.9	1013.7	26.5	331.2	247.8
1994	11712.5	0	16031.4	2830.0	962.6	218.9	357.3	170.7
1995	11748.0	0	19795.2	3174.2	908.5	215.9	389.1	158.9

A.15 Spain [Billion pesetas] (*continued*)

	CB.LOAN	TOTAL	CB.BILL	CB.BOND	CB.INV	CB.LOAN	FIX.MAT	EF.MAT
1962	11.7	154.6	0	0	0	11.7	11.8	11.8
1963	7.9	156.5	0	0	0.1	7.9	11.8	11.8
1964	8.9	174.3	0	0	0.1	8.9	11.5	11.5
1965	12.7	200.1	0	0	0.3	12.7	11.4	11.4
1966	23.0	236.8	0	0	0.5	23.0	11.1	11.1
1967	29.3	267.1	0	0	0.5	29.3	10.9	10.9
1968	25.0	306.7	0	0	0.5	25.0	10.3	10.3
1969	30.2	341.4	0	0	0.4	30.2	9.9	9.9
1970	31.4	358.5	0	4.4	1.3	31.4	9.6	9.6
1971	33.7	437.3	0	3.9	0.5	33.7	9.0	9.0
1972	12.0	476.6	0	3.0	0.7	12.0	8.4	8.4
1973	26.4	498.7	0	3.2	0.7	26.4	8.0	8.0
1974	80.8	581.7	0	3.1	0.7	80.8	7.7	7.7
1975	138.3	694.4	0	3.1	1.3	138.3	7.3	7.3
1976	86.6	826.0	0	3.0	0.7	86.6	7.0	7.0
1977	146.6	1108.8	0	2.8	72.2	146.6	6.8	6.8

1978	289.5	1350.5	0	3.8	4.1	289.5	6.2	6.2
1979	446.0	1742.6	0	5.3	64.3	446.0	5.2	5.2
1980	824.6	2313.9	0	4.8	66.7	824.6	4.2	4.2
1981	1306.6	3125.9	0.3	4.8	79.1	1306.6	3.1	2.0
1982	2176.5	4747.4	2.9	17.2	99.4	2176.5	3.0	2.0
1983	2316.1	6720.9	708.6	42.6	156.5	2316.1	1.7	1.3
1984	1660.5	9357.3	447.9	40.9	170.9	1660.5	1.1	0.9
1985	2105.6	11701.8	447.8	37.3	179.4	2105.6	1.3	1.2
1986	1528.1	13643.6	427.9	256.1	142.4	1528.1	2.0	1.9
1987	1241.1	15378.5	1236.4	160.6	92.7	1241.1	1.5	1.5
1988	917.3	15431.4	1550.9	205.9	0	917.3	1.3	1.2
1989	1156.1	16912.6	1103.4	230.4	0	1156.1	1.2	1.2
1990	1026.4	18786.5	816.6	225.6	0	1026.4	1.1	1.1
1991	1034.9	20723.6	1042.7	327.6	0	1034.9	1.5	1.4
1992	920.7	23552.4	25.1	382.0	0	920.7	1.9	1.7
1993	-1283.8	28044.9	0	502.6	0	-1283.8	2.9	2.6
1994	34.7	32318.1	0	513.4	0	34.7	2.9	2.6
1995	278.0	36667.8	0	544.4	0	278.0	3.1	2.8

A.16 Sweden [Million kronor]

	Old.BILL	TBILL	P-INDEX	FIX.BOND	T.BOND	LOT.BON	FOR.CUR	SAVING
1960	4516	0	0	13062	1177	2103	0	73
1961	4727	0	0	12328	1334	2204	0	167
1962	4176	0	0	12516	1282	2253	0	236
1963	2153	0	0	14296	1252	2350	0	243
1964	2313	0	0	14322	1207	2436	0	247
1965	2480	0	0	14043	1182	2425	0	244
1966	4468	0	0	13903	1122	2425	0	493
1967	5287	0	0	14804	1102	2725	0	820
1968	6727	0	0	16506	1100	3175	0	1041
1969	7425	0	0	18013	1015	3375	0	1317
1970	9807	0	0	18377	1325	3740	0	1510
1971	9613	0	0	20927	1335	3850	0	1566
1972	10455	0	0	24989	1324	4350	0	1715
1973	7090	0	0	32140	2198	5150	14	2386
1974	12471	0	0	36735	2209	6600	68	2855
1975	13789	0	0	44542	2136	8175	156	3485
1976	10563	0	0	50540	2297	10200	227	4495
1977	11122	0	0	54013	3158	11900	9199	5624

Year								
1978	16382	0	0	75601	4436	13950	11233	6741
1979	26542	0	0	92464	2817	17600	20272	9029
1980	33986	0	0	112865	1917	21225	42297	13282
1981	33243	0	0	166111	1280	21525	51632	16939
1982	29174	37810	0	179535	4417	23225	71808	21087
1983	2925	58301	0	232958	334	28050	97605	25465
1984	29427	70650	0	242382	330	34050	109130	28316
1985	22225	99500	0	246901	320	38100	128375	33607
1986	22100	93000	0	266202	321	53800	125551	30390
1987	18365	75510	0	266267	320	53400	126050	34576
1988	13685	90040	0	254935	30	55000	106020	32497
1989	30442	80055	0	243441	30	48900	94888	25783
1990	14862	148070	0	232522	28	46800	77537	22926
1991	-88886	329320	0	268777	11	45600	58988	9921
1992	-110073	295001	0	336958	6	49400	243503	10753
1993	-21789	212805	0	456992	6	55800	363656	5381
1994	8525	275379	3100	513266	0	60200	382071	0
1995	3825	202053	16295	662800	0	64800	391477	0
1996	4900	179900	73900	638600	0	60100	398400	0

A.16 Sweden [Million kronor] [*continued*]

	NAT.SAV	DEBT.ACC	BK.LOAN	SS.LOAN	COMPUL	TOTAL	CB.Old.BILL
1960	0	0	146	1693	0	22770	4350
1961	0	0	724	929	0	22413	4105
1962	0	0	194	668	0	21325	3200
1963	0	0	571	651	0	21516	1300
1964	0	0	567	677	0	21769	1370
1965	0	0	439	699	0	21512	2265
1966	0	0	20	776	0	23207	3650
1967	0	0	208	832	0	25778	3665
1968	0	0	0	868	0	29417	6025
1969	0	0	941	858	0	32944	6876
1970	0	0	484	912	0	36155	7100
1971	0	0	637	859	0	38787	8295
1972	0	0	1578	725	0	45136	7190
1973	0	0	1533	776	0	51287	4640
1974	0	0	127	949	0	62014	11825
1975	0	0	0	1184	0	73467	10050
1976	0	0	0	2089	0	80411	10155
1977	0	0	0	2966	0	97982	7130

1978	0	0	1717	1115	0	131175	12790
1979	0	0	200	6222	0	175146	26540
1980	0	0	0	4017	0	229589	23200
1981	0	0	15	4845	0	295590	30470
1982	0	0	3180	6854	0	377090	27169
1983	0	0	0	14558	0	460196	2921
1984	5571	0	0	14766	0	534622	29425
1985	15024	0	0	11643	0	595695	22225
1986	29943	0	0	9477	0	630784	22100
1987	39448	0	0	8334	0	622270	18365
1988	51085	0	0	11321	0	614613	13685
1989	62490	0	0	19508	1379	606916	30442
1990	54510	0	0	25472	9587	632314	14862
1991	61177	4841	0	19346	8421	717516	-88886
1992	66516	7121	0	8281	0	907466	-110073
1993	65012	9226	0	0	0	1147089	-21789
1994	52598	9785	0	0	0	1304924	0
1995	48081	11850	0	0	0	1401181	0
1996	43500	11900	0	0	0	1411200	0

A.16 Sweden [Million kronor] (*continued*)

	CB.BILL	CB.BOND	CB.TBON	IDX.FACE	CON.TOT	CON.MAT	FIX.MAT	EF.MAT
1960	0	1531	16	0				
1961	0	1539	16	0				
1962	0	1593	16	0				
1963	0	3853	16	0				
1964	0	3525	16	0				
1965	0	3224	36	0				
1966	0	2714	36	0				
1967	0	3032	36	0				
1968	0	3043	36	0				
1969	0	3750	36	0				
1970	0	3935	36	0				
1971	0	4300	16	0				
1972	0	5225	16	0				
1973	0	6200	16	0				
1974	0	7163	16	0				
1975	0	9071	216	0				
1976	0	11174	379	0	5.4	6.9	6.9	6.9
1977	0	11731	500	0	n/a	6.1	6.1	5.4

1978	0	11559	16	0	n/a	6.7	6.7	6.0
1979	0	12358	16	0	n/a	6.3	6.3	5.3
1980	0	15105	16	0	4.4	5.5	5.5	4.2
1981	0	19747	16	0	n/a	5.0	5.0	3.9
1982	8239	23442	12	0	n/a	4.7	4.7	3.7
1983	17783	23542	0	0	n/a	4.1	4.1	3.1
1984	19575	23825	0	0	n/a	4.0	4.0	3.0
1985	23675	29781	0	0	3.5	3.8	3.8	2.8
1986	54430	26722	0	0	3.6	4.0	4.0	3.1
1987	40000	34186	0	0	2.8	3.6	3.6	2.7
1988	38460	35081	0	0	2.6	3.0	3.0	2.4
1989	30660	28101	0	0	2.7	3.0	3.0	2.4
1990	21391	17300	0	0	2.7	2.9	2.9	2.5
1991	68664	40494	0	0	2.5	2.9	2.9	2.7
1992	53811	60629	0	0	2.6	2.9	2.9	2.1
1993	44215	36403	0	0	3.9	4.7	4.7	3.1
1994	43468	34775	0	6730	3.8	4.3	4.3	2.9
1995	14635	49228	0	35357	4.1	4.6	4.4	3.1
1996	0	46200	0	107861	4.8	5.6	4.6	3.1

A.17 United Kingdom [Million $]

	TBILL	VAR.BOND	FIX.BOND	P-INDEX	FOR.CUR	SAVING	IDX.SAV	TAX.CER	OTHER	PH.DEBT	OFF.HELD	TOTAL
1961.1	2908	0	14179	0	1979	3510	0	377	98	23051	7968	31019
1962.1	2759	0	14158	0	1922	3577	0	397	68	22881	8260	31141
1963.1	2495	0	14404	0	1875	3678	0	352	63	22867	8283	31150
1964.1	2595	0	14426	0	1835	3720	0	292	58	22926	8592	31518
1965.1	2094	0	14419	0	1806	3823	0	251	51	22444	8932	31376
1966.1	2305	0	14207	0	1795	3664	0	191	41	22203	9340	31543
1967.1	1722	0	15444	0	1822	3630	0	288	37	22943	9253	32196
1968.1	3077	0	15888	0	2302	3683	0	308	35	25293	9181	34474
1969.1	3218	0	15048	0	2253	3676	0	344	75	24614	9263	33877
1970.1	1443	0	16216	0	2234	3559	0	292	46	23790	8949	32739
1971.1	950	0	17149	0	2149	3574	0	326	24	24172	9133	33305
1972.1	1321	0	19558	0	1879	3967	0	372	66	27163	8759	35922
1973.1	1413	0	19393	0	1616	4178	0	218	7	26825	10194	37019
1974.1	1065	0	21268	0	1543	4075	0	78	9	28038	11805	39843
1975.1	2659	0	23854	0	2338	4014	0	28	7	32900	12802	45702
1976.1	4828	0	29148	0	3451	4062	272	23	5	41789	13644	55433
1977.1	3637	0	36813	0	4372	4757	528	18	4	50129	14418	64547

1978.1	3065	800	42697	0	4629	5048	784	452	3	57478	18364	75842
1979.1	2225	800	50725	0	4288	6070	1079	1571	4	66762	17741	84503
1980.1	2281	1200	59097	0	3949	6140	1762	618	203	75250	18161	93411
1981.1	1209	800	73736	1000	3083	8661	2895	1108	302	92794	18277	111071
1982.1	1104	400	78567	2567	2360	10538	4757	1666	302	102261	14506	116767
1983.1	1300		81996	5679	2601	13219	4541	2700	302	112338	14099	126437
1984.1	1426		93562	7033	2555	16175	4043	2465	706	127965	12206	140171
1985.1	1241		103715	9482	2909	18821	3592	3186	534	143480	11582	155062
1986.1	1365		110670	11091	3861	20531	3189	3612	593	154912	13160	168072
1987.1	2036		113564	14376	5915	23894	2689	2930	308	165712	16483	182195
1988.1	2817		119444	15151	4725	26054	2516	2909	620	174236	19364	193600
1989.1	3290		105468	16739	5272	27035	2844	2273	595	163516	30147	193663
1990.1	9026		90534	17478	6455	26096	3038	2542	1049	156218	32514	188732
1991.1	10295		87819	19176	7885	27036	4105	2692	697	159705	35027	194732
1992.1	9069		99790	20924	8648	29226	5159	2713	562	176091	34396	210487
1993.1	4826		126528	27483	18893	32591	6287	2385	1719	220712	23324	244036
1994.1	3077	2500	164306	34709	16861	37014	6769	2133	1843	269212	32654	301866
1995.1	7887	5100	180091	39201	16913	39990	7090	1612	2435	300319	43618	343937
1996.1	10781	5700	201739	46127	16789	44411	7620	1222	4009	338398	47244	385642

A.17 United Kingdom [Million $] (*continued*)

	MAT.BOND	MAT.FX.B	CON.MAT	FIX.MAT	EF.MAT
1961.1	n/a	n/a	n/a	n/a	n/a
1962.1	n/a	n/a	n/a	n/a	n/a
1963.1	13.5	13.5	11.5	11.5	10.4
1964.1	12.9	12.9	11.0	11.0	9.9
1965.1	12.8	12.8	11.2	11.2	10.1
1966.1	12.7	12.7	10.9	10.9	9.9
1967.1	12.9	12.9	11.6	11.6	10.5
1968.1	12.6	12.6	10.6	10.6	9.4
1969.1	13.3	13.3	11.0	11.0	9.8
1970.1	13.1	13.1	12.0	12.0	10.7
1971.1	13.3	13.3	12.6	12.6	11.3
1972.1	13.7	13.7	12.8	12.8	11.8
1973.1	14.5	14.5	13.5	13.5	12.6
1974.1	13.3	13.3	12.7	12.7	11.9
1975.1	12.0	12.0	10.8	10.8	9.9
1976.1	12.4	12.4	10.7	10.7	9.7
1977.1	12.5	12.5	11.4	11.4	10.3
1978.1	12.2	12.2	11.4	11.4	10.4

1979.1	12.5	12.5	12.0	12.0	11.1
1980.1	12.9	12.9	12.4	12.4	11.7
1981.1	12.4	12.4	12.2	12.2	11.6
1982.1	12.1	11.8	11.9	11.6	11.0
1983.1	11.6	11.0	11.4	10.8	9.9
1984.1	10.7	10.1	10.6	10.0	9.0
1985.1	10.4	9.5	10.3	9.4	8.4
1986.1	10.4	9.5	10.3	9.4	8.3
1987.1	10.9	9.7	10.7	9.5	8.1
1988.1	10.6	9.3	10.4	9.1	7.8
1989.1	10.2	8.7	9.9	8.4	7.0
1990.1	10.2	8.4	9.4	7.7	6.2
1991.1	9.9	8.0	9.0	7.2	5.6
1992.1	10.0	8.4	9.3	7.7	6.1
1993.1	10.8	9.4	10.5	9.1	6.7
1994.1	10.6	9.1	10.4	8.9	6.8
1995.1	10.4	9.1	10.0	8.7	6.7
1996.1	10.1	8.8	9.7	8.4	6.5

A.18 USA [Billion $]

	TBILL	T.CERT	NOTES	FIX.BOND	FOR.CUR	SAVING	OTH.MKT	OTH.NMK	GV.ACC	MATUR
1960.2	33.4	17.6	51.5	81.3	0	47.5	0	7.0	44.9	0.9
1961.2	36.7	13.3	56.3	80.8	0	47.5	0	5.9	45.0	0.9
1962.2	42.0	13.5	65.5	75.0	0.1	47.6	0	5.7	44.9	1.1
1963.2	47.2	22.2	52.1	82.0	0.6	48.3	0	4.6	44.8	0.9
1964.2	50.7	0	67.3	88.5	0.8	49.3	0	4.1	46.6	0.8
1965.2	53.7	0	52.5	102.5	1.1	50.0	0	4.6	48.6	0.8
1966.2	54.9	1.7	50.6	101.9	1.0	50.5	0	3.6	51.1	0.8
1967.2	58.5	5.6	49.1	97.4	0.9	51.2	0	3.3	56.2	0.7
1968.2	64.4	0	71.1	91.1	1.7	51.7	0	4.8	59.5	1.1
1969.2	68.4	0	78.9	78.8	2.4	51.7	0	4.8	66.8	1.1
1970.2	76.2	0	93.5	63.0	1.4	51.3	0	7.5	76.3	0.9
1971.2	86.7	0	104.8	54.0	1.7	53.0	0	13.3	82.8	1.0
1972.2	94.6	0	113.4	49.1	2.1	55.9	0	20.5	89.6	1.2
1973.2	100.1	0	117.8	45.1	1.7	59.4	0	30.5	101.7	1.0
1974.2	105.0	0	128.4	33.1	1.6	61.9	0	27.7	115.4	1.1
1975.2	128.6	0	150.3	36.8	1.6	65.5	0	25.3	124.2	0.9
1976.2	161.2	0	191.8	39.6	1.6	69.7	0	24.8	130.6	1.1
1977.3	156.1	2.5	241.7	45.7	1.3	75.4	0	34.7	140.1	1.3
1978.3	160.9	0	267.9	56.4	0.8	79.8	0	47.9	153.3	4.5

1979.3	0	161.4	274.2	71.1	4.1	80.4	0	51.3	176.4	7.6
1980.3	0	199.8	310.9	83.8	6.4	72.7	0	42.8	189.8	1.5
1981.3	0	223.4	363.6	96.2	5.0	68.0	0	39.2	201.1	1.4
1982.3	0	277.9	442.9	103.6	2.4	67.3	0	36.3	210.5	1.1
1983.3	0	340.7	557.5	125.7	0	70.0	0	47.1	234.7	1.5
1984.3	0	356.8	661.7	158.1	0	72.8	0	50.7	259.5	12.7
1985.3	0	384.2	776.4	199.5	0	77.0	0	69.9	313.9	2.2
1986.3	0	410.7	896.9	241.7	0	85.6	15	106.9	365.9	2.6
1987.3	0	378.3	1005.1	277.6	0	97.0	15	134.1	440.7	2.5
1988.3	0	398.5	1089.6	299.9	0	106.2	15	154.3	536.5	2.3
1989.3	0	406.6	1133.2	338.0	0	114.0	15	165.8	663.7	21.1
1990.3	0	482.4	1218.1	377.2	0	122.2	15	216.5	779.4	22.4
1991.3	0	564.6	1387.7	423.3	0	133.5	15	230.1	908.4	2.5
1992.3	0	634.3	1566.3	461.8	0	148.3	15	225.0	1011.0	2.8
1993.3	0	658.4	1734.2	497.4	0	167.0	15	222.3	1114.3	2.9
1994.3	0	697.3	1867.5	511.8	0	176.4	15	209.8	1211.7	3.2
1995.3	0	742.5	1980.3	522.6	0	181.1	15	184.7	1324.3	23.3
1996.3	0	761.2	2098.7	543.5	0	184.1	15	163.6	1454.7	4.0

A.18 USA (Billion $) *(continued)*

	TOTAL	GV.MKT	GV.NMK	GV.OTH	CB.BILL	CB.CERT	CB.NOTE	CB.BOND	FIX.MAT
1960.2	284.1	6.0	44.8	2.2	2.5	8.5	13.0	2.5	4.3
1961.2	286.4	6.5	45.0	2.2	2.8	6.5	14.6	3.3	4.5
1962.2	295.4	7.2	44.9	2.2	2.8	5.6	17.2	3.8	4.9
1963.2	302.7	9.0	44.4	2.2	3.3	14.5	9.8	4.4	5.1
1964.2	308.1	9.9	46.5	2.2	5.2	0	24.9	4.7	5.0
1965.2	313.8	10.4	48.5	2.2	7.8	0	25.7	5.4	5.3
1966.2	316.1	12.0	50.2	2.1	10.4	0	25.3	6.4	4.9
1967.2	322.9	13.6	56.1	2.1	14.0	4.4	21.7	6.5	4.6
1968.2	345.4	14.7	59.4	2.1	18.4	0	27.7	6.1	4.2
1969.2	352.9	16.0	66.7	2.1	19.5	0	30.5	4.1	4.0
1970.2	370.1	17.0	76.1	2.1	22.4	0	32.4	2.9	3.7
1971.2	397.3	18.1	82.7	2.1	27.9	0	34.4	3.2	3.5
1972.2	426.4	19.9	89.5	2.1	31.3	0	36.6	3.5	3.3
1973.2	457.3	20.1	101.2	2.1	34.2	0	37.1	3.7	3.1
1974.2	474.2	21.2	114.9	2.1	37.3	0	39.7	2.8	2.9
1975.2	533.2	20.5	122.8	2.1	37.2	0	42.9	4.5	2.7
1976.2	620.4	18.4	129.2	2.1	38.7	0	45.7	6.1	2.6
1977.3	698.8	14.6	138.8	2.1	41.5	2.5	49.9	8.5	2.9

1978.3	771.5	13.9	152.0	2.1	47.6	0	53.8	11.6	3.3
1979.3	826.5	11.4	174.2	2.1	44.2	0	56.2	14.2	3.6
1980.3	907.7	10.1	187.7	0	43.9	0	58.7	16.8	3.8
1981.3	997.9	9.0	199.1	0	46.9	0	59.4	18.0	4.0
1982.3	1142.0	7.9	208.5	0	50.3	0	62.0	18.3	3.9
1983.3	1377.2	5.9	233.1	0	62.9	0	63.0	20.2	4.1
1984.3	1572.3	5.0	258.1	0	68.5	0	64.5	22.0	4.5
1985.3	1823.1	6.1	310.4	0	79.2	0	66.1	24.4	4.9
1986.3	2125.3	20.8	362.0	0	92.1	0	66.6	25.8	5.3
1987.3	2350.3	17.5	439.7	0	105.8	0	78.5	27.6	5.8
1988.3	2602.3	14.8	535.6	0	106.6	0	87.5	29.5	5.8
1989.3	2857.4	12.9	663.8	0	98.5	0	91.9	30.6	6.0
1990.3	3233.2	15.7	780.0	0	111.8	0	91.6	30.9	6.1
1991.3	3665.1	11.3	908.3	0	128.6	0	98.4	31.6	6.0
1992.3	4064.5	5.5	1010.8	0	133.7	0	112.4	33.6	5.9
1993.3	4411.5	3.2	1113.5	0	152.0	0	128.6	38.8	5.8
1994.3	4692.8	1.4	1211.7	0	169.8	0	141.4	41.8	5.7
1995.3	4974.0	1.5	1319.3	0	177.1	0	147.9	42.7	5.3
1996.3	5224.8	1.5	1445.5	0	183.7	0	152.4	47.8	5.2

References

Agell, J., and M. Persson (1992), "Does Debt Management Matter?," *Institute for International Economic Studies Seminar Paper* No. 442, University of Stockholm, 1989; repr. in J. Agell, M. Persson and B. M. Friedman (eds.), *Does Debt Management Matter?* Oxford: Oxford University Press.

Alesina, A., M. De Broeck, A. Prati and G. Tabellini (1992), "Default Risk on Government Debt in OECD Countries," *Economic Policy*, 15: 427–63.

—— A. Prati and G. Tabellini (1990), "Public Confidence and Debt Management: A Model and a Case Study of Italy," in R. Dornbusch and M. Draghi (eds.), *Public Debt Management: Theory and History* (94–124). Cambridge: Cambridge University Press.

Bach, G. L., and R. A. Musgrave (1941), "A Stable Purchasing Power Bond," *American Economic Review*, 31: 823–5.

Bank of England (1996), *Index-Linked Debt: Papers Presented at the Bank of England Conference September 1995.*

Barro, R. J. (1974), "Are Government Bonds Net Wealth?," *Journal of Political Economy*, 82: 1095–117.

—— (1979), "On the Determination of Public Debt," *Journal of Political Economy*, 87(6): 940–71.

—— (1986), "U.S. Deficits since World War I," *Scandinavian Journal of Economics*, 88(1): 195–222.

—— (1990), "On the Predictability of Tax-Rate Changes," mimeo, 1981. Printed in R. J. Barro, *Macroeconomic Policy*. Cambridge, Mass.: Harvard University Press.

—— (1995), "Optimal Debt Management," *NBER Working Paper*, 5327, October. Printed as "Optimal funding policy," in G. Calvo and M. King (eds.), *The Debt Burden and Its Consequences for Monetary Policy*, IEA Conference Vol. 118, Macmillan Press Ltd., 1998.

—— (1997), "Optimal Management of Indexed and Nominal Debt," *NBER Working Paper*, 6197, Sept.

—— and D. B. Gordon (1983), "Rules Discretion and Reputation in a Model of Monetary Policy," *Journal of Monetary Economics*, 12: 101–21.

Barsky, R. B., N. G. Mankiw and S. P. Zeldes (1986), "Ricardian Consumers with Keynesian Propensities," *American Economic Review*, 76(4): 676–91.

Bhattacharya, S. (1982), "Aspects of Monetary and Banking Theory and Moral Hazard," *Journal of Finance*, 37(2): 371–84.

Blanchard, O. J., and P. Weil (1992), "Dynamic Efficiency, the Riskless Rate, and Debt Ponzi Games under Uncertainty," *NBER Working Paper*, 3992.

Bohn, H. (1988), "Why Do We Have Nominal Government Debt?," *Journal of Monetary Economics*, 21: 127–40.

—— (1990a), "Tax Smoothing with Financial Instruments," *American Economic Review*, 80(5): 1217–30.

—— (1990b), "A Positive Theory of Foreign Currency Debt," *Journal of International Economics*, 29: 273–92.

Bohn, H. (1991), "Time Consistency of Monetary Policy in the Open Economy," *Journal of International Economics*, 30: 249–66.

——(1994), "Optimal State-Contingent Capital Taxation: When Is There an Indeterminacy," *Journal of Monetary Economics*, 34(1): 125–37.

Breedon, F. J., and J. S. Chadha (1998), "The Information Content of the Inflation Term Structure," *Bank of England Working Paper*, 75.

Broker, G. (1993), *Government Securities and Debt Management in the 1990s.* Paris: OECD.

Brownlee, O. H., and I. O. Scott (1963), "Utility, Liquidity and Debt Management," *Econometrica*, 31(3): 349–62.

Buchanan, J. (1958), *Public Principles of Public Debt: A Defense and Restatement.* Homewood, Ills.: Richard D. Irving, Inc.

Calvo, G. A. (1988), "Servicing the Public Debt: The Role of Expectations," *American Economic Review*, 78(4): 647–61.

——and P. E. Guidotti (1990a), "Indexation and Maturity of Government Bonds: An Exploratory Model," in R. Dornbusch and M. Draghi (eds.), *Public Debt Management: Theory and History*: 52–93. Cambridge: Cambridge University Press.

————(1990b), "Credibility and Nominal Debt," *IMF Staff Papers* 37 (Sept.): 612–35.

————(1992), "Optimal Maturity of Nominal Government Debt: An Infinite-Horizon Model," *International Economic Review*, 33(4): 895–919.

————(1993), "Management of the Nominal Public Debt: Theory and Applications," in H. Verbon and F. van Winden (eds.), *The Political Economy of Government Debt*: 207–32. Amsterdam: North-Holland.

————and L. Leiderman (1991), "Optimal Maturity of Nominal Government Debt: The First Test," *Economic Letters*, 35: 415–21.

——and M. Obstfeld (1990), "Time Consistency of Fiscal and Monetary Policy: A Comment," *Econometrica*, 58(5): 1245–7.

Campbell, J. Y. (1995), "Some Lessons from the Yield Curve," *Journal of Economic Perspectives*, 9(3): 129–52.

——and R. J. Shiller (1987), "Cointegration and Tests of Present Value Models," *Journal of Political Economy*, 95(5): 1062–88.

————(1996), "A Scorecard for Indexed Government Debt" in B. Bernanke and J. Rotenberg (eds.), *NBER Macroeconomics Annual 1996*: 155–97. Cambridge, Mass.: MIT Press.

Carracedo, M. F., and P. Dattels (1997), "Survey of Public Debt Management Frameworks in Selected Countries," in V. Sundararajan, P. Dattels and H. J. Blommestein (eds.), *Coordinating Public Debt and Monetary Management*: IMF: 96–162.

Chamley, C., and H. Polemarchakis (1984), "Asset Markets, General Equilibrium and the Neutrality of Money," *Review of Economic Studies*, 51(1): 129–38.

Chan, L. K. C. (1983), "Uncertainty and the Neutrality of Government Financing Policy," *Journal of Monetary Economics*, 11: 351–73.

Chari, V. V., L. J. Christiano and P. J. Kehoe (1994), "Optimal Fiscal Policy in a Business Cycle Model," *Journal of Political Economy*, 102(4): 617–52.

Dale, S., A. Mongiardino and D. Quah (1997), "A Modest Proposal for Structuring Public Debt," mimeo, Bank of England.

De-Broeck, M. (1997), "The Financial Structure of Government Debt in OECD Countries: An Examination of the Time-Consistency Issue," *Journal of Monetary Economics*, 39: 279–301.

De-Cecco, M., L. Pecchi and G. Piga (1997), *Managing Public Debt: Index-Linked Bonds in Theory and Practice*. Cheltenham: Edward Elgar.

Deacon, M., and A. Derry (1998), *Inflation-Indexed Securities*. Hemel Hempsted: Prentice Hall Europe.

De Fontenay, P., G. M. Milesi-Ferretti and H. Pill (1995), "The Role of Foreign Currency Debt in Public Debt Management," IMF Working Paper, 95/21 revised version May 1995.

De-Haan, J., B. J. Sikken and A. Hilder (1995), "On the Relationship between the Debt Ratio and Debt Maturity," *Applied Economics Letters*, 2: 484–6.

Detemple, J., P. Gottardi and H. M. Polemarchakis (1995), "The Relevance of Financial Policy," *European Economic Review*, 39(6): 1133–54.

Devereux, M. B., and G. W. Smith (1994), "International Risk Sharing and Economic Growth," *International Economic Review*, 35(3): 535–50.

Diamond, P. A. (1965), "National Debt in a Neoclassical Growth Model," *American Economic Review*, 55: 1226–50.

Drudi, F., and A. Prati (1997), "An Incomplete Information Model of the Optimal Maturity Structure of Public Debt," IMF Working Paper.

Eichengreen, B. (1990), "The Capital Levy in Theory and Practice," in R. Dornbusch and M. Draghi (eds.), *Public Debt Management: Theory and History*: 52–93. Cambridge: Cambridge University Press.

Fischer, S. (1983), "Welfare Aspects of Government Issue of Indexed Bonds," in R. Dornbusch and M. H. Simonsen (eds.), *Inflation Debt and Indexation*: 223–46. Cambridge, Mass.: MIT Press.

——(1990), "Rules versus Discretion in Monetary Policy," in B. M. Friedman and F. H. Hahn (eds.), *Handbook of Monetary Economics*: 1155–84. Amsterdam: North-Holland.

Frankel, J. A. (1985), "Portfolio Crowding-Out Empirically Estimated," *Quarterly Journal of Economics*, 100.

Friedman, B. M. (1981), "Debt Management Policy, Interest Rates and Economic Activity," *NBER Working Paper*, 830; repr. in J. Agell, M. Persson and B. M. Friedman (eds.), *Does Debt Management Matter?* Oxford: Oxford University Press.

——(1985), "Crowding Out or Crowding In? Evidence on Debt-Equity Substitutability," *NBER Working Paper*, 1565.

——(1986), "Implications of Government Deficits for Interest Rates, Equity Returns, and Corporate Financing," in B. M. Friedman (ed.), *Financing Corporate Capital Formation*. Chicago: University of Chicago Press.

Friedman, M. (1959), *A Program for Monetary Stability*. New York: Fordham University Press.

Gale, D. (1990), "The Efficient Design of Public Debt," in R. Dornbusch and M. Draghi (eds.), *Public Debt Management: Theory and History*: 94–124. Cambridge: Cambridge University Press.

Gerlach, S., and F. Smets (1995), "The Term Structure of Euro Rates: Some Evidence in Support of the Expectations Hypothesis," *Journal of International Money and Finance*, 16(2): 305–21.

Giavazzi, F., and M. Pagano (1990), "Confidence Crises and Public Debt Management," in R. Dornbusch and M. Draghi (eds.), *Public Debt Management: Theory and History*: 94–124. Cambridge: Cambridge University Press.

Giovannini, A. (1997), "Government Debt Management," *Oxford Review of Economic Policy*, 13(4): 43–52.

Goldfajn, I. (1995), "On Public Debt Indexation and Denomination," Brandeis University Working Paper, 345.

Gottardi, P. (1987), "Asset Structure and the Irrelevance of Government Financial Policy," *Economic Theory Discussion Papers*, 122, University of Cambridge, Dec.

Haliassos, M., and J. Tobin (1990), "The Macroeconomics of Government Finance," in B. M. Friedman and F. H. Hahn (eds.), *Handbook of Monetary Economics*: 889–959. Amsterdam: North-Holland.

Hardouvelis, G. (1994), "The Term Structure Spread and Future Changes in Long and Short Rates in the G7 Countries," *Journal of Monetary Economics*, 33: 255–83.

Hart, O. (1975), "On the Optimality of Equilibrium when Markets are Incomplete," *Journal of Economic Theory*, 11: 418–43.

Hawkesby, C., and J. Wright (1997), "The Optimal Public Debt Portfolios for Nine OECD Countries: A Tax Smoothing Approach," mimeo, University of Canterbury, New Zealand.

HM Treasury and Bank of England (1995), "Report of the Debt Management Review," London: Publishing Unit, HM Treasury.

Judd, K. L. (1991), "Optimal Taxation in Dynamic Stochastic Economies: Theory and Evidence," mimeo, Hoover Institution, Standford University.

King, R. (1990), "Observable Implications of Dynamically Optimal Taxation," *Working Paper*, University of Rochester.

Levhari, D., and N. Liviatan (1976), "Government Intermediation in the Indexed Bond Market," *American Economic Review*, 66(2): 186–92.

Lucas, R. E. (1976), "Econometric Policy Evaluation: A Critique," in K. Brunner and A. H. Meltzer (eds.), *Carnegie-Rochester Series on Public Policy*, 1. Amsterdam: North-Holland.

—— and N. L. Stokey (1983), "Optimal Fiscal and Monetary Policy in an Economy Without Capital," *Journal of Monetary Economics*, 12: 55–94.

Mackinnon, J., "Critical Values for Cointegration Tests," in R. Engle and C. W. J. Granger (eds.), *Long-Run Economic Relationships*. Oxford: Oxford University Press: 267–76.

Masson, P., and M. Mussa (1995), "Long-Term Tendencies in Budget Deficits and Debt," in *Budget Deficits and Debt: Issues and Options*, Federal Reserve Bank of Kansas City.

Milesi-Ferretti, G. M. (1995), "Do Good or Do Well? Public Debt Management in a Two Party Economy," *Economics and Politics*, 7(1): 59–78.

Miller, V. (1997), "Political Instability and Debt Maturity," *Economic Inquiry*, 35(1): 12–27.

Missale, A. (1994), *Public Debt Management*, MIT Ph.D. thesis, May.

—— (1996), "Public Debt Indexation and Liquidity Constraints," *Discussion Paper*, 9603, Università di Brescia.

—— (1997a), "Tax Smoothing with Price Indexed Bonds: A Case Study of Italy and the United Kingdom," in M. De Cecco, L. Pecchi and G. Piga (eds.), *Managing Public Debt: Index-Linked Bonds in Theory and Practice*: 50–92. Cheltenham: Edward Elgar.

—— (1997b), "Managing the Public Debt: The Optimal Taxation Approach," *Journal of Economic Surveys,* 11(3): 235–65.

—— and O. J. Blanchard (1991), "The Debt Burden and Debt Maturity," *NBER Working Paper,* 3944.

——— (1994), "The Debt Burden and Debt Maturity," *American Economic Review,* 84(1): 309–19.

—— F. Giavazzi and P. Benigno (1997), "Managing the Public Debt in Fiscal Stabilizations: The Evidence," *NBER Working Paper,* 6311, Dec.

Morcaldo, G., and E. Salvemini (1984), "Il Debito Pubblico; Analisi dell'Evoluzione nel Periodo 1960–83 e Prospettive," *Rivista di Politica Economica,* 74(11): 1407–45.

Mundell, R. A. (1971), "Money, Debt and the Rate of Interest," in R. A. Mundell, *Monetary Theory.* Pacific Palisades, Calif.: Goodyear.

Musgrave, R. A. (1959), *The Theory of Public Finance.* New York: McGraw-Hill.

Obstfeld, M. (1990), Discussion to: "Confidence Crises and Public Debt Management," in R. Dornbusch and M. Draghi (eds.), *Public Debt Management: Theory and History:* 146–52. Cambridge: Cambridge University Press.

——(1994), "The Logic of Currency Crises," *NBER Working Paper,* 4640, Feb.

Pagano, M. (1988), "The Management of Public Debt and Financial Markets," in F. Giavazzi and L. Spaventa (eds.), *High Public Debt: The Italian Experience:* 135–76. Cambridge: Cambridge University Press.

——(1989), "Endogenous Market Thinness and Stock Price Volatility," *Review of Economic Studies,* 56: 269–88.

Pecchi, L., and G. Piga (1999), "The Politics of Index-Linked Bonds," *Economics and Politics,* forthcoming.

Peled, D. (1984), "Stationary Pareto Optimality of Stochastic Asset Equilibria with Overlapping Generations," *Journal of Economic Theory,* 34: 396–403.

——(1985), "Stochastic Inflation and Government Provision of Indexed Bonds," *Journal of Monetary Economics,* 15(3): 291–308.

Persson, M. (1996), "Swedish Government Debts and Deficits, 1970–1995," *Swedish Economic Policy Review,* 3(1): 21–59.

——(1997) "Index-Linked Bonds: The Swedish Experience," in M. De-Cecco, L. Pecchi and G. Piga (eds.), *Managing Public Debt: Index-Linked Bonds in Theory and Practice:* 18–32. Cheltenham: Edward Elgar.

—— T. Persson and L. E. O. Svensson (1987), "Time Consistency of Fiscal and Monetary Policy," *Econometrica,* 55(6): 1419–32.

——— and L. E. O. Svensson (1989), "Time Consistency of Fiscal and Monetary Policy: A Reply," *Institute for International Economic Studies Seminar Paper,* 427, University of Stockholm.

Piga, G. (1998), "In Search of an Independent Province for the Treasuries: How Should Public Debt be Managed," *Journal of Economics and Business,* 50: 257–75.

Roley, V. V. (1979), "A Theory of Federal Debt Management," *American Economic Review,* 69(5): 915–26.

—— (1982), "The Effect of Federal Debt-Management Policy on Corporate Bond and Equity Yields," *Quarterly Journal of Economics,* 97: 645–68.

Rolph, E. R. (1957), "Principles of Debt Management," *American Economic Review,* 47: 302–20.

Sahasakul, C. (1986), "The U.S. Evidence of Optimal Taxation Over Time," *Journal of Monetary Economics*, 70(1): 251–75.

Samuelson, P. A. (1958), "An Exact Consumption Loan Model of Interest with or without the Social Contrivance of Money," *Journal of Political Economy*, 66: 1002–11.

Sargent, T. J. (1987), *Dynamic Macroeconomic Theory*. Cambridge, Mass.: Harvard University Press.

—— and N. Wallace (1982), "The Real Bills Doctrine versus the Quantity Theory: A Reconsideration," *Journal of Political Economy*, 90(6): 1212–36.

Shiller, R.J. (1990), "The Term Structure of Interest Rates," in B. M. Friedman and F. H. Hahn (eds.), *Handbook of Monetary Economics* i. 627–722. Amsterdam: North-Holland.

——(1993), Macro Markets, Creating Institutions for Managing Society's Largest Economic Risks. Oxford: Clarendon Press.

—— J. Y. Campbell and K. L. Schoenholtz (1983), "Forward Rates and Future Policy: Interpreting the Term Structure of Interest Rates," *Brookings Papers on Economic Activity*, i. 173–217.

SNDO (1995), *Annual Report Fiscal Year 1994/95*, Stockholm: Swedish National Debt Office.

Stiglitz, J. E. (1983), "On the Relevance or Irrelevance of Public Financial Policy: Indexation, Price Rigidities, and Optimal Monetary Policies," in R. Dornbusch and M. H. Simonsen (eds.), *Inflation Debt and Indexation*: 183–220. Cambridge, Mass.: MIT Press.

Sundararajan, V., P. Dattels and H. J. Blommestein (1997), *Coordinating Public Debt and Monetary Management*, IMF.

Tobin, J. (1963), "An Essay on the Principles of Debt Management," in *Fiscal and Debt Management Policies*, prepared for the Commission on Money and Credit, Englewood Cliffs: Prentice-Hall; repr. in J. Tobin, *Essays in Economics*, i. Amsterdam: North-Holland, 1971.

Uhlig, H. (1997), "Long-Term Debt and the Political Support for a Monetary Union," CEPR Discussion Paper, 1603, Mar.

Wallace, N. (1981), "A Modigliani-Miller Theorem for Open Market Operations," *American Economic Review*, 71(3): 267–74.

Watanabe, T. (1992), "The Optimal Currency Composition of Government Debt," *Bank of Japan Monetary and Economic Studies*, 10(2): 31–62.

Weiss, L. (1980), "The Effects of Money Supply on Economic Welfare in Steady State," *Econometrica*, 48(3): 565–76.

Woodford, M. (1990), "Public Debt as Private Liquidity," *American Economic Review, AEA Papers and Proceedings*, 80(2): 382–88.

Zhu, X. (1992), "Optimal Fiscal Policy in a Stochastic Growth Model," University of Chicago, *Journal of Economic Theory*, 58: 259–89.

Zilcha, I. (1991), "Characterizing Efficiency in Stochastic Overlapping Generations Models", *Journal of Economic Theory*, 55(1): 1–16.

Index